Barriers Down

Barriers Down

*How American Power and Free-Flow
Policies Shaped Global Media*

Diana Lemberg

Columbia University Press   New York

Columbia University Press
Publishers Since 1893
New York   Chichester, West Sussex
cup.columbia.edu

Library of Congress Cataloging-in-Publication Data

Names: Lemberg, Diana, author.
Title: Barriers down : how American power and free-flow policies shaped global media /
   Diana Lemberg.
Description: New York : Columbia University Press, [2019] | Revised and expanded
   version of the author's thesis (doctoral)—Yale University, 2014, titled "The free flow
   of information" : media, human rights, and U.S. global power, 1945–1984. |
   Includes bibliographical references and index.
Identifiers: LCCN 2018056847 | ISBN 9780231182164 (cloth : alk. paper) |
   ISBN 9780231544030 (e-book)
Subjects: LCSH: Communication, International. | Mass media—Political aspects. |
   Mass media and culture—United States. | Mass media—United States.
Classification: LCC P96.I5 L46 2019 | DDC 302.2309/045—dc23
LC record available at https://lccn.loc.gov/2018056847

Cover design: Noah Arlow

For Mom and Dad

Contents

Introduction

LIBERALIZING MISSIONS

The United States had been at war with Nazi Germany for only a year in December 1942, but already Kent Cooper was making plans for the postwar peace. Cooper was general manager of the Associated Press (AP), the powerful American news cooperative that served thousands of domestic newspapers with daily news items from the United States and abroad. The war had given him rhetorical ammunition with which to attack the AP's chief foreign competitors, especially the British news agency Reuters—leader of "the greatest and the most powerful international monopoly."[1]

The news operations of the United States' staunchest ally might have seemed like a peculiar target with total war raging across the globe. But Reuters and other European rivals, Cooper contended in his 1942 history of the AP, had actually contributed to Hitler's rise. Decades earlier, Reuters, along with the French agency Havas and the German Wolff, had partitioned the world into spheres of influence, operating such that only Reuters could furnish international news to Japan, only Havas to South America, and so on. In the punitive settlement following the First World War, Reuters and Havas had cut Wolff out of the picture by severing its influence in the territories it had formerly served (Scandinavia, Russia and the Slavic states, and Austria) and by seizing control of the provision of news to Germany's neighbors. According to Cooper, these "news barriers" had isolated the German people from international news flows, leaving them vulnerable to fascist propaganda and thereby helping to provoke the Second World War. "Surely in another peace treaty there will be something about freedom of the press and international news exchange," he wrote. "Or will there?" The way to prevent future conflicts, Cooper argued, was to ensure the flow of "true and unbiased news" around the world—the "greatest original American moral concept that [has] ever been exported from America."[2]

Kent Cooper was not alone in outlining a sweeping global mission for the United States to "liberalize" the international exchange of information after the Second World War. This mission gained the support of individuals and organizations that were opposed on most other matters: newspapers and publishers ranging from the liberal Arthur Hays Sulzberger of the *New York Times* to the arch-conservative Robert McCormick of the *Chicago Tribune*; the AP's domestic competitors, the United Press (UP) and the International News Service (INS); and both major American political parties. All agreed on the need for a "freer flow" of news across borders in the postwar period.[3]

This mission, moreover, encompassed more than just print media. While accounts of press freedoms in the United States have typically focused on the newspaper industry, the 1940s were a moment of transformation in what was signified by terms like "information" and "the press." In the wartime scientific community, Claude Shannon was busy conducting seminal work that would define communication as the transmission of discrete "bits" of information amid distorting noise—an insight which made it possible for the first time to conceptualize, with a single model, the operations of technologies ranging from the telegraph and the telephone to radio and television broadcasting. Shannon's work laid the theoretical basis for the subsequent emergence of digital communications.[4] Meanwhile, in discussions geared toward the general public, many Americans, witnessing the contribution of film and radio to the Allied war effort, were beginning to consider them to be providers of important information, like newspapers, and not just entertainment. "[We] are using the word press in its broadest definition: to include not only all things that are printed but also the radio, the newsreel, the documentary film, etc.," stated an early set of guidelines for the Commission on Freedom of the Press, a high-profile inquiry into the state of press freedoms in the 1940s United States. The political significance of these midcentury new media was especially evident abroad, where radio and newsreel propaganda had drummed up support for fascism. Americans ranging from the left-liberal film producer Walter Wanger to the powerful radio magnate David Sarnoff responded by championing the antitotalitarian influence of transnational flows of broadcasting and audiovisual media.[5] Together these journalists, media producers, intellectuals, and policymakers were laying the groundwork for a distinctively American approach to global press and speech freedoms, one which would guide U.S. foreign policy for more than half a century after 1945: more flows, more information, more freedom.

The title of this book borrows from Kent Cooper's 1942 volume on the AP, *Barriers Down: The Story of the News Agency Epoch*. What Cooper and others were seeking to change was not only an international scene dominated by cartels, censorship, and protectionism but also the national policy outlook. Prior to the Second World War, Americans' international communications links, through undersea cables and then radio, had been dominated by the private sector—in cable communications by British firms no less. What governmental interest did exist focused mostly on Latin America, the United States' self-proclaimed sphere of influence. Following the First World War, during which Washington had temporarily nationalized radio operations, the Republican administrations of the 1920s reverted to prioritizing private-sector expansion, convinced that powerful American corporations were the best guarantors of the national interest. Only the economic contraction and ideological polarization of the 1930s—during which Nazi Germany curtailed then eliminated Hollywood imports and the AP saw its carefully cultivated ties to Japan wither—spurred a rethinking of this status quo. Even the libertarian Cooper recognized the need for some kind of governmental commitment to reopening and maintaining cross-border channels of trade and ideas after the war ended.[6]

In pressing the case for bringing informational "barriers down," Kent Cooper got his wish—and then some. During the 1940s and beyond, the United States committed itself to projecting American influence on a global scale.[7] Washington fulfilled Woodrow Wilson's deferred dream of institutionalizing diplomatic interchange by joining the United Nations. It also extended this dream to economic and cultural matters through its membership in bodies including the World Bank, the International Monetary Fund, and the UN Educational, Scientific, and Cultural Organization (UNESCO).[8] These commitments were integral to the postwar expansion not only of international trade but also of international communications. Where the private sector would or could not go, the federal government did, becoming involved for the first time in underwriting international communications in peacetime. The Voice of America was perhaps Washington's best-known postwar mouthpiece: created in 1942 to combat Nazi radio propaganda, the U.S. station survived demobilization, morphing into an anticommunist operation during the Cold War. In a less overtly propagandistic vein, this work was also accomplished through bilateral and multilateral assistance to expand television broadcasting in Latin America, Asia, and Africa and even efforts to spread the English language overseas. Washington also poured money into the development of new communications technologies, including broadcasting satellites.

This book tells the story of how the United States worked to reduce cross-border restrictions on information exchange and to maximize the flow of American media abroad in the decades following the Second World War—in other words, to promote "freedom of information" and the "free flow of information," as this constellation of trade and diplomatic policies would come to be known by the late 1940s. After 1945, generations of Americans maintained that abundant and varied information promoted democracy and undermined regimes that sought to control what people read, heard, and watched. They mobilized "free flow" talk in order to battle not only fascist and communist autarky but also protectionism in Europe and European empires and (later) postcolonial demands for greater autonomy from Western media. The products of this discourse ranged from the creation of new professional organizations devoted to researching the international press to foreign aid that enabled developing countries to receive satellite broadcasts. Its ramifications even stretched into the digitally interconnected, post–Cold War world. When, in the hopeful days of the Arab Spring, the U.S. State Department championed the free flow of information online as a weapon against autocracy, it was extending the grooves of arguments made by Kent Cooper, Walter Wanger, and others in the analog age.

Embedded within the history of these political and economic contests is another transformation: the changing epistemology of information and of what constituted the press in the mid-twentieth-century United States. Decades before digital communication was a technical reality, the Second World War pushed many Americans to begin to adopt a more inclusive approach toward *which* media they considered "informational" (i.e., not only print media but also newer formats like film) and thus worthy of civil-liberties protection. This increasingly capacious understanding of information also helped to shape international discussions of press and speech freedoms. Article 19 of the United Nations' 1948 Universal Declaration of Human Rights reads: "Everyone has the right to freedom of opinion and expression; this right includes freedom to hold opinions without interference and to seek, receive and impart information and ideas through any media and regardless of frontiers."

To date, our picture of this historical process has been obscured by disciplinary divisions that have encouraged the production of narrower studies, often of a single medium or technology—so film historians have tended to write on film, communication scholars on radio and television, and science-and-technology historians on satellites and information theory. In twentieth-century U.S. history, there are important exceptions to the single-medium approach, but they tend to end in the 1940s or 1950s—the very moment when the United States was becoming a global superpower.[9] So far no study has analyzed the symbiosis between the mutable epistemic status of information and the expansion of U.S. power in the post-1945 period. *Barriers Down: How American Power and Free-Flow Policies Shaped Global Media* recovers this history by adopting a capacious conception of information media as a structuring principle. The chapters that follow examine episodes ranging from 1940s advocacy to include film and broadcasting in international press-freedoms guarantees (chapter 1) to Anglophone efforts during the following decade to define English as the medium uniquely equipped to carry cutting-edge technical information to the postcolonial world (chapter 3) to developmental projects to diffuse television and satellite broadcasting in the name of freedom of information in the 1960s and 1970s (chapters 4 and 5) to American ambitions for digital free flow in the 1980s (chapter 7).

Contemporary American discussions of "freedom of information" and the "free flow of information" often fall into one of two patterns, what we might dub the digital-determinism fallacy and the libertarian fallacy. The first situates these ideas chiefly in relation to the spread of digital communications in the 1980s and 1990s. The title of MIT political scientist Ithiel de Sola Pool's 1983 study of communications *Technologies of Freedom: On Free Speech in an Electronic Age* suggested as much, as did futurist Stewart Brand's contemporaneous and much-cited quip that "information wants to be free."[10] The second portrays these selfsame concepts as the self-evident and inevitable outgrowth of the First Amendment of the U.S. Constitution. This book shows how these ideas, on the contrary, were forged by analog-era political, economic, and cultural conflicts—conflicts over civil liberties and the repression of print and other media by illiberal censors, to be sure, but also over Americans' latitude to circumvent other countries' regulatory systems in their quest to expand markets and their capacity to represent these struggles, through media, to foreign publics.

Out of these midcentury conflicts, the ideology of American free-flow globalism was born.[11] Advertising the political and socioeconomic benefits of greater cross-border information exchange, this ideology aimed to attract both domestic and international support, beginning in the immediate postwar period and continuing into the digital age. But it also met with criticism and resistance—from U.S. allies as well as U.S. adversaries. *Barriers Down: How American Power and Free-Flow Policies Shaped Global Media* tells this story and, in doing so, exposes the analog antecedents of contemporary debates over the politics and ethics of transnational information exchange.

From the 1940s onward, "freedom of information" and the "free flow of information" acted as leitmotifs of American internationalism. Beneath the surface of this strikingly consistent discourse, policymakers and media professionals experimented with a range of tactics to achieve greater global flows of information. For industry insiders like the AP's Kent Cooper and film producer Walter Wanger, freedom of information was to emerge chiefly from the overseas operations of American businesses: they argued that private-sector journalists and filmmakers operating uncensored could sell the American way of life to foreign publics far more credibly than any government agency. This approach, which dovetailed with what the anti-communist philosopher Isaiah Berlin called "negative freedom" in his famous 1958 lecture "Two Concepts of Liberty," held that only independence from government could secure press and speech freedoms at home and abroad.[12]

But there was another way of looking at the problem of freedom of information. Since the early American era, the federal government had exhibited what scholar Paul Starr describes as "strong positive commitments to information and communications, not merely the 'negative liberty' of individual rights to free expression," for instance, through postal subsidies that facilitated the national spread of newspapers.[13] Too, in the post-1945 era, the idea that press and speech freedoms might be enhanced through government action—or what has been called "positive freedom"—formed an important counterpoint to the better-known refrain of negative freedom. In the 1940s the Commission on Freedom of the Press—funded chiefly by Henry Luce, publisher of *Life*, *Time*, and *Fortune* magazines—debated whether the government had a prerogative to ensure the American public access to an adequate variety of information. While possibilities for domestic reform shrank in the late 1940s amid rising Cold War tensions, governmental action to enhance information flows found an outlet in U.S. foreign policy, as superpower competition for global influence bolstered the case for information diplomacy abroad. Liberal cold warriors such as the publisher, advertising veteran, and diplomat William Benton (who also funded the commission) argued that the United States should mobilize both federal agencies and international institutions in order to "tell the glorious story of freedom" to the world, as Benton described his vision for UNESCO in 1950.[14]

This book shows how—more often than American libertarianism—positive freedoms exerted international appeal, linking up with reconstruction and modernization plans in the UN forums of the post-1945 period. The hands of governments became especially visible in the 1960s when President Kennedy and the United Nations announced a global "Development Decade" designed to promote socioeconomic growth in Asia, Africa, and Latin America. According to American social scientists and policy intellectuals such as Stanford's Wilbur Schramm, inadequate public access to books, newspapers, radios, films, and televisions in new and developing states was undermining a universal "right to know." The scholarship of Schramm and other media-development advocates drew on quantitative standards announced by UNESCO in 1962 that called for every country to be equipped with a minimum of ten newspapers, five radios, and two cinema seats per one hundred residents.

The discourse of positive information freedoms shaped development initiatives from the Pacific Rim to South America. Under Presidents Kennedy and Johnson, the United States helped to fund educational television in places ranging from Colombia to Nigeria to American Samoa. It encouraged the construction of ground stations for satellite reception across the developing world. It funded efforts overseas to spread and institutionalize the English language—the "key which opens doors to scientific and technical knowledge indispensable to the economic and political development of vast areas of the world," according to the Johnson administration.[15] Recovering the history of U.S. media-development initiatives helps us to see how international information flows have emerged from concrete material circumstances, which were themselves shaped by policymaking and diplomacy.

Why, given the prominence of positive or developmentalist freedoms in the 1960s, has this history today been largely forgotten? *Barriers Down* traces this amnesia to the renaissance of antistatist politics in the 1970s, a pivotal period marked by disappointment with the results of the Development Decade and cynicism toward the federal government in the wake of the United States' chaotic retreat from Vietnam and the Watergate scandal. Even for many liberal and left-leaning Americans, the social and economic guarantees pursued by postwar welfare states and 1960s development programs came to seem less and less vital in comparison with civil and political liberties. Meanwhile, around the same moment, the profusion of new communications technologies—including broadcasting satellites and digital networking protocols—appeared to undermine governmental regulation of terrestrial broadcasting and phone systems, which in the United States had previously been justified by conditions of scarcity in the case of broadcasting spectrum and of naturally occurring monopoly in the case of telephony. Champions of negative free flow trumpeted the power of new technologies to render regulation obsolete and to undermine censorship in the Soviet Union and other authoritarian states. "[Electronic] technology is conducive to freedom," wrote Ithiel de Sola Pool in *Technologies of Freedom*, helping to banish regulation from American conceptions of information freedoms in the dawning neoliberal era.[16]

Had he lived to witness this era of renewed information libertarianism, Kent Cooper likely would have been pleased. The neoliberal turn did not mean, however, that governments ceased to shape information flows or structures. This is particularly true when we turn to examine Washington's role in fostering American economic and cultural power outside U.S. borders.[17] Which U.S. government policies facilitated—and continue to facilitate—flows of American information and media abroad? What happened when market competition yielded monopoly or oligopoly control by a few powerful corporations? Why did the United States tend to export more media than it imported, and was this situation desirable or fair in the eyes of foreign producers and publics? These questions, infrequently considered by American commentators, would be posed more forcefully by international actors.

Whether libertarian or developmentalist in outlook, Americans debating freedom of information during the Cold War had the same overarching strategic aims: to limit communist expansion and to spread American influence overseas. Abroad, not everyone shared these objectives. Even Britain and France, two of the United States' most important Cold War allies, had a history of seeking trade restrictions on Hollywood films in order to protect their domestic industries, and they sanctioned greater government involvement in broadcasting as an alternative to American-style commercial media.[18] Over the years, policymakers in Washington and journalists in New York amassed an arsenal of pejoratives to deploy against resistance to U.S. free-flow policies: crypto-communism, European vanity, Third World venality, and so on. Addressing primarily

American audiences, and often using exclusively English-language sources, these American commentators painted varied criticisms of U.S. information expansionism in the same light: as obstructionist and essentially political gestures that were destined to fail.

But political obstructionism is not the only way of interpreting international freedom-of-information disputes—nor, this book contends, the one that best illuminates how global information flows have evolved since 1945. These disputes illustrate the significance of what scholars call "positionality," a term that refers to how people's geographical and institutional contexts shape their worldviews.[19] Overseas actors more often represented international information debates as being freighted with genuine social and cultural significance: the forms information would take, the audiences it would reach. When, for instance, the Scottish filmmaker and UNESCO official John Grierson criticized American consumption of newsprint during the paper shortage that followed the Second World War, the scarcity of print media and economic austerity afflicting postwar Europe—and their potentially disastrous political consequences—were foremost in his mind. And when, a few years later, France's Jacques Kayser and Fernand Terrou dismissed the expensive, data-intensive methods favored by American social scientists studying the press, they pointed out that key concepts in American communication research did not always translate neatly into other languages: in French, even the seemingly simple phrase "mass communication" did not have a single, unambiguous translation. The examples of Grierson, Kayser, and Terrou reflect two recurring concerns for overseas actors who criticized U.S. free-flow policies: material disparities and cultural and linguistic power.

This book draws on far-flung voices to illustrate the material and cultural facets of international information debates, with a particular focus on French and Francophone critics of U.S. information policies. As a power much diminished by the world wars but with a tradition of cultural and linguistic diplomacy that still made William Benton envious, France had a particular stake in these questions and played an outsize role in resisting U.S. ambitions to oversee the liberalization (and Americanization) of postwar information flows. This was all the more irritating to Benton and other U.S. elites because of France's—often prickly—alliance with the United States in the Cold War.[20] Whether challenging the American presence in postwar institutions like UNESCO or planning their own regional satellite-broadcasting system, French policymakers and intellectuals articulated ideas about information flows and freedoms that frequently did not fit into the East-West template of American anticommunists, who tended to see information issues in terms of a black-and-white contest between capitalist liberties and communist oppression.

The political alignments around information issues were far from static, particularly regarding the quantitative and material aspects of information freedoms. As the process of decolonization gained momentum in the 1950s, British and French officials, previously eager to defend imperial communications systems that tended to constrain information flows, looked for new ways to preserve their influence in Asia and Africa. The broad developmentalist consensus on positive information freedoms that emerged in the following decade included not only the United States and many new states but also the ex-colonial powers. France, in particular, invested heavily in broadcasting and educational initiatives in its former colonies in sub-Saharan Africa—thereby opening itself to accusations of cultural imperialism. When disillusionment about the disappointing results of many development projects set in in the late 1960s and early 1970s, blame fell not only on the United States but more broadly on the industrialized West.

Cultural and linguistic concerns—put another way, qualitative concerns—more consistently wedged the United States apart from other countries. This split became especially prominent in the late 1960s and 1970s when persistent European suspicion of U.S. free-flow policies began to generate unexpected synergies between ex-imperial Europe and the global South. Journalists and scholars such as Hervé Bourges from France and Armand Mattelart from Belgium immersed themselves in postcolonial and anti-imperial political movements abroad (in Algeria for Bourges and Chile for Mattelart), calling for the decolonization of mass culture. Policymakers from Dakar to Paris to Quebec, concerned by the rise of global English, popularized the cultural cartography of a postcolonial "Francophone world"—in French, *le monde francophone* or *la francophonie*. Diplomats from Argentina, Brazil, and Mexico joined counterparts from

France in advocating for the international regulation of satellite broadcasting. None of these examples reflected quite the same political or intellectual configuration: Bourges, for instance, was a critic of French as much as American neocolonialism, while Dakar's embrace of French had as much to do with its concern to manage Senegal's multilingualism as it did with the incursion of global English. But all suggested new points of agreement between actors from Europe, Latin America, Africa, and elsewhere who opposed the unchecked globalization of information flows—a prospect that in the 1970s appeared synonymous with U.S. power as the arrival of technologies like satellites capable of broadcasting directly to home receivers drew near.

Ultimately, these realignments contributed to the United States' growing isolation over the question of how, if at all, to regulate producers and providers of information. By the late 1970s, many Democrats as well as Republicans were embracing the idea that the proliferation of satellite and digital media would foster a competitive marketplace of ideas, thereby diminishing the need for regulation at both the national and the international levels. This marked a shift away from the principles of international cooperation cemented in the 1940s and expanded in the development programs of the 1960s—for even the antiregulatory Kent Cooper had championed an international accord on (negative) press and speech freedoms. But just as Cooper's idealism had been cut with pragmatism, so was the liberalizing mission of the digital age bound up with the goal of breaking open new markets abroad. And, as in the 1940s, Americans of diverse political persuasions took the American model for a global gold standard, in the process often neglecting to differentiate between democratic regulation and authoritarian repression. From privacy and hate-speech legislation to film quotas to public broadcasting abroad, all have been portrayed as a threat to freedom of information. The questions that often get lost in day-to-day coverage of these issues in the American press are How global is the First Amendment? How global should it be? And how has the American model itself evolved in response to historical pressures and opportunities?

The chapters that follow track these three aspects of U.S. information policies—the dominant theme, free-flow globalism; the fluctuating counterpoint of positive freedoms; and international responses to both—from the 1940s to the early 1980s. This era, which coincided with the short "American century" of U.S. international hegemony, was also the period when what Brian T. Edwards calls the "American century logic of broadcasting" dominated American understandings of the function of information freedoms: that they existed to maximize flows of information from the United States abroad, or, in other words, to broadcast American power globally through the analog media of the day.[21] In this project, advocates of free-flow globalism, a supple ideology, selectively incorporated positive freedoms into their proposals, embracing them in development aid in the 1960s and then marginalizing them by the late 1970s, by which point the promises of development seemed exhausted. Over the same period, an international consensus around development blossomed and withered. But overseas critics also rendered the diacritics of U.S. power legible by confronting Washington's claim to spread universal values with facts of material and embodied difference.

Chapter 1 examines the spread of the ideas of "freedom of information" and the "free flow of information" in the United States, and analyzes how these concepts became embedded in U.S. foreign policy in the 1940s. The turmoil of the decade was matched by rhetorical creativity on the home front as American policymakers, intellectuals, and industry elites sought to reinvigorate rights language to fight fascist regimes that had shrewdly manipulated mass media for political ends. The press-freedoms discourse of the 1940s did not merely rehash laissez-faire notions of minimizing government interference in print media. Its interlocutors lobbied for the inclusion of midcentury new media—radio and film—in domestic civil-liberties guarantees and in discussions of press freedoms taking place at the new United Nations.

Along with this expansiveness on questions of what constituted information media, many Americans in the early to mid-1940s also exhibited a willingness to experiment with how information freedoms might be realized. Advocates of positive freedoms pressed for a robust governmental role to ensure publics an adequate variety and quantity of information in the event that private-sector incentives or foreign pressures opposed it. The chapter traces the disparate domestic and international fates of this discourse of positive freedoms. Despite tight wartime coordination between executive-branch agencies and the business sector, positive freedoms made powerful corporate enemies, who likened them to the enemy systems of fascist Germany and Italy—and, a few years later, of Soviet Russia—thereby helping to dampen enthusiasm for domestic antimonopoly reform. But, less noted by historians of the domestic media, the onset of the Cold War in the late 1940s also cemented Washington's commitment to overseeing the global circulation of information, through new forms of diplomacy, investment, and social-scientific research.

Chapters 2 and 3 track Washington's newly institutionalized information diplomacy into the international arena of the early Cold War, where American free-flow metaphysics collided with two grounded realities: the materiality of information media and infrastructure, and embodied linguistic difference. The United States was the only combatant to gain economically from the Second World War, which had compromised the press in many countries and disrupted supply chains of newsprint, film stock, and other commodities. Chapter 2 analyzes international efforts to rejuvenate the cross-border circulation of information—through research and professional exchanges as well as diplomacy—amid conditions of widespread austerity in Europe, then the locus of East-West tensions. In the late 1940s, UNESCO began a series of groundbreaking surveys to measure media capacity in war-devastated countries. To many observers, the surveys appeared to embody the values of the postwar peace: information shared across borders for the common good. But they also exposed the starkly uneven distribution of newsprint supplies, with the United States consuming vastly disproportionate amounts per capita. In a Europe where rationing was still the norm, many commentators argued that intergovernmental redistribution of newsprint was the only way to ensure information flows and freedoms. These flows and freedoms could not exist, they argued, in the absence of the physical media that conveyed information—in this case, paper.

While in hindsight the newsprint crisis might appear to be a mere hiccup in postwar Europe's economic recovery, at the time, proposals for multilateral redistribution of a scarce commodity posed an existential challenge to Washington's free-flow designs. The United States vetoed demands to reallocate newsprint supplies, equating redistribution with statism. It also refused to back any but the most negative liberties in proposals for U.N. freedom-of-information conventions, which died a slow death in the early 1950s. Told from the purview of diplomatic history, the tale of the United States' postwar freedom-of-information campaign typically ends with American efforts to liberalize global information flows short-circuiting amid escalating East-West tensions and the emergence of a nonaligned bloc at the United Nations.[22] But *Barriers Down* shows that ideas about information freedoms—and American efforts to shape them abroad—overflowed the corridors of traditional diplomacy. Even as the State Department retreated from UN convention talks in the early 1950s, American policymakers, journalists, and social scientists turned to alternative channels for broadcasting American informational superiority. At two new institutions incubated by UNESCO, the International Press Institute (the IPI, founded in 1951) and the International Association for Mass Communication Research (the IAMCR, founded in 1957), Americans attempted to secure institutional and epistemic beachheads in Europe, emphasizing private enterprise as the universal sine qua non of press freedoms.

Interactions outside U.S. borders repeatedly tested American assertions of global mastery. At the IPI and the IAMCR, French speakers countered that the concepts and methods by which Americans understood communication concepts were culturally and linguistically marked. In chapter 3, questions of language and linguistic difference move to the fore of our exploration of the history of American free-flow globalism. In addition to material inequalities, postwar UN surveys also helped generate a new consciousness of global literacy disparities. Coupled with the reality of multilingualism in many new states, these disparities appeared to present another blockage to American free-flow principles, this time in embodied human form: increasing information flows would do no good if people could not understand the information itself.

This chapter identifies a transition between late-colonial and postcolonial attitudes toward language learning. While late-colonial administrations—in Africa especially—had aimed to contain popular access to Western languages, postwar Anglophone modernizers believed they could overcome multilingualism in Asia and Africa through new language-teaching peda-gogies using radio, film, and television. By the late 1950s and early 1960s, Anglophone experts had begun to promote English as a global lingua franca, reasoning that comprehension of such a "language of wide commu-nication" would ensure that postcolonial populations could take advan-tage of global media flows. In many places, American language aid was welcomed by postcolonial elites who were eager to shed remnants of the colonial past and to access the new forms of technical assistance available in English. But it also contributed to suspicions that the Anglophone pow-ers were seeking to displace local vernaculars and other potential lingua francas.

Divergent responses to the medium of vehicular English captured in microcosm what decolonization signified for U.S. free-flow ambitions: new opportunities in the postcolonial world, but also new sources of potential opposition. Chapters 4 and 5 analyze U.S. efforts to shape post-colonial information flows through the spread of two technologies first widely deployed in the postwar period: television and broadcasting satel-lites. Although today the diffusion of new technologies is commonly asso-ciated with market demand, in the cases of television and especially satel-lite reception, their introduction in many places was fueled less by preexisting demand than by the bilateral and multilateral development-aid programs that were beginning to supersede territorial empire by the early 1960s.[23]

Chapter 4 exposes the connections between information freedoms and development in U.S. foreign policy in the 1960s. Commonly treated as a paradigm of economic growth, development was also fundamentally bound up with discourses about the media, which leading scholars such as MIT's Daniel Lerner and Stanford's Wilbur Schramm framed as a key psychosocial stimulus to modernization. It was also a program for global media expansion cloaked in the language of positive freedoms. Chronic information shortages, experts in the United States and Europe could agree, undermined a universal "right to know"—a right used to help jus-tify an ongoing role for the industrialized powers in postcolonial Asia and Africa and in Latin America. In sites as disparate as American Samoa, El Salvador, and Nigeria, U.S. aid programs promoted television as a tool that would revolutionize teaching, enabling developing countries to educate their citizens more inexpensively than through conventional schooling.

For Wilbur Schramm and much of the American policy establishment, the development process was contingent on essentially one-way vectors of expertise flowing from the industrialized world (especially the United States) to the global South. Unsurprisingly, many Americans viewed communications satellites as a tantalizing tool for the further expansion of U.S. influence. Not everyone, however, found this possibility appealing. Chapter 5 explores how the advent of satellite broadcasting began to destabilize the development consensus by the mid-1960s. The United States, quickly the preeminent power in the new technology, pushed for the creation of a global system of satellite communications, framing this as another way to help developing states expand their education systems in a cost-effective manner. But Washington's dream of a "single global system" of satellite communications—and American dominance in this system— also provoked alternative geographies of cooperation and cultural affinity, even among U.S. allies. In 1967, France and West Germany began to discuss a joint program to build their own communications satellites independent of U.S. involvement. Confronting the perceived threat of vehicular English in Africa, France also began to reimagine its relationship to its former colonies, embracing the discourse of a postcolonial Francophone world, which it hoped to knit together through investments including the Franco-German satellites.

Broadcasting satellites, in particular the prospect of satellites that could transmit directly to home receivers, also spurred international efforts to regulate transnational information flows. These efforts have at times been conflated with maximalist demands for cultural sovereignty by Third World autocrats. In fact, hardcore cultural-sovereignty demands were merely a subset of a much more capacious array of criticisms linking commentators in the developing world and Europe. Chapter 5 concludes by examining the United States' isolation in the face of mounting international demands to regulate satellite transmissions. Chapters 6 and 7 map how these pressures reconfigured both North-South relations and American free-flow globalism. Chapter 6 brings together a transnational array of intellectuals from North America, Europe, Latin America, and elsewhere who voiced concerns in the late 1960s and 1970s over the socially and affectively disruptive tendencies of unrestrained capitalism and its international avatar, the United States. Even a figure so well disposed to the American media as the French television policymaker and UN veteran Jean d'Arcy sought to broker compromise between competing demands for liberal flows, redistributive justice for the global South, and cultural integrity. The concluding chapters of *Barriers Down* discern a partial convergence between the ex-imperial powers and many postcolonial and developing states in favor of media regulation in the 1970s, as these concerns became incorporated into international discussions through initiatives including UNESCO's International Commission for the Study of Communication Problems (also known as the MacBride Commission).

In the face of international anxieties over unregulated information flows, the U.S. response in the late 1970s and early 1980s, rather than compromise, was to subvert internationalism itself, which is the focus of chapter 7. American free-flow talk, which had previously targeted censorship and trade restrictions, now met its nemesis in multilateral institutions more generally. In 1984 the United States quit UNESCO, citing the Mac-Bride Commission's final report as proof of the organization's desire to muzzle the free press. This exit has commonly been ascribed either to an ideological conflict between liberal individualism and Third World authoritarianism or to the domestic ascent of Ronald Reagan and the New Right. The chapter, while acknowledging these approaches, relates the American exit to the broader transformation of U.S. global power underway at the time: away from development aid and toward structural adjustment; away from the one-country, one-vote democracy of the UN General Assembly and UNESCO and toward the World Bank and the International Monetary Fund, where votes were allocated on a shareholder basis; away from multilateralism and toward disciplining overseas rivals with markets facilitated by deregulated and privatized digital communications technologies.[24]

Rights talk, the late historian Kenneth Cmiel observed not so long ago, is one of the "lingua francas" of the contemporary world, "used to communicate across cultures around the globe, just like statistics or money or pidgin English." We mobilize concepts like freedom of information and the free flow of information as if they are self-evident values shared around the world. As Cmiel also noted, however, part of what makes human-rights concepts compelling to far-flung activists and policymakers is that they are "remarkably pliable," able to "mean remarkably different things to different people."[25] Since the 1940s, this quality has led to many moments of sharp international misunderstanding over what constitutes genuine freedom of information.

But the fungible quality of freedom of information has also led to some surprising twists in the post-2016 world. Not since the early Cold War, with its anxieties over Soviet propaganda, have Americans engaged in as much discussion as they do today of the darker aspects of information flows—how they may function not only to inform publics but also to sow misinformation, stir up racialized paranoia, and abet money laundering and the trafficking of people, weapons, and drugs. Seen in an international context, these concerns are unusual only in terms of who is voicing them: policymakers abroad have long harbored suspicions of unregulated information flows. "[False] reports can easily be propagated on an immense scale so as to confuse public opinion throughout entire regions," observed France in a 1969 paper on the coming era of direct-to-home satellite-television transmissions.[26] At the time, such concerns were marginalized by Ithiel de Sola Pool and other Americans who were secure in their country's dominance in high-speed communications technologies. They might appear more prescient to us in light of the "new normal" of the post-2016 era: an age in which cyberattack operatives working for foreign governments—or entrepreneurial Macedonian teenagers churning out reams of fake-news clickbait—have the potential to shape democratic elections in the United States and elsewhere.

Has free flow finally had its backlash? Are we entering a period in which American commentators return to the notion, long dormant in the United States but more actively explored elsewhere, that information freedoms might entail a consideration of the quality of the information provided, not just its quantity? Or that government might have an affirmative role to play in fostering these freedoms? While it is beyond the scope of this book to answer these questions, exploring some of the forgotten byways and paths not taken in international information diplomacy may help to illuminate fresh possibilities.

I

Freedom for Every Medium, Everywhere

INFORMATION POLITICS IN
THE 1940S UNITED STATES

Since America in 1942 is at war, America has a story to tell the world.
The question is, how can that story best be told?
—Kent Cooper, *Barriers Down* (1942)

The claim of right for speech and press has an interesting peculiarity:
it involves two persons or groups while mentioning only one. A person who claims freedom to address the world, pictures the world in
the attitude of an auditor.
—William E. Hocking, 1944

In May 1946, Eric Johnston, head of the powerful film-industry lobbying group the Motion Picture Association of America (MPAA), sent a letter to Eleanor Roosevelt, chair of the United Nations Commission on Human Rights, which was soon to draft the landmark postwar statement on human rights, the Universal Declaration of Human Rights. Touting film as "one of the three prime media of communication," Johnston argued that it was just as important as "the press and radio" in facilitating the international exchange of information. He pressed Roosevelt to include it in the commission's definitions of international press and speech freedoms. "As a result of experience gained in the recent World War, it is now universally agreed that the motion picture is one of the most potent instruments ever devised for the dissemination of ideas, information and mutual under-standing between peoples," argued Hollywood's promoter in chief. "The motion picture is no longer looked upon solely as a device for mass entertainment. Its power to inform, to instruct and to teach is just now being realized."[1]

To a reader in the digital age, inhabiting a world where film, radio, and print media are all convertible into bitstreams of ones and zeroes, Johnston's rationale might seem quaint. Not only do we possess the technological means of treating film as "information" in the sense meant by computer scientists; we also live in a world where film—like newspapers—enjoys First Amendment protections that render the distinction between entertainment and news largely moot. In the 1940s, however, it was neither obvious nor inevitable that the American film industry would begin to market itself as a purveyor of information vital to world affairs. In the 1930s it had tended to put profits ahead of politics: in the face of repeated Nazi threats to boycott film studios that portrayed Germany in a negative light, Hollywood produced very few anti-Nazi features before 1939. During the interwar era, the industry had institutionalized content self-regulation in order to facilitate the approval of foreign, state, and local censors.[2] Eric Johnston's plea to the UN Commission on Human Rights in 1946 thus reflected how the Second World War had reshaped Hollywood's own image of its work. As the major movie studios lined up behind the fight against fascism, they underscored the capacity of midcentury new media—in this case, film—to act like newspapers by informing and educating audiences about war-related developments.

Despite its whiff of special pleading, Johnston's letter also participated in wider efforts to expand the meaning of press and speech freedoms in the postwar world. The same year, 1946, Radio Corporation of America (RCA) president David Sarnoff proposed that the United Nations adopt "freedom to listen" as an international guarantee. Promoting global access to mass media including radio, thought Sarnoff, would help to "advance the cause of peace." The Commission on Freedom of the Press, a two-year inquiry largely underwritten by magazine magnate Henry Luce that featured well-known public intellectuals including theologian Reinhold Niebuhr, propaganda scholar Harold Lasswell, and First Amendment expert Zechariah Chafee, likewise defined the "press" as encompassing audiovisual and broadcast media.[3] At a moment when film and radio were often treated as being distinct from print media, this inclusive vision—which framed them as vectors of information as opposed to mere entertainment—signaled a new politics of information in the United States, by which the free circulation of all media was to serve the cause of liberal democracy on a global scale.

The 1940s press-freedoms crusade had roots in earlier efforts to secure an international role for U.S. cable and radio communications and to open new markets to American news agencies and films.[4] During the First World War, Woodrow Wilson had expressed hope that voice radio, then in its infancy, might help international publics transcend narrow nationalism and achieve mutual understanding by facilitating the exchange of ideas across borders. On the supply side, Eric Johnston's predecessor as the country's motion picture czar, Will Hays, had championed American film exports in the 1920s and 1930s, finding backing from the State Department. However, during the interwar era, the inheritance of nineteenth-century economic liberalism continued to circumscribe Washington's investments in communications. Even Wilson hesitated to involve the government too closely in peacetime economic matters, and radio, which had been nationalized during the First World War, reverted to private-sector control with the creation of RCA in 1919, against the wishes of Secretary of the Navy Josephus Daniels. Seeking to reinforce this industry structure, at the new corporation Sarnoff was soon deploying freedom talk to oppose domestic broadcasting regulation. Hays, meanwhile, promoted film primarily as entertainment, not as a medium crucial to informed democratic deliberation. Americans' interwar ventures in international communications were driven above all by capitalist profit seeking, not by the normative or institutionalized free-flow advocacy that would come to characterize the post-1945 era. They formed the seed of the crusade but not its mature expression.[5]

This chapter analyzes attempts to update press and speech freedoms in the 1940s United States in order to promote a liberal-democratic world order. The freedom talk of the decade was not limited to newspapers, and it did not merely rehash classical liberal notions of freedom from government interference. Nor was this discourse restricted to domestic affairs. Rather, its interlocutors sought to expand rights language to include the "new media" of the era (film and radio) and to apply to cross-border contexts, mobilizing federal power and international institutions as needed. "[Governments] should impose no barriers, economic or otherwise, to impede exchange of information by word and image throughout the world," wrote Eric Johnston in his letter to Eleanor Roosevelt. In an effort to enact these updated freedoms, advocates publicized them in print, on screens, and over the airwaves in catchphrases like "freedom of communication," "freedom of the screen," "freedom to listen," and "freedom to look," with the terminology eventually stabilizing and settling on "freedom of information" and the "free flow of information."[6]

The press- and speech-freedoms advocacy of the era was multifaceted. One approach that many of its contributors had in common was that they linked individual civil liberties to the media, construed in inclusive terms. Joseph Goebbels's Nazi Ministry of Propaganda provided Americans with a convenient foil for excoriating censorship—not only of print media but also of newer formats such as film. A second strand, related but not identical to the first, addressed economic restrictions on the circulation of media. Just as critics of political censorship argued that the best antidote to fascism was robust and open argumentation, advocates of the "free flow of information" contended that free flow thwarted autarkic systems and pressurized any regime that attempted to control the dissemination of news. The targets of free flow were numerous: although Nazi Germany was a prime offender, Americans also criticized governments in the Allied camp for violating the spirit of free flow. Thus the cable tariffs and film quotas that, from a British or French perspective, might appear sensible ways of protecting national or imperial interests became, in the eyes of Associated Press head Kent Cooper and Federal Communications Commission (FCC) chair James Lawrence Fly, "barriers" and "bottlenecks," ugly artificial features interfering with the otherwise frictionless movement of American media into the global marketplace.[7]

A third distinctive feature of 1940s press-freedoms discussions was an emphasis on what the government might do to promote press freedoms, which the Commission on Freedom of the Press referred to as "positive freedom." Antitrust regulation to ensure competition between media producers furnished one example of positive government action to bolster press and speech freedoms. More generally, proponents of positive freedom argued that wise government policy could help to ensure popular access to plentiful and diverse media. The yoking of freedom to government action drew on New Deal precedents and President Roosevelt's "Four Freedoms" rhetoric, which framed "freedom from want" as an organically American value of universal relevance: applied to information, "want" might connote an inadequate supply and variety of news. While Roosevelt's domestic legacy was contentious, setting their sights abroad even business leaders could espouse a more activist approach to communications. Positive freedoms also pointed toward the international-development approach announced by President Truman and later embraced by the Kennedy and Johnson administrations.

Unsurprisingly, the freedom talk of the 1940s—vocalized by corporate magnates, New Deal regulators, and civil-liberties scholars alike— coexisted with deep divisions over concrete policy matters. Historians of the domestic scene have analyzed how the coming of the Cold War in the late 1940s marginalized domestic reform proposals like those of the Commission on Freedom of the Press, which were pilloried as crypto-communist, and elevated corporate prerogatives instead. What has been less noted is how fledgling information freedoms were enlisted in postwar U.S. foreign policy over isolationist and libertarian objections but otherwise by broad consensus.[8] From civil-liberties advocates like Harvard's Zechariah Chafee to regulatory liberals like FCC chair James Lawrence Fly to corporate media tycoons like RCA's David Sarnoff, all supported the United States' assertive pursuit of freedom of information abroad after 1945.

CIVIL LIBERTIES AND MIDCENTURY NEW MEDIA

Between the First World War and the Second, new media technologies revolutionized the ways in which information was produced and consumed in the United States and abroad. During the 1920s and the 1930s, the radio and the newsreel transformed the way Americans encountered national and international affairs. No longer did print media hold a monopoly on current events. The ordinary woman or man could tune in to news stories on the airwaves or see jackboots thumping at Nazi Party rallies on the newsreels typically shown in theaters before feature films.[9]

The emergence of these formats broached difficult questions about the relationship between mass media and government in a liberal democracy. Should radio and film be accorded the same freedom from government interference as newspapers? Or did the domestic and international crises of the interwar period necessitate a rethinking of how to protect press and speech freedoms *tout court*? Advocates of the first approach sought to extend First Amendment protections to the era's new media by arguing that radio and film behaved like newspapers, conveying ideas that were critical to public debate. Others flipped this logic on its head, arguing that American newspapers—increasingly consolidated into oligopolistic (and editorially conservative) newspaper chains—were no model of a healthy democratic press. Rather, concentration in the domestic news industry suggested that regulation might be necessary to protect the press and speech freedoms of ordinary Americans.[10]

In the film industry, civil libertarianism married a technologically expansive interpretation of the "press" to a classically liberal philosophy of freedom. It grew out of disappointment with both Progressive Era jurisprudence and interwar corporate pliancy. In its 1915 *Mutual Film Corporation v. Ohio Industrial Commission* decision, the Supreme Court had upheld state-level censorship of film on the grounds that film was an entertainment business, not "part of the press of the country." The ruling meant that the many state and municipal film-censorship boards that had emerged across the country were perfectly lawful. By the early sound era, Hollywood was colluding in its own muzzling, consolidating a system of self-regulation that aimed to eliminate controversial material at the point of production in order to preempt costly postproduction cuts (which, in the analog era, were physically and irreversibly perpetrated upon fragile reels of celluloid). Its Production Code Administration, established in 1934, banished interracial and same-sex relationships from the screen. Contentious political topics, such as the mounting crisis in Europe, were also subject to Production Code interference. In the era of Will Hays's leadership, the film industry's profit motive trumped any commitment to fostering a free market of ideas. This institutionalized self-regulation may have helped to obscure film's significance to the nascent interwar community of civil-liberties activists. The American Civil Liberties Union

(ACLU), founded in 1920, hesitated to address film debates beyond making tepid anticensorship statements. At the time, many of its members distinguished between protected political speech and entertainment.[11]

Even a Production Code seal of approval did not guarantee a film immunity from postproduction pressures. A 1938 film about the Spanish Civil War, *Blockade*, won its industry imprimatur only to be tarred by Catholic and anti-interventionist groups as "Leftist propaganda." The Knights of Columbus lobbied exhibitors and local censors to ban the film. The independent producer Walter Wanger, who was behind *Blockade*, framed the problem of censorship in stark terms in a 1939 article for the influential foreign-policy journal *Foreign Affairs*: as Europe descended into war, wrote Wanger, Hollywood was "[living] in mortal fear" of offending censors and lobbying groups.[12]

Paradoxically, the darkening international picture of the late 1930s provided civil libertarians like Wanger with an opening to argue that film deserved First Amendment protections. "Foreign nations have been dictating American screen policy and stifling what free speech had been left after the incursions of domestic pressure groups and censors," the outspoken left-liberal producer wrote. Thumbing his nose at these political pressures, Wanger repeatedly advocated expanding the scope of the First Amendment in order to protect cinematic speech. "Victory for democracy, understanding and peace is bound up with freedom *for every medium of expression*," he argued in *Foreign Affairs* in 1939. He reiterated in *Public Opinion Quarterly* in 1943, "*[Freedom] of the screen is every whit as cogent as freedom of the press.*" Wanger's writings anticipated the direction of film advocacy after the war. By the late 1940s, the ACLU had joined the battle to overturn film censorship.[13]

Civil-liberties advocates in the field of broadcasting confronted a somewhat different set of technical constraints than those facing the newspaper or film industries. Newspaper publishers in the mid-twentieth-century United States had to navigate fluctuating paper prices, but on the whole, American print media was not gravely threatened by conditions of scarcity (particularly when seen in light of the newsprint shortages, discussed in the following chapter, which ravaged the press abroad after the Second World War). The capital costs of producing a film were high, but neither was it a zero-sum game: if one studio made a film, this did not tend to impinge on another studio's ability to do the same. By contrast, broadcasting spectrum appeared to be a much scarcer resource in the early to mid-twentieth-century United States.[14] By the mid-1920s, extensive signal interference between competing radio stations had prompted Americans ranging from the technocratic Republican commerce secretary (and soon-to-be president) Herbert Hoover to the Democratic future Supreme Court justice and First Amendment stalwart Hugo Black to agree on the need to regulate broadcasting. To address the technical problem of spectrum interference, the Federal Radio Commission was created in 1927, and for much of the 1930s this was what the commission—renamed the Federal Communications Commission and expanded to cover telecommunications as well as broadcasting in 1934—continued to focus upon, notwithstanding its mandate to protect the "right of free speech by means of radio communication." Some interwar industry voices, likening radio to the press, argued that the new medium should enjoy freedom from government censorship, with David Sarnoff of RCA warning against the dangers of "over-regulation." But these demands coexisted with broad support for some form of radio regulation, which was sanctioned by the Supreme Court and backed by prominent members of that bellwether of civil-liberties discourse, the ACLU.[15]

For not everyone believed that the principles of classical liberalism could guarantee press and speech freedoms over the airwaves. An alternative understanding of civil-liberties protections gained particular traction in debates over radio regulation, by which some form of government involvement was seen as essential to preserving these liberties for ordinary Americans. As ACLU cofounder Morris Ernst stated in 1926, "short of government ownership and control of the stations, some machinery should be set up to insure as far as possible the presence on the air of minority points of view." Civil-libertarian arguments for radio regulation grew louder in the 1930s, a period when radio stations were becoming increasingly integrated into national chains and when newspaper owners were snapping up stations in many markets, stoking fears of local news monopolies. In a study released in 1936, in the midst of industrywide consolidation, the ACLU concluded that the range of opinions expressed on American radio was highly constricted. Three years later, in 1939, the FCC appointed a new chair, the Texan lawyer and committed New Deal liberal James Lawrence Fly, who departed from the narrowly technical approach that the commission had previously favored. Fly argued that powerful commercial actors, if left unchecked, could easily elbow small and local stations off the airwaves, thereby restricting the press and speech freedoms of less advantaged Americans. For Fly and his fellow regulatory liberals, government involvement was therefore necessary to protect these freedoms in the field of broadcasting. The compatibility of regulation and civil liberties in midcentury American liberalism was evident in Fly's career trajectory; after leaving the FCC, he went on to work as a director of the ACLU.[16]

The global conflagration of the Second World War sparked what the historian Daniel Rodgers has called an explosion of "Freedom talk" in American society. President Roosevelt's "Four Freedoms" speech in January 1941 lionized "freedom of speech and expression" as a core American value—and one the United States should pursue "everywhere in the world."[17] The Pearl Harbor attacks eleven months later cemented Washington's commitment to securing the United States' communications networks on a worldwide scale.[18] The wartime expansion of U.S. communications capabilities happened most prominently through military action and through the creation of emergency executive agencies such as the Office of War Information (OWI). James Fly, who coordinated the FCC's work with the military, industry, and executive-branch agencies through the Defense Communications Board, also set his sights abroad. "[We] must have a free ingress and egress of information, and freedom for all peoples of the world to communicate with each other," he announced to a meeting of the pro–New Deal National Lawyers Guild in November 1943. Fly included cable and radiotelegraph communications and radio and television broadcasting in proposals for how to achieve "freedom of communication" internationally after the war.[19]

Media industries also rapidly mobilized to support the war effort. In Hollywood, the days of the Production Code Administration appeasing fascist regimes and right-wing lobbying groups were over. Established directors like Frank Capra, John Ford, William Wyler, and John Huston turned out films for the U.S. military that were intended to explain the roots of the global conflict to newly conscripted soldiers. Walt Disney—who before Pearl Harbor had been a member of the anti-interventionist America First Committee—volunteered his studios to contribute animated maps to Capra's award-winning *Why We Fight* films. Meanwhile, Walter Wanger, then president of the Academy of Motion Picture Arts and Sciences, threw his energies into fundraising activities for European Jews and efforts to invigorate home-front morale. Fusing anticensorship liberalism to racial liberalism, Wanger proposed domestic reforms befitting the experience of American soldiers who had fought abroad, "side by side with people of all nations and all colors." Wanger's ambition was to cultivate this war-born cosmopolitanism domestically in the postwar era.[20]

One measure of the widespread support for American proposals to globalize information freedoms lay in how they formed a common cause for domestic antagonists in government and industry. David Sarnoff, the long-time head of RCA, had clashed furiously with Fly and the FCC over television broadcasting in the early 1940s when the FCC—hoping to prevent RCA domination of the infant industry—had refused to authorize technical standards as quickly as Sarnoff wished. In response, Sarnoff and RCA had launched what Fly decried as a public-relations "blitzkrieg" against the commission. Addressing the international picture, by contrast, the two men sounded more alike. An RCA advertisement that appeared in *Life* magazine in 1947 announced that *"Freedom to Listen"* and *"Freedom to Look"* were "as important as *Freedom of Speech* and *Freedom of the Press*" to achieving a lasting peace, adding that "[as] the world grows smaller, the question of international communications and world understanding grows larger."[21]

The "freedom to listen" that RCA proposed to *Life*'s mass readership was undoubtedly minimalist: it amounted to a right to "turn [the] receiver off," essentially an antiauthoritarian freedom to refuse to listen to government propaganda. In pitting individual liberties against governmental abuses, the ad offered no hint of Fly's argument that substantive freedom demanded robust regulation of powerful corporate interests. In a speech on these freedoms given in honor of the U.S. National Commission for the UN Educational, Scientific, and Cultural Organization (UNESCO) in 1947, Sarnoff underscored the tension between individual freedoms and government power, stating that only the "beacon of freedom which shines through a free press and free radio in democratic nations" could correct for "what a treacherous government may seek to hide."[22]

Yet, in parallel to domestic quarrels, there was emerging a consensus between regulatory liberals and many corporate actors around the objective to promote greater international communications in the postwar world. Domestically in favor of robust regulation, Fly attacked foreign obstructions to the international interests of American corporations, including RCA. For instance, Fly castigated British imperial barriers to direct communications that forced an RCA radio link between the United States and Australia to pass through Canada. Fly's broader postwar agenda entailed leveraging U.S. aid to break Britain's hold on communications within its empire. Meanwhile, Sarnoff, a frequent opponent of domestic regulatory authorities, backed governmental and even intergovernmental efforts to develop international broadcasting. In 1944 Sarnoff was named communications adviser to General Eisenhower, and after the war, RCA's own "general" (as Sarnoff liked to be called thereafter) pressed for the establishment of a UN radio station—a "Voice of the United Nations"—to be broadcast by a global network of shortwave transmitters. At various points, both Sarnoff and Fly proposed that American international communications be handled by a single, government-sanctioned monopoly.[23] Libertarianism in the international arena this was not.

In addition to endorsing the idea that midcentury new media could convey vital information—not just diverting entertainment—to both domestic and foreign audiences, proposals to dissolve the British imperial communications dominion pointed to another signal aspect of 1940s press-freedoms talk: the promotion of the "free flow of information" from the United States into foreign markets.

THE "FREE FLOW OF INFORMATION" AND THE GLOBAL MARKETPLACE

At the same time that a technologically expansive interpretation of press and speech freedoms was being yoked to antiauthoritarian civil liberties, many Americans in industry were making a parallel case for breaking down foreign trade restrictions in order to achieve the "free flow of information" abroad. What was the opposite of the Nazis' autarkic European empire and its premise of continental self-sufficiency? A world of borderless and seamless exchange—a world in which news and media flowed freely, like a pristine river, untrammeled by man-made barriers such as political borders or economic sanctions.

The quest to open markets abroad was not a new ambition for American business elites or policymakers in the 1940s. Since the late nineteenth century, U.S. trade, transportation, and foreign policies had been conditioned by the quest to find international outlets for the country's booming agricultural and industrial sectors—an imperative used to rationalize U.S. imperial interventions in the Philippines, Latin America, and China.[24] Nor were abstract notions of "flow" a twentieth-century invention. The historian Augustine Sedgewick has traced the genealogy of liberal-capitalist flow metaphors back to Adam Smith's Enlightenment case against mercantilism. By the mid-nineteenth century, commodity flows had joined riverine ones in the lexicon of American newspapers such as the *New York Times*, which refuted that the Northern economy was beholden to the "free flow of cotton" in one 1861 article. Following the 1929 crash, references to the "free flow" of "credit," "commerce," and "capital" rose sharply in the *Times*. What all these variations had in common was a tendency to make the cross-border movement of monies and materials seem like part of a beneficent natural order rather than contingent transactions conducted by specific historical actors. Sedgewick and media-studies scholar Nicole Starosielski, noting the tendency of flow talk to obfuscate politics, have analyzed the coercive labor systems and environmental interventions that have conditioned the movement of goods and ideas in space and in time. They show that the imagery of flows, however pastoral, is just that—imagery, discursive rather than natural, as man-made as the barriers it has historically decried.[25]

What *was* new in the 1930s and 1940s was the widespread use of flow metaphors to describe the movement of news and information across borders and—from the mid-1940s onward—the gathering insistence upon the importance of these flows in the postwar settlement. In 1934, Columbia University journalism-school dean and Kent Cooper intimate Carl V.

Ackerman proposed the "free flow of information to the American press" as the key to international harmony in a speech to the American Society of Newspaper Editors (ASNE). Three years later, former president Herbert Hoover identified the "free flow of words" as something that distinguished the United States from other countries, characterizing the American experience as a daily confrontation with a veritable torrent of broadcast as well as print media: Americans consumed "more billion words per capita or per minute or per decibel than any other people on earth." During a time of widespread deprivation, such rhetoric conjured up the familiar image of America as a land of abundance, with newspapers and radio sets joining comestibles in the twentieth-century Thanksgiving cornucopia. Just months before Europe plunged into war, the Pulitzer Prize committee specially praised America's foreign correspondents for surmounting various obstacles to the "free flow of information" erected by foreign governments.[26]

Free-flow language continued to multiply in the ensuing decade. With zero mentions between 1920 and 1929 and five between 1930 and 1939, the phrase "free flow of information" received sixty-six mentions in the *New York Times* in the 1940s. The phrase "freedom of information" also spiked in popularity, with zero mentions prior to 1940 versus 509 between 1940 and 1949. By the early 1940s flow talk had become institutionalized in the United States' wartime communications policies. The OWI's 1942 mandate included ensuring an "accurate and consistent flow of war information" to domestic and international audiences.[27]

Soon Washington found itself responding to concerted pressure from news professionals to prioritize free flow in its postwar aims. ASNE, an influential trade group, pressed the Democratic and Republican conventions to take a stand on worldwide press freedoms in their platforms leading up to the 1944 elections. Both did. The United States planned to give a prominent place to the "free flow of news" in ceasefire negotiations with Germany and Italy, James Reston reported in a front-page story in the *Times* in 1944. As victory over the Nazis was secured, Soviet control in Eastern Europe began to displace Goebbels's propaganda machine as a central concern for American journalists and editors worried that the "news blackout" to the east would foil postwar cooperation. In 1945 ASNE sponsored an international tour of three news veterans to advocate for the "free flow of news" across borders. The organization, which reported its findings directly to President Truman, warned of the noncommittal attitude of officials in Moscow.[28]

While 1940s free-flow talk was intertwined with critiques of authoritarian censorship, for the news industry's most vocal free-flow proponents it signified more than just anticensorship measures. For Kent Cooper of the AP and Hugh Baillie of the United Press (UP), it meant open markets. The heads of the two news agencies—in Cooper's words, "ardent business competitors" but "allies in the high principles of honest journalism"— together lobbied Washington to use its leverage against European news and cable cartels. For nearly three decades, Cooper had been a vocal and persistent critic of cooperative agreements that had, since the late nineteenth century, divvied up the globe among a few major international news agencies, notably British Reuters and French Havas. These cartelized arrangements, which were, according to Cooper, a symptom of Europe's anticompetitive streak, had, he charged, closed American agencies out of international markets, most vexingly in South America. Meanwhile, Baillie battled French attempts to establish a government news monopoly after the liberation. A related irritation for the AP and the UP was the difference in rates levied by British cable concerns, which—dominant outside the Western Hemisphere—charged American news agencies a higher rate per transmission than they did communications within the British Empire. Cooper emphasized that "uniform communications rates" were key to promoting peace.[29]

Like the AP, by the 1940s the American film industry had been protesting protectionism in European markets for decades, even as it had bowed to the wishes of foreign censors in order to maximize its share of those markets. As president of the Motion Picture Producers and Distributors of America (the MPPDA, the precursor to the MPAA), Will Hays traveled to France in 1928 to oppose a proposed system of quotas, which would have permitted four American imports per every domestically produced film. In 1936 Hays called on Mussolini in Rome to object to an Italian plan to cut the country's Hollywood imports.[30] While Hays's visit to Il Duce was ostensibly motivated more by profits than it was by principles, America's film czar would strike a patriotic tone in the years ahead. In his 1944 report to the MPPDA, Hays declared that the "most vicious censorship which any Government could exert against its own people would be to dam the free flow of screen entertainment." Eric Johnston, who took over the organization from Hays in 1945, the same year it was renamed the MPAA, added that films contributed to the "free flow of ideas and information" as well as entertainment.[31] Flow talk provided Hollywood with a powerful rhetorical tool that conflated the tariffs and quotas of U.S. allies with the political censorship of authoritarian systems. If Hays and Johnston were to be believed, both needed to be abolished in order to achieve true "freedom of the screen."

As the tide of the war turned, the question of how to translate this globalist rhetoric into foreign policy became ever more pressing. Did ensuring the "free flow of information" abroad entail primarily private-sector activity? Alternatively, what role should the U.S. government play in ensuring this war-born value in the postwar era? Kent Cooper backed private-sector news dissemination, having gone so far as to reject Washington's 1941 request to make AP Latin America correspondents available for government work under the Office of the Coordinator of Inter-American Affairs. Following Pearl Harbor, Cooper had agreed to provide Washington's wartime propaganda branches with free AP coverage for distribution abroad—but he maintained that "[if] government-backed news dissemination displaces the American news agencies abroad, a loss to the American war effort and to the American way will have occurred." Cooper also criticized governmental management of information at home, likening government secrecy to totalitarianism and acting as an early advocate of the transparency principles that crystallized two decades later in the Freedom of Information Act (FOIA).[32]

Not everyone agreed that freedom of information was synonymous with economic or political libertarianism, however. Cooper's seemingly high-minded stance was compromised by the profit motive, particularly after 1945, when an antitrust decision by the Supreme Court upended the AP's domestic business model and intensified its need to cultivate foreign markets.[33] For many commentators, the sheer human cost of the war effort necessitated an appeal to a higher good—to something more inspiring and less obviously self-interested than profits. Even as Cooper lobbied for free flow on behalf of American news agencies, the Henry Luce–funded Commission on Freedom of the Press was exploring another means of updating press and speech freedoms for the postwar era: the notion that government might promote these freedoms through positive action.

THE COMMISSION ON FREEDOM OF
THE PRESS AND POSITIVE FREEDOMS

At the same time that figures in the news and media industries like Kent Cooper, Walter Wanger, and David Sarnoff were attempting to rebrand press and speech freedoms with new catchphrases, the Commission on Freedom of the Press was treating them as a philosophical and policymaking dilemma of the highest order. Formed in 1944, the commission—also called the Hutchins Commission, after its chair, the influential University of Chicago administrator Robert Hutchins—framed its inquiry into the state of press freedoms in the United States as an urgent intellectual endeavor, potentially "of the first-order of significance" in defining the "fundamental operating conditions of democracy," as member Charles Merriam put it in an early commission memorandum.[34]

Much of the commission's discussion centered on industrial concentration in the domestic American press. As Kent Cooper's AP battled antitrust regulations in federal court, some commissioners questioned oligarchic ownership patterns that appeared to have stymied healthy debate and the pluralistic sourcing of information, particularly (though not exclusively) in the news industry. Revealing a gap between the press and public sentiment, participants noted Franklin Roosevelt's electoral success despite widespread opposition from the country's newspaper editors. They also pointed out the lack of discussion of anti-Semitism in mainstream American newspapers in the 1930s, even as evidence of Nazi depredations mounted.[35] Could such a press really be trusted to report accurately and impartially on either the domestic mood or international affairs?

A major question facing the commission was whether the unreliability of private-sector media justified an expanded governmental role in collecting and disseminating information. Overseas, wartime agencies had become deeply involved in news distribution, furnishing voice broadcasting to international audiences where private companies like RCA would not. Domestic government information programs were also set up to furnish the American public with war-related news and information. But the programs, consolidated under the OWI in 1942, were contentious. In 1943 congressional conservatives, charging that OWI was engaging in pro-Roosevelt and pro–New Deal propagandizing, forced major budget cuts upon the agency, with its domestic branch absorbing the bulk of the cuts. The OWI abruptly terminated its efforts to ascertain American public opinion through polling, for instance.[36]

The commission's take on government polling was more positive. Political scientist Harold Lasswell backed government-conducted polls. Foreign adviser John Grierson, the Scottish-born documentary filmmaker who headed Canada's National Film Board during the war, was also enthusiastic. Grierson noted that in Canada the national government, curious about popular sentiment toward wartime price controls, had bypassed both the press and the legislature through direct polling. According to Grierson, the Canadian government had concluded—contrary to press and legislative findings—that there was widespread public support for price controls.[37] And commission member Archibald MacLeish noted that work by the U.S. Office of Facts and Figures (OFF) to gather public-opinion data had offered valuable insights on the reception of the federal government's wartime rationing plans. MacLeish spent the war years coordinating information resources for defense purposes at the Library of Congress, the OFF, and the OWI.[38]

More generally, the Hutchins Commission's discussions about government polling revealed the openness of some members toward activist government policy in the realm of communications and their willingness to frame such activity as furthering, not hindering, press freedoms—an important intellectual contribution to the press-freedoms discussions of the 1940s. Again and again in discussions and memos participants stressed that press and speech freedoms might involve more than "freedom from" state interference: they might also entail government action to address deficiencies in private-sector media.

The philosophical rationale for this challenge to laissez-faire liberalism was articulated most forcefully by commission member and emeritus Harvard philosophy professor William Hocking. In his 1947 commission publication, *Freedom of the Press: A Framework of Principle*, Hocking called government the "greatest instrument for achieving the common purposes of the human community." Other participants similarly deployed the language of positive liberties in commission discussions. Hunter College president George Shuster acknowledged that the group was directed by a "positive definition of freedom" that applied to "community integrity and usefulness" in addition to the "free individual," while exiled German philosopher Kurt Riezler, who with John Grierson numbered among the commission's four foreign advisers, differentiated between "freedom from" and "freedom for" and contended that "the former is not an end itself."[39] Harold Lasswell in particular insisted on what the government could do to promote press and speech freedoms—unsurprising given the approval his interwar writings had expressed regarding elite management of the masses. Over the course of two years of deliberations, Lasswell hammered away at the "urgency of clarifying the positive and negative meaning of freedom of communication," of defining "*both* a *positive* and a *negative* meaning" for freedom of the press, which embraced both " 'freedom from' and 'freedom to.' "[40]

In part, this discourse of positive freedoms indicated the compatibility of media reform and civil libertarianism in the early- to mid-1940s United States. Harvard Law's Zechariah Chafee, whose scholarship had helped to define liberal First Amendment jurisprudence after the First World War, supported cultivating "positive forces" to foster diversity in the American media. But Chafee also noted grounds for caution. "We can speak with much less assurance about affirmative governmental action [in the field of press freedoms] than was possible in dealing with governmental restrictions," he wrote in 1947. "Here we have no abundant material to guide us, either in judicial decisions or in writers like Milton and Mill."[41] On the domestic front, commission members repeatedly expressed suspicion of government censorship of media content. Even the participants who were most in favor of robust government regulation of the press—William

Hocking and Archibald MacLeish—pointed to industrial self-regulation as a potential alternative to governmental oversight, with Hollywood's Production Code Administration furnishing a real-world example.[42]

In addition to censorship, antitrust regulation also raised the hackles of some commission members. Reinhold Niebuhr warned that when government played too heavy-handed a role in the media, it "creates totalitarianism." Zealous regulators, eager to enforce the government's prerogative to ensure competition between media producers, might in fact do more harm than good. Chafee had supported the Justice Department's antitrust case against the AP, but a few years later he expressed a more circumspect attitude toward regulatory authorities. "Freedom of the press is always in danger when press laws are enforced by wide-awake officials who know their job thoroughly," Chafee concluded sardonically in his 1947 commission study, *Government and Mass Communications*. "Witness the Nazi Propaganda Ministry or Russia under the czars." Moreover, for some participants, industrial concentration in and of itself did not appear to be an evil. Banker and economist Beardsley Ruml took pains to differentiate monopolistic tendencies in the American news industry from Soviet-style "centralization" and defended a certain level of concentration in the industry in spite of the AP's recent prosecution.[43]

If the commission's discussions of the domestic scene produced lively debate, the international situation, by contrast, seemed to throw the strengths of the American press into relief. For, in spite of their differences over the nitty-gritty of domestic policy, all the American commissioners shared a firm commitment to liberal democracy such that chair Robert Hutchins could credibly claim at one meeting that "no one seriously contended there was a real difference among members of the Commission on the kind of society we want." The commission's meditations on the postwar settlement were marked by that curious combination of exceptionalism and universalism that characterized the liberal American weltanschauung in the mid-1940s. For Zechariah Chafee, soul searching at home was a prerequisite for action abroad: it was necessary to investigate the domestic press, he thought, before America could go about "filling the intellectual gap . . . brought about by the collapse of Europe." Reinhold Niebuhr dispensed with Chafee's pretense of humility. Given the "inchoate world community," Niebuhr thought, one of the Hutchins Commission's jobs was to "determine what freedom means from the global standpoint." Addressing the international situation, the American intellectuals on the commission echoed voices in the news, film, and broadcasting industries in advocating for the global dissemination of American media after the war, which would serve as both instance and agent of worldwide press freedoms.[44]

Two strands of analysis that were at times contradictory ran through the commission's final report, which was published in March 1947 under the title *A Free and Responsible Press: A General Report on Mass Communication: Newspapers, Radio, Motion Pictures, Magazines, and Books*. First, in tackling domestic issues, the report insisted on the existence of a moral right to expression that transcended state and corporate prerogatives and on the protection of legal rights to expression even in the absence of moral claims. The report's bolder suggestions included extending First Amendment protections to film and radio; FCC encouragement of "diversity" and competition on FM radio frequencies, which were newly available thanks to advances in broadcasting technology; and the protection of the rights of revolutionary minorities in the absence of a clear and present danger. The last item, written by Chafee, explicitly took issue with the Alien Registration Act of 1940, which had criminalized revolutionary groups and which would be used after the war in anticommunist prosecutions. "[If] we are to live progressively," the commission asserted, "we must live dangerously."[45]

Second, the final report framed its recommendations as part of a distinctly American vision of what a free press should look like. Its critical attitude toward the domestic press sat somewhat awkwardly alongside its faith in the American press's exemplary characteristics in international context. During the commission's deliberations, foreign adviser Kurt Riezler had insisted that a "two-way process of mutual response between the members of a community" was the sine qua non of press and speech freedoms, elaborating that though the "[First] Amendment to the Constitution takes the universe of discourse for granted," it was "doubtful whether and to what extent it can be taken for granted under the conditions of life in a modern industrial society."[46] *A Free and Responsible Press* translated this "two-way" language into the vernacular of American exceptionalism: according to the report, the "two-way" process of exchange that characterized Riezler's ideal of public engagement in fact reflected the "American faith" in the "way public opinion should be formed." Suggesting the merits of the American model vis-à-vis the United States' wartime enemy (Nazi Germany) and emerging Cold War nemesis (the Soviet Union), the report contrasted this open, democratic process to systems in which public opinion was "manufactured by a central authority and 'sold' to the public." The American press, despite its myriad weaknesses, was presented as being preferable to foreign alternatives.

This contrast was more than just a bit of patriotic cheerleading. On the contrary, in the eyes of the Hutchins Commission, it justified the U.S. government's "special obligations in international communications." The report refuted the argument made by congressional conservatives and corporate libertarians that Washington should get out of the information business after the war. Far greater than the danger of partisanship on the part of executive-branch agencies, *A Free and Responsible Press* insisted, was the "danger that the people of this country and other countries may, in the absence of official information and discussion, remain unenlightened on vital issues." More than their corporate peers, the intellectuals of the Hutchins Commission recognized that postwar communications would stand on the shoulders of the U.S. government's wartime efforts.[47]

Two studies authored by commission members and published under the commission's imprimatur underscored the ways in which the war had fundamentally reshaped the global information landscape. The United States' archipelago of military bases, expanded by its bloody wartime conquests from Japan in the Pacific theater, was also an archipelago of communications bases. *Peoples Speaking to Peoples* (1946), coauthored by commission staff members Robert D. Leigh and Llewellyn White, noted that Allied communications "reached seven times as many points as were reached before the war" at "eighteen times the pre-war volume." While for many other countries—even Britain—government involvement in overseas communications was nothing new, for the United States it marked a dramatic shift. In a few short years, the OWI and the Office of the Coordinator of Inter-American Affairs (OCIAA) had grown out of nothing to reach an estimated audience of one billion people around the world. Military communications had come to dwarf private American holdings: White and Leigh reported that during the war, the army and navy had built up a communications-coverage capacity that was "many times greater" than that of private American corporations and had "done wonders" in maximizing channel capacity and improving signal reach. Zechariah Chafee's massive two-volume study for the Hutchins Commission, *Government and Mass Communications* (1947), likewise adduced quantitative evidence of the impressive increase in global communications during the war. Chafee, Leigh, and White agreed that Washington could not afford to return to its prewar posture of aloofness given the enthusiastic use of shortwave broadcasting by other governments.[48]

As the Hutchins Commission prepared its final report, controversy was brewing over Washington's overseas information services. The State Department had concluded that some continuation of American voice-radio broadcasting to audiences abroad was necessary after the war ended. Yet there was no precedent for peacetime information diplomacy in the annals of U.S. foreign policy, and it remained unclear as to who would or should furnish the content.[49] In 1945 the State Department brought in *Encyclopedia Britannica* publisher and former advertising executive William Benton to oversee the continuation of government information services after hostilities had ceased—"the job of selling America to the world," as *Life* magazine put it—and also to sell this plan to the American public. Liberal democracy, Benton explained to *Life*, could not be left "voiceless except for diplomatic exchanges and the erratic interplay of private communication." On the commission, White, Leigh, and Chafee wrote sympathetically of Benton's work, arguing that the U.S. government might step in to provide communications facilities and, as a last resort, content when the private sector lacked market incentives to do so—envisioning a kind of internationalization of positive information freedoms.[50]

But not everyone was happy with Washington's proposals. For news agencies in the business of disseminating information, the prolongation of government information programs seemed to augur unwelcome competition. In 1946, Kent Cooper's AP rescinded the wartime agreement by which it had provided free news to the government for shortwave broadcast abroad. Its directors cited concerns that Washington could become a rival news distributor—or worse. "We hold that any broadcast designed to promote our way of life will of necessity be propaganda—good propaganda possibly . . . but certainly not objective news presentation," the AP asserted.[51] By suggesting that government information programs might damage the reputation of the American press, the AP challenged a key tenet of both the Hutchins Commission's and Benton's work: namely, the idea that government might promote press freedoms through positive action.

INFORMATION FREEDOMS AND INFORMATION DIPLOMACY FROM WORLD WAR INTO COLD WAR

American responses to the publication of the Hutchins Report in 1947 captured the winds of change traversing American politics and culture in the late 1940s amid intensifying hostility between the United States and the Soviet Union. Robert McCormick's *Chicago Tribune*, known for its right-wing editorial line, red-baited the commission, calling its report "a major effort in the campaign of a determined group of totalitarian thinkers" to take over the press. More surprisingly, centrist outlets also discounted the commission's work. Writing off his earlier subvention of the commission, Henry Luce disavowed *A Free and Responsible Press*, and Luce publications *Time* and *Fortune* were critical. *Time* noted that the program favored by the commission had been called a "long step toward a U.S. or U.N.-dominated press." *Fortune*, meanwhile, cited McCormick, who called *A Free and Responsible Press* the "outpourings of a gang of crackpots."[52]

Scholars of the Hutchins Commission have noted how these shifts rendered the kind of forceful antitrust regulation envisioned by James L. Fly and Archibald MacLeish politically impossible by the late 1940s. Conservatives and corporate interests successfully tarred domestic antimonopoly reform as a dangerously statist program, with the House of Representatives launching an investigation of the FCC in 1948. By then, Fly had long since departed the FCC.[53]

In addition to undermining regulatory reform, rising anticommunist anxieties also threatened domestic civil liberties. The Soviet threat was portrayed as coming not only from high-level espionage but from the way

concealed propaganda could infiltrate the fabric of everyday life. Even resolutely anticommunist cultural producers confessed their inability to extir-
pate such propaganda from the American media. When asked in a 1947
radio seminar whether the United States should allow broadcasting from
Moscow on American radio, David Sarnoff fretted that the country was
"already accepting it."[54] Likewise, the 1949 *Britannica Book of the Year*
apologized that not even its carefully edited selections could be fully
trusted, for propaganda was "often as difficult to discover as truth." In a
climate of ever-growing paranoia, freedom of expression was no content-
neutral proposition; it comprised "freedom from such propaganda."[55] The
early Cold War was transforming the idea of freedom in American mass
culture, narrowing it into a byword for anticommunism.

Erstwhile Hutchins Commission member Zechariah Chafee belonged
to a principled minority in arguing that the antidote to Soviet propaganda
was more free speech, not less. Exposing Soviet ideas to the pitiless scrutiny
of the press and the American public would defang them, Chafee thought,
echoing earlier civil-libertarian arguments about whether Nazi and British
propaganda should be allowed into the United States.[56] More typical was
the response of Chafee's fellow liberal William Benton. By the time of the
Korean crisis, civil liberties were of secondary importance to Benton and
other Democrats eager to prove their anticommunist credentials. "[The]
communist issue is much more serious, in my judgment, than the public
understands," Benton, then a U.S. senator representing Connecticut, concluded in 1950, defending his vote in favor of the McCarran Internal Security Act, which greatly increased the government's power to impinge upon
civil liberties in the name of national security. "This is no mere question of
civil rights." President Truman's veto of the act—on the grounds that it
would threaten freedom of expression domestically—was handily overrid-
den in Congress. The domestic reforms envisioned by the Hutchins Commission in 1947 thus seemed by 1950 to be a dead letter. "I do not think
you can do much with the phrase 'freedom of the press' or 'freedom of
information,' *applied to this country*," John Howe, Benton's trusted assistant, wrote to his boss in January of that year.[57]

But while liberals quietly set aside the cause of press reform at home,
they persisted in promoting information flows and freedoms abroad.

"Freedom is a basic human right," Howe stated in his memo to Benton. "Internationally, you should find opportunities to speak out against obstacles of all kinds to the free flow of information, notably to censorship." By the late 1940s liberals had successfully folded anticensorship politics into U.S. diplomacy at the United Nations. At the UN Subcommission on Freedom of Information—which was tasked with drafting freedom-of-information language for both the Universal Declaration of Human Rights and a legally binding human-rights covenant—U.S. delegate Zechariah Chafee successfully opposed a Soviet proposal to ban "warmongering" and fascist propaganda, denouncing it as cover for state censorship.[58] (Ironically, Soviet proposals echoed the language deployed by American isolationists just a decade earlier in their attempts to quash Walter Wanger's *Blockade* and the "warmongering" Anglophile *March of Time* nonfiction film series.) At the United Nations' 1948 Geneva Conference on Freedom of Information, the U.S. delegation, featuring Benton and Chafee, was joined by delegations from Western Europe, Latin America, and Asia in opposing Soviet attempts to legitimize state control of the press.[59]

Early UN press-freedoms initiatives were also seeded with language that appeared to apply to broadcast and audiovisual as well as print media, presumably to the approbation of American industry figures like Eric Johnston and David Sarnoff. In December 1948 the UN General Assembly adopted the Universal Declaration of Human Rights. Article 19 of the declaration—closely modeled on a U.S. draft—presented an expansive guarantee of press and speech freedoms: "Everyone shall have the right to freedom of thought and expression; this right shall include freedom to hold opinions without interference and to seek, receive and impart information and ideas by any means and regardless of frontiers."[60]

Some policymakers even suggested outlets for positive freedoms abroad despite their status as a domestic nonstarter. William Benton explicitly applied the Hutchins Commission's work to U.S. foreign policy, arguing that the "inadequacy of existing facilities" for media worldwide required "positive action" by governmental and intergovernmental agencies to "increase the flow of information and knowledge between peoples." One of UNESCO's main tasks, according to Benton, who led the U.S.

delegation to UNESCO's 1947 Mexico City conference, was to reduce barriers to "free flow" by "[remedying] deficiencies in the physical facilities of the radio, the press, and the motion pictures" in war-damaged countries and "countries that technically are less well advanced."[61] Deficient physical infrastructure obstructed the natural advance of information flows, Benton suggested, like craters that rendered a bombed-out road impassable—or like a dirt path that asphalt had never touched. This suggestion foreshadowed President Truman's 1949 "Point Four" speech, in which Truman announced a program of U.S. aid to "underdeveloped areas" of the world, as well as the logic of many 1960s media-development initiatives (discussed in chapter 4).

While what media scholar Victor Pickard calls "corporate libertarianism" was taking root at home, then, a somewhat different picture was emerging in U.S. foreign policy. International historians have shown how mounting tensions with the Soviet Union in the late 1940s led the United States to institutionalize peacetime information diplomacy for the first time in its history. The AP's wish to demobilize government news dissemination abroad after 1945 and conservative opposition to peacetime information diplomacy more generally were eclipsed by Cold War concerns. In 1948 Congress passed the Smith-Mundt Act, which authorized Washington to disseminate propaganda outside U.S. borders. Erwin Canham of ASNE and the *Christian Science Monitor*—who just a few years earlier had backed Kent Cooper's effort to demobilize government news dissemination—chaired the commission that the act created to advise the government on international information matters. The Voice of America, its future in doubt after President Truman abolished the OWI in August 1945, survived to launch Russian-language broadcasts in 1947, in part thanks to William Benton's timely intervention during his tenure at the State Department. Benton's career also epitomized the epochal shift toward government information diplomacy; he had been a member of the anti-interventionist America First Committee before Pearl Harbor.[62]

Softening the apparent contradiction between procorporate policies at home and Washington's burgeoning information apparatus abroad was the conception of information freedoms that was crystallizing in the early–Cold War United States: freedom of information as a capitalist

weapon against the global communist threat. A 1950 Walter Wanger article encapsulated this transformation. In "Donald Duck and Diplomacy,"
published in the journal *Public Opinion Quarterly*, Wanger took aim at
one of his accustomed targets—domestic film censorship. At a moment
when Hollywood had come under congressional scrutiny for allegedly har-
boring communists and disseminating Soviet propaganda, some critics
favored export censorship of American films in order to burnish the
United States' image abroad (the idea was to block films that might give
foreign audiences a negative impression of the country). Unsurprisingly,
Wanger argued that export censorship was a mistake. The United States,
he thought, had to allow its flaws as well as its strengths to be seen by publics abroad. To show only its good side would be to imitate the Goebbels
model. Wanger thus pled for liberal American cultural exports in two
senses of the word *liberal*: ample and uncensored.

This argument dovetailed with the anticensorship stance that the
United States had taken at the United Nations as well as the free-flow
maxims favored by corporate American media. It was also familiar from
Wanger's writings and political activities of the previous ten-plus years.
The key difference was that by 1950 any reference to the flow of information *into* the United States was absent. Gone were Wanger's statements of
faith in the critical judgment of the American public, such as when he
asked in his 1939 *Foreign Affairs* essay, "Is it not better for Americans to
read and understand 'Mein Kampf' than for the book to be banned?"
Gone, too, was his expansive wartime vision of a United States rendered
more cosmopolitan and tolerant through two-way contact with other
countries and cultures. Instead, "Donald Duck and Diplomacy" emphasized only Hollywood's capacity to export films—and "enlightenment"—
overseas: a one-way vector of anticommunist cultural diplomacy.[63]

This pared-down understanding of information freedoms was compat-
ible with both the profit motive and the Cold War security state. In the
same article, Wanger connected Hollywood exports to a proposal William
Benton had made to the Senate earlier that year for a "Marshall Plan of
Ideas," which called for a "greatly expanded program of information and
education" and a "steady and steadily increasing pressure in behalf of
world-wide freedom of information" in the name of the "struggle now

raging between freedom and communism." In international organizations, meanwhile, Benton was busy adapting the lessons of his advertising career to the imperatives of Cold War anticommunism. "A salesman is smart when he gets someone else to tell his story for him," Benton wrote to a State Department contact in late 1949, arguing that the United States should seek to use the United Nations and its agencies as proxies for U.S. interests.[64]

One question, however, remained unanswered: what to do when audiences abroad did not buy the stories the United States was selling about information freedoms.

2

Quantifying and Qualifying Freedom of Information During the Early Cold War

> With all the deficiencies of the United States press and radio ... the fact remains that the American people are the best-informed great people in the world, and they are better informed than they have ever been before. These are plain historical facts.
>
> —Erwin Canham, "International Freedom of Information" (1949)

> Having become a standard formula in the postwar diplomatic and professional lexicon, [freedom of information] is an extension and perhaps a deviation from ideas of freedom of expression and opinion and of the press.... Certain governments fight for freedom of information as others formerly battled against freedom of the press, because they think they can thereby attack, limit, and hinder freedom of opinion.
>
> —Jacques Kayser, *Mort d'une liberté* (1955)

In December 1947 the Scottish documentary filmmaker and producer John Grierson wrote a long letter to one of his contacts in the United States, Harvard Law professor and fellow Hutchins Commission participant Zechariah Chafee. Besides serving on the commission, Grierson had spent much of the Second World War coordinating film propaganda for the Canadian government, and so when Chafee was preparing the commission study *Government and Mass Communications*, he had unsurprisingly looked to Grierson's Hutchins contributions for material on Canadian information services. In October 1947 *Government and Mass Communications* was published. The kerfuffle that soon arose over Grierson's account captured in microcosm the fate of positive information freedoms in early–Cold War North America: Grierson stood accused of having misrepresented Canada's wartime information apparatus as being a permanent feature of its media landscape when, as one of his critics countered, "the trend since the war has been toward the steady contraction of government enterprise in the information field."[1]

By the time of his letter to Chafee, Grierson had returned to Europe, having quit Canada's National Film Board shortly before the eruption of a red scare there. Still, he was eager to tell his side of the story. "I am, as you know, most respectful of your own views and you were right to say that you do not associate yourself or the Commission with me," Grierson wrote to his liberal American counterpart. But he also took the opportunity to stress the United States' international isolation in its Cold War turn against social reform. "The American position . . . is going to have trouble all along the line," Grierson predicted, "not only from the left, and not only from those who are accused of being 'totalitarian,' but from all, who, with me, believe in the European conception of the State." According to Grierson, the Allies had won the war not through the "pursuit of those abstract liberal considerations" that were a "simple reflection" of North America's "superior wealth in the world and its special capacity to relax" but rather through the "concept of planned total effort . . . which economic conditions must progressively [continue to] justify" even after hostilities had ceased.[2]

Grierson's observations about the material differences between North America and the rest of the world in 1947, though idiosyncratically expressed, were not academic. Alone among the major powers, the United States had emerged economically strengthened from the Second World War. In Europe, on the other hand, six years of total war had decimated housing and transportation infrastructure, disrupted trade networks, and generated foreign-exchange shortages among combatants. While postwar austerity most famously entailed shortages and rationing of food staples— quite literally Europe's bread and butter—it also touched on commodities essential to the press, such as newsprint and paper pulp. The Soviet Union, previously the source of 70 percent of the wood pulp purchased in France, had not renewed its pulp exports since 1939, and other major pulp producers, foremost among them Canada and the Scandinavian countries, preferred to export to hard-currency countries. To make matters worse, many governments in Western Europe, seeking to conserve scarce dollar reserves, slashed imports that they deemed inessential to reconstruction— including paper products. Britain rationed newsprint until 1957. Newspapers that did not disappear outright shrank to a fraction of their prewar size: in Britain, the average newspaper in 1950 was six to eight pages long, compared to twenty pages before the war. This was "not a shortage" but a "famine," wrote the British *Daily Express*. In France, meanwhile, austerity posed both material and existential challenges to the reincarnated republic. The French state's statistical bureau, revamped in the spring of 1946 to play down its connection to the wartime collaborationist government, continued to use Vichy-era letterhead until the early fall.[3] In postwar Europe, information did not flow, it trickled.

It was in this climate of political uncertainty and economic austerity that the institutions of the postwar international system—including UNESCO, based in Paris; the Food and Agricultural Organization (FAO), in Rome; and the World Health Organization (WHO), in Geneva—emerged, both agents and instances of the effort to reopen channels of communication, movement, and trade that had been closed by the Second World War. In the broadest terms, the United States looked to this system to foster the global liberalization of trade and capital: to rebuild capitalism in what had been Hitler's autarkic continental empire but also to open up the domestic and imperial economies of its European allies. For other actors, however, this same international system constituted an arena in which to assert *their* political aspirations and understandings of human rights. The location of many of the United Nations' so-called soft-power agencies in Europe was a particular point of pride for policymakers there, who were then confronting their own diminished geopolitical statures in the face of postwar American hegemony and looming superpower conflict.[4] Examining the conflicts and controversies that beset UNESCO in the years after its founding illuminates the partial triumphs and ongoing trials of U.S. information diplomacy in Europe (discussed in this chapter) and in the decolonizing and developing worlds (in chapters 3 and 4).

International institutions housed a variety of freedom-of-information initiatives and agendas in the immediate postwar era. At the UN Subcommission on Freedom of Information, Zechariah Chafee and others set to work drafting definitions of press and speech freedoms for planned international agreements, including what became Article 19 of the Universal Declaration of Human Rights. Simultaneously, the United Nations' specialized agencies tackled pressing matters of wartime reconstruction. As UNESCO's first director of mass communications and public information, John Grierson oversaw the launch of a series of pathbreaking surveys of worldwide newspaper, radio, and film resources—part of an unprecedented global operation to amass social and economic data that one historian of the United Nations has called "[perhaps] the most significant practical achievement" of its early years.[5] As one contemporary, the French legal scholar Fernand Terrou, explained in 1951, UNESCO's work to gather international press and media data and documentation—"never previously equaled for completeness and co-ordination"—made possible his own comparative study of press and media laws. UNESCO also incubated new professional and social-science organizations, including the International Press Institute (the IPI, established in 1951) and the International Association for Mass Communication Research (the IAMCR, founded in 1957), which were dedicated to promoting professional exchange and research about the media—and were viewed by leading American participants as a means of internationalizing American journalistic and social-scientific norms.[6]

New data and new forms of contact did not always produce Washington's desired results, however. The data revealed, among other things, a sharp contrast between the United States and the rest of the world in terms of newsprint consumption. During a period when many of its allies were still suffering from shortages, the United States painted requests to redistribute newsprint supplies as fundamentally incompatible with liberal capitalism. But to Grierson, Terrou, and others based outside North America, the United States' free-flow and free-market stance seemed impracticable at a time when many governments remained intimately involved in the provision of raw materials like newsprint and in the rebuilding of war-devastated industries. These competing aspirations for the postwar political economy intersected with epistemological disputes: the very categories by which American journalists and social scientists analyzed and advertised information freedoms were challenged by their counterparts elsewhere, particularly in France. Even after newsprint short-ages had begun to ease, tensions lingered at UNESCO, the IPI, and the IAMCR over American economic and cultural power in the postwar world.[7]

Clashes over information freedoms during the early Cold War thus revealed both the strengths and the limitations of U.S. free-flow diplo-macy. Even as the United States consolidated its influence over the political economy of media and knowledge production about the media, its critics in Western Europe—who stood on the front lines of early U.S. contain-ment strategy—insisted that information was materially embodied and culturally conditioned.

THE NEWSPRINT CRISIS AND
THE MATERIALITY OF INFORMATION

In the task of postwar reconstruction, the United Nations and its agencies found a raison d'être and a ready-made challenge. Following its 1946 Gen-eral Conference, UNESCO initiated a series of far-flung surveys of press and media capacity, starting with twelve "war-devastated" countries in Europe and Asia: Belgium, China, Czechoslovakia, Denmark, France, Greece, Luxembourg, Norway, the Netherlands, the Philippines, Poland, and Yugoslavia. As John Grierson announced in the inaugural issue of the *UNESCO Courier* in February 1948, "The [1947 Technical Needs] survey . . . gave the first detailed picture of its kind of losses and deficiencies in equipment, manpower and raw materials in the press, film and radio industries." If the period from 1933 to 1945 in Europe had been character-ized by economic autarky and rampant misinformation, the surveys seemed to instantiate the values of the peace: countries sharing reliable fig-ures for the common good. The final Technical Needs survey, published in 1951, reiterated that UNESCO's work marked the first time that such information had been collected in many countries and touted its use by numerous organizations and researchers.[8]

This new emphasis on cross-border data sharing lent itself to various causes. Journalism professor Ralph Casey, an American member of the 1948 Technical Needs Commission, declared that "without adequate supplies and equipment," there could be "no comprehensive free flow of information." Other Americans in government and industry stayed abreast of the Technical Needs reports, alert to the possibilities they described for exporting low-cost radio receivers and other equipment.[9] Meanwhile, anti-colonial activists were hopeful that by institutionalizing reporting require-ments for non-self-governing territories at the United Nations, social and economic data would help to undermine colonialism: the idea was that international monitoring would expose the rift between the civilizing rhetoric of the colonial powers and the extractive and exploitative nature of colonialism in practice.[10]

The numbers also exposed sharp divergences in international paper and pulp consumption. *Paper for Printing—Today and Tomorrow*, a 1952 study jointly presented by UNESCO, the FAO, and the *Economist*, found that in 1950 the United States was consuming 51 percent of the world's supply of wood pulp, the key raw material in newsprint manufacture. In terms of newsprint, the statistics were even more staggering: "With only six per cent of the world's population, the United States uses 59 [percent] of the world's newsprint." The same year, Europe was home to 17 percent of the world's population and consumed 22 percent of its newsprint. *World Communications*, a 1950 atlas designed to publicize the findings of UNESCO's Technical Needs reports for a broad audience, illustrated the imbalances in worldwide newsprint consumption in stark graphical form.[11]

Most striking to the contemporary reader in this chart (figure 2.1) may be the gaping disparity between per capita newsprint consumption in Asia and Africa versus that elsewhere; these groupings would soon become divided into the developing and developed worlds. As we shall see in chap-ters 3 and 4, the European powers, responding to pressures from both above and below, sought to reform and reinvent their postwar presence in Asia and Africa, in part through revamped information policies. "[We] are not a nation of 50 million people to-day but a nation of 113 million people, white, black and others," wrote John Grierson in *Sight and Sound* in 1948, calling for enhanced educational and technical facilities in British colonial Africa.[12] At the same time, however, European resentments festered inward and bubbled upward, with the newsprint data lending fuel to criticisms of

WORLD NEWSPRINT CONSUMPTION IN RELATION TO WORLD POPULATION IN 1950

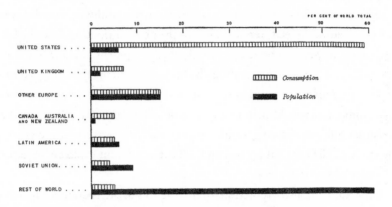

FIGURE 2.1 "World newsprint consumption in relation to world population in 1950."
Paper for Printing—Today and Tomorrow (Paris: UNESCO, 1952), 75.

postwar American power and prosperity. "[Nobody] in Europe believes in the American way of life," declared the English historian and public intellectual A. J. P. Taylor over BBC Radio in the fall of 1945. Grierson echoed that despite "growing acceptance of the principle of two-way flow" in the United States, the fact was that Americans' "use of 65 per cent of the world's output in newsprint [created] a problem when you are talking of freedom of the press, not to mention two-way, three-way or x-way flows of information."[13] For Grierson, American hyperconsumption of newsprint contradicted the very values that the United States was touting internationally.

Similarly, in France, Jacques Kayser, journalist and delegate to the United Nations' 1948 Geneva Conference on Freedom of Information, singled out the United States for absorbing Canadian newsprint production—and then some. Kayser bolstered his case with statistics: "In terms of newsprint, India consumes annually what the United States consumes in one day. As for France, it consumes in one year what the United States consumes in twenty days." He summed the matter up succinctly: "[It] is from a single country that the [newsprint] problem arises."[14] In a manner that recalled the earlier regulatory proposals of American New

Dealers like James L. Fly and Archibald MacLeish, Kayser drew on American research to argue that the country's consumption neither benefitted the quality of American newspapers—advertising tended to occupy the extra pages—nor correlated with a diversification of news outlets since ownership of the American press was more concentrated in 1945 than it had been in 1910.[15]

The Americans tasked with negotiating international freedom-of-information agreements were not unaware of the harsh material realities of European reconstruction. Newsprint in particular was acknowledged to be a major source of vulnerability leading up to the 1948 Geneva conference, with even Britain criticizing the U.S. position. Publisher and State Department veteran William Benton, who chaired the U.S. delegation to Geneva, wrote confidentially of the "soul-sickness and depth of despair of many European peoples" and admitted that newsprint and other shortages were so "tragic" that "'freedom of information' becomes almost meaningless." Zechariah Chafee, a member of the UN Subcommission on Freedom of Information who also accompanied Benton to Geneva, noted amid growing U.S.-Soviet tensions that it was "small comfort to [Europeans] to be told that we shall win in the end and bring them liberation after their cities have been ruined." At the same time that the conference was taking place, Chafee's own book *Government and Mass Communications* was facing distribution hurdles in Britain due to British import restrictions on dollar goods.[16]

Benton and Chafee were also aware that aggressive maneuvers to liberalize markets could alienate allies. This had been the U.S. experience with the film trade in the years after the war. In France, the Blum-Byrnes Accords of 1946, named for signatories Léon Blum and U.S. Secretary of State James F. Byrnes, had erased France's war debts partly in exchange for the reduction of import quotas on Hollywood films. But the accords spurred protests in the French film industry. In January 1948 ten thousand film industry workers gathered to demonstrate against them, and later that year the French government reinstated import quotas on dubbed films. In Britain, meanwhile, Hollywood had pursued a months-long boycott of the British market in 1947 and 1948 when the British government—strapped for hard currency—tried to limit its dollar remittances.[17] Washington came to understand that such episodes had not endeared it to its allies and attempted to rein in Hollywood in multilateral freedom-of-information negotiations. In the leadup to the Geneva conference, the State Department conceded that UN efforts to draft international freedom-of-information agreements should focus initially on news, not entertainment, excluding—among other things—Hollywood films; including them would have opened the United States to charges of "cultural imperialism" from putative U.S. allies as well as the Soviet Union.[18]

Shared acknowledgment of austerity in Europe, however, did not make for consensus about solutions to the newsprint crisis. UNESCO's 1947 Technical Needs report had offered a hodgepodge of possible fixes, ranging from stimulating production in Europe to voluntary consumption cutbacks in paper-rich countries.[19] But the latter, a superficially commonsensical suggestion, ran against the grain of American designs on the postwar political economy, which prioritized economic growth. The United States wished to induce recovery in Europe by encouraging trade liberalization and production increases, not by redistributing existing resources—in other words, by making the pie bigger rather than by reslicing it. "This is no Conference about money or wheat or radio frequencies where divergent viewpoints must and should be compromised," Benton intoned at the Geneva conference in 1948. "This is a Conference about principles essential to free men." Benton's point was accurate insofar as the conference had been tasked with discussing press- and speech-freedom language for a non-binding declaration of human rights—what became the Universal Declaration of Human Rights—as well as for a binding international human-rights covenant. The conference also debated several proposals for discrete conventions focused on news and information. But Benton was eager to shift the discussion away from material questions for another reason, too: Washington's immediate goal with newsprint was to maintain American access to newsprint imports.[20]

As Washington battled restrictions on trade in paper pulp and newsprint, some commentators appealed to the American conscience in an effort to redress shortages. "How many people read the lengthy supplements to the United States papers?" asked the British delegate to the 1948 Geneva conference, suggesting voluntary redistribution of newsprint supplies. Others took a tougher line, interpreting liberalization as a cause of, not a solution to, material asymmetries between countries. John Grierson argued that most countries were little served by laissez-faire information policies that would have them stand by and watch American business interests colonize their media. The fact that the United States could pursue such policies constituted "the American liberal mistake," he wrote to Zechariah Chafee.[21]

As an alternative, Grierson and Julian Huxley, UNESCO's first director general and Grierson's longtime friend, touted the positive freedoms that had fallen sharply out of favor in the United States by the late 1940s. In his 1947 annual report for the organization, Huxley outlined two interpretations of how UNESCO could foster freedom of information. One—the American option—was an "essentially negative method of abolishing or reducing the barriers which exist to that flow, especially as between nation and nation, and thus allowing existing agencies of information greater scope to penetrate every quarter of the globe." The second option, favored by Huxley and Grierson, involved the "positive" creation of "new channels and new agencies of information" on national and regional bases. These alternative avenues for flow, which would prevent "smaller nations or technically less advanced regions" from being "flooded or even propagandized by the more powerful and more advanced," would enable nonsuperpowers to achieve "cultural self-determination." Freedom was "hostile to abstraction," Huxley announced at the Geneva conference in 1948 in a speech that Grierson had helped to write, and it could "only be defined in concrete terms."[22]

At a moment of intensifying Cold War tensions, Grierson and Huxley's materialist interpretation of freedom of information made them targets for U.S. anticommunists. William Benton singled out the two men as the culprits for what he considered to be UNESCO's poor showing at Geneva. He noted with relief in a confidential report to the U.S. secretary of state that "UNESCO introduced a few resolutions regarding newsprint, which were voted with little enthusiasm or attention by the Conference. Attempts to build up UNESCO into the 'continuing machinery' [for redistributing newsprint supplies] were defeated by large majorities." Benton also alleged that Grierson was openly "supplying the Eastern bloc with ammunition for attacks on the U.S. press." Such accusations helped to seal Grierson's ouster from UNESCO later in 1948 as Washington worked to purge suspected communists from the organization. Huxley exited the same year, his director generalship limited from the outset to two years (instead of the standard six) by covert U.S. pressures.[23]

Slightly more durably than the pair of left-leaning Anglophones, France resisted U.S. free-flow diplomacy in UN forums, continuing to seek international regulation of newsprint distribution. In 1950, as negotiations for freedom-of-information conventions at the United Nations dragged on, the United States proposed a "right to be free from governmental interference" in the holding and transmitting of information, conveying the generally negative approach then dominant in U.S. foreign policy. By contrast, the French delegation called for the elimination of "obstacles of a political, economic, technical, or other kind tending to put freedom of information at risk"—a positive task anticipating the creation of an international apparatus to monitor such obstacles.[24] For France, newsprint was the key example of why such an apparatus was needed. As Jacques Kayser explained in a 1950 newspaper editorial under the headline "The Worldwide Newsprint Crisis Endangers Freedom of the Press in Europe," long-term plans to boost worldwide production were well and good but would not solve the present emergency. The immediate remedy, for Kayser and his compatriots at the French Foreign Ministry and the French Ministry of Information, was redistribution away from the United States and toward countries in need. The French minister of information estimated in early 1951 that if the United States made a voluntary sacrifice of less than 7 percent of its consumption of paper products, the surplus would fill European deficits, leaving U.S. consumption levels "still five times greater than French consumption." In connection with this, Kayser prepared to ask the governments of the UN Economic and Social Council (ECOSOC) to attract attention among their nationals to the need for voluntary cooperation.[25]

France's interventions in the newsprint debates stemmed in part from the strategic imperative to maintain its international influence in the postwar world. Multilateral regulation through UN institutions appeared to be one means of offsetting superpower influence. As Kayser put it in a 1951 letter to his fellow Geneva veteran Fernand Terrou, shortages were "not only technical" but were also "political and diplomatic." French representatives advocated that both short- and long-term action to resolve paper shortages be undertaken by the United Nations. They also expressed a marked desire to exert independence vis-à-vis the United States and the Soviet Union—much to the annoyance of William Benton.[26] "Like a sick and aging beauty," Benton wrote after France had insisted on putting forth its own information convention instead of supporting a joint Franco-American text at Geneva in 1948, "the French want flattery and limelight." Benton's dismissal, while pointing to a real decline in French power after 1945, coexisted uneasily with an equally real anxiety: as he admitted in the same report, the French delegation "usually presents the most difficult problem" for the United States, even more so than the Soviet Union, partly due to French prestige in Latin America. French calls for an "intensification of [international] coordination" in the face of newsprint shortages won support from Mexico and Uruguay as well as Egypt, India, and Italy, suggesting the appeal of such coordination to disparate nonsuperpower states.[27] While it has been suggested that the emergence of a bloc of new and developing states at the United Nations in the early 1950s was what frustrated postwar efforts to globalize the press freedoms of "the West," an analysis of the French position suggests that—though small and new states did form important contacts and alliances at this time—the reified categories of "the West" and "the Third World" do not fully capture the contested politics of information during the early Cold War. The newsprint debates also reflected competing visions for the postwar political economy that isolated the United States from many of its allies across the Atlantic: liberal capitalism versus economic planning.[28]

Like John Grierson and Julian Huxley, French commentators contested American anticommunists' largely negative conception of freedom of information. Under the postwar Fourth Republic, France was undergoing a marked turn domestically toward centralized economic planning. This transformation was reflected in contemporary attitudes toward the political economy of the press. The legal scholar Fernand Terrou, no communist, considered government subventions essential to maintaining a free press in times of austerity in that they tended to "attenuate the economic obstacles" to "freedom of information": "Liberty is a hollow word if we do not give the means of its exercise to those in whom we purport to recognize it." Terrou also challenged American anticommunists' Manichean worldview. In his 1951 UNESCO-published study, *Legislation for Press, Film and Radio*, he noted that, though it had become "customary" to "contrast two main systems" of information legislation—those of the United States and Soviet Russia—there were nevertheless, "[side] by side with these concepts, or between them," other bodies of legislation, "representing traditions and aspirations which it would be dangerous to ignore or neglect." Scrupulously parsing manifold varieties of media legislation, Terrou sketched "shades of meaning" in freedom-of-expression legislation and jurisprudence and "great variety" among systems of public broadcasting, which included the BBC (a public corporation responsible to Parliament) and France's RTF (Radiodiffusion-Télévision Française, managed by appointees of the French prime minister). Terrou's conclusion about state involvement in film industries reflected his overall modus operandi to delink regulatory systems from ideology: "[The] principle of nationalizing or otherwise specially regulating the film industry is not indissolubly bound up with the political regime of the State concerned."[29]

U.S. cold warriors were keen to portray French proposals as the product of vanity and the rest as crypto-communism. In this endeavor, the liberal anticommunist Benton was joined by conservative rags such as the *Chicago Tribune*, which wrote of stalemated UN freedom-of-information negotiations that "the American press certainly stands in no need of instruction from the French press." Unsurprisingly, one of the few Americans to acknowledge that press freedoms were not an autochthonous American (or Anglo-Saxon) invention also rejected the glib red-baiting of figures who dissented from the U.S. line: Zechariah Chafee pointed out that French negotiators considered press freedom part of *their* revolutionary heritage, and he wrote memorably of Grierson, "I do not believe that he is a Communist. He is too much himself to be identified with Marx or Lenin or any other person or group. He is a 'Griersonist.'" But the First Amendment expert was an outlier to anticommunist conventional wisdom, having departed the UN Subcommission on Freedom of Information after the Geneva conference in 1948 when the State Department had declined to renew his nomination. It replaced Chafee with Carroll Binder, a veteran foreign correspondent and editor at the *Minneapolis Star Tribune*, who was less inclined to seek compromise with foreign counterparts.[30]

Soon the United States was seeking to circumvent UN negotiations altogether. By the early 1950s, Washington was committed to torpedoing negotiations for binding freedom-of-information agreements. As the State Department's Walter Kotschnig concluded in 1952, "We can simply say this is not the climate for conventions."[31] It was also committed to rejecting the international redistribution of newsprint. Admitting that a "completely free market" in newsprint did not exist, *Paper for Printing*, the joint 1952 UNESCO-FAO-*Economist* study, nevertheless vetoed multilateral redistribution of existing supplies: redistribution was not a viable option because the American public "jealously guards free competition as its inalienable birthright." (More convincingly, the study forecast that even if the United States voluntarily restricted its own consumption, currency imbalances would persist in hindering European newsprint imports.) The fact of U.S. hegemony was driven home in the early 1950s when inflation brought on by the Korean War redoubled European newsprint shortages. The United States oversaw the export to Western Europe of so-called strategic materials—ranging from metals and minerals to newsprint—through the Marshall Plan and the International Materials Conference, the latter having been established in 1951. But French and British hopes for the international reallocation of newsprint were once again disappointed as the International Materials Conference redirected only a small fraction of worldwide supplies.[32]

Scholars of human-rights diplomacy have typically portrayed the early 1950s as a dark age for freedom of information, a time when Cold War polarization and an emergent Third World bloc led to the shelving of freedom-of-information convention talks and the dissolution of the UN Subcommission on Freedom of Information.[33] But international human-rights law was not the only avenue by which American journalists and policy intellectuals sought to widen information flows. The United States quickly began to seek more amenable platforms from which to promote its anticommunist, antimaterialist interpretation of human rights, including UNESCO. As William Benton argued, UNESCO was "more available"

to U.S. foreign policy than other branches of the United Nations because
the Soviet Union was not then a member (it did not join until 1954).
Benton also observed that compared to the United Nations proper, the
Paris-based specialized agency had a "much broader" mandate on freedom
of information, which included reducing trade restrictions in addition to
attacking political censorship.[34] At UNESCO's 1950 General Conference,
held in Florence, Italy, Benton drove these points home to an international
audience, declaring that the "occasionally expressed theory that UNESCO
must soften its policies so that it could be a bridge between East and West
was a chimera," and instead called on the organization to "tap all the
resources of the free world" and "use every means of mass communication
to tell the glorious story of freedom."[35] At the same time, U.S. Geneva delegate and *Christian Science Monitor* editor Erwin Canham, who by 1949
found himself second-guessing the "possibility of freedom coming through
governmental action," called upon media professionals to take up the task
of "reducing information barriers." While intergovernmental negotiations
on press and speech freedoms stretched on, echoed Zechariah Chafee, "a
great deal of good can be accomplished by informal bodies . . . through
exchange of ideas, mutual acquaintance and raising of standards in the
western countries."[36]

These comments pointed to the way in which freedom-of-information
advocacy overflowed the conventional limits of interstate diplomacy.
Although not everyone shared in their anticommunism, the tactical flexi-
bility advocated by Benton and Canham dovetailed with the thinking of
actors elsewhere who were frustrated with the impasse at the UN Human
Rights Commission. At UNESCO an international array of functionaries, journalists, researchers, and policymakers began to circumvent stalled
diplomatic negotiations by creating new, nongovernmental networks and
institutions dedicated to cross-border information exchange, including the
International Press Institute and the International Association for Mass
Communication Research.

But this "professional" approach to freedom of information also engendered new forms of opposition to U.S. information diplomacy. Even as
American elites attempted to bend UNESCO and the professional institutions it launched to the goals of U.S. anticommunism, an array of

European journalists and intellectuals would identify cultural and linguistic biases in U.S. free-flow policies.

THE PROFESSIONAL APPROACH TO
FREEDOM OF INFORMATION

The seeds of the International Press Institute had been sown by UNESCO's 1947 Technical Needs report, which envisioned the creation of an International Institute for Press and Information (IIPI) to further journalism training, encourage international exchange between press professionals, and serve as a research and reference center for "journalists, publishers, and all others connected with the professions of mass communications." These recommendations, which construed the "press" broadly to include radio and film in addition to print journalism, were subsequently endorsed by UNESCO and the United Nations. Although little progress had been made by the following year—by which time the communist coup in Czechoslovakia and the commencement of the Berlin airlift were contributing to Cold War polarization—the 1948 Technical Needs expert committee reiterated its support for the proposed institute. "It may be said that most of the experts realised that the field of professional training offered a fair opportunity, and considerable scope of immediate action—unlike newsprint," a UNESCO functionary reported to future director general René Maheu, then of the organization's Free Flow Division.[37]

Maheu was pragmatic, opportunistic even, about attracting support for the IIPI, flattering American vanity and British pretensions as needed. In particular, Maheu fell in line with a UNESCO resolution stating that financial support from American foundations was crucial to nurturing the institute. The American Press Institute at Columbia University was, Maheu wrote to Fernand Terrou, "on a national scale, the best example from which we can draw inspiration." At the same time as his compatriots Fernand Terrou and Jacques Kayser were battling in UN forums to advance French freedom-of-information proposals, Maheu indicated the need to move away from such seemingly insoluble diplomatic debates. "[The] inter-governmental approach on the political plane, to the problem of freedom of information, has failed," Maheu wrote in September 1948 to

Lyman Bryson, educational broadcasting expert at the American network CBS, asking for Bryson's feedback on the IIPI draft proposals.[38]

Technical and professional approaches to freedom of information, as opposed to "political" ones, seemed like one way to break the impasse.[39] Writing to University of Chicago chancellor Robert Hutchins, Maheu deftly noted the synergy between the IIPI proposals and the conclusions of the American Hutchins Commission. Here was an approach, superficially depoliticizing, in which Maheu's American colleagues could join him as pressure built to solicit funding for the IIPI on the eve of UNESCO's 1950 General Conference.[40] Writing to a Ford Foundation liaison to request his support, UNESCO deputy director general Walter Laves reasoned that after the failure of "political discussions" to "promote [freedom of information] in a practical way," collaboration between press professionals at the IIPI offered a means of furthering freedom of information.[41]

But the task of setting up such an organization would prove more difficult and more political than either Maheu or Laves had intimated. Wheels were soon turning to create a press institute under firmly American auspices. Jacques Kayser and Fernand Terrou first picked up on something suspicious in the fall of 1949 while on a trip to New York as part of the French delegation to the United Nations. Kayser had requested a meeting with *Christian Science Monitor* editor Erwin Canham to discuss the IIPI plans. However, Canham put him off, suggesting that plans for an international press institute were already underway in the United States. "Various American newspapermen are taking a lively interest in the proposals looking in the direction of an international press institute. It is our view that such an activity should be privately financed and operated," Canham explained. "We are therefore contemplating inviting various distinguished European editors to come to the United States at the time of the next annual meeting of the American Society of Newspaper Editors. On that occasion we would like to invite them to discuss the possibility of an international press institute."[42]

A miffed Kayser copied Canham's letter to Philippe Desjardins at UNESCO. Desjardins and his colleagues soon confirmed that the powerful American press organization ASNE had decided to study for itself the possibility of creating an international press institute—an institute that was to have no direct connection to UNESCO.[43] Before long, ASNE had secured support from the Rockefeller and Carnegie foundations, which UNESCO had also contacted, to hold a preliminary meeting of international editors on the subject, which was slated for the fall of 1950. "There is deplorably little contact between working newspaper men across national frontiers," Canham had written in his demurral to Kayser. "We hope at least to intensify these contacts."[44]

Beneath this veneer of transnational cooperation, the ASNE initiative constituted a power play to establish American control over the incipient institute. As with the United States' renewed economic and military commitments in Europe in the late 1940s, for Erwin Canham and Lester Markel, the *New York Times*' hard-driving Sunday editor, it was cold war, not tepid multilateralism, that justified American engagements abroad. In view of the connections that Canham in particular was developing with the Cold War security state, this rationale was not especially surprising. Canham, a U.S. delegate during the bitter UN General Assembly debates over a freedom-of-information convention, had also recently been named acting chair of the U.S. Advisory Commission on Information—created by the Smith-Mundt Act of 1948 with a mandate to counsel the government on its new information-diplomacy programs—and in 1951 the CIA floated his name for consideration for a high-level directorship pertaining to Cold War psychological warfare.[45]

Cold War competition also shaped the Americans' research agendas. Contrary to the UNESCO IIPI proposals, ASNE wanted to slash the word "Information" from the new International Press Institute, in part because states so frequently encroached upon broadcasting (a reservation which did not prevent Americans from requesting feedback from the CIA on a project shortly after the institute was up and running). And ASNE rejected the obligation to take the views of states or news organizations that were not considered "free" into account: no bridge between East and West here.[46] The ASNE initiative instead emphasized the need to study the role of communist propaganda in the press, for, according to Markel, "many of the falsehoods spread by the Communists [have] not been effectively challenged." More than anyone else, Markel seemed responsible for the ASNE group's hostility toward UNESCO: if governmental or international organizations got involved, Markel argued, then the new institute "becomes prey to all the [bickering] and disputes that have marked the debates in any branch of the United Nations over any press issue." Markel's anticommunism was shot through with national exceptionalism, and he hinted in early planning documents that the institute might usefully tutor European editors in the enlightened ways of American journalism. Canham embraced a similarly exceptionalist worldview. "[The] status of the press must be lifted up in other countries," Canham thought, just as ASNE had "helped to lift up the status of the press" in the United States.[47]

Tensions between American editors and their foreign colleagues came to a head at the gatherings arranged by ASNE in New York in October 1950. There, the two French editors present—Claude Bellanger, who helmed the daily *Parisien libéré*, and Hubert Beuve-Méry, the *Le Monde* editor known for his staunch defense of an independent French foreign policy—aired their displeasure about the ASNE plans, noting that ASNE had overlooked UNESCO's prior work on the subject. Beuve-Méry also voiced substantive concerns about the makeup of the proposed institute. "Markel seems to have made up his mind that nothing could be accomplished by an institute in which there was participation by [Eastern European] satellite journalists. This to Beuve-Mery, who is notably anti-Communist, simply is uncourageous," wrote a representative of the Rockefeller Foundation who had been dispatched to sit in on one of the New York meetings. The pair of Rockefeller Foundation observers present concluded that Markel—"an arbitrary and even dictatorial chairman"—had, in effect, railroaded the foreign editors.[48]

Canham and Markel remained undeterred. Excluding UNESCO from its meetings from the outset, the ASNE group also repeatedly suggested to reporters and others that UNESCO was planning to abandon its own project if ASNE's initiative got off the ground. The latter maneuver appears to have stymied even its American funders for a time.[49] However, by early 1951, ASNE could present its organization as a fait accompli to outflanked UNESCO functionaries and European editors. The International Press Institute was to be supported in its first three years by the Rockefeller and Ford Foundations, with a headquarters in Zurich—not in Paris as

facts about the

INTERNATIONAL

PRESS

INSTITUTE

THE HISTORY of the International Press Institute is this: in April, 1949, it was first sponsored by the American Society of Newspaper Editors; in October, 1950, thirty editors from fifteen countries, after a week of discussion, decided that the project was both "highly desirable and highly feasible"; in April, 1951, the Ford and Rockefeller Foundations made grants totaling $270,000 to cover the cost of the first three years of operation; in Paris, in May, 1951, the Institute was formally established with the adoption of a constitution by the Organizing Committee; in August, 1951, headquarters was established in Zurich and the Secretariat began functioning.

FIGURE 2.2 Early International Press Institute (IPI) promotional materials made no mention of the institute's contested origins. "Facts About the International Press Institute," [early 1950s], Rockefeller Foundation Records, FA387, Record Group 1.2, series 100, box 13, folder 84. Courtesy of Rockefeller Archive Center, Sleepy Hollow, NY.

UNESCO had initially planned (John Kenton of the *New York Times* explained to Claude Bellanger that while he personally would have preferred a headquarters in Paris, Swiss tax and incorporation law were more amenable to establishing an international nonprofit). Meanwhile, Markel and Canham pressed UNESCO to remove the IIPI plans from its agenda, arguing that so long as they remained, European editors would be "uncertain" about the two plans and would "[hold] off from cooperation" with the ASNE institute. Canham condescended to UNESCO's Douglas Schneider in April 1951: "Can you let me know when and in what way it is likely that this item will be marked up 'Objective Accomplished' to prevent this misunderstanding?" Its hand forced, UNESCO's executive board voted to suspend its involvement in June 1951.[50]

The ASNE power play engendered lingering bitterness, particularly among French-speaking functionaries and press professionals. Even before

ASNE's machinations came to light, UNESCO's Philippe Desjardins had expressed concern that too much of the feedback that UNESCO had gathered on its IIPI draft proposals had come from "four Anglo-Saxon countries": by Desjardins's count, fifty-one out of seventy-eight responses had come from the United States, Britain, Canada, and Australia. He wrote to René Maheu, "This proportion does not seem to correspond to the real needs of different regions of the world." At the 1951 executive board meeting that brought UNESCO's involvement to a close, Roger Seydoux, a diplomat and political scientist who had represented France at the United Nations' San Francisco Conference in 1945, protested that UNESCO "could not consider its work completed in this connexion, but only 'temporarily suspended.'" Meanwhile, Claude Bellanger complained that ASNE's finalized institute did not reflect what had been discussed during the international meeting it had hosted the previous fall.[51] In response, that same year, Terrou, Bellanger, Beuve-Méry, and others founded the Institut Français de Presse (IFP), which declared that it "conformed to the initial plan proposed by UNESCO" for a press institute (UNESCO's 1951 Technical Needs report clarified that both of the rival institutes, by excluding radio and cinema from their purviews, were less inclusive than what had been envisioned in UNESCO's earlier IIPI proposals).[52]

Desjardins's complaints were revealing of more than just the political pressures that led to the IPI-IFP split. By mobilizing the category of "Anglo-Saxon countries" ("*pays anglo-saxons*")—despite marked British indifference to UNESCO's early journalism education initiatives—Desjardins hinted at how the politicization of the IPI, for French speakers, was bound up with language concerns.[53] These concerns were not allayed once the IPI was up and running. Personal correspondence between Jacques Kayser and Armand Gaspard, an Armenian-Swiss staff member at the new institute, reveals the connections between language politics and the workings of institutions that were created to pursue freedom of information during the 1950s. Despite the fact that French was, along with English, an official IPI language, Gaspard lamented that "letters are written in English to French-speaking recipients" and expressed horror that an editor at *Le Figaro* (an important French newspaper) "had received letters . . . written in English." A few months later Gaspard complained to Kayser,

"[Notice] that after three years, we still don't have letterhead in French." Kayser, for his part, promised to broach the issue of the " 'French presence' or more precisely the 'French language' each time the opportunity presents itself in meetings or conversations."[54]

French concerns about Anglophone dominance at the IPI pointed to the entanglement of language and strategy in postwar information debates. For one, money was at stake in the choice of which languages to use in international institutions. The linguist Claude Hagège has postulated that countries where an internationally dominant lingua franca is spoken reap economic benefits, as resource-intensive language education is absorbed as a transaction cost by other countries.[55] In the case of international institutions, we might fruitfully adapt this idea to examine how concerns over the resources required for translation and interpretation affect their operations. In his director general's report for 1947, the Anglophone Julian Huxley had made note of the "manpower" required for the "important but heavy task of translating all Conference documents into Spanish" for UNESCO's General Conference in Mexico City that year. More explicitly, William Benton's blunt opposition to adding Spanish to UNESCO's roster of working languages demonstrated how, from the perspective of speakers of a dominant language, other languages could be collapsed into superficial cost analyses. "I see the Latins finally won out on making Spanish a working language," Benton wrote to a State Department contact in June 1950, during the director generalship of the Mexican writer and diplomat Jaime Torres Bodet. "Is it still estimated that this will cost an extra $500,000 annually?" Benton's bluster may have belied some anxiety over the status of English at the organization, for his worst school subjects had been foreign languages.[56]

French speakers were also quick to point out when language policies appeared to contradict fiscal common sense. Particularly "appalling," in Armand Gaspard's eyes, was how the IPI flouted budgetary prudence for the sake of its Anglophone members: Gaspard outlined an incident whereby coverage of a Franco-German meeting, based on minutes in French and German, was written first in English for the English-language version of the IPI's newsletter and then retranslated for the French and German editions. Gaspard commented to Kayser that his opposition to this redundancy was "not even a question of chauvinism or 'cultural' touchiness but a simple issue of economizing." But the situation at the IPI only seemed to keep getting worse. Robert Salmon of *France Soir* reported to Kayser that at the IPI's 1957 annual congress, "one only heard people speaking English and German."[57]

At a moment when France was eager to reassert its cultural and intellectual prestige on the world stage, it, too, was hostile to adding new working languages at UNESCO.[58] While Gaspard and Salmon, on the defensive at the IPI, denied any Francophone "chauvinism" in their complaints, Jacques Kayser and Fernand Terrou soon adopted another approach to fighting American influence in international freedom-of-information initiatives: the overt embrace of French cultural and linguistic specificity.

THE METHOD IS THE MESSAGE

The pressures that had fissured UNESCO's original plan for a press institute and produced the IPI-IFP split reappeared a few years later at the International Association for Mass Communication Research. The IAMCR germinated from a 1956 UNESCO General Conference resolution to "promote co-ordination of the activities of national research institutes in the field of mass communication, in particular by encouraging the creation of an international association of such institutes." Impetus for the new organization grew in part out of dissatisfaction with the IPI's limited focus and membership. On the French side, the IAMCR counted several of the same figures who had been involved at UNESCO leading up to the creation of the IPI and the IFP, namely Fernand Terrou, Jacques Kayser, and Claude Bellanger.[59] This time, though, they resisted American influence more successfully. The IAMCR's research orientation and protracted infighting—frustrated Americans were calling for its dissolution a decade on, in 1966—make investigating its first decade particularly fruitful for understanding how political and cultural conflict could mutually reinforce one another in international debates over information flows. Such tensions would continue to shape the association in the decades ahead, making the IAMCR one of the most prolific institutional sources for criticism of U.S. free-flow diplomacy by the late 1960s and early 1970s.[60]

In its early years the IAMCR was marked by European, especially French, influence. Its first president was Terrou, and its first mailing address was that of the IFP headquarters in Paris. This siting almost immediately became a source of contention. Critics charged that it compounded the problem of French overrepresentation in the organization's activities, which were concentrated in subfields and methodologies in which the French were particularly strong—legal and historical research. At a moment when American social scientists were seeking to educate their foreign peers in behaviorist and empirical methods, which (they argued) produced knowledge that transcended cultural differences, this concentration must have been frustrating, for these subfields were two of the most difficult to abstract from cultural and linguistic contexts. Within a few years, the IAMCR would move its administrative headquarters out of France, relocating to Amsterdam in 1961.[61]

The assertive French presence at the nascent institute concerned more than just the Americans involved. An "expansion of the geographical and cultural basis" of the IAMCR was hoped for by UNESCO's Norwegian mass-communication director, Tor Gjesdal, who, like René Maheu with the earlier IIPI proposals, was eager to attract the support of American foundations and participants. The Dutch journalist and communication scholar Maarten Rooy, who became the IAMCR's secretary general, complained repeatedly of French intransigence after the French refused to recognize the organization's new seat in Amsterdam.[62]

It was the Americans, however, who most emphatically stressed the universal scope and objective merits of their large-scale, quantitatively based research, all while chafing at the multilingual and multicultural aspects of conducting and disseminating such research in Europe. "[The] U.S.A. is the country in which most of the mass communication research has been done up to the present time," wrote incoming IAMCR president Raymond Nixon in 1959. As with earlier tensions at the United Nations and the IPI, Americans viewed language differences as a barrier to clear, first and foremost. William Benton had complained in his report from Geneva in 1948 that the French "cling most tenaciously to the prestige of the French language" by insisting that everything be translated into French. Eleven years later, at the IAMCR, Americans remained impatient with multilingualism. Nixon offered to help edit the English-language version of the IAMCR's bulletin, but behind the scenes he was critical, sniping to Gjesdal that he hoped the "English [would] be intelligible" in its first issue. The University of Minnesota journalism professor also complained of the "utterly inadequate" interpreter "assigned to me by Terrou" for IAMCR meetings, voicing suspicion that the interpreter was behind the "wretched English . . . in communications from the IAMCR secretariat to English-speaking members." Meanwhile, Stanford communications professor Wilbur Schramm, who under Nixon took charge of the organization's Section for Psycho-Sociological Studies, confidently dismissed the idea that there existed "more than a dozen real research publications on television and children in Italy"—an assumption he admitted to making without knowing Italian. It does not seem a stretch to suggest that tensions between Raymond Nixon and Fernand Terrou, the association's first president and outgoing secretary general, were compounded by Nixon's self-proclaimed "inadequate knowledge of French."[63]

More explicitly than at the IPI, methodological differences marked the battle for control over the IAMCR, a battle which paralleled anticommunist efforts to discipline domestic American research. Historians of Cold War social science have shown how psychological warfare and government funding shaped the emergent field of communication studies within the United States. Wilbur Schramm was an especially influential figure in the field's formative years in the late 1940s and 1950s. Schramm spearheaded new programs at the University of Illinois and Stanford; helped to popularize Claude Shannon's work on information theory by encouraging the University of Illinois Press to publish the coauthored Claude Shannon–Warren Weaver volume *The Mathematical Theory of Communication* (1949); and, most importantly, linked the new field to Washington's anti-communist foreign policy by emphasizing the power of mass communication to change behaviors and shape societies.[64]

Less commonly explored by scholars is how, overseas, these methodological battles were enmeshed in the politics of language. On the eve of taking over the IAMCR presidency from Terrou in 1959, Nixon wrote to him in English, requesting an "assistant who is an expert at English-French-English translation and who is also thoroughly familiar with the psychological and sociological approaches to mass communication research," suggesting how language suffused methods and hinting at French incomprehension of both the language (English) and the methods: "You are well aware of my eagerness that this first issue [of the IAMCR bulletin] make a good impression upon those persons interested in 'mass communication research' as the term is understood in the United States."[65] Crucially, Nixon was not implying that American research offered a particular political or intellectual perspective worth representing within the organization's broader matrix. Rather, for the American journalism professor and his compatriots, mass-communication research as it was "understood in the United States" *was* the objective foundation for all such research. Whereas Norwegian Tor Gjesdal, though aware of the need for American backing, had cautioned that attaching the association to an American research center would "leave the rest of the world even more isolated from the nucleus of the organization than is presently the case," for Nixon, the Americanization of the IAMCR was the sine qua non of its internationalization. "It is highly important to the future of our Association that we win and retain the confidence of groups like the Executive Board of IPI, as well as of individual scholars like [Paul] Lazarsfeld, [Daniel] Lerner, [Ithiel de Sola] Pool, [Robert] Silvey, [Wilbur] Schramm, etc.," Nixon wrote to Terrou. "Indeed, I would say that their full co-operation holds the key to our success as a truly international organization."[66] Of the five scholars Nixon listed, four were based in the United States (Silvey, head of audience research at the BBC, was the exception).

The geopolitical thaw following Stalin's death in 1953 had helped to melt the kind of hardline anticommunism expressed in William Benton's 1950 UNESCO General Conference speech, in which he had dismissed as a "chimera" the notion that UNESCO "could be a bridge between East and West."[67] This shift enabled Americans like Nixon and Benton to travel east of the Iron Curtain and to assert an ever more objective, global perspective on information issues. Having vaunted his "world-wide view of research in mass communication" enabled by "around-the-world" voyages to the Eastern bloc and elsewhere, Nixon framed the IAMCR's move from Paris to Amsterdam as something that would help make it a "truly international organization." But rather than yielding fruitful two-way exchange, increasing international contact for Nixon was a means of laying claim to "objectivity" in order to further U.S. objectives. "[There] is a clear and definite relationship between the status of communication research in any given country and the degree of freedom enjoyed by its journalists and scholars," he declaimed to the International Federation of Newspaper Editors and Publishers in the spring of 1960. "[The] unrestricted search for truth about mass communication provides the only realistic basis for a rational faith that our free society itself can be maintained and extended." Promoting themselves as arbiters of the "truly international," American diplomats and researchers like Benton, Nixon, and Schramm tended to associate cultural and linguistic concerns with immaturity and backwardness—and thereby to naturalize the English language's postwar ascent as the global lingua franca of research as well as diplomacy.[68]

To other participants in UNESCO's mass-communication projects, however, the prospect of wholly neutral or objective social research, modeled after the hard sciences, appeared to be the real chimera. The point of social-scientific internationalism was rather to incorporate cultural and linguistic diversity.[69] Fernand Terrou and Jacques Kayser countered American mass-communication discourse with alternative, finer-grained interpretations of the relationship between language, method, and freedom of information. One of the IAMCR's first projects was to be a glossary that indexed translations of various mass-communication concepts in different languages. According to Kayser and Terrou, the task was harder than it seemed "due to the sheer diversity and complexity of languages." Even in the same language, different milieus used different terminologies; for instance, British and American vocabularies differed. For Terrou, the very phrase "mass communication" posed a conundrum to translators working from English to French. He considered *information collective* a better translation than the more literal *communication de masse* to describe the process of mass communication: while in French *communication* connoted one-way transmission, Terrou argued, *information* invoked a larger social reality.[70] In French, UNESCO's Department of Mass Communication was the Département de l'Information.

Terrou's emphasis on social context pointed to a more general critique of American mass-communication research. Elsewhere, Terrou had written that on its own, content analysis—a method innovated by Harold Lasswell, Paul Lazarsfeld, and other U.S.-based researchers to ascertain the psychosocial motives and impact of propaganda and other mass-mediated messages—offered little help in studying the political and economic forces that shaped the diffusion of information. The Cold War American research community tended to overvalue expensive empirical studies while undertheorizing the political economy of the media, this line of thinking went (a similar criticism would be leveled at Lazarsfeld's "personal influence" paradigm, which had unseated content analysis as a dominant model in 1950s American media sociology).[71] These political and economic structures were presumably not a trivial matter to Terrou, who had been closely involved in the purge of Vichy collaborators from the French press after the Second World War. For the legal scholar, the American tendency to contrast quantitative and qualitative research and the attendant notion that the "substitution of the first for the second" was "the condition of scientific progress" were misleading. "In the social sciences, these two research categories are not, cannot be, opposed; they complement each other, work together, and theory is the instrument of this collaboration," Terrou explained. "The theory of mass communication . . . is based on the establishment and measurement of facts. It has, if you will, a descriptive and quantitative basis. But it inevitably leads to . . . a qualitative result."[72] At the IAMCR, Terrou was keen to contest the notion that behaviorist methods—in which American dominance at the time was universally recognized—were analytical and explanatory while the historical and legal fields in which France was strong were merely descriptive. The latter were long-established disciplines, Terrou added in an early IAMCR report.[73]

Jacques Kayser pushed this criticism further, suggesting that the methods used in mass-communication research were not universally valid due to the reality of social and cultural difference. According to Kayser, French researchers read the "excellent American journal" *Journalism Quarterly*—then edited by Raymond Nixon—"with the greatest interest." Nevertheless, Kayser thought that "certain methods that are described in it and that are well suited to the American worldview and manner of organization would fail in France if one tried to introduce them there." Frequent recourse to statistics, which gave American findings the appearance of objective rigor, was flawed due to the inexact categories upon which the statistics were based. Kayser gave the example of American research that presumed to calculate how much space newspapers devoted to political, economic, and financial news, objecting that the categories intersected messily: there was no way to neatly differentiate economic from financial news, for instance.[74]

In part, these arguments over methodological (un)translatability were part of a shift during the 1950s in French responses to U.S. power. As the historian Richard Kuisel has written, as the Cold War stabilized in Europe, anti-Americanism among French elites shifted from attacking the United States as a "political menace" to questioning whether, on a "socio-cultural" plane, its models and mores could or should be imported to France.[75] Here we might group public opinion polling and behaviorism with more familiar targets of French cultural anxiety like Coca-Cola and Hollywood films.

Kayser's and Terrou's struggles at the IAMCR also possessed a wider international resonance. During the 1940s and 1950s, diverse intellectuals, many of whom were European and all working on the periphery of main-stream American social science, criticized American biases toward quantitative methods and costly studies. Theodor Adorno's break with Paul Lazarsfeld in 1941 over the empirical methodology of the Princeton Radio Research Project yielded foundational concepts in sociology and communication research: the dichotomy of "administrative" research versus critical theory. So did Raymond Williams's searching rejection of formulas such as "the masses" and "mass-communication" in 1958's *Culture and Society*, a touchstone of Britain's nascent cultural-studies movement: "[Much] of what we call communication is, necessarily, no more in itself than transmission: that is to say, a one-way sending. Reception and response, which complete communication, depend on other factors."[76] Less well remembered, perhaps, is Siegfried Kracauer's demolition of the scientistic pretensions of content analysis, published in the influential American journal *Public Opinion Quarterly* in 1952. Like Kayser and Terrou, Kracauer argued that "quantification processes themselves often require much conjecturing which is not in actuality tied to objective, impersonal definitions." Harold Innis, a Canadian economist who pioneered the study of the political economy of communication, similarly sought to resist what he termed, in the 1951 essay collection *The Bias of Communication*, the "quantitative pressure of modern knowledge."[77] These insights would become the tributaries of a forceful reaction against anticommunist social science and U.S. free-flow diplomacy in the 1960s and 1970s, which is discussed in chapter 6.

But despite this emerging constellation of critiques, which linked a starry set of intellectuals, institutional efforts to resist the "quantitative pressure of modern knowledge" in general proved less effective during the early Cold War. These critiques might be seen as a kind of negative capture of American power in the 1950s, when, as the French sociologist Edgar Morin later recalled, a "questionnaire-fetish held sway" in French sociology and when—in North America especially—rejecting behavioral and quantitative approaches could spell intellectual isolation, as it did for Harold Innis, who was largely overlooked by his American contemporaries in the late 1940s and early 1950s. Linguistic and national frontiers could not contain methodology as neatly as Kayser and Terrou might have liked. The connections they had drawn between language and method were tenuous at best at a time of flux in French sociology, as modernizers emphasized the mutually constitutive relationship of modernity and data and pushed to create institutions capable of administering large-scale quantitative studies. The coordination of research by the French state, a process begun tentatively during the 1930s, was furthered during the Vichy period and then by the Fourth Republic.[78] After 1945, the empirical and inductive approaches championed by U.S.-based social scientists, which encompassed behaviorism and public opinion polling, established footholds in France, changes that were of a piece with broader currents in European social research. Where existing faculties of higher education resisted these changes, new ones—such as France's École des hautes études en sciences sociales (EHESS)—were created to circumvent them.[79]

Meanwhile, in the United States the anticommunist desideratum continued to mold how leading American scholars conceptualized information freedoms. In 1960 IAMCR president Raymond Nixon, writing in *Journalism Quarterly*, asserted a "systematic" correlation between the qualitative "degree of freedom in a national press system" on one hand and quantitative variables including per capita income and newspaper circulation on the other. Like Fernand Terrou before him, Nixon credited UN and UNESCO data for enabling his broad cross-national comparisons. But unlike Terrou's earlier study *Legislation for Press, Film and Radio*, Nixon's research reflected a bipolar worldview, mapping countries along a two-dimensional continuum of "freedom" versus "control." According to Nixon, a "free press system" was "one in which private owners are free to supply news and opinion to the general public," and "the chief criterion" in determining the status of a nation's press was the state's "power to interfere" (Nixon credited prior research by the IPI for this schema). Such counterarguments as Kayser—and American New Dealers—had raised about the potentially negative impact of corporate concentration on media went unaddressed, as did Terrou's case that state involvement did not necessarily equate to state control. In practice, Nixon's model could be a Procrustean bed. He rated the press of apartheid South Africa, where "democratic institutions have been developed to the highest level," as largely free, noting only in passing the "pressures and suspicions" generated by the apartheid regime. Kracauer and Kayser could not have invented a starker example to illustrate the subjective attitudes and assumptions structuring anticommunist American mass-communication research in the 1950s and early 1960s.[80]

From the outset, postwar media research had a broader focus than just the United States and Europe. UNESCO's Technical Needs surveys, which first appeared in 1947, quickly expanded their focus from war-devastated countries to the "less developed" regions of the world. The 1948 survey included countries in the Caribbean and Latin America, anticipating the global development imperatives announced by President Truman the following January in his "Point Four" speech. The snowballing process of decolonization, coupled with the stabilization of the Cold War blocs in Europe, eventually shifted the focus of U.S. free-flow diplomacy, and that of the Cold War more broadly, away from Europe and toward Asia and Africa. Chapter 4 treats this shift and the United States' embrace of a developmental approach to press freedoms. As Raymond Nixon wrote in 1960, while "international treaties" remained ineffective at spreading press freedoms, the development experts who "urge more assistance to newly developing countries . . . are probably much closer to the heart of the problem."[81]

At the same time, the postwar vogue for quantification was amplifying other kinds of differences that spanned continents. On a scale previously unequaled, researchers and policymakers were producing globe-spanning studies not only on media access but also on literacy, in which language and language comprehension were subjects of inquiry, not just obstacles to it. The new data helped to generate new problematics. At the same moment when diplomatic and professional approaches to freedom of information were being tested during the early Cold War, another facet of information policymaking targeted illiterates worldwide as being deprived of the freedoms guaranteed to them under the Universal Declaration of Human Rights. The burning questions for researchers and policymakers interested in literacy education thus became In which languages should literacy be pursued? And how? As the 1950s progressed and decolonization became a fait accompli in much of Asia and a sure bet in Africa, these questions would engage not only educators but also governmental and private-sector actors with vested interests in widening cross-border information flows.

3

Information Flows and the Conundrum of Multilingualism

I have found it extremely difficult [to communicate] with Africans and one very simple and obvious reason for it then, now, and this will be the case for some time to come, is that if we talk as fast as I'm talking now people in many foreign countries just cannot follow it, any more than I can follow French when it's talked this way.

—Melvin Fox, recalling a 1956 trip to Africa

Diacritics are best avoided wherever possible.

—UNESCO report, 1952

Information, no matter how freely flowing, was of little use if the people of the world could not comprehend it. During the Second World War, the U.S. military had confronted this dilemma head on in its efforts to train tens of thousands of non-Anglophone Allied personnel in the latest aerial and naval warfare techniques. The military had a choice: hire interpreters to translate for foreign military personnel or teach them in remedial English. While, traditionally, the former method was preferred, during the war, qualified interpreters in critical languages like Mandarin Chinese were scarce, so the military also conducted experiments in giving instruction in and through English. The Harvard-based literary critic and language educator I. A. Richards, for instance, oversaw the English-language training of one thousand Chinese sailors, some of whom were illiterate in their native language, at the U.S. Naval Training Center in Miami in the spring and summer of 1945. Richards's project was doubly experimental in that he was not teaching just any variety of English; he was using a stripped-down, 850-word lexicon called "Basic English" invented by his former Cambridge colleague C. K. Ogden in the interwar period. The Miami project formed part of a broader, ad hoc array of English-language training initiatives encouraged by Washington and scattered over dozens of military bases and universities in the wartime United States.[1]

It is common knowledge that the United States' military and economic supremacy formed the bedrock of the U.S.-dominated world order after 1945. For many U.S.-based educators and social scientists as well as hard scientists and engineers, wartime techniques and technologies fueled postwar ambitions. Richards, a British subject, viewed his work in Miami as a step toward establishing a global auxiliary tongue; in the coming "Air Age" of heightened international contact, he hoped the rapid teaching of Basic English would foster "common understanding" among disparate individuals and societies. American foundations and news outlets took notice of the potential of English and variants like Basic English to shape the postwar peace. The Rockefeller Foundation, which had funded Richards's efforts to spread Basic internationally since the 1930s, continued its subventions, while *Life* magazine called Basic English a potential "secondary or auxiliary language for men in all lands—scientists, businessmen, scholars—whose activities transcend national boundaries." If peace between nations was to be secured, this line of thinking went, the rest of the world's language skills might require some reengineering.[2]

International forays into education during the postwar and early Cold War period have typically been analyzed in terms of the diplomatic history of development aid. Less commonly considered is how these initiatives entailed a reimagining of global information and language landscapes: from a world riven by trade barriers as well as "language barriers" (a phrase which took off in popularity in the 1940s and 1950s) to a world of widely circulating—and readily understood—books, periodicals, broadcasting, and films.[3] Language and literacy work forced policy elites to grapple with information as an embodied entity and to relate their educational goals to the linguistic questions that inevitably arose. Was vernacular literacy the objective of international aid to education? Or was it merely a springboard for aid recipients to be able to read and speak a more widely diffused, "vehicular" language that enabled them to communicate with speakers of other languages?

Most American policymakers did not have immediate answers to these questions in the late 1940s and early 1950s. Unlike postwar efforts to liberalize trade or to inject American expertise into the institutions that monitored and measured global information flows and freedoms, Washington was slow to incorporate language training into its free-flow diplomacy. I. A. Richards, whose most enduring source of support was not the U.S. government but rather the Rockefeller Foundation, was typical of the ad hoc, experimental spirit of the immediate postwar years. Modernizers' visions of smooth global communication through Western languages also clashed with alternatives that prioritized linguistic difference over cross-border exchange. Late-colonial conservatives in Britain, for instance, repeatedly invoked the dangers of creating a class of politicized Africans through English-language education as had emerged in India.[4] This faction, along with counterparts from France and Belgium, favored policies designed to contain social change in colonial territories, including limiting education in Western languages. In the late 1940s and 1950s the three European powers colluded to block UN involvement in the colonies. As the process of decolonization gathered steam, a more enduring challenge to the globalization of English was posed by anticolonial and postcolonial nationalists who stressed the cultural value of non-Western languages. Of what use were the tongues of foreign imperialists in nation-states that were newly freed from their yoke?

Over the course of the 1950s, Anglophone language reformers honed answers to this question designed to complement the goals of postcolonial elites—and to attract support from Washington's burgeoning aid apparatus. Felix Walter of UNESCO advertised English as the premier "language of wide communication," both a link to the outside world and a means of uniting multilingual territories. In the United States, the Ford Foundation's Melvin Fox built on Walter's case for education in Western auxiliaries, presenting English as a tool of socioeconomic development in Asia and Africa. As the United States expanded its investment in informational and educational diplomacy from the mid-1950s onward, it institutionalized these rationales for English-language education overseas in the work of new executive-branch agencies including the U.S. Information Agency (USIA, founded in 1953), the U.S. Agency for International Development (USAID, established 1961), and the Peace Corps (also established 1961); English was the "communication instrument" most suited to the task of "transferring needed knowledge, skills and activities" to the developing world, as one USAID report put it in 1967. In an era clamoring for development expertise, American policy elites began to embrace English as the most convenient medium for channeling vital information flows to the developing world.[5]

THE "CURSE OF BABEL" AND POSTWAR LANGUAGE-EDUCATION DEBATES

The dream of conducting politics through language education was not new in 1945. Literacy and language-education projects launched by the United Nations and its agencies were part of a broader transformation—the heightening organization of education by governments and intergovernmental bodies—pursued by reformers and revolutionaries alike from the late nineteenth century onward. As a secular project, modernizing states ranging from France's Third Republic to revolutionary Mexico to the Soviet Union had aggressively promoted mass literacy and language acquisition. After the First World War, language education became entwined with internationalist ideals at the League of Nations, which studied whether Esperanto or some other auxiliary language might promote peace between countries.[6]

The political potential of language teaching was not unknown to the United States either. Following the Spanish-American War, American officials had disputed European colonial policies over the question of who should learn Western languages, promoting English as a language not just for circumscribed classes of cultural intermediaries—as it had been described by an influential 1835 East India Company communiqué—but for the masses in the United States' newly won imperial archipelago.[7] The United States attempted to spread English in the Philippines and Puerto Rico. At this stage, however, Washington's goals remained geographically circumscribed. The rising power acted primarily out of a desire to compete with its European rivals by acquiring access to China and by asserting its authority in Latin America.[8]

What was new after 1945 were both the targets and the tools of international language-education reform. The League of Nations' efforts had been restricted as much by a focus on elite intellectual exchange as by the United States' absence from the organization, the latter of which emblematized the constraints on U.S. global engagements during the interwar era. By contrast, the post-1945 international institutions, symbiotic with what Mark Mazower has called the "blisteringly fast emergence of American global power after 1945," embraced education for the masses. Notably, illiteracy—a condition affecting roughly half the world population in the late 1940s—was identified as a threat to global peace and well-being. Under Julian Huxley, the first director general of UNESCO, the organization undertook an ambitious pilot project in Haiti's Marbial Valley intended to redress adult illiteracy and rural poverty and to promote public health among the valley's residents. Two years later Huxley's successor, the Mexican educator and statesperson Jaime Torres Bodet, announced a global campaign against illiteracy. Observers of the new United Nations and its agencies took note. A 1952 *New Yorker* article reported that though "universal literacy" had been unheard of in the late 1920s, thirty years later it was "not only regarded as feasible" but had been "given priority by UNESCO."[9]

The post-1945 international institutions also benefitted from a tool kit that was, in technological terms, far superior to that of their interwar predecessors. Promoting the United Nations after the war, one seasoned American observer recalled that "when we started the League of Nations in 1920, there just wasn't any such animal as radio, film, or NGO. . . . Woodrow Wilson practically killed himself taking his story personally throughout the country."[10] Advances in mass communications and audiovisual aids shaped international relations almost from the moment the UN Charter was signed. The technology of simultaneous translation—which entailed a customized network of microphones and headsets linking listeners to human interpreters translating in real time—was first developed for the Nuremberg trials and was subsequently perfected at the United Nations and other international bodies. Similarly, many enthused over the possibilities of using audiovisual aids for language teaching. During the war I. A. Richards had collaborated with Disney Studios and with Time Inc.'s *March of Time* nonfiction-film outfit to produce experimental language-teaching films. Richards showed his *March of Time* films at a seminal 1947 gathering that UNESCO organized on language teaching, officially titled the Meeting of Experts on Language Problems in Fundamental Education.[11]

Given its expansive mandate and technological inheritance, some early insiders thought that UNESCO's ambition should be nothing less than to revolutionize the global cartography of languages. One contributor to the 1947 meeting optimistically announced that international language-education efforts could make Europe more "European-minded," give the United States a better understanding of Russia, and provide an "indigenous and neutral 'lingua franca' for the whole [Indian] sub-continent."[12] In particular, many areas of the world afflicted by high illiteracy rates were also areas where multiple languages predominated. In Haiti, for instance, a small elite who were literate in French dominated economic and political life amid a largely illiterate Creole-speaking majority. Director General Julian Huxley, an evolutionary biologist by training and a social-engineering enthusiast by conviction, envisioned UNESCO's Marbial Valley project as a living laboratory for the "teaching of an auxiliary language which would enable inter-communication of people with different main languages," and in this vein, the organization's Haiti team inquired with I. A. Richards about using the project to translate teaching techniques previously tested in Basic English into French. Ultimately, project leaders concluded that it would be easier for illiterates to learn to read in their native language, and the team worked to produce teaching materials in Haitian Creole. But this solution was viewed as merely a stopgap measure. Alfred Métraux, the well-known Swiss-born anthropologist heading the project, and education expert Yvonne Oddon envisioned the Creole materials as a stepping stone toward cementing broader literacy in French—which they called a "language of civilization," in contrast to Haitian Creole.[13]

The Marbial Valley project was intended as the flagship of UNESCO's Fundamental Education Division, which targeted areas outside Europe and the United States. This geography was meant to signify linguistic as well as socioeconomic need: according to preparatory documents for the 1947 language meeting, while the "curse of Babel" hung heavily over UNESCO's efforts to promote international understanding, "on the plane of Fundamental Education," the "language problem [was] an even greater barrier to international understanding." The very same "less developed areas of the world" that Fundamental Education targeted—areas where "ignorance, disease and poverty are a barrier to human progress"—were also areas where a "multiplicity of vernacular languages and dialects" tended to predominate. The Marbial Valley project ultimately faltered amid political squabbles and logistical difficulties, and by the late 1950s the Fundamental Education Division had been renamed and folded into UNESCO's burgeoning development work. But in spite of practical challenges and organizational mutations, the framing of multilingualism as a policymaking challenge continued as the process of decolonization accelerated: multilingualism remained a "problem" to solve, a "barrier" to clear.[14]

Particularly for Anglophone language reformers, the so-called language barrier was to be cleared via methods and technologies advanced during the Second World War. Modernizers were inspired by wartime military initiatives that had used native-speaker instructors, small classes, and intensive instruction schedules to stimulate rapid language acquisition among select groups of American soldiers. When UNESCO's Walter Laves asked the 1947 meeting, "What [is] the quickest way to teach people who [speak] a number of different languages or dialects to communicate

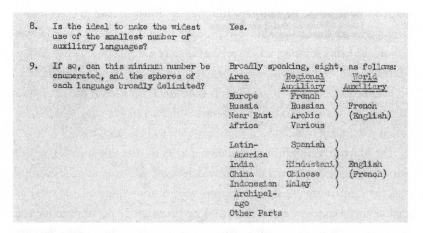

8. Is the ideal to make the widest   Yes.
    use of the smallest number of
    auxiliary languages?

9. If so, can this minimum number be   Broadly speaking, eight, as follows:
    enumerated, and the spheres of
    each language broadly delimited?

Area	Regional Auxiliary	World Auxiliary
Europe	French)	
Russia	Russian)	French
Near East	Arabic)	(English)
Africa	Various	
Latin-America	Spanish)	
India	Hindustani)	English
China	Chinese)	(French)
Indonesian Archipelago	Malay)	
Other Parts		

FIGURE 3.1 UNESCO defines "world auxiliary" languages, 1947: English and French. "Answers to Questions Raised by Papers 2, 5 and 6 (Educ./31—36/1947)," July 10, 1947. Educ./Com.Exp./S.R.7.&8./Annex B, UNESCO Archives, Paris, France, 375:4.A.064.'47.'

with each other?" participants did not lack for answers. One document announced that various "[war-born] experiments in rapid and effective second-language teaching" made it possible "for the first time in history" to "'mass-produce' bilinguals" through primary education.[15] This Whiggish understanding of advances in language-teaching pedagogies was somewhat misleading; decades earlier, fin de siècle reformers had emphasized oral communication in living languages over translation skills.[16] Yet the enthusiasm at UNESCO's 1947 gathering reflected the undeniable impact of wartime language work, which helped to shift the dominant emphasis of American language education away from reading and translation and toward listening and speaking skills. The "audiolingual" or "oral-aural" method popular after the war used rote repetition as a means of enabling students to render language patterns without the need for conscious reflection. For meeting participants, the "principles" advanced by wartime research included repetitive verbal exercises, and "all possible visual and aural aids to assist both teacher and learner": language acquisition as high-tech drill.[17]

At times, excitement about the contribution of new technologies to language acquisition outshone the military's more mundane findings. Animated films, thought I. A. Richards, "could be shown to an audience of as many as 400 learners, and this was mass education indeed." Likewise, British colonel Adolph Myers, who had worked with the Indian army, advocated using filmstrips in language teaching. Optimistic about the prospects that new technologies seemed to hold for social engineering—and overlooking the low student-to-teacher ratios of wartime military programs—many 1940s modernizers thought that the appearance of radio and other new media heralded the possibility of spreading a genuinely global lingua franca on the cheap.[18]

The quest for magic bullets ranged into the choice of languages as well. Some modernizers advocated artificial languages such as Esperanto as the best target languages in which to "'mass-produce' bilinguals." These alternatives seemed to offer a clean slate to those who, with Julian Huxley, worried that "making more people literate in more languages may not create further barriers to international understanding rather than promoting it." André Martinet, professor at the Sorbonne and Columbia University and member of the New York–based International Auxiliary Language Association, called for an artificial tongue to become the new worldwide auxiliary language—"a language which would serve no imperialism." Similarly, I. A. Richards's intellectual collaborator C. K. Ogden rejected using one of the great powers' languages as a global lingua franca. The British linguist instead proposed Basic English as a scientific means of stripping away the political and cultural baggage of preexisting languages: "The only alternative to this dilemma is a non-cultural compromise; a nucleus, simple but scientific, clear but free from literary entanglements . . . and above all embodying such analytic and normative principles as alone can lead us away from the traditional mystification and complacent psittacism of the ages."[19]

Artificial languages had many critics at the 1947 meeting; they soon fell by the wayside of UNESCO's language work. Stripped-down languages such as Basic English were also sharply criticized. As the French linguist and meeting participant Aurélien Sauvageot put it, "the history of thought was the history of vocabulary," and he would "dissent from any proposal to limit or condense the French language," which, in any case, he considered richer than everyday English: French workers, according to Sauvageot, used "four or five times as many [words] as the American soldiers he had met" (Sauvageot went on to express his sympathy for the " 'man on the street' in England and America," whose "limited vocabulary meant a limited spirit"). Even I. A. Richards admitted the limitations of Basic English, which he considered no replacement for regular English. "It's too dull," Richards told *Time* magazine, "and you can't swear in it."[20]

More consequentially, modernizers like Huxley and Richards encountered determined opposition from colonial conservatives who wished to limit popular access to metropolitan languages in their empires. The moment was a tense one in many colonies, coming on the heels of the 1946 general strike in Senegal, the Sétif massacre in Algeria, and a decade of social mobilization across the British Empire. While officials on the spot were beginning to acknowledge the intractable reality of educated and urban colonial subjects, others were still clinging to interwar policies that vested authority in rural elites in an effort to contain change.[21] According to Aurélien Sauvageot, educating colonial subjects in French from an early age had been shown as "not ideal" by the "events in Indo-China and North Africa": this policy had "formed a caste" that "mistakenly thought itself an elite" ready for self-government. Late-colonial antipathy to educating Africans in Western languages was underscored by another Francophone at the 1947 UNESCO meeting: Jean-Jacques Deheyn, formerly an education official in the Belgian Congo. Current policy in the Belgian Congo was education in the vernacular first, then in French. Deheyn blasted opportunistic schoolmasters who, flouting this policy, offered primary schooling exclusively in French—thereby producing students who "consider themselves an elite but will never be anything more than malcontents." Citing a study of education in French-colonial West Africa, Deheyn stingingly compared these Francophone Africans to one of French literature's most infamous social climbers: they were "ridiculous," "odious," akin to Molière's "parody of the *bourgeois gentilhomme*." To conservative defenders of empire in France and Belgium, language education reflected a broad problem that was, as Deheyn put it, "sociological and psychological rather than purely technical": how to manage and control colonized populations.[22]

British opinion, meanwhile, was highly fragmented. As early as 1929, Member of Parliament Josiah Wedgwood had labeled English the "language of the future" before the House of Commons. Wedgwood viewed teaching English in non-Western territories as a means of reforming British imperial rule: "If the native is to defend himself in this world, he must be able to speak a civilised language and to read civilised books." The same wish to reform the empire was shared by many who supported investing in Basic English abroad—a hope belied by C. K. Ogden's promise of "noncultural compromise." During the Second World War, arch-imperialist Winston Churchill endorsed the teaching of Basic English, and the British war effort encompassed teaching Basic to unify Britain's far-flung possessions.[23] Other Anglophones, including the influential League of Nations official (and former governor general of Nigeria) Lord Lugard, expressed doubts about teaching Western languages in Africa, pointing to anticolonial agitation in India to demonstrate its dangers. By the late 1940s the latter approach to colonial education stood in stark contrast to the antiracist internationalism that was becoming prevalent in many corridors of the United Nations, and the colonial powers knew it. Britain and

France agreed to cooperate in order to stymie UN interference in their empires.[24]

Modernizers and conservatives at the 1947 UNESCO meeting did demonstrate one important commonality, however: a patronizing attitude toward non-Western languages and cultures. For late-colonial conservatives, European rule was the natural and rightful outcome of cultural backwardness in the colonies. For modernizers, meanwhile, local practices appeared to be obstructing the forward march of progress. C. K. Ogden, arguing that illiterates should not be educated in their mother tongues, put it bluntly: "When Henry Ford diagnosed the troubles of Europe as due to the need for 50 more dead languages, the problem seemed relatively simple." If, for Ogden and other artificial-language advocates in the 1940s, the languages of the great powers were politically unacceptable to serve as global lingua francas, then the vernacular tongues of Asia and Africa were culturally unacceptable options. According to Adolph Myers, another promoter of Basic English, it was "too late now to rely on undeveloped native languages" to act as vehicular languages. A preparatory report for UNESCO's 1947 meeting asked whether vernaculars should be "abandoned" or "modified" when "unfitted" to convey modern knowledge. Another document referenced "certain primitive languages [that] do not lend themselves easily to writing on account of their phonological complexity or irregularity"; these languages "cannot carry a modern (technical and scientific) educational content." Was it possible, the document asked, to establish "general principles" for the "desirability of working for a gradual elimination of smaller or more primitive languages?" The clinical tone of most documentation from the 1947 meeting was occasionally—but tellingly—interrupted by a more transparent antagonism: "It is estimated that 200 languages and dialects are spoken in French West Africa alone, while in one small area of Northern Rhodesia primers have been printed in six languages to carry vernacular education. . . . (I am told that one of these African languages cannot really be spoken unless the two middle teeth are prized out with a spear-head.)"[25]

Such racially tinged rhetoric soon fell by the wayside of UNESCO's language-education efforts. The international order that emerged as colonial regimes waned after 1945 was many things to many people; one thing scholars have noted was its rejection of ethnic and racial hierarchies as organizing social principles.[26] In the field of language education, this transformation signified the formal equality of all languages, Western and non-Western—their common capacity to express complex and abstract concepts and to adapt to new conditions. It did not, however, mark a complete break with colonial practice. In parallel to mounting international antiracism, one key late-colonial postulate endorsed by attendees of UNESCO's 1947 meeting would persist: the notion that social and political change in the non-Western world could and should be managed through language education.

DECOLONIZATION AND THE INVENTION OF "LANGUAGES OF WIDE COMMUNICATION"

As the crumbling of European empires accelerated and newly independent states expanded the United Nations' membership, new entrants transformed internationalism. Postcolonial states, anticolonial movements, and nonsuperpowers began to use the UN General Assembly and the Economic and Social Council (ECOSOC) to challenge the great powers, which maintained a stranglehold on the Security Council. This produced unexpected alliances in the language field. From UNESCO's inception, Hispanophones pushed to make Spanish the organization's third "working language" (one of William Benton's bêtes noires, also opposed by French officials). By 1950, wrote UNESCO language-education specialist Felix Walter, the "Spanish group," which was "backed on this occasion as on previous ones by the representatives of the Arabic-speaking States," had won a "substantial majority" at UNESCO's General Conference.[27]

This political reconfiguration also reshaped international debates about language education. Language could and would no longer function as a means of separating populations from colonial overseers. In 1949 the UN General Assembly resolved that member states should make vernacular languages "the languages of instruction in elementary, primary and secondary schools." UNESCO soon followed suit, organizing a pair of meetings that addressed the "use of vernacular languages in primary and adult education." In preparing for the 1951 Meeting of Experts on the Use of

Vernacular Languages, UNESCO cast its net widely, consulting experts from the Philippines, India, Mexico, Peru, and the United States. On the cultural plane, decolonization secured growing recognition that non-Western languages were not hopelessly backward but were rather dynamic instruments of communication—part of what Felix Walter called the "reaction in Asia and Africa against linguistic imperialism and the old-fashioned idea that native cultures—and hence native languages—are inferior." Based on surveys it gathered in the early 1950s—which included frank criticism of colonial authorities for their neglectful treatment of non-Western languages—UNESCO concluded that the mere fact that some languages lacked scientific and technical vocabularies was neither proof of their inadequacy nor an insurmountable obstacle to progress. Governments in the Philippines, Indonesia, and India were working to modernize Tagalog, Bahasa Indonesia, and Hindi respectively.[28]

While colonial efforts to preserve stable ethno-cultural hierarchies faded from international language-education debates, decolonization did not necessarily resolve the question of which languages to use in education. Many postcolonial elites had attended prestigious universities in Europe and the United States. Some, such as the Filipino official who called English a "linguistic bridge to the outside world," shared in the view of Western languages as a way of accessing developments outside their borders. English might even signify the shaking off of the colonial past in places like Indonesia, which, after a bitter four-year struggle for independence from the Netherlands, pointedly declared English—not Dutch—its official primary foreign language.[29]

As the Philippines gained independence, followed by India, Pakistan, Burma, Indonesia, Cambodia, and Laos, Western policymakers would develop new strategies for sustaining their international influence. Historians of decolonization have shown that, more often than not, the end of political colonialism did not amount to a complete rupture between new states and the ex-colonial powers. Their relations encompassed the ongoing transfer of expertise and the persistence of economic ties.[30] These relations extended as well into the realm of language education. The end of colonial oversight of schooling occasioned growing American, British, and French interest in promoting their languages as transnational lingua francas.

These would, it was argued, ease language conflict in new states and speed their integration into the international community.

Felix Walter, a leading figure in UNESCO's early language-education work, was on the vanguard of this discursive shift. In Walter's eyes, the anticolonial pushback "against linguistic imperialism" presented Western language-education reformers with a challenge—and an opportunity. In 1952 Walter prognosticated that the wave of nationalism that was unsettling the privileged status of European languages in Asia was likely to pass on to Africa, where it would create a "multitude of new language problems." The education specialist repeatedly advised UNESCO to prepare for this eventuality, for, as he put it, "language barriers constitute [a] chief source" of international tension.[31] Walter counterposed these barriers to UNESCO's freedom-of-information guarantees: "[An] international organization which, to quote Article One of its constitution, aims 'to promote the free flow of ideas by word and image,' 'to give fresh impulse to . . . the spread of culture,' 'to diffuse knowledge,' 'to encourage cooperation among the nations in all branches of international activity,' must at every stage encounter these barriers."[32]

In the early 1950s Anglophone researchers and policymakers began to promote cross-border lingua francas—particularly English—as a means of countering the upheavals they associated with postcolonial multilingualism. A language-education meeting held by UNESCO in 1952 in Jos, Nigeria (then part of British West Africa), reflected both the international impact of anticolonial antiracism and the reconfiguration of Western strategies to maintain ties to Asia and Africa. The Jos meeting downplayed the concerns of a few years earlier, when late-colonial actors had worried that Western education posed a danger to colonial control and when modernizers had contended that African languages were not culturally "developed" enough for modern societies. Increasingly, discussion centered instead on the question How could language education in multilingual areas mollify political tensions and promote societal cohesion?

To fulfill these ambitions, Western experts repurposed an existing idea for the postcolonial masses: the spread of a few lingua francas, or even a single lingua franca, worldwide. Integrating the concerns of two emerging fields, applied linguistics and communication, Felix Walter argued that spreading "languages of wide communication," particularly in Asia and Africa, could promote understanding both within nation-states and internationally. Foremost among the candidates was English ("widely used at the Bandoeng [Bandung] Conference," Walter noted a few years later). Throughout the 1950s Walter promoted international cooperation to ensure the vitality of Western languages in so-called underdeveloped areas, in particular drawing attention to research emanating from the United States. American researchers had pioneered advances in the use of audiovisual tools and audiolingual methods in language teaching, and Walter thought that these tools and methods should be considered for use in UNESCO's educational and technical-assistance programs.[33]

The title of the Jos meeting, however convoluted, could not wholly obscure this shift: the Meeting of Experts on the Use in Education of African Languages in Relation to English, Where English Is the Accepted Second Language. In addition to covering issues pertaining to vernacular-language education, the meeting also addressed the use of English as a potential lingua franca in Africa—much to the annoyance of Iraqi functionary Matta Akrawi, who countered that UNESCO's mandate from the UN General Assembly had been to study education in "indigenous languages," not in "secondary European languages." ("Another point which requires a big question mark is the limitation of the study of secondary languages in 1952 to English, while other secondary languages, say, French, Spanish, Portuguese, are also involved," he added in a memo to a British colleague.) For Akrawi, UNESCO's exploration of vernacular literacy had seemingly ended before it could begin.[34] He had exposed a fundamental ambiguity in the pursuit of "languages of wide communication": while ensuring that vernacular literacy was not prima facie incompatible with spreading vehicular languages, in practice, the two objectives amounted to a resource-allocation problem as well as a political conundrum for education planners in many places. In large swaths of South and Southeast Asia and Africa, moreover, the politics of language in new states were doubly complicated by the existence of a multitude of local languages—meaning that language planning often entailed identifying a smaller number of regional vernaculars to elevate within the educational system as well as choosing a national vehicular tongue.

These complications were of secondary concern to Anglophone experts who saw vernacular languages primarily as barriers to diffusion and flow. Akrawi's criticisms, though astute, had little immediate impact on UNES-CO's plans. The Jos meeting recommended that African schools begin teaching spoken English early, preferably "in the first or second year of school life," and use audiovisual aids "wherever possible."[35] This emphasis on vehicular English was a sign of things to come as Washington's restrained involvement in international language-teaching initiatives during the early Cold War gave way to greater American support for English-language teaching outside U.S. borders.

DEVELOPMENT AND THE IDEOLOGY
OF INSTRUMENTAL ENGLISH

Though it was a locus of innovation in applied linguistics during the Second World War, the United States appeared officially uninterested in overseas language-education work in the late 1940s and early 1950s. The intensive military and government programs that had contributed much to research in language acquisition had been scaled back after 1945. And the first, haphazard forays of the Fulbright Program—American English-literature teachers were sent abroad to teach the English language without specialized training—testified to the nascent status of English-as-a-foreign-language pedagogies and applied linguistics in the United States in the late 1940s. In 1951 UNESCO's Education Department found itself chiding the U.S. delegation for its slow response to inquiries about the teaching of foreign languages for international understanding.[36]

Behind the scenes, however, liberal-internationalist elites were exploring links between language education and foreign assistance such as those outlined by UNESCO's Felix Walter. I. A. Richards maintained contacts in Washington after the war, fielding an inquiry from the State Department in 1946 about the possibilities for private language aid to Turkey and Afghanistan.[37] Within a handful of years, the Rockefeller and Ford Foundations would become significant funders of language-education initiatives in postcolonial states. Their nominal independence from the U.S. government provided operational latitude at a moment when

McCarthyism was debilitating the State Department. Moreover, foundation work tended to be more stable than activities supported by the government, the budgets of which were subject to the whims of Congress. The foundations' pronounced personnel overlaps and ideological commonalities with the Washington establishment, meanwhile, rendered them de facto agents of U.S. power. Actors on either side of the public-private divide recognized that foundation action could be preferable to government involvement in situations where populations were suspicious of Washington.[38]

The Ford Foundation's earliest intervention in the English-language field came in Southeast Asia. Starting in the early 1950s, Ford supported English-language teaching in Indonesia, dispensing $1.8 million on it between 1951 and 1956 alone. Although the project began with a request from President Sukarno's government, Ford's activities in Indonesia also had clear strategic value for U.S. containment policy in the wake of the Chinese Revolution of 1949 and the outbreak of the Korean War the next year. The language project was exhaustive, amounting to what Melvin Fox described as the "nationwide reorganization of the whole system of teaching English": training 1,500 teachers in the latest audiolingual teaching methodologies, preparing new teaching materials, and establishing facilities in Indonesia where teacher-trainers could pursue graduate study, which were intended to make Indonesia less dependent on stopgap foreign aid to fill its English-teaching needs. Around 1957 Ford's English-language activities expanded once more, into Africa, where a team of visiting foundation representatives concluded that the lack of English competence was "[one] of the greatest obstacles to accelerated education." In Kenya, Ford supported teacher training and the creation of materials for elementary English teaching. In Nigeria it backed broadcasting designed to bolster the English-language skills of both teachers and students.[39]

With the exception of a small-scale investment in Egypt, the Rockefeller Foundation's English-language initiatives in the 1950s hewed closer to historic regions of U.S. power. The foundation made a substantial investment in the Philippines, where observers worried that the status of English was under siege both from linguistic nationalism and from shortages of personnel and materials. (Despite Manila's efforts to furnish Tagalog with a scientific lexicon, the foundation concluded that neither Tagalog nor other languages spoken in the Philippines possessed "the vocabulary or the tradition which could make them the medium of advanced instruction at any time in the near future.") In 1957 the Rockefeller Foundation and UCLA helped to found a new institution in Manila, the Philippine Center for Language Study, which trained teachers, created literacy materials, and engaged in language-education research. Borrowing an image from fluid dynamics, UCLA likened English to a "channel through which the

FIGURE 3.2 "English Texts Used in Philippine Public Schools as of 1958–59," Philippine Center for Language Study, Manila. The book the woman on the left is pulling off the shelf is *The General Basic English Dictionary*. Photograph in Rockefeller Foundation Records, Record Group 1.2, series 200, box 41, folder 993. Courtesy of Rockefeller Archive Center, Sleepy Hollow, NY.

substance of education must flow"; if the channel were "blocked," all efforts to raise educational standards in the Philippines would come to naught.[40]

Obstacles, blockages, channels, flows: policy elites were embracing English as an instrument of American power in the 1950s. All that was missing was the official imprimatur. Internationally minded Americans were optimistic that the waning of McCarthyism and Stalin's death in March 1953 would rekindle governmental support for language-teaching efforts. One encouraging sign was President Eisenhower's establishment of the USIA in August 1953. By the early 1960s, the USIA could report more than 200,000 students enlisted in the English-language classes it supported overseas. The Peace Corps and USAID, both founded in 1961, also became involved in overseas English teaching. Thousands of Peace Corps volunteers provided stopgap teaching assistance to developing countries, while USAID intervened in teacher training, reporting that it had trained more than six thousand foreign teachers of English in the 1964 fiscal year alone, mostly in Africa. By 1965 the Johnson administration could declare Washington's intention "to be of active and friendly assistance to countries that desire . . . help in the teaching and utilization of English."[41]

The Ford Foundation meanwhile sought to harmonize its work with evolving federal priorities by refining its rationale for funding language education. In 1959 Ford, together with the Modern Language Association, established the Center for Applied Linguistics (CAL), the mission of which encompassed "[improving] the teaching of English around the world." The center, based in Washington, DC, would soon issue a report that identified *Second Language Learning as a Factor in National Development in Asia, Africa, and Latin America*. The report admitted that in many places, "the immediate, urgent problem" was education in local or national languages. However, "all developing countries" shared one thing in common: "the need for increased learning of a language of wider communication (LWC) such as English or French."

The concept of languages of "wide" or "wider communication"—advocated by Felix Walter at UNESCO and then by Walter's contacts at Ford and the CAL—affirmed the role of Western languages in postcolonial spaces. Whereas less than fifteen years before, late-colonial conservatives could portray the teaching of English and French in Africa as a political threat to European rule, the CAL's very existence was premised on cross-border communication in these languages, particularly English—"the most important of the LWC's."[42]

This instrumental understanding of language differed sharply from the thinking of older generations of Anglophone language reformers. In interwar Britain liberal imperialists had framed English as a language of enlightenment for the colonies. During the Second World War, *Life* magazine had contrasted English—the "richest, most intellectual and perhaps most delicate of all languages"—with "[tortuously] inflected languages like German and Japanese," suggesting that qualities inherent to these languages had shaped (even deformed) their societies.[43] By contrast, to growing numbers of policy intellectuals in the 1950s and early 1960s, English appeared useful less because of any intrinsic merit or cultural patrimony than because it made the greatest amount of scientific and technical know-how available to the largest number of people around the world. American conceptions of the place of English in the world had diverged, too, from the arguments of 1940s modernizers like Julian Huxley, under whose leadership UNESCO had mapped contemporary languages onto an evolutionary time line.[44] No longer was it in fashion to contest the fitness of non-Western languages to express scientific content. Rather—given the time and resources required to create educational materials in different languages—it was the pace of change that rendered vehicular English useful in a world in which development seemed to march to the drumbeat of innovation. As the Johnson administration proclaimed in 1965, declaring Washington's support for English-language teaching abroad, "The rapidly growing interest in English cuts across political and ideological lines because of the convenience of a *lingua franca* increasingly used as a second language in important areas of the world. . . . English is a key which opens doors to scientific and technical knowledge indispensable to the economic and political development of vast areas of the world."[45]

By the 1960s, in the public proclamations of developmentalist liberals, the mother tongue of the American elite and much of the American public had become a neutral and apolitical mechanism for conveying information, a "key which opens doors," everywhere in the world.

In 1959 the Center for Applied Linguistics, with Ford Foundation funding, began an ambitious World Second Language Survey. The survey had originated in the work of the Ford Foundation and the CAL, but—lest it appear too "American"—Ford's Melvin Fox and the CAL's Charles Ferguson took pains to attract international participation. They reached out first to British policymakers, who expressed interest in drawing on American "skills and funds" in the field of English as a foreign language. Second, they targeted France, with its well-known reputation for language diplomacy. To mollify potential Anglophone-Francophone tensions, Fox and Ferguson tapped Felix Walter of UNESCO to lead an early meeting of the survey committee, for Walter was old hat at dealing with French policy elites whom the Americans were leery of provoking. But these fears proved overblown, Fox reported happily to his colleagues: all the survey participants were "strongly action-oriented" and recognized the importance of research that could link up with their burgeoning international-development plans. The field of second-language teaching, glossed Fox, was "for a variety of quite obvious reasons a matter of considerable importance to the foreign policy interests of England, the United States and France."[46]

On the eve of the 1960s, development aid was becoming a big-tent issue. For new states, it held out the promise of technical and financial assistance. For forward-thinking Europeans, it offered a means of maintaining cultural and economic ties with the rest of the world as their empires shriveled. For the United States, finally, embracing development meant fighting Soviet influence in postcolonial Asia and Africa. This convergence of interests also entailed a burgeoning consensus over the ways in which people's material and social welfare shaped their beliefs and ideas: experts and policymakers around the world could agree that the developing world would never achieve genuine freedom of information if its citizens did not have regular access to abundant books, periodicals, and broadcasting—or if they could not read or comprehend the media to which they did have access.[47]

But there was another side to U.S. involvement in far-flung aid projects. American social scientists had been blocked from conducting fieldwork in colonial India and lacked experience in much of the decolonizing world. The paradigm of development offered Americans a means of asserting an understanding of places where they had little cultural and linguistic knowledge. Area expertise mattered less when every society, from Southeast Asia to West Africa, was presumed to want the same things—economic growth and improved social welfare. This elision was evident in American language work abroad. Americans "know little about African problems," admitted the UCLA linguist Clifford Prator after a 1959 trip to Ghana. But this lack of area-specific knowledge appeared unimportant when the International Meeting on Second Language Problems, an extension of the World Second Language Survey, was predicting "administrative chaos and economic stagnation" if the developing world were not soon graced with better second-language training. Despite his reservations, Prator, who had spent formative years working on English-language teaching in regions of historic American influence—Latin America and the Philippines—began to investigate setting up a program somewhere in Africa modeled on UCLA's work in Manila.[48]

The irony was apparent to at least a few language experts. Charles Ferguson of the CAL contrasted American leadership in the field of applied linguistics with lagging American interest and ability in actually learning foreign languages. Ferguson, a scholar of Arabic, was uniquely placed to observe this contradiction, which was baked in to U.S. foreign policy on the eve of the Development Decade announced by President Kennedy and the United Nations in 1961. For if mainstream American policymakers had begun to admit that there was a material basis for political allegiances, they proved slower to grasp the policymaking significance of cultural and linguistic differences. "I sort of felt he was like a thick layer of glass," remarked Melvin Fox of one high-ranking Ghanaian official whom he met on a 1956 Ford Foundation visit to Africa.[49] The solution that Fox did so much to advocate for in the ensuing decade captured, in microcosm, the optimistic calculus of many of his fellow American policy elites during that period: more English, more flows, more freedom.

4

Capacity as Freedom During the Development Decade

[The] greater and freer the flow of information, the less likely it is that manipulative communication will have any effect.... This is what the United Nations Commission on Human Rights meant when it called information one of the basic rights. The process of national development illustrates it admirably. An adequate flow of information is required for knowledge to be shared between those who have more of it and those who have less on any given subject.
—Wilbur Schramm, *Mass Media and National Development* (1964)

In 1959 Henry Cassirer of UNESCO produced a sixteen-millimeter short film, *Television Comes to the Land*, which told the story of television's arrival in the rural French village of Nogentel, sixty miles outside Paris, in the early 1950s. Despite initial skepticism about the new technology, television was soon embraced by the villagers, who pooled money to purchase a set that was then installed at the local school. Television, the film suggested, was more than mere entertainment for the men, women, and children who gathered regularly at the school to watch; it "opened to the people of Nogentel a new window on the world" and enlightened them about modern conveniences. A program about rural life in France, coproduced by UNESCO and Radiodiffusion-Télévision Française, the French broadcasting monopoly, spurred the villagers to install a water-pumping station in their valley. "Water in the house brings contentment to all," chorused a group of children on the screen. Cassirer's film also noted the efforts of local teachers to stimulate discussion and debate after Nogentel's communal television-viewing sessions—the first chapter in what became known as the "tele-club" movement. Soon similar tele-clubs had gotten started in Italy and Japan, with plans in the works, the film announced, to "use television as an aid to social and cultural progress" in Latin America, Africa, and other parts of Asia.[1]

In its great faith in the power of media to foster enthusiasm for development projects, *Television Comes to the Land* captured the mindset of many media professionals and policymakers on the eve of what President Kennedy and the United Nations declared the world's first Development Decade. In the United States earlier broadcasting diplomacy had been consumed by the mission to wage psychological warfare against the Soviet Union, especially in occupied Germany. By the late 1950s, however, thawing cultural relations between the superpowers plus the imperative to win hearts and minds in the decolonizing world were shaping a less overtly paranoid, more globally oriented understanding of broadcasting's foreign-policy potential among American policy elites. This shift was evident in one of the era's landmark works of modernization theory, Daniel Lerner's *The Passing of Traditional Society: Modernizing the Middle East* (1958). Presenting a fresh interpretation of Voice of America listener surveys taken during the early Cold War, the MIT sociologist—and psyops veteran— argued that modernization was a psychosocial process as well as an economic one, advanced by factors such as radio ownership, newspaper consumption, and rising literacy rates. Media sowed the seeds of curiosity and empathy, those characteristically modern traits. Give people a "window on the world," Cassirer and Lerner seemed to agree, and they will modernize themselves.[2]

With this optimism about the developmental potential of media came a recognition of how far much of the world still had to go to obtain access to it. Presenting the findings of four years' worth of research and meetings to the UN Human Rights Commission in the spring of 1962, Tor Gjesdal, head of UNESCO's Department of Mass Communication, reported, "No less than 70 per cent of the world's population lack adequate information media. They are without a 'window on the world' and are thus denied effective enjoyment of one of the basic human rights—the right to know." Gjesdal proceeded to announce bold targets for global media capacity, calling for ten daily newspapers, five radio sets, and two movie seats per one hundred people in every country. If, during the 1940s newsprint crisis, attempts had been made to link media rights to material capacity, during

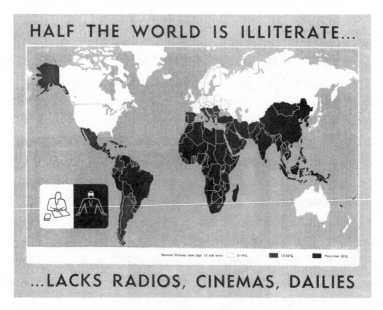

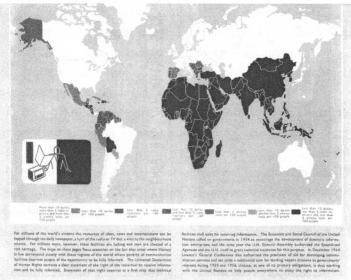

FIGURE 4.1 "Half of the World Is Illiterate...Lacks Radios, Cinemas, Dailies."
Reprinted from the *UNESCO Courier*, May 1956. In the top map, areas in white indicate
less than 10 percent illiteracy among residents fifteen or older; gray, between 10 and 50 percent illiteracy; and black, more than 50 percent illiteracy. In the bottom map, darker the
area, the worse it was served by media.

the 1960s there emerged a genuine, if thin, international consensus that chronic shortages of "information media" undermined a universal "right to know."[3] This positive conception of information freedoms was embraced by actors in the United States, Europe, and the developing world alike.

In addition to its optimism about the positive social effects of media, *Television Comes to the Land* was a microcosm of postwar development thinking in another way, too: in the vector of expertise that it traced from industrialized countries to the rest of the globe. While before 1945 the United States had honed protodevelopmental tactics of governance in the Philippines and Latin America, it had a relatively small footprint in Asia and Africa. In the case of the European colonial powers, the organization of social programs for ordinary colonial subjects matured only after the Second World War, in response to demands by these subjects for full citizenship.[4] By 1959, by contrast, Cassirer's film could contend that a practice that had developed in France—watching television in group settings—was a portable development technique offering insights to educators, broadcasters, and ordinary people elsewhere, notably "in Latin America, in Asia, [and] in Africa." For the United States and its allies in Western Europe, the announcement of the Development Decade crystallized a postcolonial rationale of global involvement; remedying endemic shortages, it seemed, required maintaining or expanding relationships with new states.[5]

In existing histories of postwar human rights, the episode of media development has rarely figured. Its absence is partly an artifact of methodology: human-rights history, a relatively recent field, has been dominated in its first two decades by legal and diplomatic historians and is less often addressed by cultural historians or historians of media or technology.[6] Diplomatic historians have shown how the emergence of postcolonial states at the United Nations transformed internationalism in the 1950s and 1960s, but at times these scholars have done so with a narrow institutional focus that has obscured rather than clarified the broader picture. One historian goes so far as to treat development as the pet cause of corrupt developing-world autocrats.[7] It is true that the development consensus was fueled largely by the aspirations of policymakers and activists in Asia, the Middle East, Africa, and Latin America, many of whom viewed economic growth as taking precedence over political and civil liberties. But this account overlooks the persistence of social and economic concerns across time and space and their various entanglements with human-rights claims in the postwar era. Not only did such concerns motivate, for instance, Latin American social-democratic human-rights advocacy in the mid-1940s or the Western European varieties of "social citizenship" concretized a few years later by postwar governments.[8] Social and economic factors also drove U.S. development policies in the 1960s, which were justified with reference to positive rights.

Few figures embodied the development consensus more than the American communication scholar Wilbur Schramm, whose work for UNESCO and the U.S. government during the 1960s helped to spread the gospel of development communication to far-flung corners of the world. Schramm was, in one sense, an unlikely fit as an international consultant. Like Lerner's, Schramm's research agenda in the late 1940s and 1950s had been molded by the imperatives of Cold War psychological warfare, in particular by the task of measuring the effectiveness of U.S. propaganda overseas.[9] The Stanford professor had little esteem for communication research conducted outside the United States or in languages other than English—even when he could not read them. Nor did Schramm have much tolerance for the intricacies of polyglot, polycultural organizations like UNESCO's spin-off the International Association for Mass Communication Research (IAMCR, discussed in chapter 2). Yet Schramm's impatience with cultural and linguistic differences was beside the point. His international collaborations in the 1960s marked a period when efforts to increase developing countries' material capacities for information flows seemed to provide a bridge—however narrow or shaky—over prior international impasses regarding information freedoms. By the lights of the media-development paradigm, state power was not a threat to these freedoms but rather their conduit. Schramm's 1964 opus, *Mass Media and National Development*, commissioned by UNESCO and copublished by UNESCO and Stanford University Press, would become one of the best-known expressions of this paradigm.[10]

This chapter sets Schramm's work in the context of unfolding debates about television and development in the 1960s. Not everyone was so sanguine about centralized power or expertise. Henry Cassirer was nearly as well connected as Schramm, consulting for the Ford Foundation, the World Bank, and other influential institutions during his many decades working in broadcasting and educational media. Cassirer was likewise a believer in the power of media to promote positive social change. But Cassirer's peripatetic career differed from Schramm's in crucial respects. Born in Berlin to a family whose Protestantism was recent (his paternal grandfather had been Jewish), Cassirer fled the Third Reich and spent much of the Second World War translating and debunking Nazi radio propaganda for Anglophones in the United States, where he became a citizen. More suspicious than Schramm of state power, Cassirer—a native German speaker who was fluent in French as well as English and literate in Spanish—was also more cognizant of the ways in which linguistic and cultural diversity factored in to media reception. For media development to work, Cassirer contended, policymakers needed to encourage information to flow from ordinary viewers and listeners back up the governmental chain of command. Others went further than Cassirer, challenging the very presumption that "vertical" communication managed by states—government-funded educational television, for instance—could act as a constructive force for change. Taken together, these exchanges pointed to the limitations of organizing information freedoms around material capacity.

SHAKING THE WEB, BURNING THE STEPS: DEVELOPMENT AND THE PROMISE OF TELEVISION

The Development Decade was marked by dramatic statements about the role of new media technologies in the development process. In an era obsessed with quantification, these technologies functioned as knowledge multipliers, a way of spreading vital educational content and information on hygiene and productivity even to populations largely excluded from existing education systems. As one Wilbur Schramm–directed study concluded, "The new media offer . . . a means of shaking the whole web of traditional attitudes and practices, thus contributing to the modernization and advancement of any educational system." Henry Cassirer, who was often more guarded, cited the French expression "*brûler les étapes*" (literally, "to burn the steps") to dramatize the desire for rapid progress in developing countries and to suggest the ways in which educational media could help societies attain it.[11]

Television in particular attracted admiration. It was "the most powerful force of any of the media," according to Leonard Marks, director of the U.S. Information Agency (USIA, founded in 1953), which disseminated information about the United States abroad on behalf of the U.S. government. The American educational economist Philip Coombs, a collaborator of Schramm's, noted that television could help to streamline educational bureaucracies when used in the classroom, where more pupils could be instructed while holding down staff costs. In Vietnam, U.S. authorities enthused about the potential of television to "project the Governmental presence" and to display the shiny fruits of development ("housing developments, health clinics, new schools") to the Vietnamese public.[12]

It was not just Americans who sang the medium's praises. With Americans, voices from Europe emphasized the relevance of Euro-American television experience and expertise to the rest of the world. The veteran French producer and UN media specialist Jean d'Arcy noted in 1964 that until recently, many rural parts of Europe might have been considered "underdeveloped." Nogentel's first collective television screening in 1951 happened at a moment when postwar austerity remained a fact of life in France, Britain, and elsewhere. But by the late 1950s austerity was giving way to a more robust consumer economy, which was starting to bring household appliances, televisions, and cars within the reach of the average Western European family. D'Arcy interpreted the spread of the small screen as more than just evidence of development. It was also a cause of development: "It is worth noting to just what degree in the remote areas of France, England, or Italy, for example, where television has recently penetrated, women are better groomed, more elegant and more assertive in daily life." According to d'Arcy, television, "an excellent generator of new desires and needs," reduced people's resistance to change even in what experts considered the locus of traditional practices—the home.[13]

Policymakers and media specialists enumerated three basic ways in which television could be used for development purposes. The first was for training teachers. The cost of educating teachers formed a substantial part of any education budget, presenting one of the most significant limitations to educational expansion. Writing to a State Department contact in 1965, William Benton—by then the U.S. Ambassador to UNESCO—criticized "orthodox" teacher-training methods, dismissing them as too expensive for developing nations: "We've got to rely on other techniques." Although, as Wilbur Schramm was careful to point out, the use of new media could not totally eliminate teacher-training costs, it could help to save money in contexts of educational expansion. It could also redress shortages generated by political upheaval. Newly independent Algeria had embarked on a teacher-training program using television "to meet the desperate shortage of teachers after independence," a rupture which had, it was reported, provoked the departure of roughly half of the country's twenty thousand teachers.[14]

A second, more direct way of reaching populations in developing countries was to broadcast school courses via television. Proponents argued that this technique, when properly applied, reduced the need for skilled teachers altogether. As Benton put it, the "weaker the teachers . . . the more they urgently [need] the 'new tools' which are developing through modern technology." UNESCO's Ignacy Waniewicz was more explicit: television might act as a "substitute for teachers, provided that . . . programmes are viewed under the guidance and in personal contact with monitors who are at least partially instructed." With French assistance, Niger had conducted a television-teaching experiment using educational television in classrooms for four hours per day to make up for a shortage of trained staff. This technique rendered the on-the-ground expertise of teachers—"a discontented element in so many countries," as Harold Lasswell commented suspiciously—less critical to educational planning.[15]

The third use of television was to reach children and adults who were no longer in school or had never attended it. Television could reach groups "impervious to those forms of education and training which enjoy more traditional methods," according to the French National Commission for UNESCO. By marrying "sight with sound," echoed the American technology company IBM, television offered a way to "leap the barriers of illiteracy." Although many experts were careful to qualify that media alone offered no panacea for instructing undereducated or illiterate populations,

Waniewicz noted that television might "weaken the natural reluctance to return to the school benches," acting as both a pedagogical aid and a publicity tool for literacy campaigns. In Italy, for instance, children who left school because no further education was available in their villages had been successfully reached through the Telescuola program of broadcast courses—an initiative with "direct significance for developing countries," according to Henry Cassirer. Meanwhile, in the Ivory Coast, televised literacy courses were broadcast for workers.[16]

The catch with these optimistic assessments of television's pedagogical potential was, as Schramm noted, that television was "the most costly of the media to capitalize." Television broadcasting required production studios and transmitters as well as trained personnel to manage the equipment. Moreover, television sets were substantially pricier than radio receivers and in the developing world usually needed to be imported—a drain on foreign-currency reserves. In the absence of easily obtainable battery-powered sets, television reception was limited to electrified areas, restricting its range absent costly infrastructural improvements.[17] Thus fetishized by development experts as both invaluable and impossibly expensive, the medium of television was more than the message. It involved, for the United States and other industrialized countries, concerted efforts to maintain their presence in recently decolonized areas—even ones actively nationalizing or Africanizing their resources and personnel.[18]

Wilbur Schramm's work for UNESCO during the 1960s exemplified this convergence of interests. In spite of behind-the-scenes tensions between American and European policymakers, Schramm made an effort to put a consensual veneer on media development in his published writings. His 1964 UNESCO-published *Mass Media and National Development* was bookended by paratextual compromise. Schramm dedicated the book to the French journalist Jacques Kayser, who had passed away the year prior to its publication and whom the dedication called a "[sturdy] fighter for free flow of information." The volume also included a separate section authored by Kayser's compatriot and Raymond Nixon's erstwhile nemesis at the IAMCR, Fernand Terrou (predictably, this arrangement did not go completely smoothly; alluding to their "occasional trouble" communicating, Schramm admitted, "Undoubtedly I am guilty, because of my faulty command of French").[19] In the book's body text, Schramm embraced the French concept of *formation*: "As a French word for education, *formation*, suggests, education aims at the formation of a new person, with new horizons, new skills, new goals. It does indeed take a long time. All the kinds of human change required for economic development take long, and are costly and difficult."[20]

Throughout, *Mass Media and National Development* referred to data and media-capacity standards produced by UNESCO in order to corroborate its recommendations. Developing countries suffered a "shortage of trained personnel; . . . a shortage of newsprint; . . . a shortage of radio receivers, with which information might leap the literacy barrier and bring modern life to the villages; . . . [and] a shortage of printing, broadcasting, and film-making and film-showing equipment." In a strong expression of the positive, material aspects of information freedoms, Schramm extrapolated from the data the impossibility of achieving genuine freedom under shortage conditions. Although the United Nations' 1948 Geneva Conference on Freedom of Information had termed freedom of information "'one of the basic freedoms,' and free and adequate information 'the touchstone of all the freedoms,'" Schramm insisted that "before there can be free and adequate information in any country, there must be adequate development of mass communication." For Schramm, then, development was the a priori condition for fulfilling the promises of the Universal Declaration of Human Rights, and UNESCO's quantitative benchmarks were the measuring stick.[21]

Some of Schramm's solutions for increasing communication capacity in the developing world rehashed classic liberal formulas about reducing trade barriers in an echo of the postwar newsprint debates. "There are only two real solutions to shortages. One is to manufacture the goods within the country. The other is to ease the import restrictions—tariffs and quotas—so as to increase the flow from other countries," he wrote. Though desirable, the former solution—in-country manufacture of printing presses, radios, televisions, and other equipment—would take time to achieve, a lag that justified interim international aid, much as the Marshall Plan had contributed to the rebuilding of Europe after 1945 by helping participating countries to import scarce items such as fuel and foodstuffs.[22]

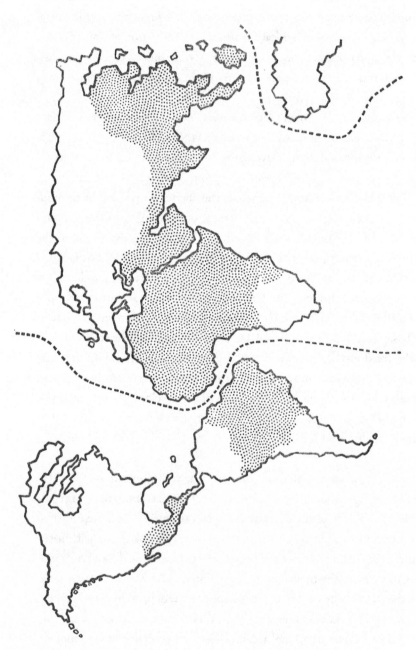

FIGURE 4.2 Wilbur Schramm's "band of scarcity," 1964. Schramm, *Mass Media and National Development: The Role of Information in the Developing Countries* (Stanford, CA: Stanford University Press, 1964), 92. Courtesy of the Board of Trustees of the Leland Stanford Jr. University.

The geography of shortage, however, appeared to have shifted considerably since the 1940s. By the early 1960s the Western European recovery was maturing into an economic boom, with average workers for the first time enjoying disposable income and spending it on home appliances, automobiles, and leisure items like televisions. In tracing a "band of scarcity"—really more of a selectively distended sine wave—curving across parts of Latin America and most of Africa, the Middle East, and Asia, Schramm avoided Europe entirely.[23] Scarcity, moreover, had a temporality as well as a geography. Using UNESCO survey data from 1950 and 1962 to establish rates of media growth, he projected that it would take until 1981 for Asia to attain the UNESCO minimum for cinema seats and Africa until 2035 to attain the minimum for newspapers. Schramm commented in *Mass Media and National Development* that these were areas "used to living in the past and present, although [their] policy is to live in the future." However condescending this might have sounded to later critics, Schramm's thinking was of a piece with that of his peers Walt Rostow and Daniel Lerner, who indexed postwar transformations in the developing world to prior developmental stages of the industrialized West. The assumption central to the modernization theory propagated by Rostow and Lerner, that every country could follow the same path toward an advanced industrial economy, merged racial liberalism and Western hubris: new and developing states might eventually achieve Euro-American modernity—if they followed Euro-American (especially American) guidance.[24]

For every dramatic claim about television's potential as a development tool there came equally dramatic admonitions about the perils of its premature introduction in developing countries. Despite divergences between American and European broadcasting models—France as well as Britain having rejected commercial broadcasting along American lines—American and European media specialists could agree that entertainment should not be the primary goal of television in developing countries, where audiences were not ready for it. Rather, education should come first. Henry Cassirer and Jean d'Arcy hammered home this point in their contributions to a 1964 UNESCO meeting of television experts in Nigeria. Cassirer wrote, "In Africa . . . the needs for the education of children and adults alike are so pressing that everything else takes by comparison second place." D'Arcy, then director of the UN Radio and Visual Services Division, likewise asserted that television's "value as an entertainment medium" was "in no way comparable to its potential power as an instrument for national unification, social development, education and the general dissemination of information." In case the consequences of ignoring developed-world know-how were not obvious, experts warned that poor planning could yield disastrous results. Cassirer emphasized to a Nigerian colleague that the "excessively rapid" and "inadequately planned" introduction of television would undermine a country's development program.[25]

Schramm's variation on this theme in *Mass Media and National Development* killed two birds with one stone. First, he repeated the familiar trope that developing-world audiences were too fickle and inattentive to process entertainment and information at once. Second, and more creatively, he used this to justify continuing research of the type he specialized in:

> Common sense, based on long experience with entertainment programs in well-developed cultures, advises that an audience should be sent away "happy." ... A comedy at the end of an instructional film showing is probably good public relations. ... But when this is tried in developing countries, development officers began to have doubts. They began to wonder how much of the health or agriculture or literacy taught in the earlier films was forgotten in the final comedy. "How many times," a film officer wrote ruefully, "have I seen the whole effects of teaching disappear in the gusts of laughter greeting Charlie Chaplin!" The problem, therefore, is to balance the loss in learning against the increased motivation to come back for more. ... How much was learned over a period of time with, and how much was learned without, the final comedy; and how many people lasted through the course? Questions like these are research questions, for which common sense does not provide an adequate guide.[26]

The tactic worked. By the mid-1960s, Schramm had become a kind of guru for the burgeoning development bureaucracy in Washington. The

USIA heaped praise on *Mass Media and National Development*, recommending its findings to "every Agency officer." The agency planned to translate the book into more than thirty languages, including Vietnamese, Chinese, Greek, and Turkish. William Benton, then the U.S. ambassador to UNESCO, likewise sang Schramm's praises. "I've just had two days in Washington as your publicity agent . . . promoting you as a cutting edge," Benton joked in a 1965 letter to Schramm. Schramm may not have needed the help; he was then advising the executive-branch Task Force on Educational Television in Less Developed Countries.[27]

Unsurprisingly, given Schramm's stature among establishment anticommunists, the development heuristic he had sketched in *Mass Media and National Development*—essentially a one-way vector of knowledge to countries in the band of scarcity—was adopted in Washington. The Task Force on Educational Television in Less Developed Countries, chaired by USIA's Leonard Marks, recommended that U.S. foreign-aid efforts in the field of education move away from "conventional methods" in order to give more weight to new teaching technologies. "[We] in America know more about educational television than anyone else," White House aide Joseph Califano explained to President Johnson in a 1967 memorandum, reflecting the confidence that Washington vested in its development-communication expertise to shape the world for the better. The U.S. government put its rhetoric into action. The governor of American Samoa, a future FCC commissioner, introduced classroom television in both primary and secondary schools there in order to "implement an abrupt and revolutionary change in the [educational] system," as the project evaluation coauthored by Schramm noted. In El Salvador, the U.S. Agency for International Development (USAID), founded in 1961, contributed to a television-teaching initiative designed to overhaul teacher training as well as classroom instruction, with Schramm and dozens of other American experts consulting on the project. USAID also helped to finance educational television in Colombia and Nigeria among other places.[28]

Scholars of modernization and development have underscored the illiberal implications of the development paradigm that reigned in the 1960s. Viewing world events in terms of global anticommunist struggle, leading American modernization theorists were content to see economic growth as something that preceded civil liberties in the developing world and not the other way around.[29] This order of priorities was implicit in parts of Schramm's *Mass Media and National Development*. It also inflected the thinking of Schramm's repeat collaborator Daniel Lerner, who began to doubt the media-effects model he had outlined in the late 1950s in *The Passing of Traditional Society*. During the 1960s Lerner expressed concerns that unchecked commercial broadcasting in the developing world would create consumer expectations among the masses that could not be satisfied, leading to popular dissatisfaction and, ultimately, political instability—a "revolution of rising frustrations." From this he concluded that expectations in the developing world needed to be more carefully managed by policymakers: "The news that must be spread is that reward goes with effort."[30]

During the Johnson administration these illiberal tendencies became institutionalized in U.S. aid to television abroad. At the State Department, bureaucrats entertained the tantalizing notion that an educational system built around television would give centralized authorities greater influence over what students encountered in the classroom—a factor in American Samoa and El Salvador among other places. But the foremost "reason for the urgency" regarding educational television, explained administration insider Matthew Nimetz to Joseph Califano, was Southeast Asia. In Vietnam, Washington scrambled to set up television broadcasting following high-level recommendations for an "intensified" campaign of psychological warfare. Although U.S. authorities wished to minimize the appearance of American domination, they acknowledged that the South Vietnamese regime (Republic of Vietnam, or RVN) was not prepared to operate television on its own. More to the point, the Americans did not trust it.[31]

Through the cooperation of USAID, USIA, the Defense Department, and the RVN, television service in Vietnam began in February 1966 with an inaugural broadcast featuring an "attractive female" who "invited continued interest" among audiences. An initial one thousand television sets were purchased for group viewing in and around Saigon, the site of the first television station, with more to be distributed once three other planned stations—one in the Mekong Delta and two farther north—were operational. By the end of the year, the Saigon station was broadcasting for up to three hours each night. USIA advised the South Vietnamese government on programming, which was to focus on informational and educational content, with English-language instruction "covered from the start."[32]

Early observers reported hundreds of people, sometimes more, turning out to watch on a single television set. The crowds were at once a testimony to television's appeal, a sound-engineering challenge, and a Vietcong target. One intelligence communiqué described a knifing at a communal viewing session as proof that the medium was reaching an audience. This time was no case of guerrilla warfare, however; the assailant was trying to get closer to the television set. American authorities projected that the broadcasts would reach two-thirds of the population by the end of 1967—an impressive feat for the crash program, though not impressive enough for General William Westmoreland, commander of U.S. forces in Vietnam, who called for each village to be served by television.[33]

The rapid-fire, top-down introduction of television in Vietnam pushed up against the limits of statist efforts to build media capacity. Even Wilbur Schramm appeared to retreat from some of the ways in which development expertise was being mobilized by the U.S. government. In comparison with General Westmoreland, Schramm was cautious about what media on their own could accomplish, highlighting the "*human and social* problems" associated with new technologies. "Often it is no favor to a country simply to give it a magnificent set of educational hardware," he wrote to presidential adviser Douglass Cater. Schramm recommended closer collaboration with international organizations such as UNESCO in order to spread American know-how, partly because multilateralism was cost-effective—and partly because many states preferred multilateral aid to bilateral aid (which tended to come with more strings attached). And Schramm privately acknowledged the ways in which one-way flows did not always produce the consequences intended by aid experts. "As a nation begins to develop economically and socially, its educators develop a predictable pride and sensitivity," he told Cater. "They resent Americans doing research in their country while local professors have neither the time nor the money to do similar research."[34]

Unleashed in the international arena, Schramm's ideas about media and development would be multiplied—and transformed.

"HENRY'S 'FEED-BACK' ": TWO-WAY COMMUNICATION AND INFORMATION FREEDOMS

While still in its draft stages, Wilbur Schramm's *Mass Media and National Development* had provoked sharp debate at UNESCO, which was copublishing the book. In particular, Henry Cassirer was critical of the way in which Schramm conceptualized the communication process: it was "too hierarchical, from top to bottom." Information not only "[filtered] down to the village level" but also flowed up the social hierarchy and laterally across regions. "Freedom of information," Cassirer insisted, "includes freedom of expression and access of those who wish to express themselves to communications media." Cassirer suggested that in revising the manuscript for publication Schramm pay more attention to ordinary media audiences, who needed and wanted to have a sense of participating in the communication process.[35]

Cassirer also challenged Schramm's conception of how to evaluate media effects. "People are not only objects of research," Cassirer wrote to Schramm in 1963. Behind the scenes, Cassirer elaborated to UNESCO's Tor Gjesdal that "organized feed-back, which may not qualify to be called scientific research, is of great value and should not be discarded by an alternative between no research or expensive and highly scientific research." This criticism resonated as Schramm prepared a shorter brochure on conducting media research in development contexts for UNESCO. The point of the publication, thought UNESCO's Pierre Navaux, stemmed from "the need to convince under-staffed and under-financed broadcasting stations... that it is nevertheless worth putting some money... into setting up an audience relations section." Navaux asked, "Is there no place for what Schramm would probably consider the 'unscientific methods'—listeners' mail, ad hoc interviews by officials on tour, etc.? Can all of this be dismissed with the few paragraphs on page 6?"[36]

Schramm responded to criticisms of his work variously. Although Cassirer and others had raised the concern that media in the wrong hands could be a force for manipulation, *Mass Media and National Development* appeared to double down on the idea that increasing the quantity of media offered an adequate check on state abuses. But Schramm did grant the "need of lateral as well as hierarchical communication, and the importance of getting reports up as well as down." In revising, Schramm conceded, "I shall do my best . . . with Henry's 'feed-back.'" Some of Cassirer's points even filtered upward to Washington's executive-branch agencies, though anonymously. In its precis on *Mass Media and National Development*, the USIA credited Schramm with underlining the importance of feedback in the development process.[37]

Cassirer had not manufactured his criticisms out of thin air. They were rooted in his professional experience in commercial television at CBS and in educational media at UNESCO. The American professoriate did not have a monopoly on knowledge about television or development, he seemed to assert. As the Development Decade progressed, Cassirer would become even more convinced of the importance of audience responses to the development process, partly through his involvement in a UNESCO media project in Senegal.

The project began in 1963 with the signing of a six-year agreement between the Senegalese government and UNESCO calling for the creation of an educational television service in Dakar. On the production side, this encompassed producing programs, training local personnel, and forming film crews to capture life outside the capital city. In March 1965, once the programs were ready, the project also organized eleven tele-clubs consisting of thirty to fifty *dakaroise* women each—nearly five hundred women total, most of them illiterate. The clubs met twice a week to watch and discuss programs on health and nutrition.[38]

Cassirer's initial impressions were hopeful. "Television is proving its effectiveness as a force of adult education in urban conditions," he reported after a 1965 visit to Dakar. Its power to reach female illiterates—"the most under-privileged section of the population," in his estimation—was particularly impressive, suggesting that, programming aside, the medium by its very nature could attract and motivate adult learners. And the programs, combining live broadcasting with filmed footage, were innovative. At the time, there was no commonly taught Latin script for Wolof, the most widely spoken language in the country. Producers surmounted this hurdle by first preparing written scripts in French then handing the scripts to actors who performed loose, impromptu translations into spoken Wolof before the camera. Rather than criticizing the ad-libbed quality of these productions, Cassirer praised them for their fresh and vivid depiction of everyday life in Senegal.[39]

The major challenge, common to many development-communication initiatives, was how to spread these techniques on a larger scale and to the rural areas where a large proportion of Senegal's population lived. This was a tall order for a brand-new tool. Television production was frequently beset by logistical difficulties, such as the fact that all film (black-and-white as well as color film) still had to be sent to Paris to be developed. Cameras also needed to be imported, a further drain on tight budgets. One television camera was stuck in port for months for lack of funds until suddenly the money was drummed up from unspecified sources because it was needed to film an interview with President Léopold Sédar Senghor. On the distribution side, the hurdles were high as well. How could urban tele-clubs be replicated outside Dakar if, as Senghor pointed out to Cassirer, television service would not be widely available until 1974 at the earliest?[40]

Gradually, radio emerged as a more economical way of reaching Senegal's peasants. Cheaper to produce, it had also already diffused into the countryside; by the late 1960s villages in central Senegal's peanut-producing region were well equipped with transistorized sets. Radio, not television, was truly a mass medium in the 1960s, perhaps *the* mass medium in a country where, as of 1961, some 94 percent of the population could not read or write in French—Senegal's only official language. A radio component was added to UNESCO's pilot project in 1965, with programs designed to help educate peasants in modern agricultural techniques.[41]

The project's ambition to channel information from the government down to peasants would have been familiar to development-communication specialists the world over. For instance, when a new local fertilizer factory opened, peasants would need to be informed and educated about the fertilizer in order for the investment to actually boost production. What set the Senegalese pilot apart was that, in addition to diffusing knowledge from the governmental top down to grassroots producers, it also sought to channel feedback from the bottom back up to the government—to promote what Cassirer termed "free two-way communication" and "democratic participation in national development." Production teams were sent out into the field to gather responses and ideas from listeners—a more complex and expensive proposition than producing programs in a studio but one that gave peasants a voice. In addition, letters from listening groups were gathered into a bulletin, *Dissoo* ("dialogue" in Wolof), which was then circulated within the government. As Cassirer explained, though literacy rates were low, there was usually at least one literate adult or school-age youngster available to record the village's thoughts. The project team also took on an "old Wolof farmer and poet" to read aloud any Wolof letters written in Arabic script (which some peasants learned at Koranic schools), which could then be translated into French by another team member.[42]

The radio pilot, or Radio Educative Rurale (RER), successfully encouraged audience participation. Letters for *Dissoo* streamed in from rural listeners: hundreds in the months after the RER began broadcasting, and more than four hundred on average per year for the next several years. While some letters merely offered formulaic thanks to the government, others presented substantive questions and suggestions. One peanut cultivator, after witnessing a buyer try to cheat another grower by undervaluing the weight of his goods, asked whether the cultivator "has the right to inspect the scales before weighing his peanuts." Another grower wrote to protest a radio broadcast that he felt assigned blame unfairly to peasants for not paying their debts to the agricultural cooperatives through which the postcolonial state distributed fertilizer, farm implements, and other necessities: it was not fair to responsible growers who had paid their debts and "who have the good will to help the government in the development of the country." A third letter in the same issue came from a group that had ordered carts to transport its produce to market. When groups of more than four traveled on the same cart, police were stopping and fining them. The letter requested the government's help, otherwise people would stop ordering carts. Although some in the government felt threatened by such frank talk, it was encouraged by President Senghor, who framed the issue in stark terms: "My only choice is between dictatorship and dialogue, and I have chosen dialogue."[43]

Cassirer was at pains to clarify that two-way communication was not merely a cosmetic mask for one-directional, top-down change. While more orthodox development experts like Wilbur Schramm and Everett Rogers still considered it their primary task to manipulate the behavior of individuals and social groups in order to fulfill national development plans—reflecting a commitment to advancing U.S. foreign policy through communication research—Cassirer lambasted what he called the "conventional authoritarian concept of communication": "Feedback is not only response to messages already sent on topics chosen by the authorities but also comment . . . on issues which are foremost in the peasants' minds." At times it was the behavior of ineffective policymakers and ivory-tower experts, not peasants, that needed changing.[44] He had witnessed the importance of open-ended dialogue firsthand on a trip to a Senegalese village to observe an RER listening and discussion session. Although the program had focused on peanut cultivation, after the broadcast a peasant woman commented that what really concerned her was water. Senegal was then experiencing a prolonged drought. "What can be done about water?" she persisted. Such feedback helped to stimulate the government to adapt its agricultural policies, changes which coincided with rising productivity and falling rates of unpaid debts among peanut cultivators. Cassirer concluded, "This 'feed-back' is the essential element."[45]

As his career wound down, Cassirer was anxious to steward his intellectual legacy in the field of development communication. In 1980 he sent a letter to the Bolivian critic Luis Ramiro Beltrán to clarify his contribution. "My pre-occupation with the two-way process of communication (top-down and [down-up]) coupled with horizontal communication (interaction at the community level) goes back to 1952/54 when I was responsible at UNESCO for launching experiments in radio farm forums and teleclubs in different parts of the world. I have always been critical of Wilbur Schramm in this respect," he wrote. Cassirer noted that, though he had pushed Schramm into a superficial acknowledgment of the "role of feedback," it had "never been absorbed into his theoretical framework. In an environment in which expertise had been thoroughly fetishized by academic social scientists like Schramm and by various aid bureaucracies, Cassirer may have felt marginalized. He had been unaffiliated with any university and had, as he put it to Beltrán, always put practice ahead of theory.

Cassirer's peripatetic existence as a German exile and naturalized American based in France may have also contributed to his liminal status among development-communication specialists. Though more sympathetic than Schramm and Lerner to popular desires, he was not especially interested in analyzing the underlying political and social structures that at times controverted these desires. What Cassirer skirted in celebrating the role of feedback was the question of what happened when such feedback was not merely peripheral to the plans of modernizing elites but opposed to those plans. He was critical of Paulo Freire, who viewed mass media as a tool of domination. "By rejecting the media not only as they are but as they might be used," he wrote to Beltrán, "the field is left wide open to the autocrats." Cassirer's concern to fight autocracy and "authoritarian flow" reflected his experience refuting Nazi propaganda four decades earlier, but it did not really respond to the revolutionary thrust of Freire's work or to the popular discontent over modernization that was then brewing in many parts of the world.[46] This was the Pandora's box that Schramm, Lerner, and other orthodox development thinkers sought to keep closed for the time being by prioritizing economic growth over popular participation. But for many critics outside the United States, the trade-off rang false.

FROM DEVELOPMENT DECADE TO DECADE OF DIVERGENCE? THE END OF THE CAPACITY CONSENSUS

The medium of television had an enormous appetite for programs, but producing and diffusing them was time consuming and expensive. Throughout the 1960s developing countries relied on technical expertise and program content coming from the industrialized world to fill their broadcasting schedules. In ex-French Africa, this flow often represented a prolongation of colonial-era relationships, however irritating to nationalists; as one anticolonial journalist later admitted, the establishment of television in Africa was "inseparable from cooperation" with France and industrialized Francophone countries. Even in newly independent Algeria, the site of one of the bitterest wars of decolonization, authorities signed an accord with France to link Algerian transmitters to each other and to the French network just a few years after the war ended.[47] In many countries, broadcasters also opted to import cheap American reruns to fill the time around their own productions. This was true in Africa, Asia, and especially Latin America. In 1966 imported programs took up more than 52 percent of broadcasting time on Venezuelan commercial television, versus the roughly 20 percent occupied by domestically produced programming (the rest was advertising). By 1967 the American network NBC was selling television shows to ninety-three countries worldwide. "One program, 'Bonanza,' may well reach more people than any single communication ever produced," bragged Walter Scott, chairman of NBC's board, in a 1967 speech.[48]

But as the Development Decade failed to live up to its promises to deliver economic growth, many new and developing states demonstrated increasing unwillingness to simply receive one-way flows of media and information from their development partners. By the early 1970s some African states that had initially accepted Western aid to build up their broadcasting infrastructure began to exert increasing control over broadcasting content. The Moroccan parliament endorsed television censorship for the sake of public morality, following the lead of Tunisia, which had already reduced its live television broadcasts from France. In the wake of a coup d'etat, in the early 1970s Congo-Brazzaville declared its intention to stop importing Western cultural products in addition to nationalizing French television facilities in the country. Perhaps most irritatingly for France, Algeria announced its goal of totally Algerianizing and Arabizing its broadcasting by 1971 through a "progressive reduction of foreign programs and the expansion of national productions" (to which the French broadcasting monopoly responded somewhat lamely, "[The] use of French to explain [Arabic-language] courses remains indispensable").[49]

The widespread importation of American shows in the developing world aroused cultural concerns that mirrored earlier debates about Hollywood's presence in Europe. The United States stood accused of "dumping" its bottom-of-the-barrel productions—*Bonanza* and the like—onto vulnerable economies. In Latin America, where commercial culture industries ruled the airwaves, the Venezuelan scholar Antonio Pasquali challenged the notion that liberty meant only the liberty to make money. In situations of cultural domination, wrote Pasquali, two-way dialogue was nonexistent: "The audience is always the one listening, the broadcaster always the one speaking." Cassirer's correspondent Luis Ramiro Beltrán, who had pursued graduate work in the United States and was intimately familiar with the American development orthodoxy, questioned the notion that technology alone could improve people's lives in the developing world. Real development was a political, not merely technocratic, issue, which entailed changing the social structure of developing countries. Pasquali and Beltrán were part of a wave of Latin American thinkers who had begun to take aim at modernization theory. In particular, the emerging "dependency" critique of orthodox development models argued that under unregulated capitalism, developing countries were locked into subordinate relationships with the industrialized world, forever consigned to producing export commodities in exchange for more advanced manufactures and technologies.[50]

These intertwined forms of political discourse—postcolonial nationalism and leftist anti-imperialism—reflected the fragility of the development consensus. While new and developing states wanted access to the latest technology, they did not necessarily wish to cede their cultural influence over broadcasting. And in places where elites profited from commercial broadcasting, as in much of Latin America, oppositional intellectuals and activists bemoaned economic and cultural domination by foreign capital. By the late 1960s the idea that the capacity to receive media flows signified freedom of information was falling out of favor even in the institutions that had once supported it. "[The] decade . . . is ending with divergent instead of convergent national and international actions," commented one UNESCO economist at a 1969 seminar on development.[51]

Some Americans persisted in taking a developmental approach to information flows. For many Washington elites, commercial dumping presented a legitimate concern. "If our security and possibly survival depends on CBS, NBC and ABC, I'm afraid we've just about had it," concluded presidential adviser Charles E. Johnson, who compared American broadcasting unfavorably with its European—even Soviet—counterparts. This was a critique not only of American programs but of the American way of producing them, for as Johnson must have known, even in solidly Western-bloc allies like Britain, government subsidies for television production and greater government involvement in broadcasting were the norm. How could the United States possibly convince the developing world of the merits of liberal capitalism when what Nigerian villagers concluded from American shows was that most Americans toted guns and rode horses to work? The problem was most acute in Vietnam, where American troops clamored for entertainment but U.S. authorities fretted that a "too liberal programming policy" could result in the "[airing of] programs inimical to [the] U.S. image (crime programs)."[52]

Others countered accusations of dumping with allusions to the universal appeal of freedom from government interference. NBC's Walter Scott defended the company's exports in terms that echoed Walter Wanger's defense of Hollywood exports two decades earlier, when Wanger had argued that the relatively liberal climate enjoyed by filmmakers and audiences in the United States was what made American movies a vessel of antitotalitarianism. "[Television] programming in America emerges from the free choice of millions of viewers," said Scott, suggesting that this was what made it compelling to foreign audiences, who got to see the country warts and all. For American business elites, the task of ensuring "free expression and open channels among nations" dovetailed with foreign buyers' ability to freely choose what media they purchased. This was not quite the kind of antistatist free-market argument that would gain traction in the 1980s; Scott also called for "long-range planning" and investments in developing-world training in order to secure the worldwide exchange of television programs. Nevertheless, Scott's comments, besides recalling Walter Wanger, also pointed to a future in which American media and technology corporations appealed to the negative freedoms of foreign audiences to oppose the aspirations of foreign states.[53]

The waning appeal of positive freedoms secured through development partnerships coincided with a political realignment around the issue of cross-border information flows. By the late 1960s, debate was intensifying around a new technology that posed a serious challenge for diplomats and information policymakers: broadcasting satellites. As Walter Scott put it, "the intricate technology of international communications satellites is simplicity itself, compared to the administrative and operating arrangements for their use."[54] While early satellite broadcasting entailed the use of costly ground infrastructure to retransmit signal, American technocrats looked forward to a time when high-powered satellites could beam directly to individual users—thus bypassing the ground relays controlled by foreign governments. Anticipation of these "direct-broadcast satellites" would drive a wedge in the tripartite consensus linking the United States, Europe, and developing states around capacity, for while Wilbur Schramm and his compatriots could express enthusiasm about a technology in which the United States enjoyed global preeminence, an eclectic array of critics from both the developing world and Europe voiced concerns that direct broadcasting via satellites posed a threat to national sovereignty. International consensus, it seemed, would no longer be quite so necessary in the dawning age of satellite communications.

5

Satellites and the End of Sovereignty

The world *needs* TV on a global basis regardless of the opposition by prideful and defensive nations.
                    —Document circulated among President Lyndon Johnson's
                                satellite-communications advisers, 1966

Technically possible does not mean *politically* feasible. Communications technology does not develop in an autonomous sphere.
                    —Armand Mattelart, *Agresión desde el espacio* (1972)

In 1962, five years after the Soviet Union propelled the space race into high gear with the launch of Sputnik, the first man-made satellite to orbit the Earth, the United States achieved the world's first ever satellite television broadcast when the Telstar satellite linked television ground stations in the United States and France. Three years later the U.S. National Aeronautics and Space Administration (NASA) launched the first commercial satellite, Early Bird, which relayed signal between the United States and Europe. At the apogee of the "First Age of communication satellites," American communication scholar Wilbur Schramm projected in 1965, "low-power synchronous satellites will cover the earth, efficiently linking ground system to ground system." Despite the early Soviet lead in space technologies, by the mid-1960s the United States was coming to dominate the new field of space communications. Schramm and other anticommunist American elites fantasized about the possibility of a truly global network of high-speed communications that—unlike the British imperial telegraph network of yore or nationally and regionally fragmented terrestrial broadcasting services—would be stewarded by the United States.[1]

The new technology possessed impressive technical potentialities, to be sure. By the mid-1960s it was clear that satellite communications would have an enormous impact on broadcasting coverage. Stanford economist Ernest Wenrick ventured that compared to the seven to ten thousand square miles served by a high-power ground transmitter and the 138,000 square miles covered by a plane transmitter, satellites could easily cover one million square miles—and "up to one third of the earth's surface." Regarding data transmission, too, satellites seemed set to outdo competing technologies, namely deep-water cables. The first transatlantic cables capable of carrying telephone conversations, laid in 1956, could transmit thirty-six concurrent telephone conversations; they could not carry television signal, which required a much greater channel capacity. Early Bird, by contrast, could transmit television signal or three hundred voice channels, and a successor was in the works that was capable of relaying up to fifty thousand voice channels. Although in the twenty-first century most long-distance signal traffic passes through fiber-optic networks, it was not until the 1990s that cable technologies began to displace satellites in terms of channel capacity and cost effectiveness. In 1965 Schramm, Wenrick, and science fiction luminary Arthur C. Clarke could all agree that it was satellites that would, as Wenrick put it, "eliminate the distance factor in costs," foreshadowing the eventual commodification of data transmission.[2]

These technological advances also posed a host of diplomacy and policy questions. Who would oversee the technical aspects of satellite broadcasting? Who would furnish content? American policy intellectuals tended to portray the emerging network of satellite communications as a tremendous leap forward for the free flow of information across borders and a developmental boon to less wealthy nations. Seen from outside Washington, however, satellite broadcasting appeared far more ambiguous, largely because it was dominated throughout the 1960s and 1970s by the two superpowers (especially the United States). Voices from Europe, Latin America, and elsewhere raised concerns over the political economy of satellites as well as their cultural and linguistic impact. Even Schramm acknowledged the potential pitfalls of American space hegemony: "[Most] governments would be unwilling to have their people subject to a monopoly television service operated by foreigners."[3] In particular, the same technology that seemed to actualize freedom of information to many Americans appeared in the eyes of other countries to threaten another cherished principle of international relations—state sovereignty. As satellite technologies advanced, this division would deepen. The consensus by which development was to flow through international cooperation began to fray when discussion turned to "direct-broadcast satellites" that could bypass national regulatory systems and broadcast directly to individual receivers.

AMERICAN HEGEMONY AND THE DREAM
OF A "SINGLE GLOBAL SYSTEM"

The roots of unease over broadcasting satellites attached to how they were administered politically. Radio spectrum had been the subject of international negotiations since the early twentieth century. In the interwar era several nations had merged international telegraph and radio bodies into the International Telecommunication Union (ITU), aiming to minimize signal interference at a moment when commercial radio stations and government shortwave services were rapidly multiplying. The advent of airplanes had similarly spurred international efforts to define rules of conduct for the peaceful use of airspace. Satellites compounded the challenges associated with regulating radio and aerial technologies. Not only were new states concerned about being late on the scene to acquire frequencies for their satellites, but nearly all states save the Cold War superpowers were forced to recognize that they would not have the technological or capital capacity to launch their own broadcasting satellites for some time. In the 1950s and 1960s these issues helped to foster the emergence of a new field of international law—space law—in which diplomats and legal scholars attempted to define the relationship between state sovereignty and outer space and to divvy up the scarce resources needed for space broadcasting. These resources included orbital slots for "geostationary" satellites that orbited at a fixed location above the Earth's surface (the type of satellite that the United States quickly came to favor for communications and that operated in a band above the equator less than twenty miles wide) and the frequencies used by satellites.[4]

The international consortium set up in 1964 to manage commercial satellite traffic, Intelsat, did not offer much relief to those worried about U.S.

domination of space. Intelsat's institutional design departed from that of the iconic representative institution of the mid-twentieth century, the UN General Assembly; the space consortium did offer representation to countries participating in the Western-bloc satellite system, but rather than basing it on a one-country, one-vote principle, voting was weighted on a basis proportional to a country's investments in the system (much as it was at the World Bank and the International Monetary Fund). This meant that in the early years of satellite broadcasting, American interests dominated the consortium. Comsat—the public corporation created by the Kennedy administration to represent the United States at Intelsat and to manage Intelsat's operations—enjoyed a majority vote there throughout the 1960s.[5]

Predictably, this arrangement fueled criticisms from Europe, Latin America, and elsewhere. Intelsat was far from "truly international and universal in scope," J. J. Matras, the research director of the French broadcasting monopoly, the Office de Radiodiffusion et Télévision Française (ORTF), charged in a 1967 editorial. Matras argued that the Intelsat-Comsat system favored American high-tech companies at the expense of foreign counterparts despite the fact that "its international position [imposes] on it if not the duty—the word not existing in the parlance of 'free enterprises,' even when they enjoy a de facto monopoly—then at the very least consideration for a desirable equilibrium." Not only European tech industries but also broadcasting organizations resented the American chokehold on Intelsat. In 1969 West German broadcasters protested being charged more than twice the amount paid by their American counterparts per hour of satellite transmission.[6] Meanwhile, a coalescing bloc of developing countries and new states was arguing that any commercial profits derived from space broadcasting should be equally divided among nations. Aldo Armando Cocca, president of the Argentine Aerospace Science Association and Argentina's ambassador to the United Nations, persistently criticized the lopsided representation at Intelsat and emphasized the need for a more genuinely multilateral system to regulate space communications.[7]

Behind closed doors, U.S. policymakers expressed concerns about the criticisms directed at Intelsat from abroad. The organization had been set up on a provisional basis in 1964, with participants agreeing to renegotiate the agreement in 1969. During this interim period, substantial international attention was brought to bear on the fact that Intelsat was under de facto U.S. control. The central "problem" leading up to the 1969 renegotiation, admitted one internal Johnson administration document, was "U.S. domination"; as it stood, the agreement "provides that our interest will never be less than 50%. In other words, we control. It is difficult to maintain international cooperation on this basis." A threat equal to the one posed by a competing Soviet system was interest in regional systems by highly industrialized allies such as France and Japan. Washington carefully monitored French plans for satellite broadcasting to its former territories in Africa as well as French contacts with the Soviet Union. U.S. policymakers also found themselves having to deflect a bit of political jujitsu when France charged that the coexistence of Intelsat and the competing Soviet system actually contravened Washington's support for one globally unified system. As an alternative, France proposed that the United Nations assume control of Intelsat, much as it had absorbed the ITU in the late 1940s.[8]

Under pressure to justify its policies, the United States defended the consortium's underlying principle of a "single global system" of commercial satellite traffic. Intelsat, it was argued, represented an expansion of the principle of freedom of information to areas of the world that had been marginalized by existing regional communications systems, including cable systems. Under colonialism, much of the world had been forced to rout its communications through the colonial metropoles, often at great expense. This led to absurd situations whereby postcolonial states could communicate with each other only through the ex-imperial capitals of Europe. As of 1967, President Johnson reported to Congress, a telephone call from Dakar, in Senegal, to Lagos, farther down the coast of West Africa in Nigeria, still needed to pass through Paris and London. Even the United States did not possess direct telephone links to more than one hundred countries and territories. With satellites, by contrast, it appeared that technology had finally caught up to politics, eliminating colonial communications intermediaries for good. According to one high-ranking U.S. official, broadcasting satellites would enable information to at last "flow free of artificial constraints held over from the colonial traditions of past centuries." Observers on the ground noted that many African leaders preferred satellite communications over cables.[9]

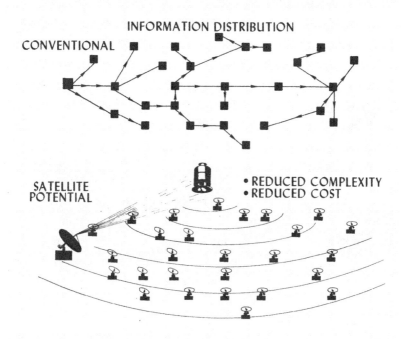

FIGURE 5.1 "The communications satellite . . . is particularly suited for carrying long distance, high capacity communications over all obstacles and inhospitable regions, such as deserts, seas, mountain ranges, and political boundaries." From a 1966 report by the White House Office of Telecommunications Management. Executive Office of the President, Office of Telecommunications Management, "Educational Television Demonstration and Interference Measurement Program: Using Advanced Communications Satellite Technology," November 1966, Lyndon B. Johnson Presidential Library, Austin, TX, Office Files of Douglass Cater, box 45.

The United States also invested in satellite facilities abroad where they were not commercially viable. Lyndon Johnson had been an early champion of the potential of satellite technologies to win hearts and minds abroad. While still in the Senate, Johnson had criticized the Eisenhower administration's cautious space policy, which—defense concerns excluded—treated satellite broadcasting as a private-sector matter. The question of whether Washington should encourage satellite broadcasting pitted the prerogatives of commercial giants, notably AT&T, against a purported national interest in reaching international mass audiences, and—as in the State Department's standoff with Kent Cooper and the Associated Press in the 1940s—Cold War competition helped to tip the scales in favor of government information diplomacy. This time, however, East-West rivalry was intertwined with North-South considerations. As vice president and then president, Johnson continued to press the principle of a "single global commercial communications satellite system," underscoring its appeal to new and developing states, even when these states needed assistance to cover the $3–5 million attached to building facilities to receive satellite signal. With National Security Action Memorandum (NSAM) 342, issued in 1966, the Johnson administration declared its intention to "take active steps to encourage the construction of earth-station links to the worldwide communications satellite system in selected less-developed countries." The construction of terrestrial ground stations thereby became folded into the administration's broader development policies. Johnson likened satellite communications to a more tangible symbol of development: satellites were a "space bridge."[10]

NSAM 342 had charged the State Department and the U.S. Agency for International Development with the task of deciding which countries to prioritize in the furnishing of funding for ground stations. Factors under consideration included a country's ability to disseminate satellite broadcasts via domestic and regional communications networks as well as how to "gain the maximum political advantage for the United States." By the summer of 1966 State and USAID had defined a list of priority countries for ground station assistance: Colombia, Chile, Brazil, Nigeria, Ethiopia, Turkey, Pakistan, India, Thailand, the Philippines, and Korea in addition to regional facilities for Central America and East Africa. Washington also publicized the benefits of satellite communications to developing countries by facilitating exchanges between developing-world policymakers and American industry experts. In May and June 1966 representatives from some thirty-five developing countries participated in an educational seminar on satellite broadcasting hosted by the State Department. The seminar included a tour of space facilities in the United States and Canada and numerous opportunities to liaise with commercial space technology representatives. While Washington expressed a preference for financing developing-world ground stations through either the private sector or development banks such as the World Bank and the Export-Import Bank, in cases where that funding was unlikely to materialize—in Africa, notably—direct financial assistance via USAID was considered.[11]

Six months later, in January 1967, the State Department reported substantial progress toward the goals set out in NSAM 342. All the priority countries save Turkey were in the process of planning for earth-station construction, with financing forthcoming in most cases from private firms or development banks. In addition, Intelsat's membership was growing steadily. The State Department anticipated that its roster would soon feature "all areas of the world except the Soviet bloc" (even Yugoslavia and Romania were "showing some interest in INTELSAT").[12]

President Johnson attempted to reassure the international community that the expansion of Intelsat posed no threat to national communications systems. Global satellite communications, Johnson stated, "[do] not mean that the United States—or any other nation—will give up vital sovereignty over domestic communications. The flow of satellite communications—both domestic and international—is to and from ground stations owned by the individual nation." Johnson's circumspection reflected the ways in which communications were handled by most countries in the 1960s. In an era when television systems in Western Europe still commonly operated as public monopolies, even staunch U.S. allies were concerned about commercial advertising beamed in from another country of origin. This represented not only a potential drain on foreign-exchange balances but also an existential threat to the principle of public broadcasting. The Johnson administration also made concessions to those who worried that powerful states would appropriate space resources exclusively for their own benefit. In 1967 the United States supported a far-reaching agreement at the United Nations, the Treaty on Principles Governing the Activities of States in the Exploration and Use of Outer Space, Including the Moon and Other Celestial Bodies, commonly referred to as the Outer Space Treaty. The treaty stipulated, among other things, that space activities be conducted for the benefit of all people and countries and that space itself could not be appropriated by states via sovereignty claims. The Soviet Union also signed the treaty, signifying relaxed relations between the superpowers as well as

FIGURE 5.2 The American dream of a single global satellite system, 1966. Image from "Statement of James D. O'Connell, Director of Telecommunications Management, Executive Office of the President, Before the Communications Subcommittee, Committee on Commerce, United States Senate," August 10, 1966, Lyndon B. Johnson Presidential Library, Austin, TX, National Security File, Files of Charles E. Johnson, box 13, folder "COMSAT—U.S. Communications Policy, NSAM 338 File #2 [2 of 2]," no. 23a.

the heightened symbolism of space communications in the quest for scientific and technical leadership.[13]

Washington also began to reconsider the U.S. role at Intelsat. By the time the Intelsat agreement was up for renegotiation in the late 1960s, its member-states were generally split over the consortium's future: one group of countries was uninterested in developing their own satellites while a second group pushed to reform the system. The latter group comprised a veritable mélange. It included a number of highly industrialized European countries, including France and West Germany, and Western bloc stalwarts Canada and Japan. It also featured postcolonial states such as India and Algeria. After two years of talks, a permanent agreement was finally settled in 1971. The United States conceded Comsat's de facto control over the system, agreeing to cap its ownership stake and management role at 40 percent.[14]

Unsurprisingly, these compromise concessions did not satisfy all parties. The Soviet Union's absence from Intelsat did not make for a unanimous front. Two U.S. allies, France and West Germany, initially refused to sign the revised agreement. It was clear that NASA's monopoly among Intelsat members on launching broadcasting satellites, coupled with American commercial leadership in the state of the art, left the United States with plenty of leverage internationally. (As Sino-American relations improved in the early 1970s, Comsat was one of three American companies contracted to upgrade communications in the People's Republic of China.)[15] From the disparate array of states that had expressed dissatisfaction with American dominance in satellite broadcasting, there emerged two potential solutions: first, regional satellite initiatives that spread cost burdens among participants and aimed to provide transnational broadcasting service and, second, diplomatic alliances to push for the regulation of satellite broadcasting.

ALTERNATIVE CARTOGRAPHIES
OF SATELLITE BROADCASTING

Even before the Intelsat renegotiations had begun, the Western European powers were exploring new forms of regional cooperation that would help break down economic and regulatory barriers between nation-states in Europe. The urgency of this cooperation was made clear from the mid-1960s onward in discussions of the "technology gap" between Europe and the United States. The bleakest of these predicted that Europe was becoming an "'underdeveloped continent,' dependent on the [United States]," particularly in high-tech fields such as aerospace. French and West German observers could agree: American hegemony made it crucial for Europe to "catch up . . . in order to integrate itself into global information flows via its own satellites." For these observers, Western Europe possessed the scientific expertise to launch its own broadcasting satellites; what remained was to hammer out the finer points of European cooperation.[16]

Discussions for the Symphonie project began in 1967. A joint Franco-German effort, Symphonie was to be a communications-satellite system primarily oriented toward television broadcasting. In early January 1971, France and West Germany successfully concluded an agreement for the execution of the Symphonie program, with France contributing 163 million francs and West Germany the equivalent of 189 million francs. Launches of two Symphonie satellites, to take place at Kourou in French Guiana, were slated for 1973 and 1974; powerful transmitting stations were to be located at Plemeur-Bodou in Brittany and Raisting in Bavaria, with less expensive receiving stations to be built in participating countries. Symphonie would possess a broadcasting capacity of either two high-quality color channels or four medium-quality black-and-white channels. In addition it would have twelve sound channels.[17]

Symphonie was driven in part by industrial imperatives. The ORTF's J. J. Matras noted that one reason France had sought bilateral cooperation with West Germany was that broader European satellite cooperation was stalling, "to the great displeasure of the [European] electronics industries" that were "losing hope of integrating themselves into the [business of] equipping... international networks."[18] Yet observers understood that Symphonie was not merely geared toward economic or technical matters. It was undertaken with mass audiences in mind. Symphonie's focus on television, according to Matras, was "easy to understand," given that the "long-distance broadcast of television programs constitutes... a political and cultural objective of primary importance." Even more so than radio, thought Matras, the "universal distribution of television programs" would have important foreign-policy consequences: Symphonie would offer Europe an instrument to secure a cultural and linguistic presence in Africa, the Middle East, and elsewhere.[19]

This was a particular worry for France, which feared growing American influence in its ex-colonial territories. Charles de Gaulle, concerned with U.S. designs in Southeast Asia, had famously denounced the United States' escalating presence in Vietnam. French worries over American influence in Africa were meanwhile exacerbated by the arrival of television and satellite broadcasting. One 1969 study by the ORTF and the Centre National des Etudes Spatiales (CNES) stressed the "inevitable

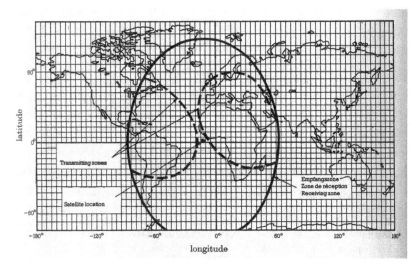

FIGURE 5.3 Symphonie's projected coverage area, shown by the unbroken oval. Image from M. Schmidbauer, "The Symphonie Project," *Proceedings of the Royal Society of London. Series A, Mathematical and Physical Sciences* 345, no. 1643 (October 7, 1975): 560. Reproduced with permission of Royal Society of London via Copyright Clearance Center.

establishment of an educational-television program for Anglophone African countries in the coming decade," adducing visits by World Bank delegations to African capitals and plans for educational television in Nigeria and in the Ivory Coast. French authorities also carefully monitored the construction of satellite ground stations in their former African colonies. The ORTF's foreign-affairs bulletin noted in the spring of 1971 that "hardly a month passes without information emerging about either the construction or the inauguration of a new ground station somewhere in Africa," projecting near-total coverage of the continent by 1972. The following issue announced that "five Francophone African countries" (Madagascar, Senegal, the Ivory Coast, Cameroon, and Gabon) all either had satellite receiving stations under construction or were on the verge of breaking ground. This was a competitive proposition, for while the Ivory Coast, Madagascar, and Senegal planned to use Symphonie in addition to Intelsat satellites, several other countries were to be served exclusively by Intelsat.[20]

Nothing better illustrates the cultural and linguistic aspirations that undergirded French broadcasting-satellite initiatives than the ORTF's phrase for describing France's former African colonies—"Francophone African countries." The imagined cartography of a Francophone world, however self-evident it seemed, was a historically contingent concept, which mingled France's imperial past and the postcolonial present. The first person to use the words *francophone* and *francophonie* in print had been a fin de siècle geographer, Onésime Reclus, who argued that spreading the French language in Africa was key to France's civilizing mission. But French colonial governance had taken a conservative turn during the interwar era, when policymakers had attempted to stymie the demands for equality being made by urban, French-educated Africans; they would have been alarmed at the thought of French being widely spoken and read by nonelite African subjects. On the eve of decolonization, only a small fraction of the population of French colonial Africa was actually literate in French.[21] The resurgence of la francophonie in the 1960s initially owed less to France itself and more to the work of postcolonial elites such as Léopold Sédar Senghor of Senegal, who viewed the French language as both a tool to unify multilingual states (Senegal was home to speakers of more than twenty African languages) and a means of attracting development aid from wealthier French-speaking countries. Despite initial skepticism from Paris—which was hesitant to open itself to charges of neocolonialism immediately after pulling out of its African colonies—the cultural cartography of la francophonie gained momentum. By 1966 or 1967, French elites led by Charles de Gaulle and Georges Pompidou had embraced postcolonial Francophone ties as a means of furthering French interests internationally.[22]

Transforming la francophonie from a policymaker's dream into a grounded reality was another matter. Early attempts reflected the top-down thrust of much of the media-development work of the period. The joint ORTF-CNES study, Projet Socrate (Project Socrates), was intended to bring educational television to seventeen African countries, "the official language of which is French," first via a modified Symphonie satellite (the launch of which was anticipated for 1974), then via direct-broadcast satellite (launch projected for 1979). Starting in forty thousand schools, the

program—elaborated in a thick report featuring ORTF maps of participant countries and six separate annexes—was to expand to reach 63,000
schools by the project's final year in 1982–1983, involving hundreds of thousands of teachers and technical and production personnel. By then, the
report estimated, satellite television could educate nearly thirteen and a
half million students per year in Africa. These projections, however grandi-
ose, echoed the cost-saving benefits advertised by American educational-
television enthusiasts like Philip Coombs and Wilbur Schramm: it was to
be an economic and pedagogical asset for newly independent nations,
enabling them to expand schooling in a fiscally efficient manner. At a
moment when the question seemed to be not if but when and how educational television would establish itself in Africa—the main alternative to
satellite broadcasting being separate, nationally owned and operated
stations—cost comparisons showed that satellite broadcasting offered a
clear "economic advantage" to new states.[23]

But Project Socrates was not only motivated by concerns for economic efficiency or pedagogical efficacy. It also aimed to ensure long-term
French-language continuity across a demographically expanding swath of
states. The seventeen "Francophone" countries to be covered in the project,
stretching for thousands of kilometers across sub-Saharan Africa, were, as
of 1969, home to a population of around sixty-five million people—"more
than France and Quebec combined." The project's authors, clearly tanta-
lized, further noted that "in 1980 it should exceed 80 million": a headcount
reminiscent of the "wider France of one hundred million inhabitants"
vaunted by fin de siècle imperialists like Jules Ferry and Onésime Reclus.
Project Socrates paid particular attention to the school-age population to
be reached by classroom television, noting that "the age group of five to
fifteen years is currently close to 16 million children." Although the possibility of transmitting other language soundtracks was acknowledged, the
report clarified that programming "will theoretically be exclusively broadcast in French."[24]

The political calculations behind this design were made explicit on
Project Socrates' last few pages, which referenced the need to "[defend]
la francophonie" against both the "attitude of the Anglophone countries"
and the "movement currently pushing certain states toward education in

vernacular languages." For ORTF insiders, Symphonie's impact in Africa was both an end in itself and the first phase of realizing broader exchanges. A later stage of *"coopération,"* the ORTF's Eliane Paracuellos thought, might involve cultural and informational programming in addition to educational broadcasts: "The way would be clear for the penetration of French culture, through the medium of the programs distributed by the Office [ORTF], in the current film form or directly via satellite." More so than American modernization advocates, who tended to describe the development process in quasi-evolutionary terms, French experts framed it as a political intervention with cultural consequences. By the lights of another ORTF report, "Recourse to satellites does not boil down to . . . a simple economic decision: it appears as a political act, a stance favoring the democratization of education and the acceleration of economic progress."[25]

As was the case with many contemporaneous educational-television projects, Project Socrates' sweeping ambitions did not come to fruition. After the costly failure of the European Europa 2 launcher, the two Symphonie satellites were launched by NASA in December 1974 and August 1975 respectively. The contract with NASA restricted Symphonie crafts to noncommercial uses, effectively proscribing their competition with Intelsat satellites. More to the point, as of the late 1970s, only a handful of the seventeen countries included in Project Socrates had participated in educational-television experiments via Symphonie hookup. By that point, the ORTF had been splintered apart by a set of reforms intended to liberalize French broadcasting initiated by President Valéry Giscard d'Estaing. The era of statist development initiatives that linked technology implantations to sweeping social change was on the wane.[26]

Symphonie's impact was also dampened by the grounded reality of linguistic diversity, which could not be wholly reconfigured by space-based technology. As commentators subsequently observed, the project team had failed to consult any African representatives, who might have challenged the team's assumption that a "single message transmitted over a vast area" was desirable or sufficient.[27] West Germany's intentions for Symphonie held up only somewhat better in this regard. It had planned to use its Symphonie channels to aid the circulation of Arabic-language and other educational and cultural programs in North Africa and the Middle East, with one observer dryly noting that the German plan had the "advantage that the Arabic language is spoken and understood by all the inhabitants" of the receiving area. But this observer omitted to mention the dialectical variation in spoken Arabic over the projected receiving zone, which stretched from Morocco thousands of miles eastward to the Persian Gulf. This variation meant that a speaker of the colloquial Arabic that was common in Cairo might have had trouble understanding a peer from Morocco or Yemen speaking his or her native dialect. Education in Standard Arabic, no one's first language, was not universal.[28]

In spite of these evident failures, what makes Project Socrates and the broader Symphonie program historically significant is that they stand as early regional and subglobal responses to American globalism in postcolonial territories. Francophone cooperation would become institutionalized in 1970 with the formation of the Agence de Coopération Culturelle et Technique (later renamed the Organisation Internationale de la Francophonie, or International Organization of La Francophonie). The organization brought together representatives of developing states, such as Senegal, Tunisia, and Cambodia, with French elites as well as actors from developed countries with large Francophone minorities, such as Canada and Belgium.[29]

More significantly, numerous regional satellite initiatives succeeded the Symphonie program. Western European cooperation persisted, and in the late 1970s the European Space Agency—a merger of the European Space Research Organization and the European launcher program—formed the European Telecommunications Satellite Organization, or Eutelsat, to operate Europe's communications satellites, the first of which was successfully launched in 1983. In the Middle East, Saudi Arabia spearheaded the creation of a regional satellite consortium, the Arab Satellite Communications Organization, or Arabsat, which launched its first satellite in 1985. Rather than a "single global system," a patchwork of systems became the reality in satellite communications, as one prescient Johnson administration official had predicted in the mid-1960s.[30]

At the same time, a new technology was on the horizon that had begun to provoke shared anxieties among many ex-colonial, postcolonial, and developing states: satellites that could broadcast directly to individuals without the need for a terrestrial relay—also known as direct-broadcast satellites. Drawn together by a common concern that direct-broadcast satellites would undermine their capacity to regulate transmissions received within their borders, these countries would seek to shore up the principle of sovereignty in the international arena.

"WILL SPACE BE OPEN TO PIRACY?": DIRECT-BROADCAST SATELLITES AND THE QUESTION OF SOVEREIGNTY

Early satellites that were dependent on ground facilities to relay signal to individual users could only do so much to widen information bottlenecks. In areas that were already well equipped with terrestrial infrastructure, these satellites would have a limited impact on the quantity and variety of media available to broadcasting audiences. Their effect was also uncertain in developing countries, but for different reasons: where capital for infra-structural investments was limited and the price of home appliances like televisions too expensive for most people to afford, they would reach only a small audience. Even in the developed world, lack of investment could limit information traffic. In France, where the state held a monopoly on telecommunications, government planners tended to prioritize large-scale industrial investments over satisfying the demands of private consumers. Into the late 1960s the average French household could spend months on a wait list for the installation of home telephone service.[31]

American experts projected that the real technical breakthrough in information flows, including television broadcasting, would come with direct-broadcast satellites that were capable of bypassing ground stations and transmitting directly into homes and schools. This advance, they promised, would save developing countries the capital costs of building extensive terrestrial infrastructure to relay signal. Wilbur Schramm was confident that direct-broadcast satellites would "notably increase the flow of information in the world," creating "opportunities without precedent to communicate and collaborate," while his Stanford colleague Ernest Wen-rick forecast that direct broadcasting would "open vast areas not now served to the benefits of the flows of information." Schramm predicted that the advent of direct-broadcast satellites would take place between 1970 and 1985 while RCA's David Sarnoff put it around 1975.[32]

American enthusiasm about direct broadcasting derived in part from its powerful technical capabilities. But it also stemmed from the United States' dominance in satellite broadcasting in the 1960s. Having lost its early lead in the space race, the Soviet Union in general appeared somewhat less interested in satellite communications than the United States, probably because the technology was less essential for communications in its contiguous Eurasian sphere of influence than for the United States' projection of power outside North America.[33]

The geopolitically marked nature of satellite communications was evident in Anglophone excitement over the potential linguistic effects of direct broadcasting. The science fiction writer Arthur C. Clarke, widely credited as the first person to imagine a global system of communications satellites, predicted, "[Communications] satellites will make a basic world language mandatory. . . . There [can be] little doubt that this language will be English." Clarke envisioned that in the near future "political objections" from non-Anglophone and postcolonial states could be literally transcended by direct-broadcast radio courses aimed at "English teaching on a global basis—if possible, over independent United Nations–owned circuits." Americans also tended to treat language difference as a hurdle to be cleared by technological means. Wilbur Schramm, only slightly more restrained than Clarke, enthused that the "problem of language" might be resolved by direct-broadcast satellites, which would "furnish precisely the incentive needed for nations to agree on one or two or a few languages which might be taught as second languages throughout the world and serve as vehicles for the world's people to talk to each other." Schramm thought this was particularly true in Asia and Africa, where the "first problem would be language." Power politics were implicit in these projections: by controlling satellite technology, the idea went, the hegemonic powers could redraw the world's language map in their favor. As early as 1961, in the lead-up to the passage of the Comsat bill in the U.S. Congress, the chair of the House Committee on Science and Astronautics had stressed that satellite television was strategically critical "because the nation that controls worldwide communications and television will ultimately have that nation's language become the universal tongue."[34]

Washington was aware that talk of direct broadcasting had raised hackles outside U.S. borders. The American embassy in Paris, cabling the State Department in 1968 to report on satellite-broadcasting discussions at UNESCO, privately expressed thanks that the technology would not be a reality for some time, "thus putting off [the] evil day" when the "political and economic implications of direct broadcasting satellites" would have to be dealt with. Others were more optimistic, viewing direct broadcasting through the lens of ongoing developmental cooperation. USAID's A. H. Moseman thought that, in Latin America at least, "most of the political and legal issues involved in a direct broadcast system would of necessity be worked out" through a "demonstrations program" showing the effectiveness of satellite educational television. Likewise, Columbia University law professor and Intelsat architect Richard N. Gardner wrote in the *Washington Post* that the way to quell political anxieties in the developing world was to demonstrate the usefulness of satellite broadcasting in education and national development.[35]

But policy elites were also well aware that the technology might also enable a more aggressive, less conciliatory approach if need be: the use of direct broadcasting to purposefully dissolve rivals' sovereignty. Gardner pointed to the "strange coincidence" that, at roughly the same moment in the 1970s "when the Chinese will be able to deliver nuclear warheads around the world," the United States might have developed the capability of "[reaching] the Chinese people with radio and TV programs sent directly from communications satellites to home receivers." Similarly, Arthur C. Clarke vaunted direct-broadcast satellites as an "end of the present barriers to the free flow of information; no dictatorship can build a wall high enough to stop its citizens listening to the voices from the stars." Deviating from the then-standard usage of piracy to refer to illegally furnishing signal, Clarke associated the *jamming* of broadcasts with piracy; rogue states that jammed satellite broadcasts would face repercussions, because "any attempt by one country to do so would result in an act of space piracy . . . which the rest of the world could not permit."[36]

While Clarke's image recalled Soviet jamming of Western radio broadcasts, in the case of satellite broadcasting, the most serious obstacle did not come from Russia. Leading up to the 1967 UN Outer Space Treaty, both superpowers opposed a proposal to restrict direct broadcasting.[37] The opposition came, rather, from international actors that did not yet possess independent satellite capabilities. For not everyone was as sunny as Arthur C. Clarke about the prospect of boundless information transmission. Other commentators applied a more standard usage—pirates were the ones *broadcasting* signal—to the novel situation of space broadcasting. As early as 1963 an article in the ITU journal *Telecommunication Review* posed the question plainly in its title: "Will Space Be Open to Piracy?" Author and ITU official Jean Persin, who painted direct-broadcast satellites as a threat to international harmony, denied that nationally controlled broadcasting systems contravened freedom of information. "[That] principle is not at issue here and we refer to another principle: that of safeguarding the sovereignty of states, which is unanimously recognized as being at the root of international relations."[38]

Although the sovereignty concerns of the 1960s and 1970s have typically been most strongly associated with Third World actors, sovereignty also preoccupied Western European participants in the satellite debates of the same period. At one 1965 UNESCO gathering of experts, the French legal scholar Fernand Terrou noted that while the current generation of satellites—dependent as they were on ground-based transmission systems—posed little threat to national sovereignty, direct transmission to homes would sap states' capacity to regulate broadcasting content. Terrou and Stockholm-based professor of international law Hilding Eek, who also participated at the meeting, agreed that this development might require a rethinking of the principles of freedom of information that had guided the United Nations since the late 1940s. Eek thought that the advent of satellite broadcasting necessitated a multilateral approach to freedom of information, one that set aside the "old terrestrial principles of unlimited freedom of information and opinion" in favor of a "careful, pragmatic approach," respectful of "different national policies." Eek noted that this approach might entail individuals' "acceptance of governmental judgments of what national interests mean." Terrou echoed Eek, emphasizing the

need for "discipline and responsibility" to counteract the potential negative effects of direct broadcasting, which threatened national authority to
"protect rights."[39]

These were more than the musings of individual scholars. They partook
of broader currents of anxiety over broadcasting and sovereignty that
were coursing through Western Europe in the 1960s, a decade when growing radio (and some television) piracy was challenging Europe's public-
broadcasting monopolies. Debates over satellite communications were
happening during the same period when the Council of Europe was defining regional regulations to outlaw broadcasting piracy from ships, artificial
islands, and planes, efforts which even relatively liberal Britain and the
Netherlands supported.[40] For many policymakers, regulating space broadcasting seemed like the logical extension of these antipiracy efforts. France
had proposed the outlawing of direct-broadcasting satellites in 1963.
While this initiative ran into opposition from both the United States and
the Soviet Union, it also heralded years of French attempts to define international regulations for direct broadcasting, which included efforts to
require broadcasters to receive prior consent from receiving states. Hilding
Eek's Sweden, meanwhile, collaborated with Canada to propose that
direct broadcasting should take place through regional systems that would
encourage cooperation and consultation among signal-receiving states.[41]

The issue of direct broadcasting was, at the same time, drawing Western
European perspectives closer to those circulating in many new and devel-
oping states. Echoing French efforts, Egypt had proposed the restriction of
direct broadcasting in negotiations for the 1967 Outer Space Treaty.[42] In
Latin America, the prolific Argentine space-law expert and diplomat Aldo
Armando Cocca approvingly explained European and Soviet criticisms of
Intelsat for a Hispanophone audience at a 1968 conference in Mexico City.
"In Europe we can observe a pronounced shift in favor of an international
organization" to replace the "commercial consortium" that was Intelsat,
Cocca reported. Cocca's own strong advocacy of multilateral regulation
echoed the French position on the need to institutionalize international,
rather than commercial, management of the system. The neo-Marxist Left,
though less enamored of interstate regulation as a solution, similarly criticized American domination of space. The even more prolific Belgian

sociologist Armand Mattelart, then based in Chile, pointed out that between 1965 and 1968, less than 20 percent of Intelsat's contracts went to non-American firms. Pressures to adopt a technology so dominated by a foreign industry affected both developing states and the European powers.[43]

As the 1960s progressed, a second tactic in addition to regional cooperation was thus emerging in response to U.S. dominance in the field of broadcasting satellites. This was pressure to internationalize the management and regulation of satellite communications. It appeared in parallel in multiple forums. UNESCO had acted as a sounding board for concerns about satellite broadcasting almost since the technology's inception. As debate over direct broadcasting intensified, the organization called upon two familiar faces, Hilding Eek and Fernand Terrou, to draft a declaration on space communication. An early iteration of the declaration stated unequivocally in its first article that satellite broadcasting was "governed by international law." The document was subsequently discussed and revised at a series of meetings in 1971 and 1972. The final version, officially titled the "Declaration of Guiding Principles on the Use of Satellite Broadcasting for the Free Flow of Information[,] the Spread of Education and Greater Cultural Exchange," called for "prior agreements" between governments on the matter of direct broadcasting to foreign publics. The declaration also elaborated the "right of all countries and peoples to preserve their cultures as part of the common heritage of mankind" and the duty of satellite broadcasters to "respect the sovereignty and equality of all States." It was adopted by the UNESCO General Assembly in December 1972 with a vote of fifty-five in favor, seven opposed (including the United States and Britain), and twenty-two abstaining.[44]

A more pronounced divide between Washington and the rest of the world was becoming evident at the United Nations proper. In 1968 the United Nations had established the Working Group on Direct Broadcast Satellites under the aegis of its Committee on the Peaceful Uses of Outer Space (COPUOS), which was charged with hashing out agreements on space matters. Regulation immediately emerged as a matter of intense debate at the working group and more broadly in COPUOS. By the early 1970s COPUOS was confronting marked dissension among its member states over the (still-hypothetical) issue of direct broadcasting. According to Aldo Armando Cocca, discussion of direct broadcasting spurred by UNESCO's declaration on the subject proved to be the "most controversial topic" at COPUOS's September 1972 meeting. Two months later the UN General Assembly held a vote on whether or not to pursue an international convention regulating the use of direct-broadcasting satellites. The result: 102 countries, including France, the United Kingdom, Canada, Sweden, the Netherlands, and Argentina, voted in favor of the principle that international law should regulate direct broadcasting. The sole no vote came from the United States.[45]

For many observers, the UN vote amounted to a referendum on—and resounding rejection of—the free-flow policies that the United States was pursuing internationally. On the left, many saw the outcome as a reflection of the cleft between the developed and the developing worlds. Writing after the first oil crisis, Armand Mattelart linked the rejection of unregulated direct broadcasting to a parallel controversy involving the remote sensing of energy resources by NASA-launched satellites; both uses broached the question of whether or not to require the permission of countries in the coverage footprint. But misgivings also emanated from Europe. The Swedish representative at the UN working group doubted that "freedom of information" would really be achieved in a situation where space broadcasting was effectively monopolized by a few countries, a criticism echoed by Austria. Even the American development guru Daniel Lerner admitted that he found "more demerits than merits in [the U.S.] position" on direct-broadcast satellites, evidenced by fact that "101 [sic] nations [had] lined up against the United States to express their distrust—and even their fear—of direct satellite broadcasting by any power with the technological capability of doing it." Lerner commented in 1976, "When anxiety is so widespread, it will take much more than technology to make world communication shape world cooperation." Lerner was prescient in knowing that flow alone would not produce agreement. Into the late 1970s and early 1980s scholars documented the international community's ongoing failure to arrive at a consensus over direct broadcasting.[46]

In another sense, the vote marked the passing of the developmental model that Lerner's work had once encouraged Washington to embrace. Merely a decade earlier, the United States had advertised satellite broadcasting as a means of helping information in the postcolonial world to "flow free of artificial constraints held over from the colonial traditions of past centuries." By the mid-1970s, in the wake of the first oil shock and the United States' messy retreat from Vietnam, American support for development aid was on the wane. Many establishment policy intellectuals instead depicted a showdown between the U.S. promotion of freedom of information on one hand and the sovereignty concerns of developing countries on the other. According to S. Neil Hosenball, who became general counsel of NASA in 1975, "The concern on the part of many of these countries is not counterbalanced at all, so it appears, by a dedication to the principle of free flow of information across national boundaries."[47] Even before the maturation of commercial direct-broadcast satellites, in other words, the debate they generated helped to polarize the United States against its former partners in development. Coupled with growing private-sector impatience with the regulatory state, this polarization would diminish Washington's commitment to positive developmental freedoms and, conversely, increase its interest in globalizing tactics and technologies that purposefully diminished rivals' sovereignty.

6

Cultural Turns in the International Arena

Largely as a reaction to the flood of American cultural material . . . a new mood with respect to the doctrine of free flow of information became observable in the international community in the late 1960s and early 1970s. Besides the free-flow view, one began to see frequent references to cultural sovereignty, cultural privacy, cultural autonomy, and even admissions of the possibility of cultural imperialism.

—Herbert Schiller, *Communication and Cultural Domination* (1976)

Where did information flows go? What was their object? What was the purpose of all the United States' activity to ensure that they crossed borders?

To American modernization theorists in the 1950s and early 1960s the target had seemed straightforward: information flowed into societies. The effects of these flows were suitably alike in far-flung places that MIT's Daniel Lerner could generalize that the "same basic model reappears in virtually all modernizing societies on all continents of the world," while Lerner's frequent collaborator Wilbur Schramm proclaimed the liberating "social effect of free information." Lerner, Schramm, and their cohort posited that as developing countries abandoned older practices and traditions (such as "Islam") in favor of the secular, forward-looking outlook transmitted by mass media, they, too, would achieve modernization. But as the experts' promises failed to materialize, their heuristic of socioeconomic change increasingly seemed incomplete, or downright inaccurate. Modernization schemes gone awry in the jungles of Vietnam; the rise of the anti-war movement and a self-conscious "counterculture"; the emergence of a forceful alliance of oil-producing states; seemingly incurable stagflation: all these factors contributed to growing unease with generalizations about how societies functioned at a moment when the experts' model society—America—seemed to be fragmenting under pressures from within and without.[1]

In the late 1960s and 1970s an alternative concept would displace society in many intellectual disputes over international development: culture. Culture was a more protean and mysterious matrix of human activity, harder to corral into a comparative framework. Cultures incubated different languages and customs. They were not necessarily impervious to flows of information and media, far from it. But they might not respond to these flows in predictable ways. Emblematic of the intellectual challenge from within the social sciences was anthropologist Clifford Geertz's break with modernization theory and his embrace of "thick description" in works including his landmark 1973 book, *The Interpretation of Cultures*. A more frontal assault came from neo-Marxist critics who conceptualized North-South relations under the rubric of cultural imperialism. One measure of the impact of these attacks lay in how American anticommunists were forced to reconsider their earlier assumption that growth would vanquish older traditions and beliefs. "I should have given more thought than I did to . . . the cultural differences that make development almost necessarily different, culture to culture, country to country," Schramm admitted in 1979.[2]

These cultural criticisms of U.S. power did not emerge out of nowhere in the 1970s. In France an array of writers and intellectuals had disparaged the transnational reach of American media in the 1920s and 1930s, foreshadowing the postwar critiques of figures like Jacques Kayser and Fernand Terrou. In the larger transatlantic community, the concept of culture was central to a tradition of mass-culture critique that dated from the same period and continued in the postwar writings of intellectuals like the Frankfurt School pessimist Theodor Adorno and the heterodox American leftist Dwight Macdonald, both of whom wrote about mass culture's tendency to deaden individual judgment.[3] In the late 1950s and 1960s the Cuban Revolution and the Chinese Cultural Revolution helped to push culture to the forefront of radical politics, with leftists across the globe contemplating images of Che Guevara and copies of Mao's *Little Red Book*. What was distinctive about the late 1960s and 1970s was not culture, per se, but its momentum in the postwar, postcolonial international arena, its capacity for bringing together diverse factions that questioned the global spread of commercial American mass media. From the anti-imperial left, concepts of cultural difference moved toward the heart of the UN establishment as policymakers and policy intellectuals from the global North grappled with Third Worldist demands including declarations of a New International Economic Order (NIEO) in 1974 and a New World Information Order (NWIO) in 1976. Their solutions ran the political gamut, but all expressed, in varied terminology, the merit of what would today be termed cultural diversity. Values and traditions that modernization enthusiasts and Maoists alike had wished to eliminate were the same ones that, according to this new set of claims about culture, merited protection.

This chapter examines the cultural preoccupations of a range of critics of U.S. free-flow diplomacy in the late 1960s and 1970s, when the modernization paradigm was falling into crisis. Neo-Marxists such as the American communication scholar Herbert I. Schiller and the Chile-based socialists Ariel Dorfman and Armand Mattelart asserted that the capitalist culture industries had colonized the developing world. Their calls to push back against what they termed American cultural imperialism resonated with the wishes of many nonaligned governments frustrated with the limited results of development cooperation. Less remarked upon, their concern to limit the power of Western governments and corporations in the developing world found echoes among an array of liberal and center-left voices in the West. The Australian-born writer Shirley Hazzard, who had worked for the United Nations in New York and Italy during the early Cold War, castigated the premise of wholesale social transformation propagated by modernization theorists. Another unlikely veteran of the UN system, the English cultural-studies scholar Richard Hoggart, framed international institutions and the cultural and intellectual exchanges they fostered as a countervailing force to multinational corporations. Pitted against the complex of commercial and political forces that Hoggart dubbed "technological neo-colonialism" and Schiller called the "technology gambit," a set of bywords emerged as shorthand for these cultural concerns, ranging from "cultural sovereignty" and "cultural autonomy" to the more modest "cultural integrity," "cultural identity," and "cultural diversity."[4]

Outside the United States even liberal policy intellectuals found themselves drawn to the concept of culture as a way of mediating between U.S. free-flow policies and other positions. In 1969 the French television pioneer and UN media director Jean d'Arcy announced a "right to communicate" in an attempt to update Article 19 of the Universal Declaration of Human Rights for the satellite era. This right was intended to encompass the free flow of information across borders, which d'Arcy generally favored. But over the course of the 1970s d'Arcy also incorporated cultural considerations into his discussions of it as he attempted to triangulate the competing communications policies of the United States, its Cold War allies in Western Europe and Canada, and the Third World bloc.[5]

Ultimately, the uptake of cultural critiques of U.S. power by moderate and establishment figures such as Hoggart and d'Arcy proved just as threatening to Washington as any alleged Soviet–Third World machinations. In a reprise of the breakdown of early Cold War freedom-of-information negotiations, the United States responded by backing away from the kinds of multilateral compromise that had characterized the Development Decade. Instead, as is shown in the final chapter of this book, Washington doubled down on technological means of dissolving rivals' claims to informational and economic authority. But before treating the ascent of neoliberalism in U.S. freedom-of-information policy in the late 1970s and 1980s, let us examine anxieties and doubts about American globalism that were cutting across the First and Third Worlds in the late 1960s and early 1970s.

THE RETURN OF POLITICAL ECONOMY AND THE RADICAL CRITIQUE OF CULTURAL IMPERIALISM

Radical opposition to U.S. free-flow policies was rooted in the reemergence of an intellectual and methodological approach that had been marginalized in American communication research during the early Cold War: political economy. Critiques of corporate concentration of the kind that had animated the Hutchins Commission's early discussions had largely yielded by the 1950s to anticommunist accommodation to corporate capitalism. This accommodation shaped the dominant approaches in

American communication research at a moment when figures like Paul Lazarsfeld and Wilbur Schramm were working to institutionalize communication as a discipline in American universities. Reliant on corporate and government backing, their vein of "administrative" research, so named by Lazarsfeld, tended to buttress rather than challenge the anticommunist consensus in corporate boardrooms and in Washington.

Outliers who persisted in criticizing the overweening power of American information industries felt the chill. The Canadian economist Harold Innis, analyzing American consumption of Canadian paper pulp, had contended that by the twentieth century, freedom of the press had become an ideological cover that "obscured [the] monopolistic characteristics" and imperial reach of the American news industry. Innis withheld the publication of his last work until shortly before his death in 1952; the work was highly critical of the United States.[6] Dallas Smythe, another Canadian with a background in economics, had cut his teeth on communications questions while working at the Federal Communications Commission in the 1940s, when the New Deal liberal James L. Fly was squarely taking aim at corporate concentration. The red scare that shook the federal government later in the decade provoked Smythe's exit from the FCC and his move to the University of Illinois's new communications research center, which was then under Wilbur Schramm's direction. But whatever sense of refuge Smythe might have had after receiving the offer from Illinois was fleeting: the appointment was nearly thwarted by HUAC (the House Un-American Activities Committee), and clues later surfaced that the FBI may have monitored Smythe through a nearby source—Schramm.[7]

Political economy, however, could not be repressed (or red-baited) indefinitely. The United States' far-flung interventions to shore up the capitalist bloc, the complicity between industry and government pointed to by President Eisenhower's warning of an incipient "military-industrial complex" in his farewell address in 1961, the transnational reach of American culture industries—all pointed toward the ways in which American capitalism intersected with U.S. foreign policy. By the early to mid-1960s political economy was reemerging across the social sciences as a means of understanding U.S. power. In *The Tragedy of American Diplomacy* (1959) and *The Contours of American History* (1961), the Wisconsin-based historian

William Appleman Williams pioneered the study of how American economic expansionism had shaped U.S. foreign policy, engendering cold war. Marxist economists Paul Baran and Paul Sweezy's *Monopoly Capital: An Essay on the American Economic and Social Order* (1966) framed the rise of powerful U.S.-based transnational corporations as the latest phase in the onward march of industrial concentration. In *The International Film Industry: Western Europe and America Since 1945* (1969), Dallas Smythe's mentee Thomas Guback analyzed Hollywood's drive to export films to Europe after the Second World War. Guback challenged the industry's standard explanation—that European audiences simply liked Hollywood films best—with evidence of diplomatic arm twisting and industrial collusion: the tributaries of transatlantic film flows were, Guback argued, the State Department and the Motion Picture Association of America.[8]

In the field of communication research, no American embraced political economy more assertively than the scholar who filled Smythe's shoes at Illinois, Herbert I. Schiller. After serving with the army in North Africa during the Second World War, Schiller had worked for the U.S. occupation forces in Germany, where he witnessed the United States' will to denazify the German economy dissipate amid rising hostilities with the Soviet Union. His resulting disillusionment with Cold War anticommunism informed his future scholarship. Schiller was drawn to international communications issues partly by the heated debates over satellite broadcasting that erupted in the 1960s. His work was also informed, from the mid-1960s on, through contact with a transnational cast of researchers associated with the International Association for Mass Communication Research—an institution which, in spite of the efforts described in chapter 2, cold warriors like Wilbur Schramm and Raymond Nixon had not been able to bend to their purposes. In 1969 Schiller produced what was perhaps the first book-length critique of the role of American media industries outside U.S. borders, *Mass Communications and American Empire*. As Dallas Smythe explained in the book's preface, Schiller's intervention was methodological as well as empirical: Schiller challenged administrative research by exposing the "economic and political" calculations undergirding postwar American power.[9]

The focus of *Mass Communications and American Empire* was the rapid expansion of American communications industries abroad since 1945.

Schiller asserted that the American military-industrial complex had ruth-
lessly colonized all aspects of modern communications, from hardware to
software to the natural resource most essential to broadcasting—radio
spectrum. The need to seek new markets determined not only the reach of
these industries but also their governing ideology. Recalling Harold Innis's
work of two decades earlier, Schiller argued that American free-flow talk
signified not greater peace and stability but rather the "unrestrained opportunity for the dissemination of messages by the American mass media in
the world arena." Free-flow ideology, underwritten by U.S. political and
economic power, had also captured international institutions: the United
States, wrote Schiller, had succeeded in making free flow UNESCO's
"designated objective."

Schiller's critique yoked together an overview of the political economy
of American communications industries with a sketch of their cultural
effects. By 1969 the American communications complex was "[impinging]
on peoples' lives everywhere"—not just through the equipment being
dumped on the rest of the world but also through exported programming
and the consumerist values embedded therein (unsurprisingly, Schiller
found little to redeem these exports: American broadcasting was a "soul-
destroying wasteland" while "[individual] expression and talent" were likewise "difficult to discover" in Hollywood films).[10] Schiller's subsequent
scholarship expanded on the cultural analysis introduced in *Mass Communications and American Empire*. In the 1970s he tracked a shift in post-
Vietnam U.S. foreign policy away from boots-on-the-ground interventions
and toward what one government panel labeled the new "premium on
persuasion," away from coercion and toward the "ideological" and "cultural"
production of consent. As evidence of this subtler form of expansionism,
Schiller pointed to phenomena ranging from the exportation of American-
style business education to the use of the English language abroad to the
global promotion of opinion-polling techniques. These exports shaped practices overseas: when, for instance, multinationals infiltrated developing-
world economies using sophisticated market-research techniques, local businesses then needed to learn the same techniques in order to compete.[11]

In Schiller's view, American empire threatened to engulf the cultural
landscape elsewhere in the world. The "cultural domination" and "cultural

penetration" perpetrated by American communications industries was exhaustive. One only needed to look to Canada, where national identity had been "practically obliterated" by its southern neighbor, to understand what was at stake in the battle to contain U.S. influence: nothing less than the "cultural integrity of weak societies."[12] Paradoxically, in his recourse to gendered and sexualized tropes to model communications effects, Schiller shared something in common with an earlier generation of arch-establishment propaganda research—namely, the premise of a one-way transmission of messages and values to a feminized target population.

The totalizing claims that Schiller made for U.S. power were not shared by all critics of cultural imperialism.[13] In the writings of many leftists working in Latin America, power and agency were distributed—albeit unevenly—across borders. The Chile-based socialists Armand Mattelart and Ariel Dorfman shared numerous assumptions with Schiller in their widely disseminated 1971 treatise on Disney comics in Latin America, *How to Read Donald Duck: Imperialist Ideology in the Disney Comic* (*Para leer al Pato Donald* in the Spanish original): the view of free-flow talk as the ideological cover for U.S. imperialism, the mechanisms by which the First World maintained the developing world in a state of economic dependency, and the emasculation of Latin American audiences. But as much as the pair were in dialogue with radicals north of the Rio Grande, they also addressed a practical question that tended to be more central to debates in Latin America than to North American neo-Marxists: How could the cycle of dependency be broken?

In many ways *How to Read Donald Duck* read as the hermeneutical complement to Schiller's broad-brush picture of American domination, neo-Marxism by a different method. Through close reading, Dorfman and Mattelart sought to demonstrate how North American capitalism maintained the United States' southern neighbors in a state of ideological as well as economic dependency. In the universe of Donald Duck, Uncle Scrooge, and Mickey Mouse, neither conquest nor productive labor existed. Wealth on the order of Uncle Scrooge's mountains of gold coins was generated not by toiling workers but by diversions like treasure hunts and prize competitions. "[Even] in the treasure hunt the productive process is lacking," the authors glossed. "The problem lies not in the actual extraction of the treasure, but in discovering its geographical location." By this sleight-of-hand, Dorfman and Mattelart contended, the seemingly innocuous children's comics—a synecdoche for American mass-culture exports—elided long histories of imperial violence and naturalized the coercive extraction of wealth from the Third World. Encouraging consumption, not honoring production, was the endgame of this culture: "[We] send copper, and they send machines to extract copper, and, of course, Coca Cola." Moreover, also like Schiller, Dorfman and Mattelart used gendered language to postulate audience passivity in the face of Disney's seductive message, which "emasculates" class conflict: not only territories and resources but also imaginations had been colonized, trained to focus on "individual goals at the expense of the collective needs."

Yet, in *How to Read Donald Duck*, Dorfman and Mattelart appeared ultimately more optimistic than Schiller about the potential of developing countries to break free of U.S. influence. Culture, they insisted, could be remade; a "mass culture built on the backs of the masses" could be displaced by an emancipatory popular culture in which collective needs took center stage.[14] To this end Dorfman spent the waning days of Salvador Allende's presidency devising a series of cartoon shorts intended to combat the acts of transportation sabotage that were then undermining Allende's government. The shorts were to star Susana the Seed, "a sort of Chilean version of Chiquita Banana," who languished inland as her lover, Federico the Fertilizer, struggled to outwit the bad guys—in real life, truckers whose strike was being subsidized by the CIA—who were then paralyzing the road from the coast. "I had scripted twenty-five one-minute TV spots to be aired week after week," recalled Dorfman, "[which were to start] in September of 1973 and [culminate] in an orgasmic finale, my two lovers coupling under the stars of March 1974." Chile was one of the few places where the socialist Left was—briefly—in a position to put its ideas into practice. This political and existential imperative to action may explain why cultural imperialism appeared more vulnerable from Santiago de Chile in the early 1970s than from Southern California, where Schiller, who had just moved from Illinois, was busy establishing a communication program at the University of California, San Diego—for what good was it to theorize imperialism if there were no possibility of toppling it?[15]

The overthrow of Allende in September 1973 by the Chilean army, backed by the CIA, dashed these hopes, sending Dorfman into exile and the Belgian-born Mattelart back across the Atlantic to Europe. American imperialism had native allies in Chile and elsewhere, and many leftist intellectuals would subsequently sharpen their focus on the role of national elites in securing U.S. hegemony in Latin America. Mattelart, who resettled in France, analyzed how the Chilean upper classes had embraced the "technocratic ideology" of the U.S. communications complex. (In an article written with Michèle Mattelart, he also noted the growing influence of the English language in France's business and education sectors and reproved Anglophone French elites for this threat to Francophone "cultural vitality.") The Mexican writer Carlos Monsiváis similarly indicted the Mexican bourgeoisie for converting popular cultural forms into instruments of ideological domination over the lower classes.[16] The 1960s had been, in Dorfman's recollection, a period of "extreme nationalism" that precluded any "soul-searching about the enigma of heterogeneous identity," even for someone like himself—born in Argentina, of Jewish ancestry, and partly raised in the United States. By the mid-1970s, however, the limitations of cultural nationalism were increasingly apparent to far-flung observers across Europe and the Americas, who could agree with the French journalist and veteran *tiers-mondiste* Hervé Bourges that the radical project to "decolonize information" was not the same as autarkic authoritarianism.[17]

For a leading critic of cultural imperialism, Herbert Schiller appeared curiously unconcerned with these intellectual and political developments delinking culture from the nation-state. Schiller did not deny that the discourse of cultural imperialism brought together a transnational network of leftist scholars. *Mass Communications and American Empire* had drawn on the writings of Frantz Fanon, and at UCSD Schiller rubbed elbows with the Frankfurt School émigré and New Left idol Herbert Marcuse. The more divisive question was where to locate the forces that could plausibly oppose First World imperialism. The Allendists, Schiller concluded, had been too respectful of existing information flows, having continued to allow bourgeois-capitalist broadcast media, film, and publications like *Reader's Digest* into Chile, revealing a laxity that ultimately undermined

Chilean democracy. "[In] the communications-cultural sphere, national sovereignty is the last defense against the forward march of the media conglomerates," Schiller reflected in his 1976 book *Communication and Cultural Domination* in a special afterword dedicated to assessing the Pinochet coup. "If the barrier of sovereignty goes down, there is absolutely no protection."[18] For Schiller, strong states formed a kind of last-ditch defense against wholesale cultural annexation.

Schiller's hardline approach was doubly curious in view of the fact that American power appeared far less monolithic by the mid-1970s than it had for much of the 1950s and 1960s. Reeling from the U.S. retreat from Vietnam, economic stagnation, and the Watergate scandal, Washington came the closest it ever would to what might be called soul searching. One upshot of the coup in Chile, specifically, was that it helped to sensitize the U.S. establishment to the influence that American communications corporations wielded outside U.S. borders. Congress opened its first-ever public review of U.S. undercover intelligence operations, the Senate Select Committee to Study Government Operations with Respect to Intelligence Activities, also called the Church Committee after its chair, Senator Frank Church. The Church Committee devoted multiple pages of its 1975 report on "Covert Action in Chile" to exposing the collusion between procoup forces in Chile, the CIA, and International Telephone and Telegraph (ITT, a U.S.-based corporation that then controlled Chile's telephone service).[19] Criticisms of the power of wealthy multinationals to intrude in the affairs of sovereign states have most often been associated with Third World radicalism. But if the conclusions of the Church Committee are any indication, by the mid-1970s these concerns had moved closer toward the political center in the heartlands of the multinationals, the United States and Western Europe.

THE CONCEPT OF CULTURAL DIFFERENCE
MOVES TO THE CENTER

At the same moment when radical intellectuals and activists were lambasting American cultural imperialism, an array of liberal, left-liberal, and center-left thinkers were also expressing concerns about the cultural aspects of U.S. power. The Australian novelist and former UN functionary Shirley Hazzard issued withering critiques of existing development policies and their technocratic approach toward far-flung societies and cultures. The English cultural-studies pioneer Richard Hoggart, who spent half a decade working as an assistant director general at UNESCO in the early to mid-1970s, took a more hopeful view of the state of internationalism while sharing Hazzard's dim view of top-down efforts to reshape cultures. Jean d'Arcy, the French television expert and UN policymaker, was the most optimistic of the three about technologies like satellite broadcasting, but he, too, incorporated cultural considerations into his policy proposals, as concerned by corporate monopolies as he was by state abuses. Though they did so less systematically than their neo-Marxist contemporaries, these UN veterans all participated in what many subsequent commentators, enthralled by what cultural studies scholar Michael Denning has called the "ahistorical logic of global cultural flow," have tended to marginalize: a period of intense international contestation over the means and ends of cross-border exchange.[20]

Hazzard's writings on the United Nations reflected two broad trends in Anglophone politics in the 1970s: growing liberal disenchantment with governmental and intergovernmental authority, and the rise of nongovernmental human-rights organizations. By then, years of corruption seemed to have drained the United Nations of its moral legitimacy. The nadir was the director generalship of Kurt Waldheim (1972–1982), whose cozy relations with autocrats like the shah of Iran Hazzard linked to Waldheim's own youthful involvement in the Austrian Nazi movement. Historians of the 1970s have highlighted how this state of affairs spurred Western liberals to look instead to nongovernmental organizations to act as beacons of human rights. As Hazzard put it, "Organizations like Amnesty International . . . mobilize inestimable resources of human fellowship and proper indignation, and have assumed the task that the United Nations, with its colossal funds and massive bureaucracy, would not attempt." Hazzard was keenly committed to civil liberties—those negative freedoms that protected ordinary citizens against governmental abuses. Like the thousands of people who were then joining Amnesty International's letter-writing campaigns on behalf of prisoners of conscience, she was a believer in press and speech freedoms, not a radical critic of their ideological biases.[21]

What distinguished Hazzard's analysis of UN venality was how she traced its genealogy back to an unaccustomed culprit: U.S. anticommunism. Unlike many in the Anglophone press who blamed the "politicization" of the United Nations in the 1970s on Soviet–Third World connivance, Hazzard argued that long-standing East-West tensions had laid the groundwork for North-South polarization. The original sin, which she unmasked in a series of trenchant articles and two books, *Defeat of an Ideal: A Study of the Self-destruction of the United Nations* (1973) and *Countenance of Truth: The United Nations and the Waldheim Case* (1990), was the system of security clearances that the U.S. government had initiated in a secret 1949 pact with then UN secretary general Trygve Lie. Having worked at the institution for a decade during the early Cold War, the budding novelist had witnessed the poisonous effects of the clearance system firsthand: it had eviscerated the independence of UN functionaries, whose sworn loyalty to the United Nations was thereafter compromised by political pressures.[22]

It was this Cold War expediency—the United States' own disrespect for the civil liberties and intellectual independence of international civil servants—that, according to Hazzard, had abetted the rise of a development technocracy that was utterly disengaged from the societies it purported to improve. She satirized this technocracy in the 1967 novel *People in Glass Houses: Portraits from Organization Life*, which depicted the workings of a—pointedly unnamed—international organization ("the Organization"). The novel skewered the Organization's bureaucratese, as in a scene where the director general thanks the staff for its "productivity illustrated by an increased flow of documentation in the five official languages." This proclivity for portable clichés was evident as well in the Organization's development work, illustrated in the character of Edrich, who scorns the conditions at his field site—"[low] level of overall production, cottage industries static for centuries, poor communications with neighbouring towns, no telegraph or telephone system, partial electrification, dissemination of information by shepherd's rumour, little or no interest in national or international events"—even as he hurriedly seeks to endow it with a road and an administration building constructed by residents who have not requested them.[23]

In her nonfiction, too, Hazzard suggested that, though buzzwords could "flow" across cultural and linguistic divides, they might do so in ways that obscured rather than clarified what was most important. Though politically and temperamentally more *New Yorker* than neo-Marxist, in discussing development in *Defeat of an Ideal* Hazzard momentarily seemed to approach Herbert Schiller by way of Edmund Burke:

> Development, as it has been practiced by such programs as those of the United Nations, is not a series of individual humanitarian alleviations over which a country may retain the sovereignty of its identity, nor is it even limited to an exchange of useful skills, or to the increase of crops or the introduction of electrification. Cumulatively, it represents the imposition of transfiguring and often alien new concepts that may well exterminate national and regional character within a generation.[24]

In Hazzard's view, the rise of an international development technocracy ran directly counter to the vital work that the United Nations *could* have been doing in the overlapping fields of culture and the environment. The writer recognized that the impulse to transform far-flung lifeways and societies was not coming only from international organizations. In a telling passage from 1974 she asserted that the United Nations had surrendered any pretense of "global power" to "technology and the multinational corporations." This was not a welcome change, for in spite of the United Nations' profound flaws, it was one of the few institutions with the potential to check the multinationals. For Hazzard, the decline of intergovernmental authority and the ascent of neoliberal forms of power were potentially disastrous in a world threatened by environmental degradation.[25]

Richard Hoggart's trajectory likewise illustrated this search for protection against the vicissitudes of global capitalism, which occupied ecologically minded progressives and social democrats as well as those further to the left in the 1970s. On the surface, Hoggart's interventions were quite different from Hazzard's. While she inscribed her high-toned work within the tradition of Western humanism, Hoggart pioneered the study of popular culture, emphasizing the rich cultural resources created and shared by working people. Yet in spite of these distinctive writerly personae, Hoggart would arrive at a similar position vis-à-vis social change in the developing world: left-liberal internationalism fused, somewhat awkwardly, to cultural conservationism.[26]

One thing Hoggart shared with Hazzard was a keen sense of how power could corrupt language. Hoggart's 1957 opus, *The Uses of Literacy*, had helped to open cultural scholarship to a thrilling new range of texts and contexts by taking the idiomatic speech and popular forms of Northern England's working classes as seriously as conventional English studies took literature. *The Uses of Literacy* also departed from the assumptions that guided behaviorist research on the social psychology of mass media. Working-class people were not the gullible, pliable masses posited by cultural mandarins and social-science behaviorists alike. The real story of cultural change, Hoggart argued, lay in how commercial mass culture had co-opted older working-class values since the early twentieth century. In Hoggart's model, profiteering media interests acted as cultural parasites: the "success of the more powerful contemporary approaches is partly decided by the extent to which they can identify themselves with 'older' attitudes."[27]

A key instance of this commercial parasitism lay in changing understandings of freedom. Exploiting the working classes' habitual "charitable allowance for human frailty and the difficulties of ordinary lives," profit-oriented "popularisers" had, between roughly 1900 and 1950, widened the concept of freedom to signify hedonism, a "refusal to admit that anyone can be judged for anything." By the mid-twentieth century, salt-of-the-earth popular tropes ("after all, it's only 'uman") were being dissolved into an expertise fetish ("scientists tell us that inhibitions are wrong"):

It was always a comfort to think that nature free is also naturally good; now we know. This becomes very soon the idea of freedom as a justification. It is always freedom from, never freedom for; freedom as a good in itself, not merely as the ground for the effort to live by other standards. One can easily see how this may spread in a class which has never before felt so free. . . . It is in the interest of the organs of mass entertainment that this attitude should be maintained.[28]

Hoggart's notion of "freedom for" resonated with the positive, socially mediated freedoms that William Hocking had touted during the Hutchins Commission's discussions in the 1940s. For Hoggart, however, "freedom for" was the established reality, and "freedom from" the newer proposition; negative freedoms were the ideological ally of mass consumerism and a degraded mass culture.

Hoggart's innovative approach to the study of culture had an impact beyond his own research. By the early 1960s it was helping to mold institutional agendas in the nascent field of British cultural studies. Early projects and seminars at the University of Birmingham's Centre for Contemporary Cultural Studies (CCCS), which Hoggart founded in 1964, included an analysis of public interest broadcasting and talks on "popularisation," popular music, and television dramas. In the years ahead the CCCS incubated the careers of a younger generation of scholars, notably Stuart Hall, who built upon the insight that popular and mass cultural forms merited scholarly attention.[29] Hoggart's suspicion of commercial culture also found an outlet in domestic policy through his participation on the British government's Pilkington Committee (1960–1962). A staunch defender of public service broadcasting, Hoggart helped to shape the committee's controversial 1962 report, which successfully advocated awarding a second television channel to the noncommercial BBC instead of its commercial rival, ITV. This anticommercial orientation, shared by many Tories as well as lifetime Labour backers like Hoggart, reflected geopolitical anxieties as well as domestic preoccupations. The Pilkington Committee's conclusions amounted to a rejection of the American model of commercial broadcasting, which had been implanted in Latin America as early as the 1920s but in the 1960s was still not dominant in Western Europe.[30]

In 1970 Hoggart left England for France in order to take up a post as an assistant director general at UNESCO, where he would spend five years working under Director General René Maheu (and briefly under his successor, the Senegalese Amadou-Mahtar M'Bow). Maheu, a Frenchman who was by then well into his twelve-year tenure, had steered the organization during the 1960s toward the development initiatives favored by the United States, thereby greatly increasing its budget. But Maheu had also actively criticized racism (to the United States' dismay) and courted the support of new states then entering the UN system. These attempts to mediate East-West and North-South tensions formed the backdrop for Hoggart's own work as head of the Sector of Social Sciences, Human Sciences, and Culture. Hoggart's duties, as befitted this expansive title, encompassed everything from reporting on the reconstruction of Warsaw to assessing UNESCO's relationship to NGOs to overseeing the organization's expanding work in the field of cultural heritage.[31]

Like Maheu, and to a lesser extent Hazzard, Hoggart struggled to triangulate a coherent position amid the competing claims of the First, Second, and Third Worlds. The complex understanding of value transfer that Hoggart had presented in *The Uses of Literacy*—where it had appeared as a process by which powerful actors imposed ideals and expectations upon subordinate groups—was less evident in *An Idea and Its Servants*, his 1978 study of UNESCO. In the latter volume Hoggart resorted to the familiar notion that the "West" possessed values that were "still worth exporting," notably the "rule of law, the freedom of the individual, democratic process, [and] free exchanges of people and ideas." As the historian Kenneth Cmiel has noted, human rights are necessarily a thin idiom designed to communicate across cultural and linguistic divides, and the kinds of thick description Hoggart had deployed in analyzing the English scene were less feasible when he turned his attention to the polyglot, multicultural arena of international relations.[32] The difficulty of replicating the insights of *The Uses of Literacy* in his UNESCO memoir may have been compounded by the distinction between his working-class upbringing and the relative privilege his race and citizenship afforded him in international context. The roles of race and empire in shaping cultural meanings, a focus of high-profile work coming out of Birmingham after Stuart Hall succeeded Hoggart as CCCS director, remained peripheral to Hoggart's thinking.[33]

Hoggart stood on firmer ground when he addressed the issue of economic inequality between wealthy and developing countries. "The call for a New International Economic Order is a call for greater distributive justice," the former scholarship boy noted in *An Idea and Its Servants*, referencing the 1974 UN General Assembly resolution spearheaded by the Third World bloc to reorient the global economy to address North-South disparities. "In a world in which 70 per cent of the population receive 20 per cent of the wealth . . . it is no wonder that the statesmen of the poorer nations are alarmed and angry." Hoggart also observed how these stark differences had been exacerbated by Western obduracy. Recalling a meeting of "high-level Western European" elites, he wrote that it "was as though they had moved from military colonialism to technological neo-colonialism without a thought beyond the purely practical and profitable"; they had "almost to a man . . . assumed that people at their level were right to be annoyed by and dismissive of Third World attitudes."[34] In Hoggart's view, pervasive Western insensitivity demonstrated UNESCO's utility as a place that institutionalized developing-world concerns, thereby making them harder for First World elites to dismiss out of hand.

Between their appeals to so-called Western values and their anxieties over the transformative forces of global capitalism, Hoggart and Hazzard exemplified an unresolved tension in the politics of the center Left in the 1970s over the proper scope of state power. On one hand, speech and press freedoms were doubly significant in the battle against governmental oppression, both targets of and weapons against it. The ordeal of the British publisher of *Lady Chatterley's Lover*, for which Hoggart had served as a defense witness when the publisher was charged with obscenity in the early 1960s, must have come to seem slight by the 1970s in the face of mounting repression of dissidents in the Soviet Union and in the dictatorships that had emerged in the Southern Cone and much of postcolonial Africa. On the other hand, what besides state and interstate regulations could guard cultures against the power of multinational corporations and their international avatar, the United States?

The philosopher and historian Isaiah Berlin once distinguished between two types of intellectual: the fox, who "knows many things," and the more single-minded hedgehog, who "knows one big thing."[35] If Herbert Schiller was a hedgehog, ceaselessly hammering away at the theme of American cultural imperialism, then Hazzard and Hoggart were foxes, willing to court inconsistency in exchange for the liberty to pursue their various interests. In Hazzard's case, seeming political irresolution might also equate to a kind of resignation to the limits of what politics might accomplish—or so she hinted in the novel *People in Glass Houses* through a conversation between two sympathetic translators employed at the Organization:

> "Got one," Algie Wyatt underlined a phrase on the page before him.
>
> "What?" asked Lidia Korabetski, looking up from the passage she was translating.
>
> "Contradiction in terms." Algie was collecting contradictions in terms: to a nucleus of "military intelligence" and "competent authorities" he had added such discoveries as the soul of efficiency, easy virtue, enlightened self-interest, Bankers Trust, and Christian Scientist.
>
> "What?" Lidia asked again.
>
> *"Cultural mission,"* replied Algie, turning the page and looking encouraged, as if he studied the document solely for such rewards as this.[36]

In sidelong fashion, Hazzard suggested that bureaucratic attempts to apprehend or mold culture resulted from a fundamental misunderstanding of what culture was.

Hoggart was more hopeful that thorny political debates might yield political solutions. Despite the myriad organizational difficulties he had confronted during his stint in Paris, he retained a sense of optimism about international institutions, writing of UNESCO as a place that facilitated a "greatly increased sense of the sheer variety of human ways of life and in particular of the many different kinds of strength and resilience people can show." The implication was that this unmastered yet delicate cultural variety merited defending. More so than Hazzard, Hoggart believed it was politically possible to do so through the United Nations and its agencies. In his eyes UNESCO acted as a "world resource centre, a complex of information banks, a set of clearing houses"; a locus of vital "work on the meaning of cultural diversity, on the needs and rights of minorities, and on the pressures on oral cultures today"; and a "market for the traffic of knowledge," especially for and between parts of the world where the actual "forces of the market" had failed to ensure dialogue and exchange.[37]

Around the time of Hoggart's writing, an attempt to foster such an alternative marketplace was winding its way through the international system in the form of a proposed update to Article 19 of the Universal Declaration of Human Rights.

UPDATING ARTICLE 19: JEAN D'ARCY AND THE RIGHT TO COMMUNICATE

Like Richard Hoggart, the French media expert Jean d'Arcy believed that growing cross-border and cross-cultural communication might be shaped through deliberate policy to serve the greater good. Having spent a decade in New York as director of the UN Radio and Visual Services Division (1961–1971), d'Arcy could appreciate the virtues of the more liberalized American audiovisual sector vis-à-vis European public broadcasting monopolies.[38] D'Arcy's initial intervention into international communication debates—the 1969 essay "Direct Broadcast Satellites and the Right to Communicate," published in the official review of the European Broadcasting Union—took a generally liberal approach to communications technologies. The article charted a dialectic of technological breakthrough and political repression at least as old as the printing press: printing's revolutionary potential had been largely overlooked by its contemporaries, save the "secular and religious authorities" who sought to control and profit from it. D'Arcy suggested sympathy for the printing-press renegades of centuries past, the " 'pirate stations' where prohibited works could be produced . . . at that time, too, located across the border." These he interpreted as an *avant la lettre* instance of a transnational public exerting pressure on authorities to more fully democratize communications technologies and information flows. D'Arcy believed that the advent of direct-broadcast satellites, which he forecast for roughly the late 1980s, offered a historic opportunity to restructure communications for the wider public benefit—if only it could be seized.[39]

However, d'Arcy's proposals were not wholly in line with the increasingly antiregulatory American approach to cross-border broadcasting.

"The closest possible intergovernmental cooperation is obviously an essential condition for the full development of direct broadcast satellites," d'Arcy argued, for only cooperation would enable the international community to strike a balance between technological advances and the prerogatives of nation-states, between freedom and "mutual restraint." This was where d'Arcy's "right to communicate" entered the picture. First, he explained, "one should work more towards a pattern of groups of neighbouring countries" exchanging and pooling broadcasting resources "rather than . . . overreach ourselves by trying to set up from the beginning a world-wide organization or system of agreements in those communications areas where the common culture or traditions of a region or a continent play a predominant part." The failure of earlier UN efforts to secure a binding international agreement on freedom of information was proof positive in d'Arcy's mind that it was better to begin gradually, on a regional scale, akin to existing European institutions like the European Economic Community and Eurovision (the latter of which he had helped to create). He presented cultural differences as something that communications planners, if they were to achieve genuine consensus, could not afford to ignore.[40]

The right to communicate soon began to attract international attention. In a 1972 letter to d'Arcy, communication scholar L. S. Harms of the University of Hawaii at Manoa—located just next door to the East-West Center where Daniel Lerner and Wilbur Schramm were producing their state-of-the-field development-communication anthologies—drew a parallel between Lerner's and d'Arcy's work: the "new theory of communication" that Lerner had discerned at a recent conference, a "two-way, interactive, information sharing and testing model," converged with "much of what you have been saying with your phrase Right to Communicate." D'Arcy and Harms subsequently agreed that "a comprehensive Right to Communicate has yet to be delineated." His interest in promoting nongovernmental, regional organizations aside, d'Arcy ambitiously announced that their "final goal" should be nothing less than "an amendment to the Universal Declaration." Harms began to outline a book of readings relevant to the right to communicate, and the two were soon working to ensure its place on the international agenda.[41]

As d'Arcy's coinage circulated internationally, it grew ever more intertwined with the question of how communications technologies shaped cultural variables—and with the North-South tensions that had been largely absent from d'Arcy's initial 1969 article. UNESCO's involvement with the right to communicate officially began at its 1974 General Conference, when Sweden put forth a resolution for further research on the subject, a resolution drafted by Harms and UNESCO's E. Lloyd Sommerlad under the auspices of the International Broadcasting Institute (IBI), which d'Arcy had helped to found.[42] UNESCO then contracted the IBI to prepare a questionnaire to solicit the opinions of member states and nongovernmental organizations. D'Arcy's right was suddenly brought into an uneasy conversation with critiques linking the "unregulated flow of information across national frontiers" to a "new colonialism, and to the subjection of peoples to foreign cultures and ideologies," as Nigeria outlined in its response.[43]

Thus began d'Arcy's decade-long effort to contain the right's meaning and implications. Even within the IBI, this entailed a certain corralling of opinion. When IBI executive director Edward Ploman argued that human rights were in essence a Western invention, d'Arcy, echoing Shirley Hazzard and Richard Hoggart, countered that even so, they had laid the foundation for the United Nations: "It is certain that embracing [human rights] leads ineluctably to the establishment of democracy, a form of government which may not correspond to the current needs of certain countries, but which, I think, is recognized by all as an objective to achieve." And he wrote to UNESCO to restate his view of cross-border information flows: "Information, by its nature, escapes frontiers. There's no such thing as an opposition between 'international' and 'national' information."[44]

But for all his liberal inclinations, d'Arcy did not reject alternative understandings of the right to communicate out of hand. He wrote to Ploman that even if the right did stem from the Western political tradition, the developing world must not see it as a neocolonial imposition. D'Arcy acknowledged Third World demands, too, in his advocacy before the French National Commission, which had declined to cosponsor UNESCO's initial 1974 right-to-communicate resolution.[45] Denying any contradiction between the individual and collective guarantees implied by the right to communicate, d'Arcy insisted that it encompassed the needs of individuals and communities alike: "We will thereby have taken a step forward . . . with regards to the idea of freedom of information, a step which developing countries will be especially receptive to, concerned as they are to preserve their culture and to share it."[46]

The mobilization of culture in d'Arcy's advocacy with the French National Commission in the mid-1970s signified a tactical and an intellectual shift from his initial position. Facing the skepticism of some French National Commission members, d'Arcy pressed his case: the right to communicate offered France an opportunity to carve out a middle path between U.S. free-flow liberalism and the Third World.[47] D'Arcy counseled his compatriots to consider the "legitimate protests of those who consider themselves the victims" of free-flow doctrine. In part, France's satellite policy inspired his call for independence vis-à-vis the United States:

> Just as, at the United Nations, during the discussions . . . on broadcasting satellites, the French delegation has never blindly gone along with the American delegation's attempts to implement the principle—inviolable, they declare—of the free flow of information, at Nairobi [the 1976 UNESCO General Conference], too, we need to distinguish ourselves from the positions that the United States will take.[48]

Whereas in 1969 statism had been his primary target, by the mid-1970s d'Arcy was stressing the value of a mixed public-private policy approach to communications like Canada's or France's.[49]

By 1979 d'Arcy's cultural thought, evident in his behind-the-scenes lobbying with the French National Commission, surfaced in a discussion paper for a UNESCO gathering in Manila. Although d'Arcy consistently rejected calls for absolute national sovereignty of the kind that had captivated Herbert Schiller, Third Worldist demands had made their mark on his conception of cross-border information flows. After restating the need to update the Universal Declaration of Human Rights, d'Arcy announced that the right to communicate would correct the deformations of free flow by adding to existing freedoms "the concepts of access, participation, [and] two-way information flow... both for individuals and for societies." D'Arcy further highlighted the "welcome which for some years has been given to the new concept at international meetings, particularly by the developing countries" and asserted that a "horizontal, inter-active flow" was still extant "in its traditional forms in the majority of Third World countries." Teasing out a theme that was peripheral to many of his earlier interventions, d'Arcy identified "one of the urgent problems of our time, namely, that of the cultural identity of peoples and nations": poorly designed media-development schemes threatened the "preservation of the cultural heritage of the various human groups."[50]

An associate of d'Arcy's, Henri Pigeat, contended after d'Arcy's death in 1983 that interpretations of the right to communicate that focused on collective rights were "dangerous" and "very distant" from d'Arcy's own.[51] It was true that d'Arcy had consistently called for the reform of powerful government monopolies and had likewise consistently stressed the importance of independent, non-state-owned media. Yet Pigeat's insistence on d'Arcy's original intent—read: antistatism—elided the ways in which d'Arcy himself had modified his proposals over time.[52] These adaptations were not an isolated response to the demands of the Third World bloc, moreover. In suggesting that mass media could undermine established lifeways, d'Arcy echoed Richard Hoggart's left-traditionalism and Shirley Hazzard's conservationist critique of development. He also exhibited the instincts of a seasoned policymaker in linking the right to communicate to France's diplomatic independence vis-à-vis the United States. In a gnomic, handwritten note filed among his papers on a UNESCO seminar on satellite broadcasting, d'Arcy had paraphrased Arthur C. Clarke's familiar prediction about satellites (discussed in chapter 5): "Before the end of this century communication satellites will have decided whether English Russian [sic] or Chinese is a second language of mankind." Presumably, d'Arcy, a native French speaker, did not fully share Clarke's sanguine technological determinism about how communications technologies would shape language practices in the years ahead: global English (or global Russian, or global Chinese) represented rather the more ominous proposition of global U.S. (or global Russian, or global Chinese) power.[53]

By the time of d'Arcy's paper for the 1979 Manila conference, the cultural tropes that had emerged in counterpoint to U.S. free-flow policies were no longer a merely academic issue. They had been officially introduced into international policy debates. At UNESCO's 1976 General Conference, held in Nairobi, nonaligned states inaugurated demands for a "new world information order" (NWIO). The NWIO, modeled after the New International Economic Order (NIEO) declaration of two years earlier, encompassed the establishment of new media outlets in the Third World, multilateral oversight of satellite broadcasting and radio spectrum, and the promotion of two-way flows between the developing and developed worlds. At Nairobi, UNESCO also created an expert commission to examine the state of global communications, the International Commission for the Study of Communication Problems, also known as the MacBride Commission, which is analyzed in the following chapter.

In the United States, the NWIO proposals attracted the attention of hedgehogs on either side of the political aisle. Herbert Schiller offered his enthusiastic support, seizing the opportunity to reiterate that "national control" was preferable to "external domination."[54] Meanwhile, American conservatives attacked the NWIO as the product of a conspiracy between the Soviet Union and its Third World clients. This polarization illustrated the political appeal of intellectual oversimplification as both hardline cultural-sovereignty advocates and their free-market foes tended to reduce the conflict into an expedient set of oppositions: state versus market, Third World versus First World, and so on. Some scholars who study this period have followed suit, associating cultural concerns with Third World authoritarianism and Soviet–Third World collusion. The historian Roland Burke offers perhaps the strongest statement of this position, asserting that cultural relativism bears a "close association with authoritarian practices" and "[provides] a powerful excuse for those who murder, torture, and abuse Third World people."[55]

For policymakers and observers caught between these poles, however, the situation did not appear so simple. As this chapter has shown, cultural concepts appealed to many left-liberal and centrist figures in Europe and elsewhere, an appeal demonstrated by Jean d'Arcy's references to "cultural identity" and "cultural heritage" and Richard's Hoggart's to "cultural diversity." On the eve of the maturation of direct-broadcast satellites capable of beaming signal directly to individual receivers, the growing chorus of cultural concerns in international institutions revealed an emerging fault line between mainstream communications discourse in the United States and elsewhere. It would yield unexpected synergies between ex-colonial and developing states—as well as growing American hostility to international regulation—in the years that followed.

7

"A Global First Amendment War"

FREEDOM OF INFORMATION ON THE VERGE OF THE NEOLIBERAL ERA

Third World vs. the Media

—New York Times (1980)

[A] bid for government control of the press.

—Newsweek (1980)

UNESCO's Protection Racket

—Washington Post (1979)

[A] Global First Amendment War

—Time (1980)

These were just a few of the reactions that appeared in the American press in the late 1970s and early 1980s to a UNESCO initiative to study media flows and freedoms around the world. The initiative was the International Commission for the Study of Communication Problems, also called the MacBride Commission after its chairman, the Irish diplomat Seán Mac-Bride. While it may seem surprising that UNESCO—an organization with a slight presence in the American media—drew such vituperative attention, the MacBride Commission pursued its work on one of the key battlegrounds of the late Cold War: the relationship between states and the media. The issues discussed by the MacBride Commission—composed of members from sixteen countries, including the United States and the Soviet Union—ranged from how to ensure journalists' safety to the proper scope of government regulation of media to whether imbalanced information flows could be remedied through international efforts. Reflecting the outlook of mainstream American media, of the 141 pieces on the commission that appeared in the *New York Times* between 1976 and 1983, the tone was, one First Amendment scholar concludes, "almost uniformly hostile."[1]

The principle of government involvement in the media had not always been so divisive. Just a decade earlier, the U.S. government had poured money into developing broadcasting infrastructure in Vietnam.[2] It had also pursued an ambitious program for public-interest radio and television broadcasting, creating the Corporation for Public Broadcasting in 1967. The controversy spurred a decade later by the MacBride Commission stemmed in part from the commission's apparent departure from principles of transparency and freedom of conscience, which animated a great deal of American civil-society and nongovernmental activism in the 1970s. Domestically, legislation designed to promote governmental transparency—the Freedom of Information Act, passed in 1966—gained real teeth in 1974 through a series of amendments passed in Watergate's aftermath.[3] In foreign policy the 1970s were the decade when nongovernmental organizations like Amnesty International began to shape interstate diplomacy by pressuring governments to respect civil liberties. The Helsinki Final Act, signed by the United States, the Soviet Union, and thirty-three other nations in 1975, mandated respect for individual human rights.[4]

But the MacBride Commission uproar also stemmed from a parallel shift that has received less attention from human-rights historians. This related to the information policies that many Republicans and some Democrats were embracing in the 1970s: deregulation and privatization, often grouped together under the term "neoliberalism." With the ascension of Ronald Reagan to the leadership of the Republican Party, negative freedoms assumed pride of place in U.S. human-rights discourse and policies. In a sign of the changing times, the Heritage Foundation, a right-wing think tank that had appeared on the scene in the early 1970s, lambasted one UNESCO meeting participant for "stating blithely that freedom of the press does not mean very much to people who cannot buy TVs or radios"—an idea that had attracted broad international consensus in the

1960s, when positive freedoms were touted by development authorities in many countries.[5]

A key factor behind American policy intellectuals' growing antagonism to positive freedoms was their anticipation of new commercial and political opportunities for digital communications technologies. The MIT political scientist Ithiel de Sola Pool epitomized this shift away from the developmental approach that had dominated Vietnam-era Washington and toward neoliberal policies that prioritized market freedoms. In the 1960s Pool, like his peers Daniel Lerner and Wilbur Schramm, had embraced communications as a tool for modernization and development, in particular championing the application of social-science research to U.S. military aims in Vietnam.[6] But while Lerner and Schramm hewed more or less to the paradigm of state-driven development as they edged toward retirement, Pool, even as he navigated a cancer diagnosis, enjoyed a late-career renaissance as a theorist of communications liberalization. His 1983 work *Technologies of Freedom*, published just a year before his death, made the case for minimizing regulations on electronic and broadcast forms ranging from cable television to business communications on computer networks. For Pool, positive government engagement in communications was out; corporate prerogatives were in. This intellectual trajectory mirrored the broader transformations underway in American politics during the late 1970s and early 1980s, as many liberals and conservatives found common ground in seeking to trim the New Deal regulatory state.[7]

The maturation of digital media technologies also had international implications, which were hotly debated at the United Nations and its agencies. The MacBride Commission deliberations were one site of this debate. Much like the French television policymaker Jean d'Arcy's work on the right to communicate (discussed in chapter 6), the MacBride Commission attempted to reconcile disparate communications policies and values and to mediate East-West and North-South tensions, which were characterized by competing claims to liberty versus equality, free flow versus balanced flow, and technological advancement versus sovereignty. In turn, its deliberations would shape American discussions of freedom of information—though not in the ways many commission members had hoped. Rather than put its stamp on developed-world information policies, the MacBride

Commission would make its biggest impact through the controversies that it generated. The commission would be portrayed as a front for Soviet–Third World conspiracy by some of the more hysterically anticommunist American media outlets and think tanks.[8] On the eve of the digital age, these right-wing critics captured the American policy imagination, helping to shift the national discussion of freedom of information away from developmental multilateralism and toward neoliberal globalization. In response to the commission's reports, even moderate American commentators could find common ground with radical-right, anti-UN Heritage Foundation lobbyists: the development of direct-broadcast satellites and increasingly fast and flexible digital data-transmission technologies might elude foreign regulatory barriers. In other words, American policy elites fantasized that these technologies could maintain or even expand the United States' influence outside its borders in the face of international opposition.

ITHIEL DE SOLA POOL AND THE EXTERNALITIES OF THE FIRST AMENDMENT

Ithiel de Sola Pool has been remembered primarily for championing two seemingly unrelated political projects: he was an ardent supporter of the Vietnam War in the 1960s, and he was a leading advocate of the liberalization of domestic American communications industries in the late 1970s and early 1980s. More than unrelated, these positions might seem discordant with respect to the role of the state that Pool envisioned. In the first case, Pool portrayed it as a driver of the modernization of "traditional societies" in Southeast Asia. In the second case, the state had become a nuisance to technologically driven progress. This transition—from conventional modernization theory to neoliberal development—was doubly significant in that Pool was not just mirroring changes in the broader American political scene. As a well-connected policy intellectual whose Beltway contacts included Walt Rostow and Henry Kissinger, he was helping to propel the changes. How and why did Pool make this intellectual and political leap?

The change was slow at first. Pool, a committed and vocal participant in the collaboration between American social scientists and U.S. defense and intelligence agencies in Southeast Asia, was loath to admit the failure of U.S. counterinsurgency efforts there.[9] Even as domestic support for the Vietnam War began to hemorrhage in the late 1960s, Pool's hawkishness— he had dubbed the Defense Department "the world's largest training and educational institution"—remained undimmed. Writing to his Washington contacts in the wake of the Tet Offensive launched by North Vietnamese and Vietcong troops in January 1968, Pool continued to promise results from fieldwork on indigenous attitudes toward the South Vietnamese government. All that was needed, Pool thought, was to Vietnamize the project. Simultaneously, Pool proposed that U.S. military authorities devolve some administrative powers from the venal Saigon regime to village leaders. One Johnson administration official noted that the latter suggestion would actually require greater direct involvement by Washington.[10]

By the time the United States extracted its last personnel from Saigon in the mid-1970s, however, even Pool, the devoted cold warrior, could see that new tactics would be needed in the country's ongoing battle for global influence. Weighing in on the international satellite-broadcasting debates in 1975, Pool declared the threat of direct-broadcast satellites overblown. Even when direct broadcasting from satellites to individual home receivers was technically feasible, it would not be "economically rational" in most contexts. But Pool also admitted that anxieties about satellites stood in for a wider set of fears about technologies that were genuinely disruptive to "traditional" societies, which included films and videotapes as well as television broadcasts. Worrisomely, though the United States "would much prefer that the issue of human rights be fought out on such important matters as emigration from the Union of Soviet Socialist Republics," Soviet and other arguments that framed direct broadcasting as a violation of human rights appeared to have gained traction with developing states that were worried about preserving their "cultural integrity." "America faces a dilemma," Pool announced. "Direct-satellite broadcasting is not a matter of much importance to us, and we would like not to pick fights with friendly countries on such minor issues, but the principles and precedents at stake in this debate are important ones in other situations."

Pool's initial solution to the satellite-broadcasting controversies was to treat them as a serious but unfortunate distraction from the real work of socioeconomic development. At the same time, he was subtly refashioning what the task of development entailed. While still presumably supportive of development aid to help countries build up their communications capacities—i.e., modernization within national borders—Pool also indicated the desirability of increasing the flow of communications across national borders, which would help to "ease the pain of social change" in the developing world. In his 1975 reflection on the satellite debates, Pool suggested that the United States offer aid to developing countries to enhance two-way information flows through satellite television and satellite data transmission.[11] Here transnational flows took the place of the local and subnational dynamics Pool had focused upon in Vietnam, where he had emphasized the United States' capacity to shape the behavior of ordinary villagers as against that of the Saigon regime. Absent boots on the ground, two-way exchanges of information through high-speed communications technologies were coming to seem like the best possible means of achieving socioeconomic change.

Emblematic of this tactical shift was the unusual lesson that the long-time MIT professor attempted to draw from television in wartime Vietnam. Pool focused on the disparate responses of rural and urban audiences to South Vietnam's two-channel television system, which had gone on the air in 1966: whereas villagers preferred the channel with Vietnamese-language programming produced by Vietnamese authorities, urbanites tended to watch the English-language channel, putatively aimed at bored American troops. "The American programs attracted more or less educated, middle-class and modern sector employees because those programs related better to their culture than did the other channel," Pool explained. The implication was that if domestic media were inadequate, audiences would turn to foreign fare. (Pool also cited the success of imported BBC productions on American public television as an example of this phenomenon.) "Thus, there is a case to be made, not so much for defense of national cultures by protectionist barriers to foreign materials, but for positive fostering of production capabilities to meet otherwise unmet needs," Pool continued. "An open market for foreign imports is likely to demonstrate the existence of an unmet demand, to offer models and a learning experience for domestic producers and thus to result in a growth of local cultural expressions."[12]

This account of the recent history of Vietnamese television was revisionism of the highest order. Largely absent was the integral part played by U.S. military authorities and foreign-aid agencies in the "fostering of production capabilities" there (prior to the completion of ground transmitters in Saigon and elsewhere, television signal had actually been broadcast from a handful of Blue Eagle planes furnished by the Defense Department).[13] By likening wartime Vietnam to a "market" where the Pentagon had discovered "unmet demand," Pool was not so much providing a credible account of U.S. foreign policy as he was signaling the retreat of the state and the ascendance of the market in his own understanding of economic development.

As the decade drew to a close, market freedoms increasingly took priority in Pool's thinking. In a 1977 contribution to a volume of essays on Jean d'Arcy's concept of a "right to communicate," Pool suggested that one way to achieve greater public access to media was to encourage market competition. He repeated this argument in stronger terms in 1979 when he concluded that "[developing] countries should insist on the freest possible access by telecommunications to the best available information resources from anywhere in the world. It is in their interest to oppose all restrictions on the free flow of information. Copyright, security restrictions, and commercial restrictions . . . all check the progress of developing countries." The real agents of positive change, wrote Pool, were not states but rather the "communicators" of the world: the journalists, producers, and "technologists" with an interest in promoting the exchange of ideas and media across national frontiers. Again Pool's libertarianism was coupled with amnesia regarding the recent history of U.S. overseas interventionism. He argued that states were the perpetrators of the "largest part of all the oppression, brutality, and sadism in the world"—but rather than taking the opportunity to criticize U.S. actions in Southeast Asia, he singled out developing states for being "among the less enlightened." With this logic Pool also aimed to discredit the intergovernmental organizations that were then dominated by a majority of developing-world states. The relationship between the U.S. state and American overseas influence, on the other hand, remained opaque in his writing.[14]

It was against this backdrop that Pool composed his magnum opus on communications liberalization, *Technologies of Freedom* (1983), which made a complex yet forceful case that it was "not computers but policy that threatens freedom." Summarized in the most general way, the book addressed domestic policy questions and mingled civil-libertarian and free-market arguments for domestic deregulation. Pool argued, for instance, that the broadcasting regulations overseen by the U.S. Federal Communications Commission were being rendered obsolete by advances in communications technologies. In its 1943 *National Broadcasting Co. v. United States* decision, the Supreme Court had upheld the FCC's authority to regulate broadcasting spectrum on the grounds that spectrum was scarce resource. Pool argued, on the contrary, that "spectrum scarcity" was the shibboleth of well-intentioned but uncomprehending policymakers who failed to grasp how advancing technologies could squeeze more and more uses out of the same spectrum through multiplexing and other techniques. Rather than assign fixed spectrum bands to specific licensees, Pool concluded that policymakers should provide incentives for innovation by creating a market for spectrum, whereby owners could sell or lease their spectrum bands (an idea earlier elaborated by the British economist Ronald Coase). As it stood, the regulatory system for broadcasting overseen by the FCC and sanctioned by the U.S. judiciary did not provide a direct mechanism for spectrum trading. Not only did this system result in an inefficient use of spectrum, charged Pool; it also undermined the United States' First Amendment tradition by giving the federal government influence over who could and could not communicate over the airwaves.[15]

Scholarship on the history of neoliberalism has underscored how the free-market ideologues who were ascendant by the early 1980s in the United States and parts of Europe did not oppose state power per se but rather advocated for the selective mobilization of governmental and supra-governmental authority to protect private property and capital movement. It might be said in this regard that "deregulation" was a misnomer as applied to Pool's domestic program, which relied on certain forms of governance in order to roll back others. In order to realize a market for broadcasting spectrum, for instance, Pool recognized that the federal government would need to define and enforce property rights in spectrum. And in the few situations where a communications medium was genuinely scarce or where monopolies were naturally occurring, as had historically been the case in the telephone business, Pool thought it appropriate for the government to regulate communications providers as common carriers in order to ensure universal access. Pool wrote, "As long as the First Amendment stands, backed by courts which take it seriously, the loss of liberty is not foreordained. The commitment of American culture to pluralism and individual rights is reason for optimism, as is the pliancy and profusion of electronic technology." Thus, even Pool's ringing invocations of technological progress and consumer choice could not wholly excise government— in this instance the American judicial system—from the domestic picture.[16] In addition, a vigorous executive authority was needed to dissolve the existing apparatus of New Deal governance. Not long after the publication of *Technologies of Freedom*, Ronald Reagan's FCC issued a report intended to hollow out its own regulatory authority from within on the Poolian grounds that prior FCC efforts to ensure a balanced presentation of viewpoints on the airwaves—to enforce what was known as the "fairness doctrine"—were unnecessary in the dawning age of media abundance.[17]

It was when Pool set his sights abroad that governance as such— "[copyright], security restrictions, and commercial restrictions"—appeared to be a greater nuisance to connectivity and to business opportunities. For, though focused primarily on the domestic American scene, the conclusions Pool drew in *Technologies of Freedom* were rife with international implications. "The [regulatory] problem is worldwide," he wrote. "What is true for the United States is true, *mutatis mutandis*, for all free nations."[18] The problem was worldwide not only because many nations faced similar policymaking dilemmas regarding their internal communications. It was also worldwide because of the existence of cross-border flows of information and media. Pool noted that growing "problems encountered at the system boundaries"—over "national security, cultural protection, and trade advantage"—were "likely to be of growing importance in the electronic era." With this offhand observation Pool hinted that dissolving the economic and regulatory authority of foreign governments might simply be considered an externality of ensuring American media industries' First Amendment protections.[19]

It is worth pausing briefly to set Pool's work in the context of the late-twentieth-century evolution of American press and speech jurisprudence in order to understand how it reflected changing ideas about both the import and the geographical scope of the First Amendment. In his writings from the period Pool was participating in a broader rethinking of press and speech freedoms, whereby these freedoms were becoming more closely intertwined with market freedoms in the minds of at least some influential Americans. By the mid- to late 1970s commercial and corporate speech were beginning to enjoy First Amendment protections. In *Virginia State Board of Pharmacy v. Virginia Citizens' Consumer Council* (1976), the Supreme Court ruled that commercial advertising merited a certain level of First Amendment scrutiny. Two years later, in 1978's *First National Bank of Boston v. Bellotti*, the court overturned a Massachusetts law against corporate contributions to ballot referenda, ruling that the law abridged the bank's First Amendment rights. In *Technologies of Freedom*, Pool noted that Chief Justice Warren Burger's concurring opinion in the latter case "argued that if business corporations could be so restricted, then so could 'media conglomerates' which are corporations too." The old distinction between protected political speech and unprotected commercial speech was eroding.[20]

The imagined geography of these freedoms was also changing. In envisioning the globalization of the—free-market—First Amendment, Pool projected its guarantees far beyond what was legally recognized by either the U.S. Supreme Court or the international community. Presumably he knew as much. But the legal reality was not really the point; the point was the fantasy of American media conglomerates unfettered by regulations. As we shall see below, by the early 1980s, the exceptionalist trope of a "global First Amendment" was one that animated the mainstream American media.[21]

The global implications of Pool's neoliberal program were most obvious in his treatment of satellite and computer communications. The domestic American satellite industry had been liberalized under the Nixon administration, when the FCC adopted an "open skies" approach that established the prerogative of private interests (not just government entities or already-operating carriers) to pursue domestic satellite broadcasting. At the same time, for international satellite traffic the United States remained treaty bound to Intelsat, the official manager of commercial satellite communications for the Western bloc. What deregulation implied, Pool wrote, was the dissolution of this "domestic-international division." In a global variation on his argument about domestic broadcasting spectrum, Pool considered fears about the scarcity of satellite orbital slots to be over-blown given the ongoing refinement of satellite technology (many develop-ing states at the time feared being shut out of available slots and frequencies in the geostationary orbit, the narrow 18.6-mile-wide strip above the equa-tor used by most communications satellites). By Pool's lights, scarcity—which undergirded the international regulation of spectrum and orbital slots—was best dealt with on a planetary scale by "market mechanisms." Pool also forecast disruptions to telegraph and telephone regulations abroad, with newer telecommunications services, ranging from specialized business networks favored by airlines and banks to fax and data services enabling different types of machines to communicate, poised to challenge the national postal, telegraph, and telephone (PTT) monopolies that con-trolled physical infrastructure in many countries. In Europe, PTTs had resisted allowing these kinds of "value-added networks" to operate inde-pendently on their lines, but Pool suggested that these restrictions were stifling communication, educational, and economic opportunities.[22]

Pool's advocacy of communications liberalization thereby incorporated a vision of transnational flow that set fallible national and intergovern-mental regulatory institutions at odds with global, technologically driven progress. Absent in this vision was any conception of public or interna-tional institutions (such as PBS or UNESCO) as arenas for speech that might be marginalized by market mechanisms. Also marginalized were regulations designed to protect competing objectives like privacy and fair-ness. The longtime cold warrior, who not long before had vaunted the Pen-tagon's "training and educational" capabilities, had pivoted decisively toward markets as the best means for disciplining foreign rivals, not only in the global South but also in Europe. In the neoliberal communications agenda that Pool began to sketch in the 1970s and that found mature form in 1983's *Technologies of Freedom*, consumer choice and corporate liberties displaced the social guarantees that had been underwritten by postwar welfare states and at least nominally promoted by 1960s development experts.

"PROBLEMS ENCOUNTERED AT THE SYSTEM
BOUNDARIES": THE MACBRIDE COMMISSION DEBATES

By the 1970s the United Nations and UNESCO had become the center of overlapping debates over information flows, media policy, and state power. A far-flung group of nonaligned states was demanding a New World Information Order, the umbrella term for an array of proposals designed to redress asymmetric information flows from highly industrialized countries to the Third World and to remedy distorted representations of the Third World in the international press.[23] The UN Committee on the Peaceful Uses of Outer Space continued to debate the future of satellite broadcasting—an issue also central to NWIO advocates, who feared that the space powers would exhaust geostationary orbits and frequencies before developing countries could develop space capabilities. And at UNESCO, the Soviet Union and Belorussia attempted to tie sovereignty to antiapartheid rhetoric in a mass-media declaration designed to attract African support. This draft declaration, critics noted, would have granted states wide latitude to control the content flowing across their borders. A few years later a Soviet-African coalition linked up with the Arab states in a UN General Assembly resolution that termed Zionism a form of racism. The United States, Britain, France, and other delegations walked out of a UNESCO meeting in 1975 during which the anti-Zionism language was inserted into proposed media guidelines. There was thus a grain of truth to the charge that some American commentators began leveling in the mid-1970s that the snowballing controversies at UNESCO were the fruit of Soviet–Third World collusion.[24]

What was less accurate, but was asserted by some of these same commentators, was that all concerns about the transnational reach of Western—particularly American—information industries were the product of authoritarianism in the Soviet Union and the Third World. As we have seen in chapters 5 and 6, direct-broadcast satellites and cultural concerns formed flashpoints of debate between the United States and many of its allies in Western Europe and Canada in the late 1960s and early 1970s. One German development expert, Dietrich Berwanger, pointed out that Third World communications concerns had been foreshadowed by

Western European resistance to U.S. information diplomacy during the early Cold War. Berwanger referred to the work of the postwar French journalist Jacques Kayser to establish European antecedents to the 1970s communications debates: already in the 1950s Kayser had been troubled by North-South disparities and the subordination of the public good to commercial considerations. Berwanger also cited Richard Hoggart: "[The] communication debate started before the New [International] Economic Order [the set of Third World demands that inspired the NWIO] was posited and so exists in its own right." The boundaries between the "West" and the "rest" were porous not only because of advancing communications technologies, these antecedents suggested. Ideas—criticisms of Western and especially U.S. information policies—also cut across borders and blocs.[25]

It was in this fraught atmosphere that UNESCO, at its 1976 General Conference, created the International Commission for the Study of Communication Problems, or the MacBride Commission, which it tasked with studying "all the problems of communication in contemporary society seen against the background of technological progress and recent developments in international relations." The Irish diplomat and Nobel Peace Prize laureate Seán MacBride was tapped to chair the commission, which also featured the influential French newspaperman Hubert Beuve-Méry and the Colombian writer Gabriel Garcia Márquez. The commission met eight times from 1977 to 1979, consulting scores of papers by a far-flung cast of scholars and media professionals as it drew up its report. The authors of these papers were politically eclectic, ranging from Ithiel de Sola Pool, Wilbur Schramm, and Leonard Sussman (director of the center-right American think tank Freedom House) to critics of American empire including Herbert I. Schiller and Luis Ramiro Beltrán. Hubert Beuve-Méry, Jean d'Arcy, and Henry Cassirer also contributed papers.[26]

The MacBride Commission was born of an issue familiar from the development programs of the preceding two decades, namely the North-South economic breach. Now, however, there was greater sensitivity to the cultural dimensions of material imbalances—the ways developing-world media were shaped by Western advertising and propaganda, for instance, or how developing-world issues went chronically underreported in the developed world. Two issues in particular triggered fierce controversy at the commission: how to ensure the safety of foreign correspondents, and the transnational activities of powerful commercial media outlets. On the first point, the imperative to protect journalists from physical harm seemed self-evident to many commissioners. Seán MacBride, himself a former journalist, advocated for a UN convention to protect journalists from state repression. "[The] need for such a convention is greater than ever," Mac-Bride explained in a 1978 speech to the International Press Institute. "[There] are, proportionately in number, more journalists killed or reported 'missing' than members of any other professions."[27]

Not everyone agreed with MacBride, however. In an echo of failed League of Nations efforts to set up an international arbitration system to counteract misinformation, proposals to codify journalists' rights and responsibilities met with fierce criticism from observers who were worried that such a convention would actually serve to empower governments to censor or harass anyone who reported unflattering stories. An "international code of conduct for journalists . . . [would] be very difficult to structure without raising all the old concerns about state control of the media," the U.S. International Communications Agency's Roland Homet wrote to Jean d'Arcy, who also opposed a code (the ICA was briefly the successor to the USIA).[28] In a long private letter to MacBride, *Time's* Henry Grunwald praised MacBride's concern for journalists' safety but similarly noted that "when correspondents are singled out for special treatment it is usually to put them under restraints." Ithiel de Sola Pool glossed, "The danger in claiming special rights . . . is that privileges which legislators give, they can easily take away." The American participant on the commission, Columbia Journalism School dean (later Stanford professor) Elie Abel, also resolutely opposed a "planetary code for journalists of all nations."[29]

A particular sticking point for American observers was how a putative code might address the responsibilities, not just the liberties, of journalists and the press. Freedom House's director, Leonard Sussman, wrote to Seán MacBride to refute the notion that press "responsibility" should accompany press freedoms. Sussman cited the 1975 Helsinki Accords: The "freer flow of information called for" by the accords "would be made a cruel

sham" by such regulations. Similarly, in his paper on the right to communicate, Ithiel de Sola Pool conceptualized responsibility as a concession to
authoritarian demands: "In response to such political attacks on the liberal
concept of freedom, there is some tendency to retreat to alternative formu-
lations, for example, 'free and responsible press' instead of 'free press,' or
'freedom to' instead of 'freedom from.'"[30]

Most immediately, this dualistic worldview—liberalism versus authoritarianism, freedom versus responsibility—spoke to the very real distance
between Western and Third Worldist viewpoints, particularly between
Americans and the commissioner associated with the most "extreme"
Third Worldist position, Tunisia's Mustapha Masmoudi. In a paper prepared for the commission, "The New World Information Order," Masmoudi backed an internationally enforceable code. "Affirmation of the
ethical principles intended to govern journalism," declared the Tunisian
diplomat, "involves as a corollary the responsibility of those in control
of information, who should be accountable for the consequences of any
violation of such principles." For Masmoudi, accountability meant much
more than industry self-regulation. It entailed a mesh of binding legal regulations: both international agreements and the modification of domestic
legislation in contracting states would be necessary in order to ensure that
the media was "accountable to the community to which it belongs." Sovereignty, in this scenario, trumped flow.[31]

But, more subtly, Pool's and Sussman's thinking also reflected the rift
between the emerging neoliberal conception of information freedoms and
earlier discussions of responsibility and regulation among American news
professionals and policymakers. In the 1940s many New Deal liberals had
contended that American newspapers had been delinquent in denouncing
authoritarianism and fascism precisely because profiteering press magnates
lacked a sense of responsibility, concerns reflected in the title of the
Hutchins Commission's 1947 report, *A Free and Responsible Press*.[32] While
in the report the Hutchins Commission had backed away from calling for
government regulation of press responsibilities (instead recommending
industry self-regulation), the issue of regulatory oversight of media content
was far from settled, particularly with regard to broadcast media. The FCC
had set the fairness doctrine into place in 1949, shortly after the Hutchins
report's publication, and it was upheld by the Supreme Court two decades

later on the grounds that the "right of the public to receive suitable access to social, political, esthetic, moral, and other ideas" trumped the right of broadcasters to exclude perspectives they did not like from the airwaves.[33] But Pool and Sussman were less concerned with fidelity to this complex historical record than with the achievement of certain policy outcomes. By treating responsibility and regulation as essentially exogenous to the American media tradition, Pool, Sussman, and others sought to justify an antiregulatory approach to information policy on both the domestic and international scales.

Amnesia was also evident in American attitudes toward industrial concentration in the media. Not so long before, New Dealers had criticized concentration in the newspaper industry as a threat to American democracy. Pool was more sanguine, forecasting that the growing reach of digital technologies would foster competition, not concentration, since in the digital age "many alternatives exist for the delivery of every service." But one constant from the New Deal liberalism of the 1940s through the antiregulatory liberalism of the 1970s was that both tended to skirt the international consequences of domestic concentration: "monopoly" was a word Americans seldom used to describe what their corporations were up to abroad. While in the 1940s this would have applied primarily to Hollywood and the American news agencies, by the 1970s American corporations were getting involved in a greater and greater range of information activities abroad, including television broadcasting and telecommunications. Commentators outside U.S. borders were more inclined to view the transnational activities of powerful media outfits—especially press agencies and television exporters—in terms of monopoly or oligopoly. Federico Mayor, a Spanish scientist and deputy director general (later director general) at UNESCO, reminded the International Press Institute in 1979 that developed countries circulated "80 per cent of the total volume of information in the world, mainly through five major [press] agencies which devote less than a quarter of this volume to the problems" of the developing world. Hence the need to challenge the "monopoly" on knowledge held by the few, and the "power conferred by that monopoly."[34]

Still, through the drafting and debating of the MacBride Commission report, Americans found common ground with others in the Western camp. The semantics of the New World Information Order drew fire from both sides of the Atlantic. In Washington, Roland Homet, recalling the dystopian fictions of George Orwell and Aldous Huxley and the real-life nightmare of Nazism, stated plainly that information was "by its nature disorderly" while the American MacBride participant Elie Abel likewise questioned the use of the word "order" to describe information dynamics. Hubert Beuve-Méry and Jean d'Arcy shared similar perspectives. Beuve-Méry expressed skepticism over the "questionable vocabulary we have inherited, notably this 'new world information order,'" which "runs a strong risk of being the cause of—or the pretext for—numerous misunderstandings." And d'Arcy wrote to Homet in 1979 that the "use of the word 'order'" in this context "is even more improper in [the] French language . . . than it is already in [English]." Even the Soviet member of the MacBride Commission pointed out its echo of the Nazi New Order.[35]

On the more politically immediate question of whether the MacBride Commission should endorse a code of journalistic liberties and responsibilities, the First World bloc also coalesced. Commentators whose countries accorded greater power to governmental authorities to regulate potentially inflammatory news tended to be more amenable than their American counterparts to balancing journalistic liberties and responsibilities. Hubert Beuve-Méry argued that certain occasions merited journalistic discretion or even government intervention, citing as an example the controversial decision by the French police to cut short-wave radio transmissions during the May 1968 protests. However, for Beuve-Méry this example broached the question of timing—would the immediate release of information do physical harm?—rather than the question of whether or not to release information in due course. In the final analysis Beuve-Méry thought that responsibility was an ethical issue best served by nourishing journalists' commitment to human rights, which he suggested a binding code could not achieve. D'Arcy likewise concluded that responsibility was never enriched by restricting liberty.[36]

The concerted efforts of Abel, Beuve-Méry, and others to defend the principle of journalistic freedoms made an impact on the MacBride Commission's work. As a delegate to deliberations on the MacBride Commission's 1978 interim report, Jean d'Arcy had offered pointed criticisms: the interim report, a "mosaic" that "lacked a unifying structure," placed "too much emphasis on sovereignty and not enough on interdependence" (he could not have been pleased by the interim report's brief treatment of the right to communicate, which expressed the hope that "recognition of [it] can constitute a step forward towards the establishment of a new world information order").[37] Revisions made between the MacBride Commission's interim and final reports, the latter published in 1980 as *Many Voices, One World*, appeared to offer some relief. The final report opposed an internationally administered code and licensing system for journalists: "Journalists will be fully protected only when everyone's human rights are guaranteed." Modifications were also evident in the treatment that *Many Voices, One World* accorded to the right to communicate, which it now treated as advancing the "democratization of communication on all levels—international, national, local, individual."[38] At UNESCO's 1980 General Conference in Belgrade, d'Arcy, acting as an official voice of the French National Commission, announced his approval of the MacBride Commission's final report:

> In affirming . . . pluralism as a duty, [and] free access to all sources as the condition of unbiased and balanced information, in requesting the removal of censorship and the abolition of monopolies, in refusing the establishment of a worldwide ethical code [for journalists] and the provision of press identification cards by governments, the Report . . . establishes, for all, the profound connection between information and democracy.[39]

Like Jean d'Arcy, American commission member Elie Abel had also expressed grave reservations during the preparation of the MacBride Commission report. Abel had charged, in correspondence with the UNESCO secretariat, that changes had been improperly smuggled into drafts of the final version without being considered by the commission. He threatened not to sign it and ultimately appended numerous dissenting footnotes, including one in which he argued that the commission had seen "[no] evidence" to back the idea that valuable scientific, technical, and industrial information might be hoarded by wealthy governments and corporations.[40] Yet in the end, Abel, too, would defend the published version,

Many Voices, One World. The final report, "for all its shortcomings, comes down hard against censorship, against licensing of journalists, against information autarky," the journalism professor concluded in a 1980 speech at the University of Pennsylvania. Later that year, Abel told the American trade magazine *Editor & Publisher* that "UNESCO was moving much more strongly toward censorship three years ago than it is today since the publication of the MacBride Report." Ongoing engagement with developing-world concerns would make the American press and the United States stronger, not weaker, internationally, he concluded. "We are dealing with a genuine Third World movement to gain control of its future," Abel reflected, noting that "35 years ago the majority was with us, while today the Third World is the majority and we are growing more isolated." Having worked as a foreign correspondent in Berlin, Belgrade, and New Delhi, Abel urged American journalists to stay at the table, to "listen to, and understand, the different cultures we are dealing with on this planet."[41]

But this conciliatory gesture, however perceptive, was ultimately beside the point. At the same moment when Abel appeared to acknowledge cultural difference as a legitimate factor in the difficult work of multilateral negotiation, the very premise of multilateralism was coming under attack as a threat to the free flow of information.

"ELECTRONICS TAKES COMMAND": THE UNITED STATES' NEOLIBERAL TURN

The reaction to the MacBride Commission's final report in the American press and the American policymaking community was highly critical. Libertarian *Reason* magazine charged, incorrectly, that the final report had backed a licensing system for journalists and a code of journalistic ethics. The *New York Times* tersely summarized the report as "part of a prolonged effort by third world nations, supported by the Soviet bloc, to break what they regard as Western dominance of international news gathering and the technical means of communication." *Time* magazine's assessment was among the more measured. It framed *Many Voices, One World*—"160,000 words of glutinous UNESCOese"—as the result of concerted efforts at "[damage] control" by the commission's liberals and moderates. The report had ultimately "rejected the wilder" demands of NWIO advocates by opposing state censorship and by backing journalists' access to diverse sources of information. Nevertheless, *Time* warned, the battle was far from over, as authoritarian states continued to seek restrictions on freedom of information through UNESCO and other channels. "All that Abel and his colleagues achieved was a postponement of the crisis," echoed *Newsweek*.[42]

A growing movement of new-right policy intellectuals, pushing for a U.S. retreat from UN institutions, delighted in exploiting the West-versus-the-rest antinomy suggested by these international confrontations over media policy. In Washington right-wing think tanks weighed in on the MacBride Report. One of the most vitriolic responses came from the Heritage Foundation, which was then lobbying the Reagan administration to withdraw from UNESCO. The foundation—established in 1973 to rebut the notion that "statist ideas would bring peace and prosperity," according to one adulatory account—framed the MacBride Commission as a Soviet–Third World conspiracy and labeled Seán MacBride one of UNESCO's "Moscow-aligned radicals." Although Heritage admitted that *Many Voices, One World* had not called outright for state control of media, it nevertheless flagged the commission's "heavy attack" on the "free market principle of Western commercial media" and tarred the right to communicate as a red herring for "government control of the press in the name of Third World development" ("They have also created the 'right to education' and the 'right to culture' for similar political motives").[43]

Whereas ad hominem vitriol suffused the polemics of the Heritage Foundation, Freedom House struck a more measured tone in its assessments of UNESCO and the MacBride Commission. Director Leonard Sussman's participation in the MacBride Commission deliberations was telling of the tactical and intellectual differences dividing moderate Republicans from new-right insurgents. In his 1978 paper for the commission, Sussman acknowledged global media dynamics that were not reducible to Cold War tensions. He admitted, for instance, that developing-world issues were underreported in the developed world and were often crammed into a Cold War framework when they were reported. However, in the final analysis, like the Heritage Foundation, Sussman hewed to a bipolar worldview. His MacBride Commission paper concluded, "[Despite] the considerable ideological pluralism among nation-states, there are only two fundamentally, philosophically opposite news media systems: the government-controlled and the government-free"—or "market" and "non-market" systems.[44] It was as if the matrix of political possibility had been compressed into a single digital bit, in which only two positions were possible: on or off, one or zero, market or nonmarket, free or unfree.

Amid Heritage Foundation fantasies of a "world without a UN," centrists and liberals remained committed to international institutions.[45] International law expert Charles N. Brower reported to the American Bar Association that though ensuring free flow remained a priority, the "appropriate solution" to NWIO demands was "not to adopt domestic legislation which would eliminate or curtail the United States' contributions to UNESCO in violation of U.S. obligations under international law." Former USIA director Leonard Marks emphasized that the United States would lose leverage—a chance to make its voice heard—if it exited international institutions such as UNESCO (a possibility that Marks nevertheless thought unlikely). On the "center-right," Sussman and Freedom House were likewise committed to keeping the United States in international institutions. A Gallup poll reported in 1984 that Americans who were already aware of UNESCO tended to support the United States staying in the organization, in the face of the Reagan administration's threats to withdraw.[46]

But the damage had already been done. The MacBride Commission debates were ultimately less noteworthy for the diplomatic accords they generated than for how they stimulated an emerging American consensus on the free flow of information: American commentators from the far Right to the liberal center were beginning to converge around the ways in which advances in communications technologies might maintain or expand information flows in the event that foreign or intergovernmental bodies opposed American globalizing ambitions. Elie Abel's writings illustrated the allure of this discourse of technologically driven globalization to American elites, including liberals receptive to multilateralism. Abel had rejected a Cold War reading of the MacBride Commission and had advocated a nuanced view of developing-world concerns. Nevertheless, even Abel could appreciate the ways in which technology might soon enable the United States to circumvent regulatory authorities abroad. A 1980 article that Abel coauthored for the *New York Times Magazine* concluded portentously:

> [The] pace of technology may well outrun the ability of international political institutions to catch up. For example, there is in force today an international treaty prohibiting direct broadcast of television signals from a satellite into a country without that country's permission. The treaty is self-enforcing because current television sets cannot receive signals from satellites without an enormously expensive dish-shaped antenna.... But both American and Japanese companies are in the process of developing dishes that may in time become so cheap that families who can afford a television set...will be able to afford a dish as well. Governments may struggle to control the flow of news and information across their borders, but satellites and the technology behind them may make such efforts futile. The jinni may already be out of the bottle.[47]

The implication was that the United States might abandon multilateralism for more unilateral exercises of power once it could circumvent international mediation through advancing communications technologies. "Electronics takes command," as Pool put it, advancing a vision of life transformed by these technologies, though his vision might more accurately be described as "electronics and neoliberal policies take command."[48]

The title of Abel's article, "Third World vs. the Media," concealed as much as it revealed. As we have seen, by 1980 the most extreme or autarkic Third Worldist information proposals, such as those of Tunisia's Mustapha Masmoudi, had met their defeat in the final MacBride report. In Abel's article the "Third World" was more red herring than impending threat. The real geography at issue in the contest for information markets was not the developing world per se. It was global, with European postal, telegraph, and telephone administrations (PTTs) as well as emerging markets targeted. Well-placed Americans in both business and government were keenly aware of the economic and strategic advantages that hinged on ongoing U.S. leadership in communications technologies and set about to link this leadership to the normative principles of free flow and freedom of information—trotting out the "Third World" straw man as needed.[49]

By a similar rhetorical sleight of hand, international opposition to unregulated information flows could be framed as a threat to domestic American values. In its 1980 article "The Global First Amendment War," *Time* magazine warned, "The information battle is widening, not narrowing, to encompass not only news but [also] . . . the images that will shortly be carried by direct satellite broadcasting." The article was notable for multiple reasons. First, for the way it implicitly included satellite television and its "images" in the realm of protected First Amendment speech. This pointed to the ways in which, in domestic jurisprudence, press and speech freedoms had expanded to encompass new formats and new kinds of speech since the 1940s. In 1952, for instance, film had been accorded First Amendment protection, while in the 1970s, as discussed above, the Supreme Court extended a level of First Amendment scrutiny to commercial and corporate speech.[50] Content and form were thus coming to matter less and less in many Americans' understanding of press and speech freedoms.

Second, for the underlying suggestion embedded in the title of "The Global First Amendment War" that the First Amendment to the U.S. Constitution was, in fact, global. This assumption signified a striking reversal from official pronouncements on satellites in the 1960s, when President Johnson had reassured foreign governments that satellite broadcasting would not impinge upon their "vital sovereignty over domestic communications."[51] It also pointed to the significance of domestic jurisprudence for the global "information battle," even if its ramifications were more aspirational and discursive than judicable.[52] When MPAA head Eric Johnston had written to Eleanor Roosevelt at the UN Human Rights Commission in 1946 to argue that film merited inclusion in international freedom-of-information negotiations, he had done so on the grounds that film helped to inform both national and international audiences, thereby preserving a distinction—common in the early to mid-twentieth century— between protected political speech and unprotected entertainment speech. In the information battle of the early 1980s, by contrast, "information" had largely shed this older, normative connotation—the "action of informing"—and referred instead to emerging technologies and communications networks. In the dawning neoliberal era it did not matter whether what was being transmitted was newscasts or Hollywood fluff or Coca-Cola commercials or financial records. Maintaining the flow of information into foreign markets *was* the battle.[53]

The discursive convergence of speech freedoms with market freedoms shaped the trade and information policies that Americans pursued in the 1980s and beyond. Like Hollywood's representatives in 1945, American media professionals in the 1980s touted the free flow of information to oppose foreign regulatory regimes. Only now a greater range of media technologies was at stake. Among the "media conglomerates" then shaping the American economy were highly integrated corporations seeking to export not only films but also television programs, videocassettes, and associated merchandise abroad. They clashed with, among others, the European regulators who held the keys to the most valuable overseas television and video market (in 1988 the European market absorbed $1.8 billion out of a total $2.5 billion in American television and film exports—the fulcrum that "[turned] many losers into big money-makers").[54] At the Uruguay round of negotiations for the General Agreement on Tariffs and Trade (GATT), which stretched from 1986 to 1994, France sought a "cultural exception" to exempt audiovisual productions from the trade liberalization measures sought by the United States—part of a broader array of antineoliberal solidarities then beginning to fuel transnational and international efforts to protect cultural diversity, which also encompassed the Slow Food movement and the rise of Europe's Green Parties.[55] Predictably, Hollywood reacted with hostility couched in freedom talk. "Filmmakers cannot exist without freedom," said Steven Spielberg. "Filmmakers can find no comfort when their film is barred, or restricted, or otherwise frustrated when they try to take work to the global public." Martin Scorsese echoed, "Whenever I hear of quotas and restrictions that would affect the free circulation of a filmmaker's work outside of his or her own country, I become alarmed." On the eve of the formation of the World Trade Organization (or WTO, which replaced the GATT), Americans touted free flow and consumer choice to combat the cultural and industrial concerns of foreign trading partners.[56]

In addition to seeking looser regulations on exporting content, power-ful American corporations in the late 1970s and early 1980s were also inter-ested in loosening the regulations that applied to transmission across bor-ders. IBM, for instance, had a substantial stake in point-to-point satellite communications technologies. These technologies were intended to enable companies to elide national PTT monopolies by exchanging communica-tions ranging from phone and video calls to faxes and data files via satellite. To those who claimed that such a setup violated the integrity of national communications systems, proponents countered that the tariffs and pri-vacy regulations erected by foreign governments violated the free flow of information.[57]

At UNESCO's 1980 Belgrade conference, Jean d'Arcy had puzzled over Americans' hardline reactions to the MacBride Report and the New World Information Order. D'Arcy thought that these uncompromising responses reflected the United States' isolation in the face of the interna-tional community, in particular the majority of developing-world coun-tries. But isolation—put another way, unilateralism—was precisely the point. As Ithiel de Sola Pool had argued, it was the "communicators" of the world, not governments or intergovernmental organizations, who offered the "best hope" that "progress will be made toward creating the global sys-tem of low cost and unfettered communication that the developing coun-tries require to progress."[58] The United States' withdrawal from UNESCO in 1984 crystallized its move away from multilateral development coopera-tion and toward globalizing strategies that purposefully diminished the sovereignty of its foreign competitors, away from the agonies of postwar liberalism and toward neoliberalism.

Epilogue

FREE FLOW BYTES BACK?

On January 21, 2010, Hillary Clinton, then U.S. secretary of state under President Barack Obama, gave a much-publicized speech at the Newseum in Washington, D.C., declaring that the time had come to "synchronize our technological progress with our principles" and make internet freedom a universal right and a cornerstone of U.S. foreign policy. Clinton treated this initiative as the latest chapter in a storied American tradition, citing the early American quest to ensure robust political discussion through the crafting of the First Amendment and Franklin Roosevelt's rhetorical appeals to globalize "freedom of expression" during the Second World War. This book, however, suggests a different genealogy for early twenty-first-century U.S. internet diplomacy: it formed the digital-age apotheosis of the free-flow policies pursued by the United States since 1945.

Clinton's Newseum speech exhibited many of the key markers of free-flow globalism explored in this book. First, it recapitulated the dualistic understanding of press and speech freedoms that had crystallized in the United States during the early Cold War. The major threat to freedom of information worldwide, in Clinton's telling, came from government censorship, which she likened to a "new information curtain ... descending across much of the world." But this framework was more a legacy of the anticommunist consensus than it was of Roosevelt's presidency; nowhere did she express concern over the kinds of monopolistic corporate power that had so worried New Deal liberals in the 1930s and 1940s. Meanwhile, Clinton's optimistic view of the developmental potential of information technologies borrowed a page from the playbook of midcentury modernization experts. "A connection to global information networks is like an on-ramp to modernity," she asserted, sounding like Daniel Lerner and Wilbur Schramm when they claimed that new broadcasting technologies would help developing societies move from a hidebound past into the modern present—as if these societies were not living in the present already. Finally, the secretary of state's historical allusions served to mask the neoliberal vintage of some of her propositions. "If corporate decision makers don't have access to global sources of news and information, investors will have less confidence in their decisions over the long term," Clinton stated. "Countries that censor news and information must recognize that from an economic standpoint, there is no distinction between censoring political speech and commercial speech." As we have seen, this conflation of corporate prerogatives with individual liberties stems not from the founding era or the 1940s but rather from the antiregulatory understanding of information freedoms that gained jurisprudential momentum in the United States in the 1970s.[1]

In 2010 this amalgam of antiregulatory and developmental policy positions was a largely bipartisan one. By coincidence, the very same day as Clinton's Newseum appearance, the Supreme Court declared in its five-to-four *Citizens United* decision that corporations enjoy a First Amendment right to pursue unlimited election spending. Although *Citizens United* nominally treated the prerogative of a right-wing nonprofit to disseminate a film attacking none other than Hillary Clinton—and although she would disparage the decision in her 2016 presidential campaign—examining the speech alongside the contemporaneous court decision suggests political consensus in certain important regards. Notably, both the liberal secretary of state and the conservative court majority implied that on the whole, the source or quality of the information mattered less than the quantity available. (Clinton: "[Information] has never been so free. There are more ways to spread more ideas to more people than at any moment in history." *Citizens United*: "[It] is our law and our tradition that more speech, not less, is the governing rule.") Neither Clinton nor the court majority dwelled overmuch on the prospect of efforts by foreign corporations or actors to influence domestic affairs.[2]

How American discussions of information flows have changed since January 21, 2010. Donald Trump's defeat of Hillary Clinton in the 2016 presidential election was facilitated by free-flow norms enabling clickbait and fake-news stories to flood American social media accounts from overseas in the lead-up to the election. In its aftermath Americans have found themselves debating the problems of misinformation and hate speech and the regulatory status of social media with new intensity. The qualitative question of "What counts as information?" has come to the forefront as journalists and scholars have striven to make sense of an election tainted by fake news and hostile hackers. For a number of years, technology critics like Evgeny Morozov, Alexander Galloway, and Jaron Lanier have expressed skepticism about the extent to which digital communications have really liberated us. In the post-2016 world, their critiques are finding a louder echo as others acknowledge that free flow alone may not be enough to secure the national interest or the greater good.[3]

But digitization is only the most recent chapter in this story. The longer history of American political, economic, and cultural power explored in this book has also helped to produce the predicament in which Americans now find themselves. The dilemmas of the digital age were structured by analog-era policies privileging quantitative metrics and antiregulatory liberties as the measure of true freedom of information. The major difference is that in the analog era, these policies were underpinned by the assumption—no longer tenable in the post-2016 world—that the information in question was flowing outward from the United States, not into it.[4]

Unsurprisingly given this state of affairs, the figures who foreshadowed our current debates most powerfully were not Americans. Rather, as we have seen, they were observers based outside U.S. borders, a better position from which to observe the upshots of American free-flow globalism. During the early Cold War, foreign scholars, policymakers, and functionaries working in new international institutions emphasized the threat that powerful commercial interests posed to media industries in smaller states. In the decades that followed, as television spread—and then as direct-to-home satellite broadcasting appeared on the horizon—some pursued legal means of regulating American television imports and satellite transmissions. Others called for new multilateral and regional media initiatives in Europe, in the Third World, and between the two in order to counter American influence.[5] Much as the rhetoric of American free-flow advocates mingled lofty ideals with self-interest, their critics pursued a variety of objectives, from fighting for a more egalitarian global distribution of resources to maneuvering defensively to protect existing cultural and linguistic hierarchies, from pushing for a strong state presence in the media to emphasizing how cross-border exchange might benefit regional and transnational publics. What they all had in common was an understanding of "free flow" as an American ideology that dovetailed with American interests if not necessarily their own.

To date, these stories have been left out of U.S. history not because positive freedoms or qualitative considerations have historically failed to animate policymakers or intellectuals; rather, their invisibility is largely an artifact of post-1945 American exceptionalism. The historian Daniel Rodgers has noted how the Second World War marked the end of a decades-long period of mutually enriching transatlantic exchange between American and European policy intellectuals: seeing their country as the righteous power that saved Europe from Hitler, and soon preoccupied by the Soviet menace, Americans became less receptive to ideas emanating from elsewhere.[6] This exceptionalist confidence was reflected in the media contests and transformations (explored in this book) in which Washington persistently disregarded criticisms emanating from abroad. Immediately after the war, Americans combatted international efforts to remedy the enormous global disparity in newsprint consumption, painting regulation (more than widespread austerity) as the fundamental threat to the free flow of information. In the 1960s Washington helped to spread television and satellite broadcasting in the developing world—but also attempted to downplay emerging controversies over the political economy of these technologies. In the 1980s and 1990s the United States began to elide the multilateral forums of the United Nations and UNESCO—the establishment of which in the 1940s had been considered an achievement even by business elites like Kent Cooper and David Sarnoff—in favor of neoliberal, corporate-friendly institutions like the World Bank and the new World Trade Organization.[7]

For roughly twenty-five years following the end of the Cold War, quantitative concerns continued to dominate mainstream American discussions of information freedoms. What has been called the "quantitative politics" of the libertarian technophiles at *Wired* magazine translated, in foreign-policy terms, into an almost unbridled enthusiasm for the global expansion and the thickening of high-speed digital communications networks. This enthusiasm reached its apex during the Arab Spring in 2011, when the American commentariat and the State Department championed online free flow as a weapon against tyranny.[8] The flip side to this was fierce criticism of any kind of international regulation on the grounds that it threatened free-flow principles, as in 2014 when the *New York Times* and the *Wall Street Journal* castigated the European Union's announcement of a "right to be forgotten," which gave EU residents the legal right to demand that search engines remove potentially damaging information about them from online searches. To explicate the historical roots of the decision, the *Times* and the *Wall Street Journal* turned to the selfsame expert, a Yale Law professor who explained that the right to be forgotten had emerged from long-standing European traditions regarding the "protection of personal honor" (the *Times*), in particular a "culture in France and Germany that once allowed individuals to protect their honor and reputation—either through duels or through the courts" (the *Wall Street Journal*).[9]

Fast forward just a few years, past the 2016 election, and the dialogue on regulation has changed. The *New York Times* editorial board sounded almost wistful describing the French presidential elections of 2017, when—by law—a blackout on election news took effect the day before polling began. "It turns out that not only France, but quite a few democracies have election coverage restrictions," commented the paper. While this "period of rumination in the homestretch," despite its "allure," was "unlikely" to take root in the United States given the country's First Amendment jurisprudence, the paper's coverage of elections in Europe and elsewhere gave the impression of a common battle being waged by democratic states against online trolls and hackers. In 2017, in contradistinction to 2014, European privacy and hate-speech rules tended to be ascribed not to a seemingly frivolous dueling tradition but to weightier twentieth-century precedents: the Holocaust and Stasi surveillance in Cold War East Germany.[10]

Many in the technology industry support self-regulation as a means of solving the problems associated with digital information flows, notably fake news and hate speech. Other voices back a more adversarial approach: regulation by the government. The *New York Times* reported in 2017 that European-style policies regulating internet privacy were being adopted in countries as far-flung as South Africa and Malaysia. Around the same moment, the case for stronger government oversight of tech corporations was gaining an eclectic range of domestic champions within the United States. On the left these included the journalist and policy intellectual Barry Lynn, a longtime advocate for stronger antitrust regulation, and Massachusetts senator Elizabeth Warren. On the far right Steve Bannon, in his time as a strategist for the Trump White House, proposed that Washington treat Google and Facebook as public utilities. Commentators noted that even big tech itself, after years of antiregulatory advocacy that echoed earlier lobbying by the film and news industries, might prove amenable to greater federal regulation if this meant avoiding a welter of state-level restrictions.[11]

This book has shown how the United States' pursuit of the global "free flow of information" emerged in the 1940s and how it captivated U.S. policymakers during the developmentalist moment of the American century and the neoliberal phase that followed. Whether or not American free-flow nostrums will endure in an age of multipolar authority and digital fragmentation remains an open question. What is clear is that engaging with this history is imperative if we wish to understand the world outside the United States—and the operations of technologies inside its borders—in the twenty-first century.

Acknowledgments

Although its flaws are all the author's doing, this book could not have been written without the support of numerous individuals and institutions. It is a pleasure to acknowledge them here. Since this project's inception Jean-Christophe Agnew has been a vital source of guidance and a supremely erudite interlocutor. The graceful ease with which Jean-Christophe traversed wide swaths of intellectual history in our conversations together called to mind the title of one of the many books he pointed me toward—*A Mind at Play*. John Merriman's passion for archival research and storytelling flair offered a model of the historian's craft, and his writing advice— "start with what you're most excited about"—has stuck with me. Deepest thanks to Jean-Christophe and John for the many recommendation letters, words of wisdom, and coffees they have provided over the years. It was Seth Fein's legendary graduate seminars that first inspired me to foray into the field of the United States in the world, and fueled by the intellectual excitement that Seth's teaching generated, my transnational adventures continued long after those seminars. For the feedback, advice, and conversational food for thought they provided at various stages of the researching and writing process, I also wish to thank Dudley Andrew, Maria Pilar Asensio-Manrique, Dan Bouk, Bruno Cabanes, Charles Capper, Alice

Conklin, Carolyn Dean, James Fichter, Mette Hjort, Rolien Hoyng, Ryan Irwin, Richard Kuisel, Peter Mandler, John Durham Peters, Quinn Slobodian, Lisa Ubelaker Andrade, Jenifer Van Vleck, and Jay Winter.

The History Department at Lingnan University provided an extremely collegial home base for a new assistant professor. I could not have completed this book without the support of department heads Richard Davis, Xiaorong Han, and William Liu. Mark Hampton generously shared his experiences with the publication process and also commented on a slightly different version of chapter 3. Grace Chou helped make Hong Kong feel like home. Thanks to them and to all my colleagues at Lingnan. Thanks are also due to the History Department's matchless administrative team, Vincy Au and Ann Wong, and to the staff of Lingnan's Office of Research Support, especially Connie Lam and Heidi Chan. In addition, the Yale University History Department's graduate registrar, Marcy Kaufman, has been an indispensable resource both during and after my time in New Haven.

The research behind this book was made possible by the generous support of the Georges Lurcy Charitable and Educational Trust, the Smith Richardson Foundation, the Foreign Language Area Studies Program of the U.S. Department of Education, the Hong Kong Research Grants Council Early Career Scheme (project number 23601015), and a Lingnan University Faculty Research Grant. The École normale supérieure in Paris, France, provided a wonderful home base during the 2012–2013 academic year. I am indebted to the Yale University French Department for arranging the exchange with the ENS. In addition, valuable conference travel funding from the Lingnan University Conference Grant and the Yale University Graduate Student Assembly enabled me to present earlier iterations of various chapters of this work. I extend thanks, too, to the organizers of the conferences and working groups where I presented, including the organizers of the Warren I. Susman Graduate Conference; the Radical Americas Conference; the Business History Conference; the Yale University Transnational History Working Group; the Connected Histories, Mirrored Empires: British and French Imperialism from the 17th Through the 20th Centuries Conference at the University of Hong Kong; the Hong Kong European Studies Association Culture and Politics in European Cinema public lecture series; and the International Association for Media and Communication Research Conference.

Thanks as well to the editors and peer reviewers of the outlets where parts of this work were previously published. Chapter 3 appeared, in a modified form, as "'The Universal Language of the Future': Decolonization, Development, and the American Embrace of Global English, 1945–1965," *Modern Intellectual History* 15, no. 2 (2018): 561–92. Parts of chapters 3 and 5 were published in "The End of Empires and Some Linguistic Turns: British and French Language Policies in Inter- and Post-War Africa," in *British and French Colonialism in Africa, Asia and the Middle East: Connected Empires Across the Eighteenth to the Twentieth Centuries*, ed. James R. Fichter (Basingstoke, UK: Palgrave Macmillan, 2019). These portions of the book are reproduced with permission from, respectively, Cambridge University Press and Palgrave Macmillan.

As a researcher I have been fortunate to work with crackerjack archivists and librarians, who have gamely fielded my questions and made hard-to-access resources available. I especially wish to thank Alexandre Coutelle, Sang Phan, and Adele Torrance for their help navigating the archives of the United Nations Educational, Scientific, and Cultural Organization (UNESCO); Karl Magee at the University of Stirling Archives and Special Collections Department; Caroline Piketty at the Archives Nationales (France); and Lara Hall of the Lyndon B. Johnson Presidential Library. I also thank the staffs of these libraries as well as the staffs of the Yale University Library, the Bibliothèque Nationale de France, the Inathèque de France, the Harvard Law School Library, the Rockefeller Archive Center, the Briscoe Center for American History at the University of Texas at Austin, and the Lingnan University Library, especially the superlatively helpful Crisy Cheung and Jenny So.

Every first-time author should be so lucky as to work with an editor like Bridget Flannery-McCoy. Bridget's thoughtful and efficient feedback tremendously enhanced this project's narrative and analytical clarity, and she expertly steered the manuscript through the peer-review process. At Columbia University Press, big thanks as well to Stephen Wesley and Kathryn Jorge, who saw the book through the production process, and Ryan Groendyk and Christian Winting for their skillful editorial assistance. In addition, the adroit copyediting of Abby Graves and the index prepared by Silvia Benvenuto were essential contributions. I also wish to thank David Ekbladh, Sam Lebovic, and two anonymous reviewers for their incisive comments on the full manuscript and three anonymous reviewers for their feedback on the book proposal and an earlier version of chapter 1.

This book was researched and written on three continents and over the course of eight years, during which many personal debts were incurred. I will mention only a few here. Every bridge-and-tunnel dreamer needs pals in the big city. For their generosity, support, and all the conversations, I wish to thank three in particular: John Dempsey, Daniel Reid, and Leah Weinberg-Moskowitz. In Paris, Renalte Mangunza Kopani and Julie Obert proved that friends are the best language teachers. From second grade onward, Becca Van Schoick kept the faith. Although Becca is no longer here, the memory of her courage and grace sustains me. I also wish to thank my teachers in the Somerset Hills School District, especially Mark Reinman and Russell Sheldon, and the professors who made the study of history so engaging for me as an undergraduate—Linda Colley, Eagle Glassheim, Anthony Grafton, Emmanuel Kreike, Gyan Prakash, and Robert Tignor.

My family has been an ongoing source of strength in the years since this project began. Eric Spear, brother-in-law and new-media phenom, kept me current on the latest memes while I was buried in old media. I spent many happy days with my grandmother, Joan Hartstein, who shared her wisdom judiciously and over the best bagels. It was suggested to me shortly after I arrived in Hong Kong that Bali might make a nice winter holiday destination. Around the same time, my niece Miriam Lemberg-Spear was born. Because of Miriam, over the past five years I have spent more time in Baltimore than in Bali, and I wouldn't have it any other way. Not only does my sister, Katie Lemberg, grasp the vagaries of the peer-review process, she also serves every day as a model of integrity and compassion. Deepest thanks to Katie for that long-ago trip to 125th Street, and all the rest. Most of all I thank my mother and father, Christine and Howard Lemberg, for inspiring me from the first with their love of learning and penchant for acquiring reading materials. Their respective interests in language education and communications technologies likely planted the seeds of this project without my knowing, but I know I could not have completed it without their love and support. It is to them I dedicate this book.

Notes

INTRODUCTION: LIBERALIZING MISSIONS

1. Kent Cooper, *Barriers Down: The Story of the News Agency Epoch* (New York: Farrar & Rinehart, 1942), 6–9, quotation on 7, see also 101–6; Associated Press, "Fight for Freedom of Press Recounted: Kent Cooper Book Deals with Old International Barriers," *New York Times*, December 5, 1942.

2. Cooper, *Barriers Down*, 3–9, 85, 96–108.

3. Cooper, *Barriers Down*, 4, 9, 158, 251; Sam Lebovic, *Free Speech and Unfree News: The Paradox of Press Freedom in America* (Cambridge, MA: Harvard University Press, 2016), 148–50.

4. Jon Gertner, *The Idea Factory: Bell Labs and the Great Age of American Innovation* (New York: Penguin, 2012), chap. 7; Jimmy Soni and Rob Goodman, *A Mind at Play: How Claude Shannon Invented the Information Age* (New York: Simon & Schuster, 2017), see esp. 138–64; John Durham Peters, *Speaking into the Air: A History of the Idea of Communication* (Chicago: University of Chicago Press, 1999), 22–29.

5. "Comments by TIME INC.," December 15, 1943, Harold Dwight Lasswell Papers (MS 1043), Manuscripts and Archives, Yale University Library, box 26, folder 334; Walter Wanger, "Donald Duck and Diplomacy," *Public Opinion Quarterly* 14, no. 3 (1950): 443–52; David Sarnoff, "Freedom to Listen and to Look" (speech to the U.S. National Commission for UNESCO, September 12, 1947, Chicago, IL), William Benton Papers, Special Collections Research Center, University of Chicago Library, box 387, folder 8.

6. Daniel Headrick, *The Invisible Weapon: Telecommunications and International Politics, 1851–1945* (New York: Oxford University Press, 1991), chaps. 2–6; Jonathan Reed Winkler, *Nexus: Strategic Communications and American Security in World War I* (Cambridge, MA: Harvard University Press, 2008); Emily Rosenberg, *Spreading the*

American Dream: American Economic and Cultural Expansion, 1890–1945 (New York: Hill and Wang, 1982), chaps. 9–10; Cooper, *Barriers Down*, 319–20.

7. Even scholars who stress the relevance of the pre-1945 period agree that the Second World War transformed U.S. involvement in international communications. See, e.g., Paul Starr, *The Creation of the Media: Political Origins of Modern Communications* (New York: Basic, 2004), 402; Winkler, *Nexus*, 4, 266; Headrick, *The Invisible Weapon*, 262.

8. Emily Rosenberg, contrasting American leadership during the two world wars, notes that even the arch-internationalist Wilson hesitated to press for government involvement in economic matters, an area he believed "proper to the private sector." Rosenberg, *Spreading the American Dream*, 190.

9. These exceptions include Rosenberg; Michael Stamm, *Sound Business: Newspapers, Radio, and the Politics of New Media* (Philadelphia: University of Pennsylvania Press, 2011). Stamm also notes the predominance of single-medium studies (7).

10. In the body of the book, Pool suggests "soft technological determinism" as a way of understanding the relationship between technology and information freedoms: "Freedom is fostered when the means of communication are dispersed, decentralized, and easily available, as are printing presses or microcomputers." Brand, on the other hand, notes in the same breath as his famous line that "information wants to be expensive." Ithiel de Sola Pool, *Technologies of Freedom* (Cambridge, MA: Belknap Press of Harvard University Press, 1983), 5; Steven Levy, "Hackers at 30: 'Hackers' and 'Information Wants to be Free,'" *Wired*, November 21, 2014, accessed September 11, 2018, https://www.wired.com/story/hackers-at-30-hackers-and-information-wants-to-be-free/.

11. On the birth of American globalism in the 1940s, see John Fousek, *To Lead the Free World: American Nationalism and the Cultural Roots of the Cold War* (Chapel Hill: University of North Carolina Press, 2000), 7–8; Jenifer Van Vleck, *Empire of the Air: Aviation and the American Ascendancy* (Cambridge, MA: Harvard University Press, 2013), 7–11, 17.

12. Isaiah Berlin, "Two Concepts of Liberty," 1958, in *Liberty*, 2nd ed., ed. Henry Hardy (Oxford: Oxford University Press, 2002), 166–217.

13. Starr, *Creation of the Media*, quotation on 16.

14. On the press and the discourse of positive freedoms in the mid-twentieth-century United States, see Lebovic, *Free Speech and Unfree News*, 23, 138–63. William Benton in *Records of the General Conference of the United Nations Educational, Scientific, and Cultural Organization—Fifth Session, Florence, 1950* (Paris: UNESCO, 1950), 342, UNESCO Archives, Paris, France.

15. "National Security Action Memorandum No. 332: U.S. Government Policy on English Language Teaching Abroad," June 11, 1965, Lyndon Baines Johnson Presidential Library website, accessed September 18, 2018, https://www.discoverlbj.org/item/nsf-nsam332.

16. Pool, *Technologies of Freedom*, quotation on 231.

17. James T. Sparrow, William J. Novak, and Stephen W. Sawyer, "Introduction," in *Boundaries of the State in U.S. History*, ed. James T. Sparrow, William J. Novak, and Stephen W. Sawyer (Chicago: University of Chicago Press, 2015), 1–15.

18. Jens Ulff-Møller, *Hollywood's Film Wars with France: Film-Trade Diplomacy and the Emergence of the French Film Quota Policy* (Rochester, NY: University of Rochester

Press, 2001); Ian Jarvie, *Hollywood's Overseas Campaign: The North Atlantic Movie Trade, 1920–1950* (Cambridge: Cambridge University Press, 1992); Adrian Johns, *Death of a Pirate: British Radio and the Making of the Information Age* (New York: Norton, 2011), 30–34; Fernand Terrou and Lucien Solal, *Legislation for Press, Film and Radio* (Paris: UNESCO, 1951), 129–208.

19. For an insightful discussion of how positionality has shaped the ways in which American history is written in the United States and Europe, see Nicolas Barreyre, Manfred Berg, and Simon Middleton, "Straddling Intellectual Worlds: Positionality and the Writing of American History," in *Historians Across Borders: Writing American History in a Global Age*, ed. Nicolas Barreyre, Michael Heale, Stephen Tuck, and Cécile Vidal (Berkeley: University of California Press, 2014), 75–92.

20. Benton maintained a keen interest in French cultural and linguistic diplomacy from his time at the State Department in the 1940s to his years serving as U.S. ambassador to UNESCO in the 1960s. See, e.g., William Benton, memo to Jesse MacKnight, January 2, 1946, Lasswell Papers, box 16, folder 202; William Benton, memo to Douglas Batson, May 11, 1965, Benton Papers, box 393, folder 6; William Benton, memo to Douglas Batson, 1 June 1965, Benton Papers, box 393, folder 6.

21. Brian T. Edwards, *After the American Century: The Ends of U.S. Culture in the Middle East* (New York: Columbia University Press, 2016), 20–22.

22. On the diplomatic history of freedom of information in the early Cold War, see Kenneth Cmiel, "Human Rights, Freedom of Information, and the Origins of Third-World Solidarity," in *Truth Claims: Representation and Human Rights*, ed. Mark Philip Bradley and Patrice Petro (New Brunswick, NJ: Rutgers University Press, 2002), 107–30; Glenn Mitoma, *Human Rights and the Negotiation of American Power* (Philadelphia: University of Pennsylvania Press, 2013), chap. 3.

23. Here I draw on Nicole Starosielski's point that the laying of submarine cables has, historically, seldom followed "market-driven logic." Starosielski, *The Undersea Network* (Durham, NC: Duke University Press, 2015), 23.

24. David R. Francis, "One-Country, One-Vote Issue Comes to Fore in UNESCO Flap," *Christian Science Monitor*, December 19, 1984, accessed September 10, 2018, https://www.csmonitor.com/1984/1219/121941.html; Quinn Slobodian, *Globalists: The End of Empire and the Birth of Neoliberalism* (Cambridge, MA: Harvard University Press, 2018), chap. 7.

25. Kenneth Cmiel, "The Emergence of Human Rights Politics in the United States," *Journal of American History* 86, no. 3 (1999): 1231–50, see esp. 1248–50.

26. Cited in Ithiel de Sola Pool, "Direct-Broadcast Satellites and Cultural Integrity," 1975, *Society*, January/February 1998, 145.

1. FREEDOM FOR EVERY MEDIUM, EVERYWHERE: INFORMATION POLITICS IN THE 1940S UNITED STATES

The epigraphs for this chapter are taken from: Kent Cooper, *Barriers Down: The Story of the News Agency Epoch* (New York: Farrar & Rinehart, 1942), 293; and William E. Hocking, "Definition and Scope of the General Problems before the Group," February 2, 1944, Harold Dwight Lasswell Papers (MS 1043), Manuscripts and Archives, Yale University Library, box 26, folder 335.

1. Eric Johnston, "Communication to Chairman of Commission on Human Rights by Motion Picture Association," May 7, 1946, Zechariah Chafee Papers, Harvard Law School Library, Harvard University, reel 15.

2. Thomas Doherty, *Hollywood and Hitler, 1933–1939* (New York: Columbia University Press, 2013), chap. 2; Ruth Vasey, *The World According to Hollywood, 1918–1939* (Madison: University of Wisconsin Press, 1997); Laura Wittern-Keller, *Freedom of the Screen: Legal Challenges to State Film Censorship, 1915–1981* (Lexington: University Press of Kentucky, 2008).

3. Commission on Freedom of the Press, *A Free and Responsible Press: A General Report on Mass Communication: Newspapers, Radio, Motion Pictures, Magazines, and Books* (Chicago: University of Chicago Press, 1947), v.

4. "Crusade" is the apt descriptor of Margaret A. Blanchard, *Exporting the First Amendment: The Press-Government Crusade of 1945–1952* (New York: Longman, 1986).

5. Emily Rosenberg, *Spreading the American Dream: American Economic and Cultural Expansion, 1890–1945* (New York: Hill & Wang, 1982), 92–97, 99–103, 190; Jonathan Reed Winkler, *Nexus: Strategic Communications and American Security in World War I* (Cambridge, MA: Harvard University Press, 2008), see esp. 193–99, 271–79; David Sarnoff, "The Freedom of the Air," *The Nation*, July 23, 1924; Ruth A. Inglis, *Freedom of the Movies: A Report on Self-Regulation from the Commission on Freedom of the Press* (1947; New York: Da Capo, 1974), 11.

6. Johnston, "Communication to Chairman of Commission on Human Rights." On the rhetorical and conceptual shift from "freedom of the press" to "freedom of information," see William Benton, "Freedom of Information: The Role of the State Department" (address to Inland Daily Press Association, Chicago, IL, February 11, 1947), Chafee Papers, reel 14.

7. Cooper, *Barriers Down*; "Monopoly Is Urged in Communications," *New York Times*, May 17, 1945.

8. On the Commission on Freedom of the Press in domestic context, see, e.g., Victor Pickard, *America's Battle for Media Democracy: The Triumph of Corporate Libertarianism and the Future of Media Reform* (Cambridge: Cambridge University Press, 2015), chaps. 5–6; Brett Gary, "The Search for a Competent Public: The Hutchins Commission and Post–World War II Democratic Possibilities," in *Democracy and Excellence: Concord or Conflict?*, ed. Joseph Romance and Neal Riemer (Westport, CT: Praeger, 2005), 75–90. Rosenberg's *Spreading the American Dream* briefly addresses the commission's foreign-policy recommendations (216–17). Sam Lebovic's *Free Speech and Unfree News: The Paradox of Press Freedom in America* (Cambridge, MA: Harvard University Press, 2016) is primarily concerned with domestic affairs but contains an excellent chapter that contrasts the dashing of the commission's domestic-reform ambitions in the late 1940s with the broad agreement that emerged around the "effort to globalize American press freedom" (138–63, quotation on 148).

9. Newsreels were less vulnerable than feature films to industry self-regulation and state and local censorship—though, because of restrictions on filming inside Nazi Germany, much of their German footage came from official Nazi propaganda reels. Besides the biweekly newsreels, the monthly *March of Time* nonfiction film series—owned by Henry Luce and known for its hard-hitting angle on European fascism—also covered international affairs onscreen. Doherty, *Hollywood and Hitler*, 78–95, 237–92; M. Todd Bennett, *One World, Big Screen: Hollywood, the Allies, and World*

War II (Chapel Hill: University of North Carolina Press, 2012), 53–88, see esp. 65–66. Radio news was also well established by the 1930s, especially on the many stations owned by newspapers. The place of news on American radio further expanded after the Munich crisis of 1938. Michael Stamm, *Sound Business: Newspapers, Radio, and the Politics of New Media* (Philadelphia: University of Pennsylvania Press, 2011), 101–3.

10. On concentration in the domestic newspaper industry, see Pickard, *America's Battle for Media Democracy*, 124–51.

11. Garth S. Jowett, "'A Capacity for Evil': The 1915 Supreme Court *Mutual* Decision," in *Controlling Hollywood: Censorship and Regulation in the Studio Era*, ed. Matthew Bernstein (New Brunswick, NJ: Rutgers University Press, 1999), 16–40, see esp. 28; Vasey, *The World According to Hollywood*, see esp. chaps. 3–4; Wittern-Keller, *Freedom of the Screen*, 12.

12. Matthew Bernstein, *Walter Wanger, Hollywood Independent* (Berkeley: University of California Press, 1994), 129–35; Walter Wanger, "120,000 American Ambassadors," *Foreign Affairs* 18, no. 1 (1939): 45–59, quotation on 46.

13. Wanger, "120,000 American Ambassadors," 55, 58 (italics in original); Walter Wanger, "OWI and Motion Pictures," *Public Opinion Quarterly* 7, no. 1 (1943): 110 (italics in original); "Court Test Sought of Film Censorship," *New York Times*, June 14, 1949, cited in Wittern-Keller, *Freedom of the Screen*, 101.

14. Scholars of the American media have framed the relationship between scarcity and regulation in various ways. Paul Starr, among others, notes that the differences perceived in the interwar era between radio and print underpinned the American rationale of broadcasting regulation. Michael Stamm acknowledges this perception but also emphasizes how scarcities confronted broadcasters and publishers alike, drawing a parallel between the "absolute limits" upon available broadcasting spectrum and the "operational economics" challenge of securing newsprint. A third, and less convincing, perspective is in the work of Ithiel de Sola Pool (discussed in chapter 7), who framed scarcity as a discursive invention that outlasted the technological conditions that gave rise to it. Paul Starr, *The Creation of the Media: Political Origins of Modern Communications* (New York: Basic, 2004), 328–30, 363–64; Michael Stamm, "The Space for News: Ether and Paper in the Business of Media," *Media History* 21, no. 1 (2015): 55–73, quotation on 58. Cf. Ithiel de Sola Pool, *Technologies of Freedom* (Cambridge, MA: Belknap Press of Harvard University Press, 1983), 112–29.

15. Sarnoff cited in Pool, *Technologies of Freedom*, 120; Stamm, *Sound Business*, 21–23, 44–48, 134–35; Starr, *Creation of the Media*, 327–84; Pickard, *America's Battle for Media Democracy*, 38–39.

16. Pickard, *America's Battle for Media Democracy*, 38–42; Pool, Ernst quotation on 122; Stamm, *Sound Business*, 24–25, 53–54, 59–81, 108–45. On interwar consolidation in the radio industry, see also Lizabeth Cohen, *Making a New Deal: Industrial Workers in Chicago, 1919–1939* (Cambridge: Cambridge University Press, 1990), 139–43; Starr, 367–70.

17. Daniel T. Rodgers, *Contested Truths: Keywords in American Politics Since Independence* (1987; Cambridge, MA: Harvard University Press, 1998), 214, 218.

18. Scholars of pre-1945 communications acknowledge the sea change ushered in by the U.S. entry into the Second World War. See, e.g., Starr, *Creation of the Media*, 402; Winkler, *Nexus*, 4, 266; Daniel R. Headrick, *The Invisible Weapon: Telecommunications and International Politics, 1851–1945* (New York: Oxford University Press, 1991), 262.

19. James L. Fly, "International Communications" (speech to the National Lawyers Guild, Washington, DC, November 19, 1943), Lasswell Papers, box 26, folder 334. On Fly and the Defense Communications Board, see Headrick, 260–62.

20. Richard Shale, *Donald Duck Joins Up: The Walt Disney Studio During World War II* (Ann Arbor, MI: UMI Research Press, 1982), 38–40; Erik Barnouw, *Documentary: A History of the Non-Fiction Film*, 2nd rev. ed. (New York: Oxford University Press, 1993), 155–64; Martin J. Manning and Clarence R. Wyatt, eds., *Encyclopedia of Media and Propaganda in Wartime America* (Santa Barbara, CA: ABC-CLIO, 2011), 1:xl; Bernstein, *Walter Wanger*, chap. 11; Walter Wanger, "Post-War Is Now" (speech to the Oregon Newspaper Publishers Association, Portland, OR, June 16, 1944), William Benton Papers, Special Collections Research Center, University of Chicago Library, box 80, folder 9.

21. Mickie Edwardson, "James Lawrence Fly v. David Sarnoff: Blitzkrieg Over Television," *Journalism History* 25, no. 2 (1999): 42–52, quotation on 46; RCA advertisement in *Life*, December 29, 1947, emphasis in the original.

22. David Sarnoff, "Freedom to Listen and Freedom to Look" (speech to the U.S. National Commission for UNESCO, Chicago, IL, September 12, 1947), Benton Papers, box 387, folder 8.

23. Fly, "International Communications"; Headrick, *Invisible Weapon*, 260–65; Sarnoff; "Sarnoff Urges U.N. to Establish 'Freedom to Listen' for the World," *New York Times*, April 5, 1946; Eugene Lyons, *David Sarnoff: A Biography* (New York: Harper & Row, 1966), 265–66, 270–72.

24. Rosenberg, *Spreading the American Dream*, chap. 3.

25. Augustine Sedgewick, "Against Flows," *History of the Present* 4, no. 2 (2014): 143–46; Nicole Starosielski, *The Undersea Network* (Durham, NC: Duke University Press, 2015), see esp. introduction, "Against Flow," 1–25.

    Overall, references to "free flow" in the *New York Times* rose from 46 in the decade of 1910–19 to 133 in 1920–29 to 409 in 1930–39 to 560 in 1940–49. References to the "free flow of credit," the "free flow of commerce," and the "free flow of capital" all peaked in the decade 1930–39. From Proquest Historical Newspapers: *New York Times* database, accessed September 18, 2018. For the "free flow of cotton," see "Our Civil War and European Trade," *New York Times*, October 2, 1861.

26. Blanchard, *Exporting the First Amendment*, Ackerman quoted on 16, see also 108; "Hoover's Speech Warning of Perils to Press," *New York Times*, November 9, 1937; "U.S. News Coverage Overseas Praised," *New York Times*, April 29, 1939.

27. Data from Proquest Historical Newspapers: *New York Times* database, accessed December 12, 2015. OWI order quoted in Zechariah Chafee, *Government and Mass Communications* (Chicago: University of Chicago Press, 1947), 2:729–30.

28. "Asks World Pacts on Press Freedom," *New York Times*, June 24, 1944; James B. Reston, "Free Flow of News by Pact of Allies Our Post-War Aim," *New York Times*, July 13, 1944; Anne O'Hare McCormick, "Abroad: News Blackouts and International Cooperation," *New York Times*, March 19, 1945; "Free Press Backing Told to President," *New York Times*, June 10, 1945; "Free Press Desire Spreads in World, U.S. Editors Find," *New York Times*, June 11, 1945. *Life* noted in 1944 that both houses of Congress had endorsed "resolutions in favor of worldwide freedom of information" (sidebar, Kent Cooper, "Freedom of Information: Head of Associated Press Calls for Unhampered Flow of World News," *Life*, November 13, 1944). On the broad political

consensus behind press-freedoms advocacy in the mid-1940s, see also Blanchard, *Exporting the First Amendment*, 20–21.

29. The AP had participated in agreements with Reuters and Havas all the same. "Kent Cooper Urges Free Press Plan," *New York Times*, July 18, 1944; "Baillie Says Press Can Prevent War," *New York Times*, November 12, 1944; Rosenberg, *Spreading the American Dream*, 89–92, 97–99.

30. Victoria de Grazia, "Mass Culture and Sovereignty: The American Challenge to European Cinemas, 1920–1960," *Journal of Modern History* 61, no. 1 (1989): 64, 74; Rosenberg, 99–103; Jens Ulff-Møller, *Hollywood's Film Wars with France: Film-Trade Diplomacy and the Emergence of the French Film Quota Policy* (Rochester, NY: University of Rochester Press, 2001), chap. 6; Steven Ricci, *Cinema and Fascism: Italian Film and Society, 1922–1943* (Berkeley: University of California Press, 2008), 74–75.

31. "Will Hays Stresses Freedom of Screen," *New York Times*, March 28, 1944; Johnston, "Communication to Chairman of Commission on Human Rights."

32. Cooper, *Barriers Down*, 293–99. On Cooper and the creation of domestic FOIA legislation, see Michael Schudson, *The Rise of the Right to Know: Politics and the Culture of Transparency, 1945–1975* (Cambridge, MA: Belknap Press of Harvard University Press, 2015), 6–7, 28–63.

33. Blanchard, *Exporting the First Amendment*, 18–20; Jonathan Silberstein-Loeb, *The International Distribution of News: The Associated Press, Press Association, and Reuters, 1848–1947* (Cambridge: Cambridge University Press, 2014), 81–87; Lebovic, *Free Speech and Unfree News*, 76–84, 150.

34. Charles E. Merriam, "Memorandum on Inquiry into Freedom of Speech," January 19, 1944, Lasswell Papers, box 26, folder 335.

35. "Comments by TIME INC.," December 15, 1943, Lasswell Papers, box 26, folder 334; "Summary of Discussion Carried on by the Committee on Freedom of the Press," February 2, 1944, Lasswell Papers, box 26, folder 336; "Summary of Discussion (cont.) Meetings, July 7–9, 1946 ... (Second Session)," August 21, 1946, Lasswell Papers, box 27, folder 347.

36. Rosenberg, *Spreading the American Dream*, 210–12; "OWI Publication of 'Victory' Stirs Storm in Congress," *New York Times*, February 11, 1943; "OWI Shakes Up Its Domestic Branch; Drops Public Opinion Polls," *Wall Street Journal*, March 11, 1943; Arthur Krock, "In the Nation: The Cash Value of a Mysterious Operation," *New York Times*, July 6, 1943; "Congress Inquiry on OWI Threatened," *New York Times*, August 13, 1943.

37. Harold D. Lasswell, memo to John Howe and Francis Russell, November 13, 1945, Benton Papers, box 75, folder 2; John Grierson, comments in session minutes, March 21, 1944, Lasswell Papers, box 27, folder 340. For a brief overview of Grierson at the National Film Board, see Andre Kuczewski, "Review: *John Grierson and the National Film Board* by Gary Evans," *Film Quarterly* 39, no. 4 (1986): 59–60.

38. Archibald MacLeish, comments in session minutes, March 21, 1944, Lasswell Papers, box 27, folder 340. On MacLeish, see Brett Gary, *The Nervous Liberals: Propaganda Anxieties from World War I to the Cold War* (New York: Columbia University Press, 1999), 131–73.

39. William E. Barry et al., *Last Rights: Revisiting Four Theories of the Press*, ed. John Nerone (Urbana: University of Illinois Press, 1995), Hocking quotation on 97; George Shuster, "Document No. 7: Memorandum by George N. Shuster," [1944], Lasswell

Papers, box 26, folder 338; Riezler cited in "Document No. 14: Synopsis of Commission Meeting of March 21, 1944," [1944], Lasswell Papers, box 27, folder 339.

40. Harold Lasswell, "Memorandum on Problems and Procedures," February 2, 1944, Lasswell Papers, box 26, folder 336; Lasswell quoted in "Document No. 16: Statement on the Importance of the Commission's Work," n.d., Lasswell Papers, box 27, folder 341; Harold Lasswell, memo to "Fellow Commissioners," March 29, 1946, Lasswell Papers, box 27, folder 345, emphasis in original. On Lasswell, see Gary, *Nervous Liberals*, 2–5, 11–12, 55–84, 167–73; John Durham Peters, *Speaking into the Air: A History of the Idea of Communication* (Chicago: University of Chicago Press, 1999), 10–11.

41. Stamm, *Sound Business*, 140–41, Chafee quoted on 140; Chafee, *Government and Mass Communications*, part 2: "Affirmative Governmental Activities for Encouraging the Communication of News and Ideas," vol. 2, quotation on 473. On Chafee's interwar scholarship, see Donald L. Smith, *Zechariah Chafee, Jr.: Defender of Liberty and Law* (Cambridge, MA: Harvard University Press, 1986), 13–35.

42. Hocking, "Definition and Scope of the General Problems Before the Group"; MacLeish in "Document No. 108C: Summary of Discussion (cont.)," July 7–9, 1946, Lasswell Papers, box 27, folder 346. On Hocking and MacLeish, see Pickard, *America's Battle for Media Democracy*, 146–51; Lebovic, *Free Speech and Unfree News*, 141–42.

43. Niebuhr and Ruml in "Document No. 108B: Summary of Discussion (cont.)," August 21, 1946, Lasswell Papers, box 27, folder 347; Chafee, *Government and Mass Communications*, 2:673; Silberstein-Loeb, *The International Distribution of News*, 81–87; Lebovic, *Free Speech and Unfree News*, 76–84, 141–42. Chafee's intermediate stance on press reform was also evident slightly earlier, in his 1941 testimony to the FCC on newspaper ownership of radio stations. Stamm, *Sound Business*, 139–41.

44. Hutchins's and Niebuhr's remarks summarized in the synopsis of the February 2, 1944, meeting, Lasswell Papers, box 26, folder 336; Zechariah Chafee, "Hopes and Fears for America," April 26, 1944, in "Document No. 16: Statement on the Importance of the Commission's Work," Lasswell Papers, box 27, folder 341. On the American press and American exceptionalism in the mid-1940s, see also Lebovic, *Free Speech and Unfree News*, 138–40, 148–50.

45. Commission on Freedom of the Press, *A Free and Responsible Press*, see esp. 6–11, 79–90. On the Alien Registration Act of 1940, see *Encyclopedia Britannica*, s.v. "Smith Act," accessed February 1, 2012, http://www.britannica.com/EBchecked/topic/549923/Smith-Act.

46. Riezler in "Document No. 16"; see also Riezler in "Document No. 14: Synopsis of Commission Meeting of March 21, 1944," [1944], Lasswell Papers, box 27, folder 339.

47. Commission on Freedom of the Press, *A Free and Responsible Press*, 52, 64–67, 88–90.

48. Llewellyn White and Robert D. Leigh, *Peoples Speaking to Peoples: A Report on International Mass Communication from the Commission on Freedom of the Press* (1946; New York: Arno, 1972), 10–12, 19–23, 27–29, 43–45; Chafee, *Government and Mass Communications*, 2: 727–31, 748–52. On the commission's advocacy of postwar information diplomacy, see also Rosenberg, *Spreading the American Dream*, 216–17.

49. White and Leigh, *Peoples Speaking to Peoples*, 29–32; "Monopoly Is Urged in Communications."

50. Milton Mayer, "William Benton," *Life*, January 14, 1946, quotations on 95; White and Leigh, *Peoples Speaking to Peoples*, 102–4, 111–12; Chafee, *Government and Mass Communications*, 2:748–52.

51. "AP Shuts Off News for Use Abroad by State Department Service," *New York Times*, January 15, 1946; "Text of the Report Presented by AP Directors," *New York Times*, April 23, 1946.

52. Frank Hughes, "Round Table of Air: Pure Propaganda," *Chicago Tribune*, November 26, 1948, Chafee Papers, reel 11; "The Press: Fight over Freedom," *Time*, April 29, 1946; Gary, "Search for a Competent Public," 85; Pickard, *America's Battle for Media Democracy*, 177–82, McCormick quoted on 179.

53. Pickard, *America's Battle for Media Democracy*, 98–123.

54. "Seminar Speakers Deplore Slash in Funds for Voice of America," *New York Times*, April 25, 1947.

55. Walter Yust, introduction to the *Britannica Book of the Year* (Chicago: Encyclopedia Britannica, 1949). These yearbooks, with circulation in the hundreds of thousands, were commonly advertised in *Life* along with more expensive *Encyclopedia Britannica* sets. The 1948 *Book of the Year* gave its circulation as more than 300,000 copies (Yust, viii). On anticommunist paranoia more generally, see Ellen Schrecker, *Many Are the Crimes: McCarthyism in America* (Boston: Little, Brown, 1998).

56. Zechariah Chafee, correspondence with Robert L. Feigenbaum and H. Peabody Nelson, January–February 1948, Chafee Papers, reel 14; Zechariah Chafee, "Freedom and Fear" (speech to the Harvard Phi Beta Kappa chapter, Cambridge, MA, June 20, 1949), Chafee Papers, reel 75. On earlier debates, see "Ackerman Fights Any Curb on Propaganda as the First Step in Ending News Freedom," *New York Times*, September 7, 1939; Hugh O'Connor, "Keep Free Speech, Say Pound, Chaffee [*sic*]," *New York Times*, March 13, 1941.

57. William Benton, letter to "Mr. Larkin," October 27, 1950, Lasswell Papers, box 17, folder 209; John Howe, memo to William Benton, January 16, 1950, Benton Papers, box 347, folder 11, emphasis in original; Ellen Schrecker, *The Age of McCarthyism: A Brief History with Documents*, 2nd ed. (Boston: Bedford/St. Martin's, 2002), 55–56, 218–20.

58. Howe, memo to Benton, January 16, 1950; Zechariah Chafee, "Statement by Zechariah Chafee Before the Subcommission on Freedom of Information," January 27, 1948, Chafee Papers, reel 70. On the subcommission, see also Glenn Mitoma, *Human Rights and the Negotiation of American Power* (Philadelphia: University of Pennsylvania Press, 2013), 84–91.

59. Kenneth Cmiel, "Human Rights, Freedom of Information, and the Origins of Third-World Solidarity," in *Truth Claims: Representation and Human Rights*, ed. Mark Philip Bradley and Patrice Petro (New Brunswick, NJ: Rutgers University Press, 2002), 112–16; "Report of the United States Delegates to the United Nations Conference on Freedom of Information" (U.S. Government Printing Office, 1948), Chafee Papers, reel 19. On *Blockade* and *March of Time*, see Bernstein, *Walter Wanger*, 133–35; Bennett, *One World, Big Screen*, 66.

60. Lebovic, *Free Speech and Unfree News*, 152.

61. William Benton, "Freedom of Information: The Role of the State Department," February 8, 1947, Chafee Papers, reel 14; "Benton Offers Five Points for Cultural Democracy," *National Commission News* 1, no. 6 (1948), Benton Papers, box 389, folder 7.

62. Blanchard, *Exporting the First Amendment*, 18–21, 99–129; Lebovic, *Free Speech and Unfree News*, 156; Frank Ninkovich, *The Diplomacy of Ideas: U.S. Foreign Policy and Cultural Relations, 1938–1950* (Cambridge: Cambridge University Press, 1981), see esp. 113–38; Rosenberg, *Spreading the American Dream*, 212–19; Seth Fein, "New Empire into Old: Making Mexican Newsreels the Cold War Way," *Diplomatic History* 28, no. 5 (2004): 704–6; Alan L. Heil Jr., *Voice of America: A History* (New York: Columbia University Press, 2003), 45–48; Sidney Hyman, *The Lives of William Benton* (Chicago: University of Chicago Press, 1969), 238–39, 247; Mayer, "William Benton," 95–105.

63. Wanger, "120,000 American Ambassadors," 57; Wanger, "Post-War Is Now"; Walter Wanger, "Donald Duck and Diplomacy," *Public Opinion Quarterly* 14, no. 3 (1950): 443–52.

64. William Benton, letter to Max McCullough, November 23, 1949, Benton Papers, box 388, folder 12; "Resolution to Be Introduced by Senator William Benton (D. Conn.)," March 22, [1950], Lasswell Papers, box 17, folder 210.

2. QUANTIFYING AND QUALIFYING FREEDOM OF INFORMATION DURING THE EARLY COLD WAR

The epigraphs for this chapter are taken from: Erwin D. Canham, "International Freedom of Information," *Law and Contemporary Problems* 14, no. 4 (1949): 585; and Jacques Kayser, *Mort d'une liberté* (Paris: Plon, 1955), 65–66.

1. Zechariah Chafee, "Memorandum on the Canadian Material in Government and Mass Communications," November 3, 1947, Zechariah Chafee Papers, Harvard Law School Library, reel 71; George V. Ferguson, letter to Zechariah Chafee with enclosed memorandum, December 22, 1947, Chafee Papers, reel 71. On the publication of *Government and Mass Communications*, see Donald L. Smith, *Zechariah Chafee, Jr.: Defender of Liberty and Law* (Cambridge, MA: Harvard University Press, 1986), 112.

2. John Grierson, letter to Zechariah Chafee, December 30, 1947, John Grierson Archive, Archives and Special Collections, University of Stirling, G5.11.38. On Grierson and North American red scares, see Lord Ritchie Calder, interview, *Journal of the Society of Film and Television Arts* 2, nos. 4–5 (1972): 22, Grierson Archive, GA.1.23; David MacKenzie, "Canada's Red Scare 1945–1957," Historical Booklet 61 (Ottawa: Canadian Historical Association, 2001), 12–15, http://www.collectionscanada.gc.ca/obj /008004/f2/H-61_en.pdf.

3. On austerity and rationing in postwar Europe, see Tony Judt, *Postwar: A History of Europe Since 1945* (New York: Penguin, 2005), 82–99, 123; Colin Jones, *Paris: The Biography of a City* (New York: Viking Penguin, 2005), 490–91. On newsprint shortages and their impact on the European press, see *Report of the Preparatory Conference on World Pulp Problems*, Fonds Jacques Kayser, 465AP, Archives nationales, Pierrefitte-sur-Seine, France, carton 25, dossier 2, p. 38; Intelligence Unit of *The Economist*, UNESCO, and the FAO, *Paper for Printing—Today and Tomorrow* (Paris: UNESCO, 1952), see esp. 29–31, 72–73, 79–80, 96–100 (hereafter *Paper for Printing*); Alan S. Milward and George Brennan, *Britain's Place in the World: A Historical Enquiry into Import Controls, 1945–60* (London: Routledge, 1996), 284–85; *World Communications: Press, Radio, Film* (Paris: UNESCO, 1950), 127; *Rapport de la Commission des Besoins Techniques: Presse, radio, film après enquête dans douze pays dévastés*

par la guerre (Paris: UNESCO, 1947); *Daily Express*, May 14, 1948, Chafee Papers, reel 15; Philip Nord, *France's New Deal: From the Thirties to the Postwar Era* (Princeton, NJ: Princeton University Press, 2010), 150–51.

4. On American designs for the postwar political economy, see Barry Eichengreen, *Globalizing Capital: A History of the International Monetary System*, 2nd ed. (Princeton, NJ: Princeton University Press, 2008), 94–104; Judt, *Postwar*, 107–8. On the siting of UN "soft-power" agencies outside the United States, see Paul Kennedy, *The Parliament of Man: The Past, Present, and Future of the United Nations* (New York: Vintage, 2006), 143–44; Chloé Maurel, *Histoire de l'Unesco: Les trente premières années, 1945–1974* (Paris: L'Harmattan, 2010), 17–18.

5. Kennedy, *Parliament of Man*, 147–48. Kennedy discusses the "burst of institution building" at the United Nations during these years on 143–51. On Grierson, see Jack C. Ellis, *John Grierson: Life, Contributions, Influence* (Carbondale: Southern Illinois University Press, 2000), 231–32.

6. Fernand Terrou and Lucien Solal, *Legislation for Press, Film and Radio* (Paris: UNESCO, 1951), 17. Terrou is credited as the author in the foreword and in his introduction thanks Solal for the latter's collaboration on part 3 of the book, so here and below, I refer to Terrou as the author. On UNESCO's role in international social science after 1945, see Ira Wagman, "Locating UNESCO in the Historical Study of Communication," in *The International History of Communication Study*, ed. Peter Simonson and David W. Park (New York: Routledge, 2016), 71–89; Johan Heilbron, Nicolas Guilhot, and Laurent Jeanpierre, "Toward a Transnational History of the Social Sciences," *Journal of the History of the Behavioral Sciences* 44, no. 2 (2008): 149–51; Perrin Selcer, "The View from Everywhere: Disciplining Diversity in Post–World War II International Social Science," *Journal of the History of the Behavioral Sciences* 45, no. 4 (2009): 309–29.

7. The French Permanent Delegation to the United Nations' European Office suggested to Jacques Kayser in the spring of 1952 that the crisis was easing. French Permanent Delegation, letter to Jacques Kayser, March 24, 1952, Fonds Kayser, carton 25, dossier 2.

8. John Grierson, "Production Unit Planned: Mass Media to Be Used for Peace," *UNESCO Courier* 1, no. 1 (1948): 3; *Rapports sur les moyens techniques de l'information: Presse, films, radio* (Paris: UNESCO, 1951), 14–15, 17–19, 23.

9. Ralph D. Casey, letter to Walter H. C. Laves, September 13, 1948, UNESCO Archives, Paris, France, 307.A.20/02, part 1; André de Blonay, letter to Arthur A. Compton, May 24, 1949, UNESCO Archives, 307.A.20/02, part 1; Pierre Navaux, letter to H. C. Edgar, August 31, 1949, UNESCO Archives, 307.A.20/02, part 2; Anne Perlman, "U.N.E.S.C.O. to Map Policy at Paris Talks," *New York Herald Tribune*, [November 1946], Grierson Archive, G5.22.10.

10. The African American diplomat Ralph Bunche was particularly influential in setting up UN reporting mechanisms. Glenn Mitoma, *Human Rights and the Negotiation of American Power* (Philadelphia: University of Pennsylvania Press, 2013), 66–73; Lawrence S. Finkelstein, "Bunche and the Colonial World: From Trusteeship to Decolonization," in *Ralph Bunche: The Man and His Times*, ed. Benjamin Rivlin (New York: Holmes & Meier, 1990), 109–31, see esp. 126.

11. *Paper for Printing*, 21–26, 74–79; *World Communications: Press, Radio, Film* (Paris: UNESCO, 1950), 24–25; *United Nations Educational Scientific and Cultural*

Organization: Report of the Director General on the Activities of the Organization from April 1950 to March 1951 (Paris: UNESCO, 1951), 86.

12. John Grierson, "The Film in British Colonial Development," *Sight and Sound* 17 (1948): 2–4.

13. Judt, *Postwar*, 63–99, Taylor quoted on 69; John Grierson, letter to Charles Thompson, December 31, 1947, William Benton Papers, Special Collections Research Center, University of Chicago Library, box 382, folder 2.

14. Jacques Kayser, "La crise mondiale du papier journal compromet en Europe la liberté de la presse," September 26, 1950, Fonds Kayser, carton 25, dossier 2; Jacques Kayser, draft ECOSOC speech, [1951], Fonds Kayser, carton 25, dossier 2.

15. Kayser cited Clara Friedman's *The Newsprint Problem: Ten Questions and Ten Answers* (New York: American Newspaper Guild, [1949]) in his editorial "La crise mondiale du papier journal." See also Claude Day, letter to Jacques Kayser, August 31, 1951, Fonds Kayser, carton 25, dossier 2; Jacques Kayser, letter to Claude Day, September 4, 1951, Fonds Kayser, carton 25, dossier 1.

16. William Benton, "Confidential Report to Secretary Marshall by William Benton, Chairman of the United States Delegation to the Geneva Conference on Freedom of Information," [1948], Harold Dwight Lasswell Papers (MS 1043), Manuscripts and Archives, Yale University Library, box 17, folder 207; Zechariah Chafee, "General Observations on the Conference" (appendix 1 to Benton's report), Lasswell Papers, box 17, folder 207; Thomas J. Wilson, letter to Zechariah Chafee, April 26, 1948, Chafee Papers, reel 72; Margaret A. Blanchard, *Exporting the First Amendment: The Press-Government Crusade of 1945–1952* (New York: Longman, 1986), 171–73, 191–92. On congressional discussion of early Cold War newsprint shortages, see also Michael Stamm, "The Space for News: Ether and Paper in the Business of Media," *Media History* 21, no. 1 (2015): 67–68.

17. Yann Darré, *Histoire sociale du cinéma français* (Paris: La Découverte, 2000), 71–72; Jens Ulff-Møller, *Hollywood's Film Wars with France: Film-Trade Diplomacy and the Emergence of the French Film Quota Policy* (Rochester, NY: University of Rochester Press, 2001), chap. 9; Ian C. Jarvie, *Hollywood's Overseas Campaign: The North Atlantic Movie Trade, 1920–1950* (Cambridge: Cambridge University Press, 1992), 213–14.

18. James Hendrick, memo to Zechariah Chafee, enclosing "Position Papers Concerning the Conference on Freedom of Information," July 23, 1947, Chafee Papers, reel 14. See also "The Mass Media and UNESCO: Report of the Committee of Consultants to the Department of State," September 24, 1946, Chafee Papers, reel 15.

19. *Rapport de la Commission des Besoins Techniques* (1947), 19–21.

20. Benton cited his Geneva remarks in William Benton, "Address" (speech to U.S. National Commission for UNESCO, Boston, MA, September 27, 1948), Chafee Papers, reel 16. On the United States' focus on growth and its exportation of GDP/GNP accounting after the Second World War, see Dirk Philipsen, *The Little Big Number: How GDP Came to Rule the World and What to Do About It* (Princeton, NJ: Princeton University Press, 2015), 117–42; David C. Engerman, "American Knowledge and Global Power," *Diplomatic History* 31, no. 4 (2007): 599–622, see esp. 615–21.

21. British delegate J. Murray Watson cited in Blanchard, *Exporting the First Amendment*, 191; Grierson, letter to Chafee, December 30, 1947.

22. Julian Huxley in *United Nations Educational, Scientific, and Cultural Organisation: Report of the Director General on the Activities of the Organization in 1947* (Paris: UNESCO, 1947), 13; Grierson, letter to Chafee, December 30, 1947. On Grierson and Huxley's friendship, see Ellis, *John Grierson*, 229, 236.

23. Benton, "Confidential Report to Secretary Marshall"; Jesse MacKnight, letter to William Benton, May 26, 1950, Benton Papers, box 388, folder 2; Maurel, *Histoire de l'Unesco*, 97–98, 115–16.

24. "Délégation Française aux Nations Unies—Texte proposé par le Gouvernement français" and "Texte proposé par les Américains" in Fonds Kayser, carton 25, dossier 1, subfolder dated "05/05/1950–21/07/1950." Kayser discussed the French and American positions in a letter to René Cassin, [1950], Fonds Kayser, carton 25, dossier 1.

25. Kayser, "La crise mondiale du papier journal"; Ministre d'Information, Bordereau d'envoi and enclosures, to Jacques Kayser, January 13, 1951, Fonds Kayser, carton 25, dossier 1; Jacques Kayser, "Premier avant-projet de Résolution sur la crise du papier journal," sent to M. de Menthon at the Ministère des Affaires Etrangères, August 14, 1951, Fonds Kayser, carton 25, dossier 1.

26. Jacques Kayser, letter to Fernand Terrou, August 3, 1951, Fonds Kayser, carton 25, dossier 1. See also Jacques Kayser, letter to Claude Bellanger, May 5, 1952, Fonds Kayser, carton 26, dossier 2; Jacques Kayser, letter to Armand Gaspard, May 11, 1954, Fonds Kayser, carton 26, dossier 2.

27. At Geneva, France proposed an international "right to reply" to published errors, similar to the right guaranteed to news subjects in domestic French law. On France's relationship to other member states, see Benton, "Confidential Report to Secretary Marshall"; Jacques Kayser, letter to "mon cher ami," November 6, 1951, Fonds Kayser, carton 25, dossier 2; Fernand Terrou, "Intervention sur la question du papier devant la Commission du programme U.N.E.S.C.O.," July 1951, Fonds Kayser, carton 25, dossier 2.

28. On the planning consensus in postwar Europe, see Judt, *Postwar*, 67–76. The case of France is a weak point in Kenneth Cmiel's argument that the emergence of the Third World foiled postwar freedom-of-information negotiations: cf. Kenneth Cmiel, "Human Rights, Freedom of Information, and the Origins of Third-World Solidarity," in *Truth Claims: Representation and Human Rights*, ed. Mark Philip Bradley and Patrice Petro (New Brunswick, NJ: Rutgers University Press, 2002), 107–26.

29. Fernand Terrou, "Aspects législatifs et réglementaires de l'intervention de l'Etat dans le domaine de l'Information," *La Revue administrative* 6, no. 33 (1953): 264; Terrou and Solal, *Legislation for Press, Film and Radio*, see esp. 25, 31, 129–210. On planning in Fourth Republic France, see Nord, *France's New Deal*, 145–213.

30. "The French Lecture the American Press," *Chicago Tribune*, January 4, 1952, Fonds Kayser, carton 25, dossier 1; Zechariah Chafee, "General Observations on the Conference," Lasswell Papers, box 17, folder 207; Zechariah Chafee, letter to A. D. P. Heeney, May 10, 1948, Chafee Papers, reel 72; Smith, *Zechariah Chafee*, 223–37; Blanchard, *Exporting the First Amendment*, 161–62, 165–66, 276–77.

31. Cmiel, "Human Rights," 123; Blanchard, *Exporting the First Amendment*, 291–98, 342–43, Kotschnig cited on 297.

32. *Paper for Printing*, 66, 94, 98–104, 130–32; Sara Nocentini, "Building the Network: Raw Materials Shortages and the Western Bloc at the Beginning of the Cold War,

1948–1951," *Business and Economic History On-Line* 2 (2004), accessed April 26, 2016, http://www.thebhc.org/sites/default/files/Nocentini_0.pdf.

33. See, e.g., Mitoma, *Human Rights*, 74–102; Cmiel, "Human Rights," esp. 123–25.

34. Benton, "Address"; William Benton, letter to Max McCullough, November 23, 1949, Benton Papers, box 388, folder 12; Blanchard, *Exporting the First Amendment*, 65–68, 328–31, 343–46; Maurel, *Histoire de l'Unesco*, 93–120.

35. William Benton in *Records of the General Conference of the United Nations Educational, Scientific, and Cultural Organization—Fifth Session, Florence, 1950* (Paris: UNESCO, 1950), 342. See also Charles Thomson, letter to Max McKenna, August 29, 1950, Benton Papers, box 388, folder 2.

36. Canham, "International Freedom of Information," 598; Smith, *Zechariah Chafee*, Chafee quoted on 236; Blanchard, *Exporting the First Amendment*, 250–51, 291–94.

37. *Rapport de la Commission des Besoins Techniques* (1947), 26; "Experts recommend to UNESCO the creation of an International Institute for Press and Information," September 8, 1947, UNESCO Press Release 315, UNESCO Archives, 307:07.A.01.IIPI, part 1; "A Draft Project for the Establishment of an International Institute of Press and Information," UNESCO/MC/2 (part 1), August 4, 1948, UNESCO Archives, 307:07.A.01.IIPI, part 1; J. P. Urlik, memo to René Maheu, August 13, 1948, UNESCO Archives, 307:07.A.01.IIPI, part 1; Judt, *Postwar*, 129–64.

38. René Maheu, letters to Lyman Bryson, Zechariah Chafee, and Robert Hutchins, September 17, 1948, UNESCO Archives, 307:07.A.01.IIPI, part 1; René Maheu, letter to John Grierson, August 24, 1948, UNESCO Archives, 307:07.A.01.IIPI, part 1; René Maheu, letter to E. H. Carr, August 25, 1948, UNESCO Archives, 307:07.A.01.IIPI, part 1; René Maheu, letter to Fernand Terrou, October 26, 1948, UNESCO Archives, 307:07.A.01.IIPI, part 1; Douglas H. Schneider, letter to Walter Laves, December 12, 1949, UNESCO Archives, 307:07.A.01.IIPI, part 3; [René Maheu], letter to Fernand Terrou, November 8, 1948, UNESCO Archives, 307:07.A.01.IIPI, part 2.

39. The failed UN freedom-of-information negotiations were commonly labeled "political" by those seeking other avenues. See also "A Draft Statement on Mass Communications—UNESCO," April 2, 1951, Benton Papers, box 390, folder 12: "It is becoming more and more apparent that conventions, instead of obtaining their objectives, may point up controversial issues. . . . [This] is one of the most complicated of all fields—with many friendly nations holding 'political' views different than those of the U.S. in regard to 'freedom of information'; and involving, in addition, such diverse related problems as the competitive struggle for radio frequencies and the availability of newsprint."

40. Maheu, letter to Hutchins, September 17, 1948. Douglas Schneider wrote to William Benton in the fall of 1949 that "unless some definite signs can be observed of an implementation of the 1949 resolution, this project will no longer be granted the sponsorship of UNESCO." Douglas H. Schneider, letter to William Benton, November 9, 1949, UNESCO Archives, 307:07.A.01.IIPI, part 3. See also Douglas H. Schneider, letter to the president of the Centre d'Etudes de Presse, December 1, 1949, UNESCO Archives, 307:07.A.01.IIPI, part 3.

41. Walter Laves, letter to Peter Odegaard, June 30, [1949], UNESCO Archives, 307:07.A.01.IIPI, part 3.

42. Jacques Kayser, letter to Erwin D. Canham, October 10, 1949; Erwin D. Canham, letter to Jacques Kayser, October 13, 1949, both in Fonds Kayser, carton 26, dossier 2.

43. Jacques Kayser, letter to Philippe Desjardins, October 20, 1949, Fonds Kayser, carton 26, dossier 2; W. Farr, memo to the Office of the Director General, February 9, 1950, UNESCO Archives, 307:07.A.01.IIPI, part 4. Cf. Blanchard's account of the IPI's origins, *Exporting the First Amendment*, 364–68.

44. Lester Markel, letter to Philippe Desjardins, March 6, 1950, UNESCO Archives, 307:07.A.01.IIPI, part 4; "Foreign News Men Will Visit the U.S.," *New York Times*, August 25, 1950, UNESCO Archives, 307:07.A.01.IIPI, part 4; Canham, letter to Kayser, October 13, 1949; Edward F. D'Arms, letter to Floyd Taylor, May 2, 1950, Rockefeller Foundation Records (RF), Rockefeller Archive Center (RAC), Sleepy Hollow, NY, FA 387, RG 1.2, series 100, box 13, folder 83.

45. Sam Lebovic, *Free Speech and Unfree News: The Paradox of Press Freedom in America* (Cambridge, MA: Harvard University Press, 2016), 156; Winthrop M. Southworth Jr., memo to Mr. Sargeant re: "PSB Staff Director," May 7, 1951, CIA Freedom of Information Act (FOIA) Electronic Reading Room, CIA-RDP80-01446R000100140040-8, accessed August 17, 2018, https://www.cia.gov/library/readingroom/docs/CIA-RDP80-01446R000100140040-8.pdf.

46. Douglas H. Schneider, memo to the Office of the Director General (ODG) and Philippe Desjardins, October 17, 1950, UNESCO Archives, 307:07.A.01.IIPI, part 4. On ASNE's contact with the CIA, see, e.g., John Desmond, letter to General Walter Bedell Smith, December 13, 1951, CIA FOIA Electronic Reading Room, CIA-RDP88-01315R000300340011-3, accessed August 17, 2018, https://www.cia.gov/library/readingroom/docs/CIA-RDP88-01315R000300340011-3.pdf.

47. "Foreign News Men Will Visit the U.S."; Lester Markel, "Memorandum for an International Press Institute," memo attached to Arthur Hays Sulzberger, letter to Chester I. Barnard, August 22, 1949, RF, RAC, FA387, RG 1.2, series 100, box 13, folder 82; Lester Markel, letter and memo to Chester I. Barnard, January 6, 1950, RF, RAC, FA387, RG 1.2, series 100, box 13, folder 83; "Interviews" (interoffice RF memo), December 26, 1950, RF, RAC, FA387, RG 1.2, series 100, box 13, folder 83. On Canham, see Mitoma, *Human Rights and the Negotiation of American Power*, 96; Blanchard, *Exporting the First Amendment*, quotation on 197.

48. See the Rockefeller Foundation's two internal "Interviews" memos on the meetings dated October 11, 1950, RF, RAC, FA387, RG 1.2, series 100, box 13, folder 83. On Beuve-Méry, see Richard Kuisel, *Seducing the French: The Dilemma of Americanization* (Berkeley: University of California Press, 1993), 43–46.

49. See, for instance, "Interviews" (interoffice RF memo), January 23, 1950, RF, RAC, FA387, RG 1.2, series 100, box 13, folder 83; Floyd Taylor, letter to Edward F. D'Arms, May 5, 1950, RF, RAC, FA387, RG 1.2, series 100, box 13, folder 83; Lester Markel, letter to Hubert Beuve-Méry, October 17, 1950, UNESCO Archives, 307:07.A.01.IIPI, part 4; Pierre Artigue, memo to Philippe Desjardins, May 16, 1951, UNESCO Archives, 307:07.A.01.IIPI, part 4; Schneider, memo to the ODG and Desjardins, October 17, 1950; John Marshall, letter to Douglas Schneider, October 27, 1950, UNESCO Archives, 307:07.A.01.IIPI, part 4. The Rockefeller Foundation files on the IPI contain extensive discussion of the relationship between the UNESCO and ASNE plans. See RF, RAC, FA387, RG 1.2, series 100, box 13, folders 82–84.

50. John Kenton, letter to Claude Bellanger, February 4, 1951, UNESCO Archives, 307:07.A.01.IIPI, part 4; Erwin D. Canham, letter to Douglas H. Schneider, April 12, 1951, UNESCO Archives, 307:07.A.01.IIPI, part 4; *Executive Board 1951 Volume*

XVII 26–27–28 Sessions [1951 Executive Board proceedings], August 24, 1951, 15–16, 26 EX/CP/SR 1–3, UNESCO Archives, 307:07.A.01.IIPI, part 4; Philippe Desjardins, letter to Claude Bellanger, September 25, 1951, UNESCO Archives, 307:07.A.01.IIPI, part 4.

51. Philippe Desjardins, memo to René Maheu, May 19, 1949, UNESCO Archives, 307:07.A.01.IIPI, part 3; Seydoux in *Executive Board 1951*, 16; Bellanger in Artigue, memo to Desjardins, May 16, 1951.

52. "L'Institut français de Presse," Fonds Kayser, carton 26, dossier 3; "L'Institut international de la Presse va voir le jour," *Le Monde*, April 17, 1951, UNESCO Archives, 307:07.A.01.IIPI, part 4; "Execution of the Programme for 1951 (Mass Communication): International Institute of the Press and Information," 26 EX/14, UNESCO Archives, 307:07.A.01.IIPI, part 4; Jean-Louis Santoro, "La liberté de l'information: Logiques institutionnelles et logiques professionnelles au plan international (1947–1972)" (PhD diss., Université Michel de Montaigne, Bordeaux III, 1991), UNESCO Archives, 145–56; *Rapports sur les moyens techniques de l'information* (1951), 21.

53. On British responses to the IIPI proposals, see Maheu, letter to Carr, August 25, 1948; Vice President, International Federation of Newspaper Proprietors, letter to René Maheu, September 20, 1948; E. H. Carr, letter to René Maheu, October 7, 1948; Candidus, "A Waste of UN Money," *Daily Graphic* (UK), October 18, 1948, all in UNESCO Archives, 307:07.A.01.IIPI, part 1. For useful coverage of tensions between the "Latin" and "Anglo-Saxon" contingents at UNESCO more generally, see Maurel, *Histoire de l'Unesco*.

54. Armand Gaspard, letter to Roger Massip (*Le Figaro* editor), with copy to Kayser, November 7, 1953; Armand Gaspard, letter to Jacques Kayser, May 6, 1954; Jacques Kayser, letter to Armand Gaspard, December 2, 1953, all in Fonds Kayser, carton 26, dossier 2.

55. Claude Hagège, *Contre la pensée unique* (Paris: Odile Jacob, 2012), 39–83, see esp. 58.

56. Huxley in *UNESCO: Report of the Director General . . . in 1947*, 94; William Benton, letter to Howland Sargeant, June 20, 1950, Benton Papers, box 381, folder 2. As a Yale undergraduate, Benton had written to his mother to confess his weak grades in Spanish: "I have absolutely no ability for languages." Sidney Hyman, *The Lives of William Benton* (Chicago: University of Chicago Press, 1969), quotation on 49, see also 27, 32–33, 37.

57. Armand Gaspard, letter to Jacques Kayser, December 31, 1954, Fonds Kayser, carton 26, dossier 2; Robert Salmon, letter to Kayser, May 28, 1957, Fonds Kayser, carton 26, dossier 2.

58. William R. Pendergast, "UNESCO and French Cultural Relations, 1945–1970," *International Organization* 30, no. 3 (1976): 459–62.

59. General Conference resolution 5.22 in *Records of the General Conference, Ninth Session, New Delhi, 1956: Resolutions* (Paris: UNESCO, 1957), 29, https://unesdoc.unesco.org/ark:/48223/pf0000114585; IAMCR interim committee form letter, May 13, 1957, UNESCO Archives, 307.A.01.IAMCR "—66," part 1; "Conférence constitutive des 18/19 Décembre 1957: Compte rendu," UNESCO Archives, 307.A.01.IAMCR "—66," part 1; Kaarle Nordenstreng, "Institutional Networking: The Story of the International Association for Media and Communication Research (IAMCR)," in *The History of Media and Communication Research: Contested Memories*, ed. David W. Park and Jefferson Pooley (New York: Peter Lang, 2008), 226–28. The International

Association for Mass Communication Research was renamed the International Association for Media and Communication Research in 1996. Michael Meyen, "The IAMCR Story: Communication and Media Research in a Global Perspective," in *The International History of Communication Study*, ed. Peter Simonson and David Park (New York: Routledge, 2016), 90.

60. On the IAMCR's turn toward critical communication research and the nonaligned movement, see Nordenstreng, "Institutional Networking," 234–35.

61. Tor Gjesdal, letter to Maarten Rooy, September 8, 1959, UNESCO Archives, 307.A.01.IAMCR "—66," part 3; Fernand Terrou, "Rapport sur l'activité de l'association au cours du 1er semestre 1959," UNESCO Archives, 307.A.01.IAMCR "—66," part 3; Fernand Terrou, "Compte rendu," May 14, 1958, UNESCO Archives, 307.A.01.IAMCR "—66," part 2; Raymond B. Nixon, "Research in Mass Communication: Its Status, Trends, Needs" (speech to the International Federation of Newspaper Editors and Publishers [FIEJ], New York, May 25, 1960), UNESCO Archives, 307.A.01.IAMCR "—66," part 3; Heilbron, Guilhot, and Jeanpierre, "Toward a Transnational History," 155. On French and European influences at the early IAMCR, see also Nordenstreng, "Institutional Networking," 229–31; Meyen, "The IAMCR Story," 91–92.

62. Gjesdal, letter to Rooy, September 8, 1959; Tor Gjesdal, letter to Raymond Nixon, April 10, 1959, UNESCO Archives, 307.A.01.IAMCR "—66," part 3; Tor Gjesdal, "Meetings in Milan," memo to the Director General, October 15, 1959, UNESCO Archives, 307.A.01.IAMCR "—66," part 3; Maarten Rooy, letter to Tor Gjesdal, July 22, 1961, UNESCO Archives, 307.A.01.IAMCR "—66," part 4; Maarten Rooy, letter to Tor Gjesdal, January 3, 1962, UNESCO Archives, 307.A.01.IAMCR "—66," part 5. On the move of the IAMCR's administrative headquarters, see "Réunion de bureau," June 26, 1961; "General Assembly Held at Vevey (Switzerland) on June 19 and 20, 1961: Report of the Main Proceedings," June 19–20, 1961, both in UNESCO Archives, 307.A.01.IAMCR "—66," part 4.

63. Raymond Nixon, letter to Tor Gjesdal, February 8, 1959, UNESCO Archives, 307.A.01.IAMCR "—66," part 3; Benton, "Confidential Report to Secretary Marshall"; Raymond Nixon, letter to Fernand Terrou, December 10, 1959, UNESCO Archives, 307.A.01.IAMCR "—66," part 3; Raymond Nixon, letter to Tor Gjesdal, December 10, 1959, UNESCO Archives, 307.A.01.IAMCR "—66," part 3; Raymond Nixon, letter to Pierre Navaux, February 21, 1961, UNESCO Archives, 307.A.01. IAMCR "—66," part 4; Wilbur Schramm, letter to Gordon Mirams (UNESCO), May 4, 1963, UNESCO Archives, 307.A.01.IAMCR "—66," part 5; Raymond Nixon, letter to Maarten Rooy, December 16, 1961, UNESCO Archives, 307.A.01.IAMCR "—66," part 3.

64. Christopher Simpson, *Science of Coercion: Communication Research and Psychological Warfare, 1945–1960* (New York: Oxford University Press, 1994); Timothy Glander, *Origins of Mass Communication Research During the American Cold War: Educational Effects and Contemporary Implications* (Mahwah, NJ: Lawrence Erlbaum Associates, 2000), see esp. chap. 5; Ronald R. Kline, *The Cybernetics Moment: Or Why We Call Our Age the Information Age* (Baltimore, MD: Johns Hopkins University Press, 2015), 122–23; Jimmy Soni and Rob Goodman, *A Mind at Play: How Claude Shannon Invented the Information Age* (New York: Simon and Schuster, 2017), 167–69.

65. Nixon, letter to Terrou, December 10, 1959.

66. Gjesdal, letter to Rooy, September 8, 1959; Raymond Nixon, letter to Fernand Terrou, March 25, 1961, UNESCO Archives, 307.A.01.IAMCR "—66," part 4.

67. Benton in *UNESCO: Records of the General Conference . . . Fifth Session, Florence, 1950*, 342.

68. Nixon, "Research in Mass Communication"; Raymond Nixon, letter to Tor Gjesdal, January 31, 1958, UNESCO Archives, 307.A.01.IAMCR "—66," part 2; Raymond Nixon, letter to Pierre Navaux, February 11, 1961, UNESCO Archives, 307.A.01. IAMCR "—66," part 4; Nixon, letter to Terrou, March 25, 1961. Benton's 1955 trip to Russia would provide material for his reports on the Soviet educational system, published as *This Is the Challenge: The Benton Reports of 1956–1958 on the Nature of the Soviet Threat* (New York: Associated College Presses, 1958).

69. American participation in other UNESCO research initiatives may have been more nuanced than in its mass-communication work. On American involvement at UNESCO's Social Sciences Department, see Selcer, "The View from Everywhere."

70. Terrou, "Compte rendu," May 14, 1958; Santoro, "La Liberté de l'information," chap. 2: "Programme de l'AIERI," 209–10, 223; Fernand Terrou, "L'étude de l'information: problèmes et méthodes," *Etudes de Presse* 18–19 [typescript copy, n.d., n. pag.], UNESCO Archives, 307.A.01.IAMCR "—66," part 2. According to Santoro, Nixon's disregard for "cultural specificity"—and the differences between French and "Anglo-Saxon" research—aggravated tensions between him and Terrou and Kayser (Santoro, "La Liberté de l'information," 252).

71. Terrou, "L'étude de l'information"; Bernard Berelson and Paul Lazarsfeld, *The Analysis of Communication Content* ([n.p.], 1948), 1–6; Simpson, *Science of Coercion*, 5–10, 22–30; Todd Gitlin, "Media Sociology: The Dominant Paradigm," *Theory and Society* 6, no. 2 (1978): 205–53.

72. Terrou. On Terrou's role in the *épuration*, see Cmiel, "Human Rights," 114.

73. Fernand Terrou, "Rapport sur l'activité de l'association au cours du 1er semestre 1959," UNESCO Archives, 307.A.01.IAMCR "—66," part 3; Santoro, "Liberté de l'information," 233–34.

74. Jacques Kayser, "Intervention de M. Jacques Kayser" (speech to the Colloque international sur l'enseignement du journalisme, Strasbourg, France, December 3–5, 1956), Fonds Kayser, carton 26, dossier 3; Kayser, *Mort d'une liberté*, iii–v.

75. Kuisel, *Seducing the French*, 100–30.

76. Martin Jay, "Adorno in America," *New German Critique* 31 (1984): 157–82; Gitlin, "Media Sociology," 224–33; Everett Rogers, *A History of Communication Study: A Biographical Approach* (New York: Free, 1994), 280–84; Raymond Williams, *Culture and Society* (London: Chatto and Windus, 1958), excerpted as "The Masses," in *The Raymond Williams Reader*, ed. John Higgins (Oxford: Blackwell, 2001), 47; John Durham Peters, "Raymond Williams's *Culture and Society* as Research Method," in *Questions of Method in Cultural Studies*, ed. Mimi White and James Schwoch (Cambridge: Blackwell, 2006), see esp. 59.

77. Siegfried Kracauer, "The Challenge of Qualitative Content Analysis," *Public Opinion Quarterly* 16, no. 4 (1952): 631–42, see esp. 636, 642; Harold A. Innis, "A Critical Review," in *The Bias of Communication*, 2nd ed. (1951; Toronto: University of Toronto Press, 2008), 191.

78. Edgar Morin, *New Trends in the Study of Mass Communications* (Birmingham: Swift Print, 1968), 6; Nord, *France's New Deal*. On Innis's chilly reception in the United

States, see Paul Heyer and David Crowley, introduction to *Bias of Communication*, xxxix–xl.

79. Heilbron, Guilhot, and Jeanpierre, "Toward a Transnational History," 155; Loïc Blondiaux, "Comment rompre avec Durkheim? Jean Stoetzel et la sociologie française de l'après-guerre (1945–1958)," *Revue française de sociologie* 32, no. 3 (1991): 411–41.

80. Raymond B. Nixon, "Factors Related to Freedom in National Press Systems," *Journalism Quarterly* 37, no. 1 (1960): 13–28, see esp. 17, 20, 27.

81. *Rapport de la Commission des Besoins Techniques: Presse, film, radio après enquête dans dix-sept pays* (Paris: Unesco, 1948); Nixon, 28.

3. INFORMATION FLOWS AND
THE CONUNDRUM OF MULTILINGUALISM

The epigraphs for this chapter are taken from: Charles T. Morrisey and Ronald J. Grele, "Interview with Melvin J. Fox for the Ford Foundation Oral History Project," October 24, 1972, Ford Foundation Records (FF), Rockefeller Archive Center (RAC), Sleepy Hollow, NY, FA618, series 4, box 34, folder 171; "Meeting of Experts on the Use in Education of African Languages in Relation to English, Where English is the Accepted Second Language: Report Presented to the Director-General of the United Nations Educational, Scientific and Cultural Organization," December 15, 1952, EJD/PZ, UNESCO Archives, Paris, France, file 375:408.8(6)Ao.64(66) "52," part 2.

1. On Basic in Miami, see William Bentinck-Smith, "How to Run a Ship with 850 Words," *Harvard Alumni Bulletin* 48, no. 5, November 17, 1945, Rockefeller Foundation records (RF), RAC, Record Group (RG) 1.1, series 200, box 235, folder 2803; I. A. Richards, letter to John Marshall, June 29, 1945; Lieut. R. H. Wittcoff, "Memorandum to the Commanding Officer," June 19, 1945; I. A. Richards, "Report on the Use of Basic English in Naval Training for Foreign Language Speaking Personnel," June 19, 1945, all in RF, RAC, RG 1.1, series 200, box 234, folder 2793. On sites where new techniques for English-language teaching were being tested during the war, see, inter alia, I. A. Richards, letter to David H. Stevens, March 8, 1944, enclosing "Basic English in American Education," RF, RAC, RG 1.1, series 200, box 234, folder 2792; Charles C. Fries, letter to David H. Stevens, April 7, 1944, RF, RAC, RG 1.1, series 200, box 286, folder 3415; John Marshall, interview with Charles C. Fries, May 10, 1944, RF, RAC, RG 1.1, series 200, box 286, folder 3415.

2. For Basic in the American press, see, inter alia, Lincoln Barnett, "Basic English: A Globalanguage," *Life*, October 18, 1943; I. A. Richards, "Idle Fears About Basic English," *The Atlantic*, [1944], RF, RAC, RG 1.1, series 200, box 234, folder 2792. On Rockefeller Foundation support for Basic, see Rodney Koeneke, *Empires of the Mind: I. A. Richards and Basic English in China, 1929–1979* (Stanford, CA: Stanford University Press, 2004), see esp. 94–95, 192–93.

3. See, e.g., Charles Dorn and Kristen Ghodsee, "The Cold War Politicization of Literacy: Communism, UNESCO, and the World Bank," *Diplomatic History* 36, no. 2 (2012): 373–98; Phillip W. Jones, *International Policies for Third World Education: UNESCO, Literacy and Development* (London: Routledge, 1988), chaps. 1–2. An exception that bridges diplomatic history with language considerations is Chantalle F. Verna, "Haiti, the Rockefeller Foundation, and UNESCO's Pilot Project in Fundamental Education, 1948–1953," *Diplomatic History* 40, no. 2 (2016): 269–95. Both the

Proquest Historical Newspapers *New York Times* database and Google Ngram show usage of the phrase "language barrier" increasing dramatically in the 1940s and 1950s.

4. Stephen Evans, "Macaulay's Minute Revisited: Colonial Language Policy in Nineteenth-Century India," *Journal of Multilingual and Multicultural Development* 23, no. 4 (2002): 277–79; Clive Whitehead, "The Medium of Instruction in British Colonial Education: A Case of Cultural Imperialism or Enlightened Paternalism?," *History of Education* 24, no. 1 (1995): 1–4, 14–15.

5. A variation of this argument and parts of this chapter have also appeared in Diana Lemberg, "'The Universal Language of the Future': Decolonization, Development, and the American Embrace of Global English, 1945–1965," *Modern Intellectual History* 15, no. 2 (2018): 561–92. The cited USAID report is "English Language Programs of the Agency for International Development," Agency for International Development, Department of State, December 1967, accessed February 8, 2016, http://pdf .usaid.gov/pdf_docs/pnaad469.pdf.

6. See, for instance, Eugen Weber, *Peasants into Frenchmen: The Modernization of Rural France* (Stanford, CA: Stanford University Press, 1976); Jean-François Chanet, *L'école républicaine et les petites patries* (Paris: Aubier, 1996); Mary K. Vaughan, *Cultural Politics in Revolution: Teachers, Peasants, and Schools in Mexico, 1930–1940* (Tucson: University of Arizona Press, 1997); Elsie Rockwell, "Schools of the Revolution: Enacting and Contesting State Forms in Tlaxcala, 1910–1930," in *Everyday Forms of State Formation: Revolution and the Negotiation of Rule in Modern Mexico*, ed. Gilbert M. Joseph and Daniel Nugent (Durham, NC: Duke University Press, 1994), 170–208; Sheila Fitzpatrick, *Education and Social Mobility in the Soviet Union, 1921–1934* (Cambridge: Cambridge University Press, 1979); Charles E. Clark, *Uprooting Otherness: The Literacy Campaign in NEP-Era Russia* (Cranbury, NJ: Associated University Presses, 2000); Jean-Jacques Renoliet, *L'Unesco oubliée: La Société des Nations et la coopération intellectuelle (1919–1946)* (Paris: Publications de la Sorbonne, 1999), 33–34.

7. Scholarship on education in the British Empire depicts protracted British ambivalence about the place of English in colonial schooling. Thomas Macaulay's Minute of 1835 famously declared the desirability of spreading English in India while at the same time clarifying that it was destined for a circumscribed "class" of indigenous interlocutors rather than the "great mass of the population." As the British expanded their presence in Africa in the late nineteenth and early twentieth centuries, the Indian case became an illustration of the political dangers of educating colonial subjects in English. Diana Lemberg, "The End of Empires and Some Linguistic Turns: British and French Language Policies in Inter- and Post-War Africa," in *British and French Colonialism in Africa, Asia and the Middle East: Connected Empires across the Eighteenth to the Twentieth Centuries*, ed. James R. Fichter (Basingstoke, UK: Palgrave Macmillan, 2019); Evans, "Macaulay's Minute Revisited," 268–72, 276–79; Whitehead, "The Medium of Instruction," 2–4, 14–15; Sybille Küster, "'Book Learning' Versus 'Adapted Education': The Impact of Phelps-Stokesism on Colonial Education Systems in Central Africa in the Interwar Period," *Paedagogica Historica* 43, no. 1 (2007): 79–97.

8. Michael Adas, *Dominance by Design: Technological Imperatives and America's Civilizing Mission* (Cambridge, MA: Belknap Press of Harvard University Press, 2006), 160, 165–67, 175–77; Glenn Anthony May, *Social Engineering in the Philippines: The Aims,*

Execution, and Impact of American Colonial Policy, 1900–1913 (Westport, CT: Greenwood, 1980), 82–84; José-Manuel Navarro, *Creating Tropical Yankees: Social Science Textbooks and U.S. Ideological Control in Puerto Rico, 1898–1908* (New York: Routledge, 2002), 31–113; Ruanni Tupas and Beatriz P. Lorente, "A 'New' Politics of Language in the Philippines: Bilingual Education and the New Challenge of the Mother Tongues," in *Language, Education and Nation-Building: Assimilation and Shift in Southeast Asia*, ed. Peter Sercombe and Ruanni Tupas (Basingstoke, UK: Palgrave Macmillan, 2014), 165–80; Amílcar Antonio Barreto, *The Politics of Language in Puerto Rico* (Gainesville: University Press of Florida, 2001), 1–33; Julian Go, "Chains of Empire, Projects of State: Political Education and U.S. Colonial Rule in Puerto Rico and the Philippines," *Comparative Studies in Society and History* 42, no. 2 (2000): 333–34, 343.

9. Mark Mazower, *Governing the World: The History of an Idea* (New York: Penguin, 2012), 191–213, quotation at xvii; Chloé Maurel, *Histoire de l'Unesco: Les trente premières années: 1945–1974* (Paris: L'Harmattan, 2010), 15–27; Renoliet, *L'Unesco oubliée*, 158–78; Jaime Torres Bodet, "Half the World's Population Is Illiterate," *UNESCO Courier* 2, no. 8 (1949): 29; "War on Illiteracy in World Is Urged," *New York Times*, December 2, 1948; Robert Rice, "The Thousand Silver Threads," *New Yorker*, February 16, 1952. On the expanding geography of U.S. power after 1945, see also Odd Arne Westad, *The Global Cold War: Third World Interventions and the Making of Our Times* (Cambridge: Cambridge University Press, 2005), 23–25; Daniel Immerwahr, *Thinking Small: The United States and the Lure of Community Development* (Cambridge, MA: Harvard University Press, 2015), 52–53.

10. Arthur Sweetser, letter to William Benton, August 17, 1950, William Benton Papers, Special Collections Research Center, University of Chicago Library, box 388, folder 2. On Sweetser, see Mazower, *Governing the World*, 145, 192–93, 196, 211, 213.

11. Tom Allbeson, "Photographic Diplomacy in the Postwar World: UNESCO and the Conception of Photography as a Universal Language," *Modern Intellectual History* 12, no. 2 (2015): 386–87; David Bellos, *Is That a Fish in Your Ear? The Amazing Adventure of Translation* (London: Penguin, 2012), 268–82; Richard de Rochemont, letter to John Marshall, July 24, 1945, RF, RAC, RG 1.1, series 200, box 234, folder 2793; John Grierson, letter to D. Stevens, July 21, 1947, RG 1.1, RF, RAC, series 200, box 234, folder 2795; David H. Stevens, letter to John Grierson, August 5, 1947, RF, RAC, RG 1.1, series 200, box 234, folder 2795.

12. Colonel A. Myers, "Education for International Understanding: The Part of Language-Teaching," July 2, 1947, Educ./38/1947, UNESCO Archives, 375:4.A.064.'47.'

13. Julian Huxley, letter to Margaret Read, April 3, 1947, UNESCO Archives, 375:4.A.064.'47'; Charles B. Fahs, "Interview with Dr. Ivor A. Richards and Miss Christine Gibson," December 9, 1948, RF, RAC, FA386, RG 1.1, series 200, box 234, folder 2796; Verna, "Haiti, the Rockefeller Foundation, and UNESCO's Pilot Project," 291–93; Yvonne Oddon, "Recommendations for the Planning of Instructional Materials in a Fundamental Education Experiment," January 30, 1949; Alfred Métraux and Yvonne Oddon, "L'éducation de base dans la vallée de Marbial," March 1, 1949, both in RF, RAC, RG 1.2, series 100, box 20, folder 135. On the Marbial Valley project, see also Julia Pohle, "Kêbê l'Inesko Fò!," *UNESCO Courier*, September 2010, 41–43.

14. "Meeting of Experts on Language Problems in Fundamental Education: Notes for Acting Director General's Opening Speech," June 30, 1947; "General Considerations of Language Problems in Fundamental Education," June 19, 1947, UNESCO/ Educ./31/1947, both in UNESCO Archives, 375:4.A.064.'47.' On the evolution of UNESCO's programs, see Maurel, *Histoire de l'Unesco*, 264–65; Joseph Watras, "UNESCO's Programme of Fundamental Education, 1946–1959," *History of Education* 39, no. 2 (2010): 236–37. Felix Walter, among others, would continue to frame developing-world multilingualism as a "barrier" and "problem" in the 1950s; see Felix Walter, "UNESCO and Language," March 31, 1952, EDIU/6/52025, UNESCO Archives, 408.3:37, part 1; [Felix Walter], "UNESCO and Language Teaching," 1955, UNESCO Archives, 408.3:37, part 2; Felix Walter, "UNESCO and the Teaching of Modern Languages," March 19, 1959, UNESCO Archives, 408.3:37, part 2. Walter's authorship of "UNESCO and Language Teaching" can be assumed based on its similarities to his signed 1952 and 1959 reports, including file location, writing style, and shared preoccupations with American teaching techniques and multilingualism in Asia and Africa.

15. "Meeting of Experts on Language Problems in Fundamental Education: Summary Report of the First Meeting," July 17, 1947, Educ./Com.Exp./S.R.1, UNESCO Archives, 375:4.A.064.'47'; "Language-Teaching and UNESCO," June 2, 1947, UNESCO Archives, 375:4.A.064.'47.' On the effects of military programs on postwar language instruction, see, e.g., Col. Henry L. Davisson, memo to Chief of Army Field Forces re: "Report Staff Visit to . . . the Army Language School, Presidio of Monterey, Calif . . .," August 27, 1952, Record Group (RG) 337: HQ Army Ground Forces, National Archives and Records Administration (NARA), College Park, MD, Army Field Forces HQs, Chief of Staff, Combat Arms Advisory Group Inspection Reports, 1952, box 71; Joseph K. Yamagiwa, *MISLS Training History, Annex No. 3: The Army Intensive Japanese Language School*, 90–91, RG 319: Army Staff, NARA, Military Intelligence Language School, Fort Snelling, MN, General Records 1943–45, box 1; Edmund E. Day, letter to Major General Clayton Bissell, January 11, 1946, RG 165: War Department General Staff, NARA, G-1: Personnel, Decimal File, 1942– June 1946, 350 to 350.09, box 532; Cheryl Brown Mitchell and Kari Ellingson Vidal, "Weighing the Ways of the Flow: Twentieth Century Language Instruction," *Modern Language Journal* 85, no. 1 (2001): 29.

16. At the turn of the twentieth century, proponents of the "direct method" had encountered pushback from classicists and from scholars who did not have oral fluency in target languages—two groups which, in the case of elite British boarding schools, overlapped. The First World War presented a more political threat to the direct method, which had roots in Germany. Scarce resources could also tip the scales in favor of reading over speaking and listening skills. One influential study of language-teaching in American higher education, the 1929 Coleman Report, concluded that reading proficiency should be stressed for the simple reason that it required less classroom time and could be taught more effectively by nonnative speakers. On the history of language-teaching pedagogies in Britain and the United States in the first half of the twentieth century, see Susan Bayley, "The Direct Method and Modern Language Teaching in England 1880–1918," *History of Education* 27, no. 1 (1998): 39–57; Mitchell and Vidal, "Weighing the Ways of the Flow," 26–30; William Parker, *The National Interest and Foreign Languages: A Discussion Guide and Work Paper for Citizen*

Consultations, rev. ed. (1954; Washington, DC: [U.S. Government Printing Office], 1957), 51–61.

17. "Language-Teaching and UNESCO." The audiolingual method was especially popular in the 1950s and the 1960s. Mitchell and Vidal, "Weighing the Ways of the Flow," 29–30; Melvin J. Fox, *Language and Development: A Retrospective Survey of Ford Foundation Language Projects, 1952–1974* (New York: Ford Foundation, 1975), 19; "Forty Years of Language Teaching," *Language Teaching* 40 (2006): 1–2; "From Audiolingual to Suggestopedia: The Varieties of Language Instruction," *Chronicle of Higher Education*, February 22, 1989, A14.

18. "Meeting of Experts on Language Problems in Fundamental Education: Summary Report of the Sixth Meeting," July 25, 1947, Educ./Com.Exp./S.R.6; "Meeting of Experts on Language Problems in Fundamental Education: Report of the 3rd Meeting," July 18, 1947, Educ./Com.Exp./S.R.3; "Meeting of Experts on Language Problems in Fundamental Education: Summary Report of the Fifth Meeting," July 22, 1947, Educ./Com.Exp./S.R.5; Col. Myers, "Education for International Understanding: The Part of Language-Teaching," July 2, 1947, Educ./38/1947, all in UNESCO Archives, 375:4.A.064.'47.'

19. Huxley, letter to Read, April 3, 1947; André Martinet, "Reflections on the Choice of a Language in Fundamental Education," July 3, 1947, Educ./41/1947, UNESCO Archives, 375:4.A.064.'47'; Walter, "UNESCO and Language"; C. K. Ogden, "Article," July 27, 1947, UNESCO Archives, 375:4.

20. "Meeting of Experts on Language Problems in Fundamental Education: Summary Report of the Second Meeting," July 18, 1947, Educ.Com.Exp./S.R.2, UNESCO Archives, 375:4.A.064.'47'; "Globalingo," *Time*, December 31, 1945.

21. Alice Conklin has shown how colonial governance in French West Africa took a conservative turn during the interwar period in response to urban Africans' demands for a more equitable distribution of power. Shedding its earlier philosophy of assimilation, the interwar French administration embraced "associationalist" policies aimed at bolstering the authority of designated tribal elites. Conklin, *A Mission to Civilize: The Republican Idea of Empire in France and West Africa, 1895–1930* (Stanford, CA: Stanford University Press, 1997), chaps. 5–6; see also Frederick Cooper, "Development, Modernization, and the Social Sciences in the Era of Decolonization: The Examples of British and French Africa," *Revue d'histoire des sciences humaines* 10 (2004): 9–38. On late-colonial violence, see Fabian Klose, " 'Source of Embarrassment': Human Rights, State of Emergency, and the Wars of Decolonization," in *Human Rights in the Twentieth Century*, ed. Stefan-Ludwig Hoffmann (Cambridge: Cambridge University Press, 2011), 237–57.

22. "Summary Report of the Fourth Meeting," July 23, 1947, Educ./Com.Exp./S.R.4, UNESCO Archives, 375:4.A.064.'47'; "Summary Report of the Sixth Meeting"; Deheyn, "Note concernant ce problème," UNESCO Archives, 375:4; "Liste des Experts," June 27, 1947, UNESCO/Educ./36/1947, UNESCO Archives, 375: 4.A.064.'47.'

23. Wedgwood quoted in House of Commons Debates, Hansard (hereafter H.C. Deb.), June 2, 1937, vol. 324, cols. 169–71. For Wedgwood's interwar language advocacy, see also H.C. Deb., July 13, 1928, vol. 219, cols. 2671–72, 2676; H.C. Deb., April 30, 1929, vol. 227, cols. 1484–86; H.C. Deb., June 26, 1930, vol. 240, cols. 1471–73; H.C. Deb., April 22, 1932, vol. 264, cols. 1826–28; H.C. Deb., July 25, 1935, vol. 304, cols. 2097–98.

On Wedgwood, see Paul Mulvey, *The Political Life of Josiah C. Wedgwood: Land, Liberty and Empire, 1872–1943* (Woodbridge, UK: Boydell, 2010), 7–12, 71–72, 117–19. On Basic, see Koeneke, *Empires of the Mind*, 186–87; Michael Gordin, *Scientific Babel: How Science Was Done Before and After Global English* (Chicago: University of Chicago Press, 2015), 297.

24. In the 1920s the Colonial Office's Advisory Committee on Native Education in British Tropical Africa (of which Lugard was a member) would recommend conducting elementary education in Africa in indigenous languages and restricting the use of English in secondary schooling. While its recommendations were nonbinding, they had a powerful standard-setting effect. F. D. Lugard, "Education in Tropical Africa," *Edinburgh Review*, July 1925, reprinted by the Colonial Office, August 1930, CO 879/123/12; *The Place of the Vernacular in Native Education* (1925), African no. 1110, CO 879/121/4; Whitehead, "The Medium of Instruction," 1–15; Evans, "Macaulay's Minute Revisited," 279. On the increasingly vexed relationship between the European imperial powers and international institutions, see Susan Pedersen, *The Guardians: The League of Nations and the Crisis of Empire* (New York: Oxford University Press, 2015), 396–99; Klose, "'Source of Embarrassment,'" 245–46; Mark Mazower, *No Enchanted Palace: The End of Empire and the Ideological Origins of the United Nations* (Princeton, NJ: Princeton University Press, 2009), chap. 4.

25. Ogden, "Article"; "Summary Report of the First Meeting"; "Fundamental Education: Common Ground for All Peoples: Chapter V: Suggested Lines of Action," March 21, 1947, UNESCO/Educ./10/1947, UNESCO Archives, 375:4; "General Considerations of Language Problems in Fundamental Education"; "Notes for Acting Director General's Opening Speech."

26. Cooper, "Development, Modernization, and the Social Sciences," 10, 26, 32–33.

27. On anticolonial and nonaligned participation at the United Nations and how it transformed internationalism after 1945, see Mazower, *No Enchanted Palace*, 185–89, 196–99; Pedersen, *The Guardians*, 396–99; Matthew Connelly, *A Diplomatic Revolution: Algeria's Fight for Independence and the Origins of the Post–Cold War Era* (New York: Oxford University Press, 2002). On language power politics at UNESCO, see Walter, "UNESCO and Language"; William Benton, letter to Howland Sargeant, June 20, 1950, Benton Papers, box 381, folder 3; William R. Pendergast, "UNESCO and French Cultural Relations 1945–1970," *International Organization* 30, no. 3 (Summer 1976): 459–62.

28. UNESCO/CL/489, circular letter to member states requesting documentation for expert meeting, [1951], UNESCO Archives, 375:408.8, part 1; Walter, "UNESCO and the Teaching of Modern Languages"; "UNESCO Project: The Use of Indigenous Languages in Education: Progress Report: January 1951," [January 1951], UNESCO Archives, 375:408.8, part 1; S. Abid Husain, letter and attached report to A. Barrera Vásquez, April 25, 1951, UNESCO Archives, 375:408.8.A.064.'51,' part 1a.

29. "Remarks Made by Hon. Gregorio Hernández, Jr., Secretary of Education, on the Occasion of the Blessing and Inauguration of the Curriculum Center of the Philippine Normal College," October 11, 1954, RF, RAC, RG 1.2, series 200, box 433, folder 3728; James E. Ianucci, "English Language Teacher Training Project in Indonesia: A Brief History and Evaluation 1959–67," FF, RAC, FA739C, box 300, report 006680.

30. Wm. Roger Louis and Ronald Robinson, "The Imperialism of Decolonization," *Journal of Imperial and Commonwealth History* 22, no. 3 (1994): 462–511; Cooper,

"Development, Modernization, and the Social Sciences," 15–19, 24–27; Gilbert Rist, *Le développement: Histoire d'une croyance occidentale*, rev. 4th ed. (Paris: Presses de la Fondation nationale des sciences politiques, 2013), 131–97.

31. [Walter], "UNESCO and Language Teaching"; Walter, "UNESCO and the Teaching of Modern Languages"; Walter, "UNESCO and Language." On Felix Walter, see H. H. Stern, *Foreign Languages in Primary Education: The Teaching of Foreign or Second Languages to Younger Children* (London: Oxford University Press, 1967), ix; "In Memoriam," *Linguistic Reporter* (published by the Center for Applied Linguistics) 2, no. 6 (December 1960): 2, accessed October 2, 2018, http://www.cal.org/content /download/1968/24926/file/LinguisticReporterVolume2.pdf.

32. Walter, "UNESCO and Language"; see also [Walter], "UNESCO and Language Teaching."

33. Walter, "UNESCO and Language"; [Walter], "UNESCO and Language Teaching"; Walter, "UNESCO and the Teaching of Modern Languages."

34. Matta Akrawi, memo to Lionel Elvin et al., January 25, 1951, UNESCO Archives, 375:408.8, part 1. When Elvin, then director of UNESCO's Education Department, responded that this was a mere "misunderstanding" and that the conference was not, in fact, dedicated to the teaching of English, Akrawi scribbled dyspeptically, "Not quite a misunderstanding!" Lionel Elvin, memo to Matta Akrawi, January 29, 1951, UNESCO Archives, 375:408.8, part 1. Akrawi's biography presumably had sensitized him to issues that his British counterparts were inclined to overlook. During the interwar period, Akrawi had spent formative years participating in a student group noted for linking Arabic-language education to political pan-Arabism and anticolonial nationalism. Following Iraq's independence in 1932, Akrawi became a high-placed figure in the Iraqi educational system. On Akrawi, see Hilary Falb Kalisman, "Bursary Scholars at the American University of Beirut: Living and Practising Arab Unity," *British Journal of Middle Eastern Studies* 42, no. 4 (2015): 599–617.

35. "Meeting of Experts on the Use in Education of African Languages in Relation to English, Where English Is the Accepted Second Language: Report Presented to the Director-General of the United Nations Educational, Scientific and Cultural Organization," December 15, 1952, EJD/PZ, UNESCO Archives, 375:408.8(6)A0.64(66)'52,' part 2.

36. Charles A. Ferguson, "The Role of the Center for Applied Linguistics, 1959–1967," [1967], FF, RAC, FA572, series 2, box 3, folder 3; W. Freeman Twaddell, "U.S. Activities of the Center for Applied Linguistics, 1959–1973," Spring 1973, FF, RAC, FA739B, box 220, report 004959; Herbert J. Abraham, memo to Charles Thomson, September 21, 1951, EDIU/224.910, UNESCO Archives, 408.3:37, part 1.

37. Francis J. Colligan, letter to I. A. Richards, September 13, 1946, RF, RAC, RG 1.1, series 200, box 234, folder 2795.

38. Inderjeet Parmar has convincingly described the Ford, Rockefeller, and Carnegie foundations' portrayal of themselves as nonstate actors as one of the characteristic "fictions" of twentieth-century American philanthropy. Ford's trustees from the early 1950s through the early 1970s included numerous individuals with ties to the National Security Council, the State Department, and the Defense Department, including Robert McNamara and McGeorge Bundy. Parmar, *Foundations of the American Century: The Ford, Carnegie, and Rockefeller Foundations in the Rise of American Power* (New York: Columbia University Press, 2012), 3–6, 53–55; see also F. C. Ward, memo

to W. McPeak et al., December 20, 1963, FF, RAC, FA548, box 3, folder 13. This did not prevent foundation representatives from expressing concern about fluctuating government support for language teaching. See, for instance, Charles B. Fahs, "Excerpt from: CBF Southeast Asia Trip," August 24, 1958, RF, RAC, RG 1.2, series 200, box 434, folder 3732; Boyd R. Compton, "Philippine Center for Language Study—Trip to the West Coast," February 26, 1959, RF, RAC, RG 1.2, series 200, box 434, folder 3733.

39. Parmar, *Foundations of the American Century*, 124–48; Melvin J. Fox, "The Work of American Foundations in English as a Second Language" (paper for the Anglo-American Conference on English Teaching Abroad, Cambridge University, Cambridge, UK, June 26–30, 1961), FF, RAC, FA739A, box 91, report 002236; Daniel S. Lev, "A Brief Review of Foreign Assistance in Indonesia's English Language Program," May 31, 1961, FF, RAC, FA739A, box 11, report 000167; William O. Brown, Melvin J. Fox, and John B. Howard, "Report of Ford Foundation Mission to Africa," January 16, 1957, FF, RAC, FA568, box 63, folder 11, report 000579; Melvin J. Fox, "Ford Foundation Foreign or Second Language Activities in the United States and Overseas 1951–1966," May 1967, FF, RAC, FA572, series 1, box 1, folder 6.

40. "CBF," memo to "DR," February 26, 1957, RF, RAC, RG 1.2, series 200, box 433, folder 3730; Rockefeller Foundation grants to UCLA, April 3, 1957, December 5–6, 1961, RF, RAC, RG 1.2, series 200, box 433, folder 3728; Sirarpi Ohannessian, "UCLA Becomes Important Center for Teaching English as a Foreign Language," *Linguistic Reporter* 3, no. 1 (1961), RF, RAC, RG 1.2, series 200, box 433, folder 3735; "Proposal for a Five-Year Program to Improve English Instruction in the Philippines," attached to Franklin P. Rolfe, letter to Charles B. Fahs, October 31, 1956, RF, RAC, RG 1.2, series 200, box 433, folder 3729.

41. Kenneth Osgood, *Total Cold War: Eisenhower's Secret Propaganda Battle at Home and Abroad* (Lawrence: University Press of Kansas, 2006), 46–75, see esp. 57–58, 70–71; William W. Raup, letter to Richard W. Cortright, March 26, 1962, Frank C. Laubach Collection, Special Collections Research Center, Syracuse University Libraries, box 100; "Report on Survey of U.S. Government English Language Programs for Fiscal Years 1964, 1965 and 1966," May 20, 1965; "Peace Corps Volunteers Employed as English Teachers as of Mar. 31, 1965," [1965], both in FF, RAC, FA548, series 3, box 3, folder 13; "English Language Programs of the Agency for International Development"; "National Security Action Memorandum No. 332: U.S. Government Policy on English Language Teaching Abroad," June 11, 1965, Lyndon Baines Johnson Presidential Library website, accessed October 2, 2018, https://www.discoverlbj.org/item/nsf-nsam332.

42. "Our History," CAL website, accessed February 2, 2016, http://www.cal.org/who-we-are/our-history; CAL, *Second Language Learning as a Factor in National Development in Asia, Africa, and Latin America: Summary Statement and Recommendations of an International Meeting of Specialists Held in London, December 1960* (Washington, DC: [n.p.], 1961), 2. On Walter's connection to Ford and the CAL, see CAL, memo to Ford Foundation, October 8, 1959; Melvin J. Fox, memo to George Gant and John Howard, January 27, 1960, both in FF, RAC, FA608, series 1, box 3, folder: "Africa—Trip to Africa."

43. Interwar restrictions on English teaching in British Africa had prompted one Labour Party member of Parliament to ask, "Is this the new Imperialism, to discourage the tongue of Shakespeare and Milton?" H.C. Deb., July 2, 1928, vol. 219, cols. 952–53. For the *Life* quotation, see Barnett, "Basic English."

44. On Huxley's connection to eugenics and his ambiguous antiracism, see Glenda Sluga, "UNESCO and the (One) World of Julian Huxley," *Journal of World History* 21, no. 3 (2010): 393–418; Perrin Selcer, "Beyond the Cephalic Index: Negotiating Politics to Produce UNESCO's Scientific Statements on Race," *Current Anthropology* 53, no. S5 (2012): S173–84; Michelle Brattain, "Race, Racism, and Antiracism: UNESCO and the Politics of Presenting Science to the Postwar Public," *American Historical Review* 112, no. 5 (2007): 1386–413.

45. "National Security Action Memorandum No. 332."

46. Melvin J. Fox, memo to John B. Howard and George F. Gant, October 2, 1959; CAL, memo to the Ford Foundation, October 8, 1959; Melvin J. Fox, memo to George F. Gant, October 13, 1959; Melvin J. Fox, memo to George F. Gant and John B. Howard, copied from handwritten letter dated November 10, 1959; Melvin J. Fox, letter to Charles A. Ferguson, November 13, 1959; Melvin J. Fox, memo to George Gant and John Howard, January 27, 1960, all in FF, RAC, FA608, series 1, box 3, folder: "Africa—Trip to Africa"; Melvin J. Fox, draft memo to F. F. Hill, May 31, 1961, FA608, series 1, box 17, folder: "Language Development: World Language Survey, 1962."

47. See, for instance, the media-development guidelines issued by UNESCO in 1962, described in Tor Gjesdal, "Statement by Tor Gjesdal, Director of the Department of Mass Communication, UNESCO, to the 18th Session of the United Nations Commission on Human Rights, 15 March–14 April 1962," [Spring 1962], Benton Papers, box 393, folder 11. These guidelines are discussed further in chapter 4.

48. Immerwahr, *Thinking Small*, 52–53; Clifford Prator, "Report on Visit to Ghana in June, 1959," August 6, 1959, RF, RAC, RG 1.2, series 200, box 434, folder 3733; minutes of the International Meeting on Second Language Problems, February 21–24, 1962, RF, RAC, RG 1.2, series 497, box 17, folder 197; "BRC," interview with Clifford Prator, March 16, 1961, RF, RAC, RG 1.2, series 200, box 434, folder 3735; cross-reference slip for Robert July, letter to Clifford Prator, May 17, 1961, RF, RAC, RG 1.2, series 497, box 17, folder 197; Clifford Prator, letter to Robert July, January 12, 1962, RF, RAC, RG 1.2, series 497, box 17, folder 197.

49. Ferguson, "Role of the Center"; "Memorial Resolution: Charles A. Ferguson," *Stanford Report*, May 19, 1999, accessed November 5, 2016, http://news.stanford.edu/news/1999/may19/memferguson-519.html; Morrisey and Grele, "Interview with Melvin J. Fox."

4. CAPACITY AS FREEDOM DURING THE DEVELOPMENT DECADE

The epigraph for this chapter is taken from: Wilbur Schramm, *Mass Media and National Development: The Role of Information in the Developing Countries* (hereafter *MMND*) (Stanford, CA: Stanford University Press, 1964), 36.

1. UNESCO (United Nations Educational, Scientific, and Cultural Organization), "Television Comes to the Land," film script, 1959, accessed July 24, 2013, https://unesdoc.unesco.org/ark:/48223/pf0000180081. On the tele-club movement, see Marie-Françoise Lévy, "La création des télé-clubs: L'expérience de l'Aisne," in *La Télévision dans la République: Les années 50*, ed. Marie-Françoise Lévy (Brussels: Éditions Complexe, 1999), esp. 110–25; Roger Louis and Joseph Rovan, *Television and Tele-Clubs in Rural Communities: An Experiment in France* (Paris: Unesco, 1955).

2. Gilbert Rist, *Le développement: Histoire d'une croyance occidentale*, rev. 4th ed. (Paris: Presses de la Fondation nationale des sciences politiques, 2013), 164–71; James

Schwoch, *Global TV: New Media and the Cold War, 1946–69* (Urbana: University of Illinois Press, 2009), chap. 4; Daniel Lerner, *The Passing of Traditional Society: Modernizing the Middle East* (New York: Free, 1958); Hemant Shah, *The Production of Modernization: Daniel Lerner, Mass Media, and the Passing of Traditional Society* (Philadelphia: Temple University Press, 2011), 1–9.

3. Quotation from Tor Gjesdal, "Statement by Tor Gjesdal, Director of the Department of Mass Communication, UNESCO, to the 18th Session of the United Nations Commission on Human Rights, 15 March–14 April 1962," [Spring 1962], William Benton Papers, Special Collections Research Center, University of Chicago Library, box 393, folder 11.

4. On the origins of postwar developmentalism in pre-1945 U.S. foreign relations, see Michael Adas, *Dominance by Design: Technological Imperatives and America's Civilizing Mission* (Cambridge, MA: Belknap Press of Harvard University Press, 2006), esp. chap. 3; Emily Rosenberg, *Spreading the American Dream: American Economic and Cultural Expansion, 1890–1945* (New York: Hill and Wang, 1982), 7–13. On African citizenship claims and social reforms in French colonial governance after 1945, see Frederick Cooper, *Citizenship Between Empire and Nation: Remaking France and French Africa, 1945–1960* (Princeton, NJ: Princeton University Press, 2014), esp. chaps. 3–4. On British and French educational reforms in late-colonial Africa, see Diana Lemberg, "The End of Empires and Some Linguistic Turns: British and French Language Policies in Inter- and Post-War Africa," in *British and French Colonialism in Africa, Asia and the Middle East: Connected Empires Across the Eighteenth to the Twentieth Centuries*, ed. James R. Fichter (Basingstoke, UK: Palgrave Macmillan, 2019).

5. UNESCO, "Television Comes to the Land," 10. On the invention of the concept of development after the Second World War, see Arturo Escobar, *Encountering Development: The Making and Unmaking of the Third World* (Princeton, NJ: Princeton University Press, 1995); Rist, *Le développement*, chap. 4.

6. With the exception of Kenneth Cmiel, most work on the connections between human rights and media has been done by media-studies scholars, not historians. Many of the former are linked to the IAMCR. See, e.g., Kaarle Nordenstreng, "Myths about Press Freedom," *Brazilian Journalism Research* 3, no. 1 (2007): 15–30; Cees J. Hamelink, "The 2003 Graham Spry Memorial Lecture: Toward a Human Right to Communicate?," *Canadian Journal of Communication* 29, no. 2 (2004): 205–12.

7. Cf. Roland Burke, *Decolonization and the Evolution of International Human Rights* (Philadelphia: University of Pennsylvania Press, 2010), 92–101, 109–11.

8. Greg Grandin, "Human Rights and Empire's Embrace: A Latin American Counterpoint," in *Human Rights and Revolutions*, 2nd ed., ed. Jeffrey N. Wasserstrom, Greg Grandin, Lynn Hunt, and Marilyn B. Young (Lanham, MD: Rowman & Littlefield, 2007), 191–212; Victoria de Grazia, *Irresistible Empire: America's Advance Through Twentieth-Century Europe* (Cambridge, MA: Belknap Press of Harvard University Press, 2005), 339–44.

9. On Schramm's close ties to the national-security state, see Timothy Glander, *Origins of Mass Communications Research During the American Cold War: Educational Effects and Contemporary Implications* (Mahwah, NJ: Lawrence Erlbaum, 2000), chap. 5; Christopher Simpson, *Science of Coercion: Communication Research and Psychological Warfare, 1945–1960* (New York: Oxford University Press, 1994).

10. On Schramm's views of international research, see, inter alia, Wilbur Schramm, letter to Julian Behrstock, October 31, 1963, UNESCO Archives, Paris, France, 307.A.53, part 1; Wilbur Schramm, letter to Julian Behrstock, May 6, 1964, UNESCO Archives, 307.A.53, part 2; Wilbur Schramm, letter to E. Lloyd Sommerlad, March 1, 1965, UNESCO Archives, 307.A.01.IAMCR "—66," part 4. On Schramm and *MMND*, see Emile G. McAnany, *Saving the World: A Brief History of Communication for Development and Social Change* (Urbana: University of Illinois Press, 2012), 24–27, 32–33.

11. Wilbur Schramm et al., *The New Media: Memo to Educational Planners* (Paris: UNESCO, 1967), 95; Henry Cassirer, "The Potential Role of Television in Developing Countries" (presented to the Third International Television Symposium, Montreux, Switzerland, May 20–25, 1963), Henry R. Cassirer Papers, Dolph Briscoe Center for American History, University of Texas at Austin, box 2G54.

12. Leonard Marks quoted in Murray G. Lawson et al., "The United States Information Agency During the Administration of President Lyndon B. Johnson, November 1963–January 1969," 1968, Lyndon Baines Johnson Presidential Library (LBJ Library), Austin, TX, Administrative History: USIA, box 1, vol. 1, pp. 5–134; Charles T. Morrissey, "Interview with Philip H. Coombs for the Ford Foundation Oral History Project," July 10, 1973, see esp. 8–9, 96–98, Ford Foundation records (FF), Rockefeller Archive Center (RAC), Sleepy Hollow, NY, FA618, series 4, box 33, folder 160; Joint United States Public Affairs Office (JUSPAO), "Television for Vietnam: A Study Paper," December 29, 1965, Personal Papers of Leonard Marks, LBJ Library, box 30.

13. Jean d'Arcy, "The Statutes and Financing of a Television Service," [1964], UNESCO Archives, 307: 384.4 (6) A06 (669) TA "64," part 4. On d'Arcy, see Michael Palmer, "Jean d'Arcy et les acteurs internationaux de l'information," in *La télévision, le temps des constructeurs*, ed. Sylvie Pierre (Paris: L'Harmattan, 2011), 83. On Nogentel, see Lévy, "La création des télé-clubs," 113. On postwar austerity and the rise of European consumer societies, see Tony Judt, *Postwar: A History of Europe Since 1945* (New York: Penguin, 2005), 226–37, 324–53; Richard Kuisel, *Seducing the French: The Dilemma of Americanization* (Berkeley: University of California Press, 1993), 149–52; de Grazia, *Irresistible Empire*, 336–75.

14. Ignacy Waniewicz, "The Contribution of Television to Education and the Dissemination of Knowledge," UNESCO Archives, 654.197 (6) MEE, part 1; René Maheu, "Memorandum by Mr. R. Maheu, Assistant Director-General, UNESCO," [1959], UNESCO Archives, CAB.1/4—Education (1959); Henry Cassirer, memo to Tor Gjesdal re: "1967/68 Programme for Educational Use of Mass Media," April 20, 1965, Cassirer Papers, box 2G54; William Benton, letter to Douglas Batson, December 27, 1965, Benton Papers, box 393, folder 6; Schramm et al., *The New Media*, 150. On Algeria, see Schramm et al., 14, 37–39, 150–51.

15. Benton, letter to Batson, December 27, 1965; Waniewicz, "The Contribution of Television"; Schramm et al., 24–25; Henri Dieuzeide, "The Possible Uses of Communication Satellites in Education," December 6, 1965, UNESCO/SPACECOM/11, UNESCO Archives, file 629.19: 621.39 MEE; Harold Lasswell, memo to William Benton, February 8, 1958, Benton Papers, box 175, folder 1.

16. The French National Commission cited in Schramm, *MMND*, 161; IBM (International Business Machines Corporation), "Teacher Plus Technology: The Team for

International Education," March 1966, LBJ Library, National Security Files (NSF), Files of Charles E. Johnson, box 12, folder "COMSAT—Educational Purposes, NSAM 342 (Domestic and Foreign) File 1," 8; Waniewicz. On the Ivory Coast and Italian programs, see Schramm et al., 46–47, 52–53; Henry R. Cassirer, "Educational Television in the World Outside Asia," August 29, 1962, Cassirer Papers, box 2G54.

17. Quotation from Schramm, *MMND*, 104. In 1965 UNESCO commissioned a lengthy report on "Television in Non-Electrified Areas of Developing Countries," which addressed alternative power sources for television. Contrary to radio, there was no preexisting market for portable, battery-powered televisions, so development experts were on their own to devise technical solutions and ways of amortizing costs. See M. Reed, "A Report on the Problems Involved in Providing for Community Reception of Television in Non-Electrified Areas of Developing Countries, and an Examination of Possible Solutions," 1965, 1–5, accessed January 31, 2017, https://unesdoc.unesco.org/ark:/48223/pf0000185542. See also Henry R. Cassirer, "Television in Developing Countries: Its Problems and Potential Contributions," reprint from *Telecommunication Journal* (December 1963), UNESCO Archives, 654.197 (6) MEE, part 1; d'Arcy, "Statutes and Financing of a Television Service."

18. For instance, Wilbur Schramm and E. Lloyd Sommerlad argued for continuing short-term financial and personnel relationships between the developed world and Africanizing states in their UNESCO mission report, "Mass Media Training Needs: East Africa," 1964, UNESCO/RP/MC/EA, accessed January 31, 2017, https://unesdoc.unesco.org/ark:/48223/pf0000157262.

19. Initially Schramm had asked Terrou to write a short memo for the book, suggesting as a potential topic the legal aspects of mass media in developing countries. "You would get full credit," he assured the French legal scholar. Terrou responded favorably, apparently conceiving of his memo as information to be interspersed and footnoted throughout Schramm's text. (Rumor at the UNESCO Secretariat had it that Terrou did not wish to accept payment for his memo because he "[wanted] to have a free hand in his attitude towards [Schramm's book] at the General Conference.") Schramm, however, insisted on treating Terrou's contribution as a stand-alone annex, with "full credit"—and compensation—given to the "great scholar." Terrou seems to have eventually softened his stance; in the published version the memo appeared as its own section, "Legal and Institutional Considerations (by Fernand Terrou)." Wilbur Schramm, letter to Fernand Terrou, April 9, 1963; Fernand Terrou, letter to Wilbur Schramm, April 24, 1963; Wilbur Schramm, letter to Fernand Terrou, July 24, 1963; Julian Behrstock, memo to Tor Gjesdal, July 31, [1963]; Julian Behrstock, letter to Wilbur Schramm, September 19, 1963; Fernand Terrou, letter to Wilbur Schramm, November 8, 1963; Wilbur Schramm, letter to Fernand Terrou, November 14, 1963; Wilbur Schramm, letter to Fernand Terrou, March 19, 1964, all in UNESCO Archives, 307 A 53 MASS, parts 1 and 2.

20. Schramm, *MMND*, 26.

21. Schramm, ix, 93–99, 112–13, 203.

22. Schramm, quoted on 223, see also 224, 264–66.

23. Schramm's map, Julian Behrstock noted, was "along the lines of the graphics" used in UNESCO's *World Communications* atlas, which had been updated in 1956 and again in 1964. Julian Behrstock, "Notes by Julian Behrstock on the Manuscript 'Mass

Communication and National Development' by Dr. Wilbur Schramm," September 17, 1963, UNESCO Archives, 307 A 53 MASS, part 1.

24. Wilbur Schramm, letter to Julian Behrstock, May 4, 1963, UNESCO Archives, 307 A 53 MASS, part 1; Schramm, *MMND*, 30, 112–13; Rist, *Le développement*, 173–90; Nils Gilman, *Mandarins of the Future: Modernization Theory in Cold War America* (Baltimore, MD: Johns Hopkins University Press, 2003), 171–74.

25. Henry Cassirer, "The Objectives and National Resources for Television Programming in Africa," UNESCO Archives, 654.197 (6) MEE, part 1; d'Arcy, "Statutes and Financing of a Television Service"; Henry Cassirer, memo to F. I. Ajumogobia, Permanent Secretary, Ministry of Information, Federal Government of Nigeria, December 16, 1963, UNESCO Archives, 307: 384.4 (6) A06 (669) TA "64," part 1.

26. Schramm, *MMND*, 182–83.

27. On the USIA's praise for Schramm, see Hewson A. Ryan, memo for Leonard Marks, June 8, 1967, with attached report, "USIA Role in National Development," see esp. "Contributions of Wilbur Schramm" in attachment to section 4: "What Effect Can Information Activities Have on Modernization—Some Scholarly Findings and Recommendations," LBJ Library, Personal Papers of Leonard Marks, box 25. On the USIA translations, see the following in UNESCO Archives, 307 A 53 MASS, part 2: Julian Behrstock, memo to Tor Gjesdal, 23/XI [1966]; Julian Behrstock, letter to Wilbur Schramm, December 2, 1966; T. Prins, letters to Vietnamese, Chinese, Greek, and Turkish National Commissions for UNESCO, December 1, 1966. For Benton, see William Benton, letter to Wilbur Schramm, November 11, 1965; William Benton, letter to Douglass Cater, November 3, 1965, both in LBJ Library, Office Files of Douglass Cater, box 44.

28. Joseph Califano, memo for the President, October 11, 1967, LBJ Library, White House Central Files (WHCF), Ex ED 5, box 24. On the American Samoa and El Salvador projects, see Schramm et al., *The New Media*; Wilbur Schramm, Lyle M. Nelson, and Mere T. Betham, *Bold Experiment: The Story of Educational Television in American Samoa* (Stanford, CA: Stanford University Press, 1981); William S. Gaud, memo to S. Douglass Cater Jr., February 27, 1968, LBJ Library, WHCF, Ex ED 5, box 24; Wilbur Schramm, "Instructional Television in the Educational Reform of El Salvador," March 1973, accessed January 31, 2017, http://pdf.usaid.gov/pdf_docs/PNAAA377 .pdf; McAnany, *Saving the World*, 51–65.

29. See, inter alia, Bradley R. Simpson, *Economists with Guns: Authoritarian Development and U.S.-Indonesian Relations, 1960–1968* (Stanford, CA: Stanford University Press, 2008); David Ekbladh, *The Great American Mission: Modernization and the Construction of an American World Order* (Princeton, NJ: Princeton University Press, 2010), chap. 6; Michael Latham, *Modernization as Ideology: American Social Science and "Nation Building" in the Kennedy Era* (Chapel Hill: University of North Carolina Press, 2000), chap. 5.

30. Daniel Lerner, "Communication and the Prospects of Innovative Development," in *Communication and Change in the Developing Countries*, ed. Daniel Lerner and Wilbur Schramm (Honolulu, HI: East-West Center, 1967), 312–17; Lerner cited in "USIA Role in National Development"; Shah, *The Production of Modernization*, 129–41.

31. Frank S. Hopkins, memo to Henry D. Owen re: "Some Preliminary Observations on Use of Educational TV in LDC's," January 25, 1968, LBJ Library, NSF, Subject

File, box 15, folder "Educational TV," no. 1a; Matthew Nimetz, memo for Joseph
Califano, September 29, 1967, LBJ Library, Office Files of James Gaither, box 201;
"National Security Action Memorandum No. 330," April 9, 1965, LBJ Library,
NSF, National Security Action Memorandum (NSAM) Files, box 6, folder 13, no. 1;
JUSPAO, "Television for Vietnam."

32. [Casler], cable to "USIA WashDC," February 8, [1966], LBJ Library, Personal Papers
of Leonard Marks, box 30; Loren B. Stone, "Television in Vietnam 1966," June 1966,
LBJ Library, Personal Papers of Leonard Marks, box 29; Sanford S. Marlowe, "TV in
Viet-Nam," January 13, 1966, LBJ Library, Personal Papers of Leonard Marks, box 30;
"Need Nielsen to Count Vietcong Eavesdroppers on Ky's ETV Weapon," *Variety*,
December 14, 1966, LBJ Library, Personal Papers of Leonard Marks, box 30.

33. Stone, "Television in Vietnam 1966"; "Need Nielsen to Count Vietcong Eavesdrop-
pers"; JUSPAO, field message to USIA Washington, February 23, 1966, LBJ Library,
Personal Papers of Leonard Marks, box 30; "Mission Council Action Memorandum
No. 221," August 31, 1967, LBJ Library, Personal Papers of Leonard Marks, box 30.

34. Wilbur Schramm, letter to Douglass C. Cater Jr., November 4, 1965, with attached
memoranda, LBJ Library, Office Files of Douglass Cater, box 44, emphasis in original. See also Leonard Marks, memorandum to Douglass Cater, December 14, 1965,
with attached cable from AmEmbassy Paris, LBJ Library, Office Files of Douglass
Cater, box 45.

35. Henry Cassirer, memo to Tor Gjesdal re: "Mass Communication and Economic
Development," [1963]; Henry R. Cassirer, memo to Wilbur Schramm, September 10,
1963; Julian Behrstock, letter to Wilbur Schramm, September 19, 1963, all in
UNESCO Archives, 307 A 53 MASS, part 1.

36. Cassirer, memo to Schramm, September 10, 1963; Cassirer, memo to Gjesdal, [1963];
Pierre Navaux, memo to Lloyd Sommerlad et al. re: "Note on the Schramm
Manuscript—'An Introduction to Communication Research in Developing Coun-
tries,'" April 20, 1965; Henry Cassirer, memo to Pierre Navaux et al., April 28, 1965;
Y. V. L. Rao, letter to Wilbur Schramm, May 21, 1965, all in UNESCO Archives, 307
A 53 MASS, parts 1 and 2.

37. Schramm, *MMND*, 36; Schramm, letter to Behrstock, May 4, 1963; Schramm, letter
to Behrstock, October 31, 1963; "Contributions of Wilbur Schramm."

38. Henry R. Cassirer, "Radio in an African Context: A Description of Senegal's Pilot
Project," reprinted from *Radio for Education and Development: Case Studies*, ed.
Peter L. Spain, Dean T. Jamison, and Emile McAnany (Washington, DC: World
Bank, 1977), 300–301, Cassirer Papers, box 2G45; Ibrahima Ba, "La télévision au ser-
vice de l'éducation des masses," *Journal des Télécommunications* 37, no. 7 (1970): 479,
Cassirer Papers, box 2G55.

39. Henry R. Cassirer, "Mission to Dakar—October 20th–30th 1965," November 5, 1965,
Cassirer Papers, box 2G54; Henry Cassirer, "Report on Mission to Senegal," sound
recording, February 20, 1969, Cassirer Papers, box 2G64. On literacy and languages in
Senegal, see also Ibrahima Diallo, *The Politics of National Languages in Postcolonial
Senegal* (Amherst, NY: Cambria, 2010).

40. Henry R. Cassirer, "Mission au Sénégal (10–17 octobre 1968)," October 31, 1968, Cassirer Papers, box 2G54; Cassirer, "Report on Mission to Senegal"; Henry R. Cassirer,
"Mission à Dakar (3 au 16 décembre 1967)," December 26, 1967, Cassirer Papers,
box 2G54; Cassirer, "Radio in an African Context," 317. Senghor's estimate turned

out to be optimistic. The educational television project ceased broadcasting in December 1969 whereas the national television service was not available in some parts of Senegal until the late 1980s or early 1990s. On the history of television in Senegal, see Tidiane Dioh, *Histoire de la télévision en Afrique noire francophone, des origines à nos jours* (Paris: Karthala, 2009), 186–93.

41. Cassirer, "Radio in an African Context," 301–5; *Literacy, 1969–1971: Progress Achieved in Literacy Throughout the World* (Paris: UNESCO, 1972), 109, accessed January 30, 2017, https://unesdoc.unesco.org/ark:/48223/pf0000001736_eng; Ibrahima Diallo, "Literacy and Education in West Africa: From *Ajami* to Francophonie," *Africa Review* 8, no. 1 (2016): 60–70, see esp. 66.

42. Cassirer, "Radio in an African Context," 303, 307–11, 335; Diallo, "Literacy and Education in West Africa," 60–70.

43. Radiodiffusion nationale [Senegal], *Dissoo: Bulletin de la Radio Educative Rurale*, December 1971–January 1972, 10, 14, 20, Cassirer Papers, box 2G59. On peanut production in Senegal during the Senghor era, see James K. Gray, "The Groundnut Market in Senegal: Examination of Price and Policy Changes" (PhD diss., Virginia Polytechnic Institute and State University, 2002), 22–28. For data on RER listener mail, see Cassirer, "Radio in an African Context," 311. Senghor cited in Cassirer, "Radio in an African Context," 313.

44. H. R. Cassirer, "Learning from Each Other," *Innovation*, October 1975, Cassirer Papers, box 2G45.

45. Cassirer, "Report on Mission to Senegal"; Cassirer, "Radio in an African Context," 331.

46. Henry Cassirer, letter to Luis Ramiro Beltrán, July 4, 1980, Cassirer Papers, box 2G57. On Freire, see also McAnany, *Saving the World*, 68–69, 72–73, 91–95.

47. Hervé Bourges, preface to Dioh, *Histoire de la télévision*, 17. On French aid to Algerian television, see the internal newsletter published by the French broadcasting monopoly's foreign relations office, *Revue de l'actualité radiophonique et télévisuelle dans le monde* (hereafter *Actualité*) 25 (October 5, 1966); *Actualité* 28 (February 20, 1967). All issues of *Actualité* consulted at the Inathèque de France, Paris, France.

48. Antonio Pasquali, "Los medios de comunicación en la educación de adultos," *Convergence* 1, no. 2 (1968): 33, Cassirer Papers, box 2G54; Walter D. Scott, "A Perspective on Global Television" (address to the Detroit Economic Club, February 6, 1967), LBJ Library, Office Files of Douglass Cater, box 48.

49. *Actualité, supplément à diffusion restreinte* 9 (January 1971); *Actualité, supplément à diffusion restreinte* 6 (July 1970); *Actualité, supplément à diffusion restreinte* 19 (December 1972); *Actualité, supplément à diffusion restreinte* 5 (May 1970). On Algerian and *arabophone* opposition to French cultural and linguistic influence, see also Pierre Alexandre, "Francophonie: The French and Africa," *Journal of Contemporary History* 4, no. 1 (1969): 121–22. On efforts by the Algerian state in the 1970s and 1980s to Arabize the educational system and to Islamicize Algerian society, see Charles-Robert Ageron, Sid-Ahmed Souiah, Jean Leca, and Benjamin Stora, "Algérie," *Encyclopædia Universalis*, accessed January 25, 2019, http://www.universalis.fr/encyclopedie/algerie/.

50. Pasquali, "Los medios de comunicación," 31; Luis Ramiro Beltrán, "La 'revolución verde' y el desarrollo rural latinoamericano," *Desarrollo rural en las Américas* 3, no. 1 (1971): 20–23, Cassirer Papers, box 2G55. See also McAnany, *Saving the World*, 66–86, see esp. 80–81 on Beltrán.

51. Malcolm S. Adiseshiah, "UNESCO and Development," December 18, 1969, Cassirer Papers, box 2G55.
52. Charles E. Johnson, memo to Bromley Smith, October 30, 1964, LBJ Library, NSF, Files of Charles E. Johnson, box 12, folder "COMSAT—Educational Purposes, NSAM 342 (Domestic and Foreign) File #1"; Lloyd Garrison, "Nigeria Doing Home-Grown Television Shows," *New York Times*, September 8, 1963; JUSPAO, "Television for Vietnam."
53. Scott, "Perspective on Global Television."
54. Scott, "Perspective on Global Television."

5. SATELLITES AND THE END OF SOVEREIGNTY

The epigraphs for this chapter are taken from: "The Negative Straw Man," October 12, 1966, Lyndon Baines Johnson Presidential Library (LBJ Library), National Security Files (NSF), Files of Charles E. Johnson, box 13, folder "COMSAT—U.S. Communications Policy, NSAM 338 File #2 [1 of 2]," no. 15b, emphasis in the original; and Armand Mattelart, *Agresión desde el espacio: Cultura y napalm en la era de los satélites* (1972; Mexico City: Siglo Ventiuno Editores, 1998), 23, emphasis in the original. "The Negative Straw Man" was circulated to members of the executive-branch Ad Hoc Intragovernmental Communications Satellite Policy Coordination Committee.

1. Hugh Richard Slotten, "Satellite Communications, Globalization, and the Cold War," *Technology and Culture* 43, no. 2 (2002): 315–50, see esp. 344–45; Slotten, "The International Telecommunications Union, Space Radio Communications, and U.S. Cold War Diplomacy, 1957–1963," *Diplomatic History* 37, no. 2 (2013): 348–49, 357–58; James Schwoch, *Global TV: New Media and the Cold War, 1946–69* (Urbana: University of Illinois Press, 2009), 13, 118–21, 159–61; Wilbur Schramm, "Communication Satellites—Some Social Implications," September 10, 1965, UNESCO Archives, Paris, France, 629.19: 621.39 MEE; "Telstar TV Satellite Launched," *Science News Letter* 82, no. 3 (July 21, 1962): 37; "Telstar II Launched," *Science News Letter* 83, no. 20 (May 18, 1963): 310.
2. Ernest D. Wenrick, "Communication Satellites and the Mass Media: Economic Aspects," October 15, 1965, UNESCO Archives, 629.19: 621.39 MEE; Schramm; Arthur C. Clarke, "The World of the Communications Satellite," November 9, 1965, UNESCO Archives, 629.19: 621.39 MEE; Slotten, "Satellite Communications," 320; Nicole Starosielski, "Fixed Flow: Undersea Cables as Media Infrastructure," in *Signal Traffic: Critical Studies of Media Infrastructures*, ed. Lisa Parks and Nicole Starosielski (Urbana: University of Illinois Press, 2015), 53–54.
3. Wilbur Schramm, quoted in Kathryn M. Queeney, *Direct Broadcast Satellites and the United Nations* (Alphen aan den Rijn: Sijthoff & Noordhoff, 1978), 118. On the American promotion of developmental satellite communications, see Slotten, "The International Telecommunications Union," 326–27, 343–46, 371.
4. Adrian Johns, *Death of a Pirate: British Radio and the Making of the Information Age* (New York: Norton, 2011), 45–50; Slotten; James Hay, "The Invention of Air Space, Outer Space, and Cyberspace," in *Down to Earth: Satellite Technologies, Industries, and Cultures*, ed. Lisa Parks and James Schwoch (New Brunswick, NJ: Rutgers University Press, 2012), 19–41; Christy Collis, "The Geostationary Orbit: A Critical Legal

Geography of Space's Most Valuable Real Estate," in Parks and Schwoch, *Down to Earth*, 61–70.

5. Documents #5 and #6 (both titled "Communications Satellite Policy"), [n.d.], LBJ Library, NSF, National Security Action Memorandum (NSAM) File, box 7, folder 6; Jack Oslund, " 'Open Shores' to 'Open Skies': Sources and Directions of U.S. Satellite Policy," in *Economic and Policy Problems in Satellite Communications*, ed. Joseph N. Pelton and Marcellus S. Snow (New York: Praeger, 1977), 144–46, 168–69.

6. J. J. Matras, "Editorial," *Revue française de radiodiffusion et de télévision* 1, no. 4 (1967): 22–4, Inathèque de France, Paris, France; *Revue de l'actualité radiophonique et télévisuelle dans le monde* (hereafter, *Actualité*), supplément à diffusion restreinte 2 (December 1969), Inathèque de France. On Euro-American tensions at Intelsat, see also Judith Tegger Kildow, *Intelsat: Policy-Maker's Dilemma* (Lexington, MA: Lexington, 1973), 43–58; Marcellus S. Snow, *International Commercial Satellite Communications: Economic and Political Issues of the First Decade of Intelsat* (New York: Praeger, 1976), 102–3, 119–25.

7. Aldo Armando Cocca, "Las Telecomunicaciones por Sátelite y su Reclamo de Ordenamiento Legal," 1968; Cocca, "Hacia la Coordinación de Sistemas de Telecomunicaciones por Satélites," 1968, both in Aldo Armando Cocca, *Consolidación del Derecho espacial* (Buenos Aires: Editorial Astrea, 1971), 283–94, 341–47; Aldo Armando Cocca, *Derecho espacial para la gran audiencia* (Buenos Aires: Asociación Argentina de Ciencias Aeroespaciales, 1970), 97–106, 123–26; Collis, "Geostationary Orbit," 68.

8. Quotation in "Communications Satellite Policy [document 6]." See also Leonard Marks, memo to S. Douglass Cater Jr., March 31, 1966, LBJ Library, Office Files of Douglass Cater, box 45; J. D. O'Connell, letter to Dean Rusk, February 21, 1967, LBJ Library, NSF, Subject File, box 6, folder "Communications (National Communications System, COMSAT, etc.), Vol. III [3 of 3]," no. 25a; Charles E. Johnson, memo to W. W. Rostow, July 10, 1967, LBJ Library, NSF, NSAM File, box 7, folder 6, no. 13c; Directorate of Intelligence, Central Intelligence Agency, "Intelligence Memorandum: New Soviet Initiatives in Communications Satellites and Television," June 1967, LBJ Library, NSF, NSAM File, box 7, folder 6, no. 2; American Embassy Paris, airgram to Department of State, June 26, 1967, LBJ Library, NSF, NSAM File, box 7, folder 6, no. 4; Katherine Johnsen, "France Backs UN Intelsat Control," *Aviation Week & Space Technology*, February 13, 1967, LBJ Library, Office Files of Douglass Cater, box 45. On French interest in a regional satellite system, see Schwoch, *Global TV*, 151.

9. Quotation from J. D. O'Connell in Slotten, "Satellite Communications," 350. See also Lyndon B. Johnson, "Special Message to the Congress on Communications Policy," August 14, 1967, in *Public Papers of the Presidents of the United States: Lyndon B. Johnson, 1967* (Washington, DC: U.S. Government Printing Office, 1968), 2:766; Executive Office of the President, Office of Telecommunications Management, "Communications Satellites: National Policy Considerations," March 3, 1967, LBJ Library, Office Files of Douglass Cater, box 45; American Embassy Addis Ababa, telegram to Department of State, February 10, 1967, LBJ Library, Office Files of Douglass Cater, box 45; Schwoch, 140–43.

10. Johnson, "Special Message to the Congress on Communications Policy"; National Security Action Memorandum (NSAM) No. 342, March 4, 1966, LBJ Library, NSF, NSAM Files, box 7, folder 11, no. 2; Lyndon B. Johnson, letter to the Congress of the

United States, March 3, 1966, in Executive Office of the President, *Annual Report on Activities and Accomplishments Under the Communications Satellite Act of 1962, January 1–December 31, 1965*, [1966], LBJ Library, NSF, Files of Charles E. Johnson, box 13, folder "COMSAT—U.S. Communications Policy, NSAM 338 File #1 [1 of 2]"; J. D. O'Connell, memorandum for the President with enclosure, July 28, 1966, LBJ Library, NSF, NSAM Files, box 7, folder 11, no. 4a. On Johnson's leadership in satellite communications, see Slotten, "Satellite Communications," 327–29, 332–37, 339–41, 348–50; Slotten, "International Telecommunications Union," 329–30; Hay, "Air Space, Outer Space, and Cyber Space," 28–29; Oslund, "'Open Shores' to 'Open Skies,'" 155–71. On North-South considerations in U.S. satellite-television policy, see also Schwoch, 127–28, 139–55.

11. O'Connell, memorandum for the President with enclosure, July 28, 1966; Annex 4 of NSAM No. 342.

12. Benjamin H. Read, memorandum for Walt W. Rostow with enclosure, January 4, 1967, LBJ Library, NSF, Files of Charles E. Johnson, box 12, folder "COMSAT—Educational Purposes, NSAM 342 (Domestic and Foreign) File #3 [2 of 2]," nos. 13b–13f.

13. In the more mundane field of terrestrial broadcasting, on the other hand, jamming of Western radio in the Eastern bloc went on much as it had since the late 1940s. Johnson, "Special Message to Congress on Communications Policy," 768; Schwoch, *Global TV*, 33–35, 126, 152–53; Collis, "Geostationary Orbit," 68–69; Serge Schmemann, "Soviet Union Ends Years of Jamming of Radio Liberty," *New York Times*, December 1, 1988.

14. Christopher Lydon, "Pact to Dilute U.S. Control of Intelsat," *New York Times*, May 21, 1971; Christopher Lydon, "Intelsat Agreement Signed by Delegates of 54 Lands," *New York Times*, August 21, 1971; Oslund, "'Open Shores' to 'Open Skies,'" 173; *Actualité, supplément à diffusion restreinte* 3 (February 1970), citing *Fernseh Informationen* (January 1970). *Actualité* was the internal foreign-affairs bulletin of the ORTF, the French broadcasting monopoly; *Fernseh-Informationen* was a West German television review.

15. Lydon, "Pact to Dilute U.S. Control of Intelsat"; Lydon, "Intelsat Agreement"; Armand Mattelart, "Communications sans frontières et impérialisme," *Le Monde diplomatique*, March 1978; Oslund, "'Open Shores' to 'Open Skies,'" 176; Richard D. Lyons, "China Developing Satellite Links," *New York Times*, January 5, 1973.

16. "The Technology Gap," *Time*, January 13, 1967, LBJ Library, NSF, Files of Charles E. Johnson, box 13, folder "COMSAT—U.S. Communications Policy, NSAM 338 File #2 [1 of 2]," no. 17a; *Actualité, supplément à diffusion restreinte* 3 (February 1970), citing *Fernseh Informationen* (January 1970). This cooperation was already underway for the ill-fated Europa launcher program. Matras, "Editorial."

17. M. Schmidbauer, "The Symphonie Project," *Proceedings of the Royal Society of London: Series A, Mathematical and Physical Sciences* 345, no. 1643 (1975): 559–62; Matras, "Editorial"; *Actualité* 7–8 (March–April 1971).

18. The Europace coalition of high-tech industries would manifest impatience with delays in the European launcher program, which the British pulled out of in 1970. Matras, "Editorial"; Snow, *International Commercial Satellite Communications*, 103. On industrial prerogatives behind Symphonie, see also M.-Y. Demerliac, "Etudes et expérimentations d'Eurospace dans le domaine de l'éducation et du service public," in

Symphonie Symposium Berlin 1980: Textes des Conférences (Toulouse: Imprimerie du Sud, 1980), 760.

19. Matras, "Editorial."

20. Richard Kuisel, *Seducing the French: The Dilemma of Americanization* (Berkeley: University of California Press, 1993), 131–53; Gordon Cumming, *Aid to Africa: French and British Policies from the Cold War to the New Millennium* (Burlington, VT: Ashgate, 2001), 58–70, 80–84; "Projet Socrate: Télévision Educative en Afrique Noire francophone: Etude économique comparative entre un Système à Satellite d'Education et des Chaines de Télévision éducatives nationales," report, Centre National des Etudes Spatiales (CNES) and ORTF, 1969, Inathèque de France; *Actualité, supplément à diffusion restreinte* 11 (March 1971); *Actualité, supplément à diffusion restreinte* 12 (April–May 1971); P. Blancheville, "Le système à satellites 'Symphonie,'" *Revue française de radiodiffusion et de télévision* 4, no. 14 (1970): 95–97, Inathèque de France.

21. Luc Pinhas, "Aux origines du discours francophone," *Communication et langages* 140 (2004): 69–82; Alice L. Conklin, *A Mission to Civilize: The Republican Idea of Empire in France and West Africa, 1895–1930* (Stanford, CA: Stanford University Press, 1997), chaps. 5–6; Diana Lemberg, "The End of Empires and Some Linguistic Turns: British and French Language Policies in Inter- and Post-War Africa," in *British and French Colonialism in Africa, Asia and the Middle East: Connected Empires Across the Eighteenth to the Twentieth Centuries*, ed. James R. Fichter (Basingstoke, UK: Palgrave Macmillan, 2019). As of the late 1960s, only roughly 5 percent of the population of the former French West Africa was literate in French; Brian Weinstein, "Francophonie: A Language-Based Movement in World Politics," *International Organization* 30, no. 3 (1976): 490.

22. Tunisia's Habib Bourguiba was another early champion of *la francophonie*. Pierre Alexandre, "Francophonie: The French and Africa," *Journal of Contemporary History* 4, no. 1 (1969): 117–25; Michel Chansou, "Politique de la langue et idéologie en français contemporain," *Mots* 6 (1983): 61–63; "Coopération: La francophonie," in *Journal de l'année: 1er juillet 1968–30 juin 1969* (Paris: Larousse, 1969), 95. On linguistic diversity in Senegal, see Ibrahima Diallo, *The Politics of National Languages in Postcolonial Senegal* (Amherst, NY: Cambria, 2010), 18–21.

23. "Projet Socrate." The seventeen countries were Burundi, Cameroon, Congo-Brazzaville, Congo-Kinshasa, the Ivory Coast, Dahomey, Gabon, Guinea, Upper Volta, Mali, Mauritania, Niger, the Central African Republic, Rwanda, Senegal, Chad, and Togo. See also Jean Sany, "Le projet Socrate" (conference proceedings from the CNES colloquium "Les satellites d'éducation," Nice, France, 3–7 May 1971), Inathèque de France, 259.

24. "Projet Socrate"; Gilbert Rist, *Le développement: Histoire d'une croyance occidentale*, rev. 4th ed. (Paris: Presses de la Fondation nationale des sciences politiques, 2013), 99–113, quotation on 103.

25. "Projet Socrate"; "La mission éducative de l'ORTF," report, ORTF, 1970, Inathèque de France; Eliane Paracuellos, "La coopération en matière de programmes avec les organismes de télévision des pays francophones: concours d'administrateur avril à juillet 1971," mémoire, ORTF, 1971, Inathèque de France. On American versus European development thinking, see Frederick Cooper, "Development, Modernization, and the Social Sciences in the Era of Decolonization: The Examples of British and French Africa," *Revue d'histoire des sciences humaines* 10 (2004): 11, 26–27.

26. Snow, *International Commercial Satellite Communications*, 102–3, 106; "L'Unesco et 'Symphonie': Documents préparatoires," documents prepared by Radio France and Institut National de l'Audiovisuel, 1976, Inathèque de France. Reports on Symphonie from the late 1970s and 1980s show that educational television experiments had been conducted in two countries, the Ivory Coast and Cameroon; as of 1976 Gabon was expected to participate as well. Demerliac, "Etudes et expérimentations," *Symphonie Symposium Berlin 1980*, 761–63; Francis Billot-Piot, "Bilan des Expérimentations Symphonie en Côte d'Ivoire," *Symphonie Symposium Berlin 1980*, 769–73; Ph. Dosiere, "Le système Symphonie et ses applications" (conference proceedings for "Les Télécommunications par satellite," Abidjan, November 21–24, 1978), Inathèque de France; "L'Unesco et 'Symphonie'"; Frédéric Engel, "L'Europe, troisième force spatiale: le cas du satellite de télécommunications européen," Mémoire de maitrise de géographie, Université Paris X, 1985, Inathèque de France. On the reforms to French television, see Sophie Bachmann, "La suppression de l'ORTF en 1974: La réforme de la 'Délivrance,'" *Vingtième siècle* 17 (1988): 63–72.

27. Quotation from Sany, "Le projet Socrate," 259. See also Paracuellos, "La coopération"; "La mission éducative de l'ORTF."

28. Cf. Schmidbauer, "The Symphonie Project," 563. On colloquial Arabics and Standard Arabic, see Tristan James Mabry, *Nationalism, Language, and Muslim Exceptionalism* (Philadelphia: University of Pennsylvania Press, 2015), chap. 4: "Modern Standard Arabs"; John Eisele, "Whither Arabic? From Possible Worlds to Possible Futures," in *Applied Linguistics in the Middle East and North Africa: Current Practices and Future Directions*, ed. Atta Gebril (Amsterdam: John Benjamins, 2017), 307–42.

29. Weinstein, "Francophonie," 496–97; Organisation internationale de la Francophonie, "Une histoire de la Francophonie," accessed April 4, 2017, https://www.francophonie .org/Une-histoire-de-la-Francophonie.html.

30. The official was E. C. Welsh, in "Memorandum for File," November 25, 1966, LBJ Library, NSF, Files of Charles E. Johnson, box 13, folder "COMSAT—U.S. Communications Policy, NSAM 338 File #2 [2 of 2]," no. 22a. On Eutelsat, see "European Space Agency Puts Commercial Satellites in Orbit," *New York Times*, June 18, 1983; Eutelsat website, accessed March 7, 2017, http://www.eutelsat.com/en/group/our -history.html. On Arabsat, see Naomi Sakr, "From Satellite to Screen: How Arab TV Is Shaped in Space," in Parks and Schwoch, *Down to Earth*, 143–55; Sakr, *Satellite Realms: Transnational Television, Globalization and the Middle East* (London: I. B. Tauris, 2001), 9–16.

31. F. Ray, "The Transmission of News," September 10, 1965, UNESCO Archives, 629.19: 621.39 MEE; Wenrick, "Communication Satellites and the Mass Media." On the "crise du téléphone" in France in the 1960s, see Elie Cohen, *Le Colbertisme 'high tech': Economie des Télécom et du Grand Projet* (Paris: Hachette, 1992), 44–54.

32. Schramm, "Communication Satellites"; Ray, "The Transmission of News"; Wenrick, "Communication Satellites and the Mass Media."

33. Slotten, "International Telecommunications Union," 348–49, 357–58.

34. Clarke, "World of the Communications Satellite"; Schramm, "Communication Satellites"; Overton Brooks (chair of the aforementioned House committee) cited in Slotten, "Satellite Communications," 336.

35. American Embassy Paris, cable to State Department, January 1968, LBJ Library, NSF, Files of Charles E. Johnson, box 12, folder "COMSAT—Educational Purposes,

NSAM 342 (Domestic and Foreign) File #3 [1 of 2]," no. 1c; A. H. Moseman, memo for Leonard H. Marks, [1966], LBJ Library, White House Central Files (WHCF), C.F. ED 5, box 14; Richard N. Gardner, "Satellites Can Link Mankind," *Washington Post*, March 10, 1968, LBJ Library, Office Files of Douglass Cater, box 47.

36. Gardner; Clarke, "World of the Communications Satellite."

37. Schwoch, *Global TV*, 74–75, 152–53.

38. Jean Persin, "Will Space Be Open to Piracy?," *Telecommunication Journal* 30, no. 4 (1963): 115n9; Johns, *Death of a Pirate*, 123.

39. Fernand Terrou, "International Co-Operation in the Use of Space Communications for Information, Education and Culture," December 1, 1965, UNESCO/SPACECOM/13, accessed April 4, 2017, https://unesdoc.unesco.org/ark:/48223/pf0000155975_eng; Hilding Eek, "The Use of Space Communication: International Co-Operation and International Control," November 26, 1965, UNESCO Archives, 629.19: 621.39 MEE. On Third World sovereignty concerns, see Roland Burke, *Decolonization and the Evolution of International Human Rights* (Philadelphia: University of Pennsylvania Press, 2010), 92–111; Samuel Moyn, *The Last Utopia: Human Rights in History* (Cambridge, MA: Belknap Press of Harvard University Press, 2010), 84–119.

40. The Council of Europe's "European Agreement for the Prevention of Broadcasts Transmitted from Stations Outside National Territories" opened for signature in January 1965. The agreement was quickly signed by France, Britain, Belgium, Denmark, Sweden, and the Netherlands among other countries. Kimberley Peters, "Sinking the Radio 'Pirates': Exploring British Strategies of Governance in the North Sea, 1964–1991," *Area* 43, no. 3 (2011): 281–87; *Actualité* 23 (May 9, 1966); *Actualité* 13 (February 18, 1965); *Actualité* 16 (September 6, 1965).

41. Queeney, *Direct Broadcast Satellites*, 27–28, 32, 46–47, 55, 70–77, 168–70.

42. Schwoch, *Global TV*, 74.

43. Cocca, "Hacia la Coordinación de Sistemas de Telecomunicaciones por Satélites"; Cocca, *Derecho espacial para la gran audiencia*, 99–101; Mattelart, *Agresión desde el espacio*, 12, 47–53.

44. "First Draft of Declaration on the Guiding Principles for the Use of Space Communication for the Free Flow of Information[,] the Spread of Information and Greater Cultural Exchange," July 30, 1971, Unesco COM-71/CONF.5/4, accessed March 10, 2017, https://unesdoc.unesco.org/ark:/48223/pf0000000702; "Declaration of Guiding Principles on the Use of Satellite Broadcasting for the Free Flow of Information[,] the Spread of Education and Greater Cultural Exchange," 1972, accessed March 10, 2017, https://unesdoc.unesco.org/ark:/48223/pf0000002136; Queeney, *Direct Broadcast Satellites*, 117–37.

45. Queeney, 32–34; Aldo Armando Cocca, "The Supreme Interests of Mankind Vis-à-Vis the Emergence of Direct Broadcast," *Journal of Space Law* 2, no. 2 (1974): 84–91; UN General Assembly, "Preparation of an International Convention on Principles Governing the Use by States of Artificial Earth Satellites for Direct Television Broadcasting" (A/RES/2916/XXVII), November 9, 1972, accessed March 10, 2017, https://documents-dds-ny.un.org/doc/RESOLUTION/GEN/NR0/269/46/IMG/NR026946.pdf?OpenElement. General Assembly voting record for A/RES/2916/XXVII, accessed March 10, 2017, http://unbisnet.un.org:8080/ipac20/ipac.jsp?profile=voting&index=.VM&term=ares2916xxvii.

46. Mattelart, "Communications sans frontières"; Queeney, 150–51, 175–76; Daniel Lerner, "Technology, Communication, and Change," in *Communication and Change: The Last Ten Years—and the Next*, ed. Wilbur Schramm and Daniel Lerner (Honolulu: University Press of Hawaii, 1976), 298–300, quotations on 300. The impasse in direct-broadcasting discussions is documented, for instance, in Carl Q. Christol, "The 1974 Brussels Convention Relating to the Distribution of Program-Carrying Signals Transmitted by Satellite: An Aspect of Human Rights," *Journal of Space Law* 6, no. 1 (1978): 19–35; Michel Bourély, "The Contributions Made by International Organizations to the Formation of Space Law," *Journal of Space Law* 10, no. 2 (1982): 139–55.

47. S. Neil Hosenball, "Current Issues of Space Law Before the United Nations," *Journal of Space Law* 2, no. 1 (1974): 11.

6. CULTURAL TURNS IN THE INTERNATIONAL ARENA

The epigraph for this chapter is taken from: Herbert I. Schiller, *Communication and Cultural Domination* (hereafter *CCD*) (White Plains, NY: M. E. Sharpe, 1976), 39.

1. Daniel Lerner, *The Passing of Traditional Society: Modernizing the Middle East* (New York: Free, 1958), 43–75; Wilbur Schramm, *Mass Media and National Development: The Role of Information in the Developing Countries* (Stanford, CA: Stanford University Press, 1964), 35–37; Nils Gilman, *Mandarins of the Future: Modernization Theory in Cold War America* (Baltimore, MD: Johns Hopkins University Press, 2003), 205; Daniel T. Rodgers, *Age of Fracture* (Cambridge, MA: Belknap Press of Harvard University Press, 2011), 198.

2. On "cultural turns" within and without the academy in the 1960s and 1970s, see Michael Denning, *Culture in the Age of Three Worlds* (London: Verso, 2004); Dan Schiller, *Theorizing Communication: A History* (New York: Oxford University Press, 1996), chap. 3: "The Opening Toward Culture"; Rodgers, *Age of Fracture*, 90–102. On culture in the social sciences, see Clifford Geertz, *The Interpretation of Cultures: Selected Essays* (New York: Basic, 1973); Wilbur Schramm, "Mass Media and National Development—1979" (paper for the MacBride Commission, 1979), accessed August 4, 2016, https://unesdoc.unesco.org/ark:/48223/pf0000037073.locale=en; Daniel Lerner, "Toward a New Paradigm," in *Communication and Change: The Last Ten Years—and the Next*, ed. Wilbur Schramm and Daniel Lerner (Honolulu: University Press of Hawaii, 1976), 60–63.

3. Richard F. Kuisel, *Seducing the French: The Dilemma of Americanization* (Berkeley: University of California Press, 1993), 2, 10–14; D. Schiller, *Theorizing Communication*, 64–68.

4. Richard Hoggart, *An Idea and Its Servants: UNESCO from Within* (New York: Oxford University Press, 1978), 193; Herbert I. Schiller, "Is There a United States Information Policy?," in *Hope & Folly: The United States and UNESCO, 1945–1985*, by William Preston Jr., Edward S. Herman, and Herbert I. Schiller (Minneapolis: University of Minnesota Press, 1989), 299–303.

5. On d'Arcy's effort to find a third way between the United States and the Soviet–Third World bloc, see Chloé Maurel, "Le 'droit de l'homme à la communication': L'action de Jean d'Arcy à l'Unesco," in *Jean d'Arcy (1913–1983): Penser la communication au XXe siècle*, ed. Marie-Françoise Lévy (Paris: Publications de la Sorbonne, 2013), 189–200, see esp. 194.

6. Harold A. Innis, *Empire and Communications* (1950; Toronto: University of Toronto Press, 1972), 5–6, 169–70; Innis, "Technology and Public Opinion in the United States," in *The Bias of Communication*, 2nd ed. (1951; Toronto: University of Toronto Press, 2008), 186-87. On Innis, see Alexander John Watson, "Introduction to the Second Edition," in *Bias of Communication*, xv–xvii, xxii–xxiii.

7. Victor Pickard, *America's Battle for Media Democracy: The Triumph of Corporate Libertarianism and the Future of Media Reform* (New York: Cambridge University Press, 2015), 44–45, 120–21, 190–205; Dallas Smythe, *Counterclockwise: Perspectives on Communication*, ed. Thomas Guback (Boulder, CO: Westview, 1994), 13–58.

8. Gilbert Rist, *Le développement: Histoire d'une croyance occidentale*, rev. 4th ed. (Paris: Presses de la Fondation nationale des sciences politiques, 2013), 202–5; Thomas H. Guback, *The International Film Industry: Western Europe and America Since 1945* (Bloomington: Indiana University Press, 1969).

9. Dallas Smythe, preface to *Mass Communications and American Empire* (hereafter *MCAE*), by Herbert I. Schiller (New York: Augustus M. Kelley, 1969), vii–viii. On Schiller, see Richard Maxwell, *Herbert Schiller* (Lanham, MD: Rowman & Littlefield, 2003), 13–31, 39–40, 62–63; Smythe, *Counterclockwise*, 50.

10. H. Schiller, *MCAE*, see esp. 1–17, 20, 93, 115–21.

11. H. Schiller, *CCD*, 1–23; Herbert I. Schiller, "Communication Accompanies Capital Flows" (paper for UNESCO's International Commission for the Study of Communication Problems, 1978), accessed April 17, 2014, https://unesdoc.unesco.org/ark :/48223/pf0000034210.

12. H. Schiller, *CCD*, 8; H. Schiller, *MCAE*, 109; H. Schiller, "Communication Accompanies Capital Flows."

13. Julianne Burton and Jean Franco discuss some of the distinctions between Schiller's work and that coming from Latin America in "Culture and Imperialism," *Latin American Perspectives* 5, no. 1 (1978): 8–12.

14. Ariel Dorfman and Armand Mattelart, *How to Read Donald Duck: Imperialist Ideology in the Disney Comic* (1971; New York: I. G. Editions, 1991), see esp. 36, 48–69, 97–98.

15. Ariel Dorfman, *Heading South, Looking North: A Bilingual Journey* (New York: Penguin, 1999), 30–40. CIA monies had made their way to the saboteurs: U.S. Senate, Select Committee on Intelligence Activities, "Covert Action in Chile, 1963–1973," IV.35–IV.39, accessed August 8, 2016, http://www.archives.gov/declassification/iscap /pdf/2010-009-doc17.pdf. On the contrast between dependency theory in Latin America and the United States, see Rist, *Le développement*, 199–211; Cody Stephens, "The Accidental Marxist: Andre Gunder Frank and the 'Neo-Marxist' Theory of Underdevelopment, 1958–1967," *Modern Intellectual History* 15, no. 2 (2018): 411–42.

16. Armand Mattelart, "The Nature of Communications Practice in a Dependent Society," trans. Dana B. Polan, *Latin American Perspectives* 5, no. 1 (1978): 13–34; Carlos Monsiváis, "Notas sobre cultura popular en Mexico," *Latin American Perspectives* 5, no. 1 (1978): 98–118; Burton and Franco, "Culture and Imperialism." For the Mattelarts on France, see Armand Mattelart and Michèle Mattelart, " 'L'aliénation linguistique,' d'Henri Gobard," *Le Monde diplomatique*, November 1976.

17. Dorfman, *Heading South*, 220; Hervé Bourges, *Décoloniser l'information* (Paris: Editions Cana, 1978), see esp. 152–55.

18. H. Schiller, *CCD*, 106-8.

19. Peter Kornbluh, *The Pinochet File: A Declassified Dossier on Atrocity and Accountability* (2003; New York: New, 2013), xii–xiii; Senate Select Committee on Intelligence Activities, "Covert Action in Chile, 1963–1973."

20. Denning, *Culture in the Age of Three Worlds*, 33.

21. Shirley Hazzard, "The League of Frightened Men: Why the UN Is So Useless," *New Republic*, January 19, 1980, reprinted in Shirley Hazzard, *We Need Silence to Find Out What We Think*, ed. Brigitta Olubas (New York: Columbia University Press, 2016), 131–32, 134–35. On the growing visibility and significance of human-rights NGOs in the 1970s, see, inter alia, Samuel Moyn, *The Last Utopia: Human Rights in History* (Cambridge, MA: Belknap Press of Harvard University Press, 2010), chap. 4; Akira Iriye, Petra Goedde, and William I. Hitchcock, eds., *The Human Rights Revolution: An International History* (New York: Oxford University Press, 2012), see esp. the editors' introduction; Kenneth Cmiel, "The Emergence of Human Rights Politics in the United States," *Journal of American History* 86, no. 3 (1999): 1231–50; Jan Eckel and Samuel Moyn, eds., *The Breakthrough: Human Rights in the 1970s* (Philadelphia: University of Pennsylvania Press, 2014).

22. Shirley Hazzard, *The Defeat of an Ideal: A Study of the Self-Destruction of the United Nations* (Boston: Little, Brown, 1973), see esp. 14–146; Hazzard, *Countenance of Truth: The United Nations and the Waldheim Case* (New York: Viking, 1990). On Hazzard's time at the United Nations, see *The Defeat of an Ideal*, xiv–xv; J. D. McClatchy, "Shirley Hazzard: The Art of Fiction No. 185," *Paris Review* 173 (2005), http://www.theparisreview.org/interviews/5505/the-art-of-fiction-no-185-shirley -hazzard.

23. Shirley Hazzard, *People in Glass Houses: Portraits from Organization Life* (New York: Knopf, 1967), quotations on 34, 48–50.

24. Hazzard, *The Defeat of an Ideal*, 217–44, quotation on 230.

25. Quotation from Shirley Hazzard, "The Patron Saint of the UN Is Pontius Pilate," *New York Times*, February 23, 1974, reprinted in Hazzard, *We Need Silence*, 111. On environmental issues, see Hazzard, *The Defeat of an Ideal*, 233–36.

26. On Hoggart's left-conservatism, see Sue Owen, "Introduction," in *Richard Hoggart and Cultural Studies*, ed. Sue Owen (Basingstoke, UK: Palgrave Macmillan, 2008), esp. 17; Charlie Ellis's contribution to the same volume, "Relativism and Reaction: Richard Hoggart and Conservatism," 198–212.

27. Richard Hoggart, *The Uses of Literacy* (1957; New Brunswick, NJ: Transaction, 2000), quotation on 128; Stuart Hall, "Richard Hoggart, *The Uses of Literacy*, and the Cultural Turn," in Owen, *Richard Hoggart and Cultural Studies*, 20–32.

28. Hoggart, *The Uses of Literacy*, 133.

29. Centre for Contemporary Cultural Studies, "Second [Annual] Report," October 1965, accessed August 16, 2016, http://www.birmingham.ac.uk/Documents /college-artslaw/history/cccs/annual-reports/1964-65.pdf; Hall, "Richard Hoggart," 20–32.

30. Jeffrey Milland, "Courting Malvolio: The Background to the Pilkington Committee on Broadcasting, 1960–62," *Contemporary British History* 18, no. 2 (2004): 76–102; Julian Petley, "Richard Hoggart and Pilkington: Populism and Public Service Broadcasting," *Ethical Space: The International Journal of Communication Ethics* 12, no. 1 (2015): 4–14. On Latin American radio as an early model for how American pressures helped to privatize broadcasting elsewhere in the world, see James Schwoch, *The*

American Radio Industry and Its Latin American Activities, 1900–1939 (Urbana: University of Illinois Press, 1990), 78–79.

31. Chloé Maurel, *Histoire de l'Unesco: Les trente premières années, 1945–1974* (Paris: L'Harmattan, 2010), 73–90; preface to Hall et al., *Culture, Media, Language: Working Papers in Cultural Studies, 1972–79* (London: Centre for Contemporary Cultural Studies, University of Birmingham, 1980), vi; Malcolm Hadley, "Promoting International Understanding and Cooperation: Richard Hoggart's UNESCO Years (1970–1975)," in *Re-Reading Richard Hoggart: Life, Literature, Language, Education*, ed. Sue Owen (Newcastle upon Tyne, UK: Cambridge Scholars, 2008), 153–74.

32. Hoggart, *An Idea*, 190–96, quotation on 195; Cmiel, "Emergence of Human Rights Politics," 1248–50.

33. See, for instance, Stuart Hall et al., *Policing the Crisis: Mugging, the State, and Law and Order* (London: Macmillan, 1978).

34. Hoggart, *An Idea*, quotations on 193, see also 160–65.

35. Isaiah Berlin, citing the Greek poet Archilochus, in *The Hedgehog and the Fox: An Essay on Tolstoy's View of History* (1953; Princeton, NJ: Princeton University Press, 2013), 1.

36. Hazzard, *People in Glass Houses*, 13–14.

37. Hoggart, *An Idea*, 22, 32, 35–37.

38. On American influences on d'Arcy's thought, see Léonard Laborie, "Jean d'Arcy entrepreneur. Satellite, câble, vidéo: Nouvelles technologies et régulation audiovisuelle," in Lévy, *Jean d'Arcy (1913–1983)*, see esp. 206, 214; Henri Pigeat, "Jean d'Arcy: Le droit de l'homme à la communication, actualité d'une vision prémonitoire," in Lévy, *Jean d'Arcy (1913–1983)*, 217–26, esp. 218, 224.

39. Jean d'Arcy, "Direct Broadcast Satellites and the Right to Communicate," *European Broadcasting Union (EBU) Review* 118 (1969): 14–18, see esp. 14, 18.

40. D'Arcy, "Direct Broadcast Satellites," 17–18; Jean d'Arcy, "Satellites d'éducation et liberté d'information" (paper collected in proceedings of "Les satellites d'éducation," CNES colloquium, Nice, France, May 3–7, 1971), 385–96, Inathèque de France, Paris, France.

41. L. S. Harms, letter to Jean d'Arcy, March 3, 1972; Jean d'Arcy, letter to L. S. Harms, April 16, 1974; L. S. Harms, letter to Jean d'Arcy, July 23, 1974, all in Fonds d'Arcy, Inathèque de France, carton 15, dossier 44. Jean d'Arcy, "Pas de société sans communication" (1979), in *Jean d'Arcy parle: Pionnier et visionnaire de la télévision*, ed. François Cazenave (Paris: La Documentation française, 1984), 165–67.

42. Desmond Fisher, "From Concept to Action," in *The Right to Communicate: A New Human Right*, ed. Desmond Fisher and L. S. Harms (Dublin: Boole, 1983), 11–12; Maurel, "Le 'droit de l'homme à la communication,'" 191; Jean d'Arcy, memo to "participants in the Mexico Group on the 'Right to Communicate,'" November 13, 1974, Fonds d'Arcy, carton 15, dossier 45; biographical note on d'Arcy in *The Right to Communicate*, xix. The IBI would later be renamed the International Institute of Communications.

43. E. Lloyd Sommerlad, letter to Jean d'Arcy, February 20, 1975, Fonds d'Arcy, carton 15, dossier 45; Nigeria comments in "Summary" of questionnaire responses, January 15, 1976, UNESCO Archives, 342.727 UNE.

44. Jean d'Arcy, letter to Edward Ploman, April 23, 1975, Fonds d'Arcy, carton 15, dossier 45; Jean d'Arcy, letter to Makaminan Makagiansar, December 5, 1977, Fonds d'Arcy, carton 10, dossier 29.

45. D'Arcy, letter to Ploman, April 23, 1975; Jean d'Arcy, letter to L. S. Harms, October 18, 1974, both in Fonds d'Arcy, carton 15, dossier 44. Despite its initial refusal, the French commission would convene a working group the following year (1975) to discuss the right to communicate. The group featured Fernand Terrou, Hubert Beuve-Méry, Claude Bellanger, and Georges Friedmann among others. See "Groupe de réflexion sur le concept de droit à la communication," September 29, 1975, Fonds d'Arcy, carton 15, dossier 45.

46. Jean d'Arcy, letter to Yves Brunswick, [October 1975], Fonds d'Arcy, carton 15, dossier 45.

47. Yves Brunswick, letter to Jean d'Arcy, January 19, 1976, Fonds d'Arcy, carton 15, dossier 45; Maurel, "Le 'droit de l'homme à la communication,' " 194.

48. Jean d'Arcy, letter to Jean Thomas, August 11, 1976, Fonds d'Arcy, carton 9, dossier 28.

49. D'Arcy, letter to Thomas, August 11, 1976.

50. Jean d'Arcy, "The Right to Communicate" (discussion paper, Meeting of Experts on the "Right to Communicate," Manila, Philippines, October 15–19, 1979), UNESCO IM/RICOM/DP/4, UNESCO Archives, 342.727 MEE, part 1. See also d'Arcy, "Pas de société sans communication," 165, where he stressed the right's applicability to both individuals and groups.

51. Henri Pigeat, preface to *Jean d'Arcy parle*, 12. On Pigeat, see Lévy, *Jean d'Arcy (1913–1983)*, 258.

52. In "Broadcasting in the Global Age" (1982), for instance, d'Arcy specified that "vertical" mass media flows endangered local cultural identities—a threat posed by top-down international-development initiatives and unreflective nationalisms alike. Jean d'Arcy, "La Radiodiffusion à l'ère planétaire," in *Jean d'Arcy parle*, 168, 172–73.

53. [Jean d'Arcy], untitled note, April 1975, Fonds d'Arcy, carton 9, dossier 27. Omitting mention of any specific countries or their languages, d'Arcy would present a toned-down paraphrase of Clarke's prediction to a 1982 conference in Tokyo. Presentation excerpted in "Radiodiffusion à l'ère planétaire," 171.

54. Herbert I. Schiller, "Decolonization of Information: Efforts Toward a New International Order," *Latin American Perspectives* 5, no. 1 (1978): 35–48, quotation on 42.

55. Roland Burke, *Decolonization and the Evolution of International Human Rights* (Philadelphia: University of Pennsylvania Press, 2010), 112–13, 143–44; see also Akira Iriye and Petra Goedde, "Introduction: Human Rights as History," in Iriye, Goedde, and Hitchcock, *Human Rights Revolution*, 9–12.

7. "A GLOBAL FIRST AMENDMENT WAR": FREEDOM OF INFORMATION ON THE VERGE OF THE NEOLIBERAL ERA

The epigraphs for this chapter are taken from: Philip H. Power and Elie Abel, "Third World vs. the Media," *New York Times Magazine*, September 21, 1980, UNESCO Archives, Paris, France, CAB 7/42; Arlie Schardt with Scott Sullivan, "Inching Toward Controls," *Newsweek*, November 3, 1980; "UNESCO's Protection Racket," *Washington Post*, April 10, 1979; and Curtis Prendergast, "The Global First Amendment War," *Time*, October 6, 1980.

1. Fred H. Cate, "The First Amendment and the International 'Free Flow' of Information," *Virginia Journal of International Law* 30, no. 371 (1990): 386.

2. Sanford S. Marlowe, "TV in Viet-Nam," January 13, 1966, Personal Papers of Leonard Marks, Lyndon Baines Johnson Presidential Library (LBJ Library), Austin, TX, box 30; Loren F. Stone, "Television in Vietnam 1966: A Report by Loren B. Stone, USIA/AID Consultant," June 1966, Personal Papers of Leonard Marks, LBJ Library, box 29.

3. On domestic FOIA legislation, see Michael Schudson, *The Rise of the Right to Know: Politics and the Culture of Transparency, 1945–1975* (Cambridge, MA: Belknap Press of Harvard University Press, 2015), 28–63. On NGOs and the 1970s in human-rights historiography, see Kenneth Cmiel, "The Emergence of Human Rights Politics in the United States," *Journal of American History* 86, no. 3 (1999): 1231–50; Samuel Moyn, *The Last Utopia: Human Rights in History* (Cambridge, MA: Belknap Press of Harvard University Press, 2010), chap. 4; Jan Eckel and Samuel Moyn, eds., *The Breakthrough: Human Rights in the 1970s* (Philadelphia: University of Pennsylvania Press, 2014).

4. By the late 1970s even conservative Republicans, traditionally leery of international commitments, were selectively embracing human rights as a lever in East-West relations. Carl J. Bon Tempo, "Human Rights and the U.S. Republican Party in the Late 1970s," in Eckel and Moyn, *The Breakthrough*, 146–65; Hauke Hartmann, "U.S. Human Rights Policy Under Carter and Reagan, 1977–1981," *Human Rights Quarterly* 23, no. 2 (May 2001): 402–30.

5. Thomas G. Gulick, "The IPDC: UNESCO vs. the Free Press," *Heritage Foundation Backgrounder* 253, March 10, 1983, UNESCO Archives, 659.3:341.232 INT.

6. Ithiel de Sola Pool, "The Necessity for Social Scientists Doing Research for Governments," *Background* 10, no. 2 (1966): 111–22.

7. Wilbur Schramm, "In Memoriam: Ithiel de Sola Pool, 1917–1984," *Public Opinion Quarterly* 48, no. 2 (1984): 525–26. In their late work Lerner and Schramm both acknowledged serious flaws in modernization theory as initially conceived. But they continued to discuss development in primarily national frameworks. In his paper for the MacBride Commission, Schramm conceived of developing-world media as serving the state—and as being bounded by national frontiers—in a manner consistent with his earlier work. Wilbur Schramm, "Mass Media and National Development—1979," 1979, International Commission for the Study of Communication Problems 42, accessed May 29, 2017, https://unesdoc.unesco.org/ark:/48223 /pf0000037073_eng; see also Hemant Shah, *The Production of Modernization: Daniel Lerner, Mass Media, and the Passing of Traditional Society* (Philadelphia: Temple University Press, 2011), chap. 6. Cf. Ithiel de Sola Pool, *Technologies of Freedom* (Cambridge, MA: Belknap Press of Harvard University Press, 1983). On bipartisan support for deregulation, see Kevin G. Wilson, *Deregulating Telecommunications: U.S. and Canadian Telecommunications, 1840–1997* (Lanham, MD: Rowman & Littlefield, 2000), 100.

8. See, for instance, Gulick, "The IPDC: UNESCO vs. the Free Press."

9. Pool's and others' efforts to bring social science to bear on anticommunist foreign policy and the U.S. war effort in Vietnam have been well documented in recent scholarship. See, for instance, Joy Rohde, "The Last Stand of the Psychocultural Cold Warriors: Military Contract Research in Vietnam," *Journal of the History of the Behavioral Sciences* 47, no. 3 (2011): 232–50; David H. Price, *Cold War Anthropology: The CIA, the*

Pentagon, and the Growth of Dual Use Anthropology (Durham, NC: Duke University Press, 2016), esp. 301–22; Nils Gilman, *Mandarins of the Future: Modernization Theory in Cold War America* (Baltimore, MD: Johns Hopkins University Press, 2003), chap. 5.

10. Rohde, "Last Stand of the Psychocultural Cold Warriors," see esp. 234–35, 243–47; Ithiel de Sola Pool, "Achieving Pacification in Vietnam," [February/March] 1968, LBJ Library, NSF, Vietnam Country File, box 60, folder "Vietnam 1 C (3)-B1 1/68-10/68 Revolutionary Development Program," nos. 17a, 17c; William Leonhart, memo for Walt Rostow, March 20, 1968, LBJ Library, NSF, Vietnam Country File, box 60, folder "Vietnam 1 C (3)-B1 1/68-10/68 Revolutionary Development Program," no. 17. For Pool on the Defense Department, see Pool, "The Necessity for Social Scientists Doing Research for Governments."

11. Ithiel de Sola Pool, "Direct-Broadcast Satellites and Cultural Integrity," 1975, *Society*, January/February 1998, 140–51.

12. Pool, "Direct-Broadcast Satellites," 147.

13. Sanford S. Marlowe, memo to the Director, March 16, 1966; Sanford S. Marlowe, memo to Mr. Marks, March 15, 1966; [Casler], cable to "USIA WashDC," February 8, [1966]; Stone, "Television in Vietnam 1966," all in LBJ Library, Personal Papers of Leonard Marks, box 30.

14. Ithiel de Sola Pool, "Scarcity, Abundance and the Right to Communicate," in *Evolving Perspectives on the Right to Communicate*, ed. L. S. Harms and Jim Richstad (Honolulu: East-West Center, East-West Communication Institute, 1977), 175–89; Ithiel de Sola Pool, "Direct Broadcast Satellites and the Integrity of National Cultures," in *National Sovereignty and International Communication*, ed. Kaarle Nordenstreng and Herbert I. Schiller (Norwood, NJ: Ablex, 1979), 120–53, see esp. 151–53.

15. Pool, *Technologies of Freedom*, 108–50, 226. On the FCC's authority and the NBC decision, see Lee C. Bollinger, *Images of a Free Press* (Chicago: University of Chicago Press, 1991), 66–71; Cate, "First Amendment," 397–98.

16. Pool, 138–48, 234–51, quotation on 251. For the recent rethinking of neoliberalism and its relationship to governance, see Manuel B. Aalbers, "Regulated Deregulation," in *The Handbook of Neoliberalism*, ed. Simon Springer, Kean Birch, and Julie MacLeavy (New York: Routledge, 2016), 563–73; Quinn Slobodian, *Globalists: The End of Empire and the Birth of Neoliberalism* (Cambridge, MA: Harvard University Press, 2018).

17. Bollinger, *Images of a Free Press*, 83–84, 120–21.

18. Pool, *Technologies of Freedom*, quotation on 8.

19. Pool, quotation on 9.

20. Pool, 66–74, quotation on 71.

21. On the First Amendment outside U.S. borders, see Cate, "First Amendment," 392n103; Timothy Zick, *The Cosmopolitan First Amendment: Protecting Transborder Expressive and Religious Liberties* (New York: Cambridge University Press, 2014), esp. chap. 10.

22. Pool, *Technologies of Freedom*, 44–45, 146, 201–5, 219–25, 236–37; Wilson, *Deregulating Telecommunications*, 130–37; Cate, "First Amendment," 398; Christy Collis, "The Geostationary Orbit: A Critical Legal Geography of Space's Most Valuable Real Estate," in *Down to Earth: Satellite Technologies, Industries, and Cultures*, ed. Lisa

Parks and James Schwoch (New Brunswick, NJ: Rutgers University Press, 2012), 61–62.

23. Hervé Bourges, *Décoloniser l'information* (Paris: Editions Cana, 1978), 9–22, 152–55. The New World Information Order was also referred to as the New International Information Order (NIIO) and the New World Information and Communication Order (NWICO).

24. Yves Brunswick, letter to Jean d'Arcy, September 13, 1977, Fonds d'Arcy, box 10, folder 29; Paul Hofmann, "UN Votes, 72–35, to Term Zionism Form of Racism," *New York Times*, November 11, 1975; Paul Hofmann, "U.S. Warns at UN on Zionism Issue," *New York Times*, April 29, 1976; Michael T. Kaufman, "Free Press an Issue at UNESCO Meeting," *New York Times*, October 28, 1976; "West Quits UNESCO's Media Talks," *Washington Post*, December 19, 1975; Power and Abel, "Third World vs. the Media."

25. UNESCO, "Aide Memoire," DADG/CC/COM/48, July 30, 1976, Fonds Jean d'Arcy, Inathèque de France, Paris, France, box 9, folder 28; Dietrich Berwanger, "The Establishment of a New International Information Order: Summary of a Worldwide Debate" (working paper, Toward a New World Information Order: Consequences for Development Policy Conference, Bonn, West Germany, December 4–6, 1978), UNESCO Archives, 659.3 (06) INT. On Berwanger, see Carol J. Williams, "Entertained into Social Change," *Los Angeles Times*, April 24, 2001, accessed June 2, 2017, http://articles.latimes.com/2001/apr/24/news/mn-54862. On the parallel between NWIO and slightly later European resistance to U.S. information diplomacy, see also Cate, "First Amendment."

26. The commission's background summarized in Amadou-Mahtar M'Bow, foreword to *Many Voices, One World: Towards a New More Just and Efficient World Information and Communication Order* (New York: Unipub, 1980), xiii–xv; Seán MacBride, preface to *Many Voices, One World*, xvii–xx.

27. Seán MacBride, "The Right to Information" (speech to the 27th General Assembly of the International Press Institute, Canberra, Australia, March 7–9, 1978), UNESCO Archives, 307 A 01 ICSCP/136/8, part 2.

28. Roland Homet, letter to Jean d'Arcy, February 12, 1979, Fonds d'Arcy, box 11, folder 32. The ICA was, in Homet's words, charged with "[encouraging] the maximum flow of information and ideas among the peoples of the world." On the ICA, see Roland Homet, "Goals and Contradictions in a World Information Order," [1978], Fonds d'Arcy, box 11, folder 32; "Records of the United States Information Agency," National Archives website, accessed April 7, 2014, http://www.archives.gov/research/guide-fed-records/groups/306.html. On the League of Nations efforts, see Margaret A. Blanchard, *Exporting the First Amendment: The Press-Government Crusade of 1945–1952* (New York: Longman, 1986), 11–16.

29. Henry A. Grunwald, letter to Seán MacBride, June 1, 1979, UNESCO Archives, 307 A 01 ICSCP/136/8 PR, part 3; Pool, *Technologies of Freedom*, 72; Elie Abel, letter to Acher Deleon, January 2, 1980, UNESCO Archives, 307 A 01 ICSCP/136/8, part 4.

30. Leonard R. Sussman, letter to Seán MacBride, August 15, 1979, UNESCO Archives, 307 A 01 ICSCP/136/8 PR, part 4; Pool, "Scarcity, Abundance and the Right to Communicate," 175.

31. Mustapha Masmoudi, "The New World Information Order," International Commission for the Study of Communication Problems 31, 1978, 17, https://unesdoc.unesco

.org/ark:/48223/pf0000034010_eng. On Masmoudi, see also Cate, "First Amendment," 377–81.

32. On the discourse of press responsibility during the 1940s, see Sam Lebovic, *Free Speech and Unfree News: The Paradox of Press Freedom in America* (Cambridge, MA: Harvard University Press, 2016), 111–45.

33. Bollinger, *Images of a Free Press*, see esp. chaps. 2, 4; Cate, "First Amendment," 396–402.

34. Pool, *Technologies of Freedom*, 28; "Address by Mr. Federico Mayor" (speech to the Twenty-Eighth General Assembly of the International Press Institute, Athens, Greece, June 18, 1979), Fonds d'Arcy, box 15, folder 46.

35. Homet, "Goals and Contradictions"; Elie Abel, "Ushering the Third World into a New Communications Order" (presentation, World Communications: Decisions for the '80s Conference, Annenberg School of Communications, University of Pennsylvania, Philadelphia, May 12–14, 1980), UNESCO Archives, 307 A 01 ICSCP/136/8, part 6; Power and Abel, "Third World vs. the Media"; Hubert Beuve-Méry, letter to Acher Deleon, July 24, 1979, UNESCO Archives, 307 A 01 ICSCP/136/8, part 4; Jean d'Arcy, letter to Roland Homet, February 5, 1979, Fonds d'Arcy, box 11, folder 32.

36. Hubert Beuve-Méry, from document labeled "Transcription de bande non-autorisée," January 9, 1979, UNESCO Archives, 307 A 01 ICSCP/136/8, part 3; Jean d'Arcy, "Intervention de M. Jean d'Arcy le 13 oct. 1980 à la Conférence générale de l'UNESCO," October 13, 1980, Fonds d'Arcy, box 11, folder 33. On radio and the French state in 1968, see also Kristin Ross, *May '68 and Its Afterlives* (Chicago: University of Chicago Press, 2002), 101–2.

37. D'Arcy's intervention summarized in an undated printout, Fonds d'Arcy, box 10, folder 31. See also "Comité Information," French National Commission, January 1979, Fonds d'Arcy, box 11, folder 32. For the interim report, see "Interim Report for the International Commission for the Study of Communication Problems," UNESCO 20C/94, September 25, 1978, 76, accessed March 18, 2014, https://unesdoc.unesco.org/ark:/48223/pf0000028576.

38. *Many Voices, One World*, 172–74, 262–65.

39. D'Arcy, "Intervention de M. Jean d'Arcy," October 13, 1980.

40. Abel, letter to Deleon, December 19, [1979], UNESCO Archives, 307 A 01 ICSCP/136/8, part 5; Abel, letter to Deleon, January 2, 1980, UNESCO Archives, 307 A 01 ICSCP/136/8, part 6; Abel, letter to Deleon, January 24, [1980], UNESCO Archives, 307 A 01 ICSCP/136/8, part 6; Deleon, letter to Abel, February 1, 1980, UNESCO Archives, 307 A 01 ICSCP/136/8, part 6. Abel footnote in *Many Voices, One World*, 144n1. Only Seán MacBride and Canada's Betty Zimmerman registered more footnotes.

41. Abel, "Ushering the Third World into a New Communications Order"; Lawrence Schneider, "Abel Sets Record Straight on UNESCO," *Editor & Publisher*, November 8, 1980, UNESCO Archives, CAB 7/131.

42. Robert W. Poole Jr., "Freedom to Suppress," *Reason*, August 1, 1981; Bernard D. Nossiter, "UN Report on Press Is Causing Concern," *New York Times*, January 8, 1981; Prendergast, "Global First Amendment War"; Schardt with Sullivan, "Inching Toward Controls." See also Edward S. Herman, "U.S. Mass Media Coverage of the U.S. Withdrawal from UNESCO," in *Hope & Folly: The United States and Unesco,*

1945–1985, by William Preston Jr., Edward S. Herman, and Herbert I. Schiller (Minneapolis: University of Minnesota Press, 1989), 281–84.

43. Gulick, "The IPDC: UNESCO vs. the Free Press." On the Heritage Foundation, see William E. Simon, "Foreword: An American Institution," in *The Power of Ideas: The Heritage Foundation at 25 Years*, by Lee Edwards (Ottawa, IL: Jameson, 1997), xi. For a critical overview of Heritage's attacks on UNESCO, see Ellen Ray and William Schaap, introduction to Preston, Herman, and Schiller, *Hope & Folly*, xvi–xx. On 1950s and 1960s antecedents to Heritage's anti-UN activism, see Bon Tempo, "Human Rights and the U.S. Republican Party," 149.

44. Leonard R. Sussman, "An Approach to the Study of Transnational News Media in a Pluralistic World" (paper for the International Commission for the Study of Communication Problems meeting, Stockholm, Sweden, April 24–27, 1978), accessed March 21, 2014, https://unesdoc.unesco.org/ark:/48223/pf0000034150; Carl J. Bon Tempo, "From the Center-Right: Freedom House and Human Rights in the 1970s and 1980s," in *The Human Rights Revolution: An International History*, ed. Akira Iriye, Petra Goedde, and William I. Hitchcock (New York: Oxford University Press, 2012), 235–38.

45. Burton Yale Pines, ed., *A World Without a UN: What Would Happen If the UN Shut Down* (Washington, DC: Heritage Foundation, 1984).

46. Charles N. Brower, "American Bar Association Report to the House of Delegates, Section of International Law," [1982], UNESCO Archives, 307:342.727, part 2; "The Debate Sharpens on a New World Information Order," *New York Times*, February 15, 1981; Bon Tempo, "From the Center-Right," 236; George Gallup, "Informed Public Leans against U.S. Withdrawal from UNESCO," *Gallup Poll*, June 21, 1984, UNESCO Archives, ARC/Research/G27.

47. Power and Abel, "Third World vs. the Media."

48. "Electronics Takes Command" was the title of chapter 3 of Pool, *Technologies of Freedom*. It was a takeoff on Siegfried Giedion's well-known 1948 study of the impact of mechanization on daily life, *Mechanization Takes Command: A Contribution to Anonymous History*.

49. Cate, "First Amendment," 387–90. Quinn Slobodian makes the point that the demonization of international demands for redistributive justice in the 1970s had less to do with the global South's actual leverage and more with the existential threat that democracy, when "scaled up" to the level of international institutions, appeared to pose to western capital and private property. Slobodian, *Globalists*, chap. 7.

50. On film, see Laura Wittern-Keller and Raymond J. Haberski Jr., *The Miracle Case: Film Censorship and the Supreme Court* (Lawrence: University Press of Kansas, 2008).

51. Prendergast, "Global First Amendment War"; cf. Lyndon B. Johnson, "Special Message to the Congress on Communications Policy," August 14, 1967, in *Public Papers of the Presidents of the United States: Lyndon B. Johnson, 1967* (Washington, DC: U.S. Government Printing Office, 1968), 2:768.

52. Zick, *Cosmopolitan First Amendment*, chap. 10.

53. Ronald R. Kline discusses historical definitions of the word "information" in "Cybernetics, Management Science, and Technology Policy: The Emergence of 'Information Technology' as a Keyword," *Technology and Culture* 47, no. 3 (2006): 515–16, quotation on 515.

54. Jonathan Buchsbaum, *Exception Taken: How France Has Defied Hollywood's New World Order* (New York: Columbia University Press, 2017), 72–96; Cate, "First Amendment," quotation on 414.

55. Victoria de Grazia identifies the 1975 Helsinki Accords as a "watershed" in the abandonment of developmentalist "collective rights to subsistence" in favor of "freedom of choice, movement, and expression" for the United States and Western European signatories alike. However, de Grazia also indicates that this liberalization of human rights would help to foment a distinctly European politics of "culture as a valuable social resource." Victoria de Grazia, *Irresistible Empire: America's Advance Through Twentieth-Century Europe* (Cambridge, MA: Belknap Press of Harvard University Press, 2005), 458–80. On Franco-Canadian efforts to pursue a cultural-diversity convention at UNESCO following the "cultural exception" debates of the 1980s and 1990s, see Stephen Azzi, "Negotiating Cultural Space in the Global Economy: The United States, UNESCO, and the Convention on Cultural Diversity," *International Journal* 60, no. 3 (2005): 765–84; Armand Mattelart, "Bataille à l'Unesco sur la diversité culturelle," *Le Monde diplomatique*, October 2005, accessed April 15, 2014, http://www.monde-diplomatique.fr/2005/10/mattelart/12802.

56. Spielberg and Scorsese quoted in Buchsbaum, *Exception Taken*, 92.

57. Robert E. Jacobson, "Satellite Business Systems and the Concept of the Dispersed Enterprise: An End to National Sovereignty?" (paper for the Transnational Communication Enterprises and National Policies, East-West Communication Institute, Honolulu, Hawaii, August 6–9, [1978]), UNESCO Archives, 658.1 (100) SEM, part 1; Richard Thomas DeLamarter, "Telecom: The New Pawn in the IBM Empire?," *Computerworld*, November 24, 1986.

58. Jean d'Arcy, "Note sur la Conférence Générale de l'Unesco à Belgrade," November 27, 1980, Fonds d'Arcy, box 11, folder 33; Pool, "Direct Broadcast Satellites and the Integrity of National Cultures," 153.

EPILOGUE: FREE FLOW BYTES BACK?

1. Hillary Clinton, "Remarks by Secretary of State Hillary Rodham Clinton on Internet Freedom" (speech given at the Newseum, Washington, DC, January 21, 2010), reprinted in Hillary Clinton, "Statement: Hillary Clinton on Internet Freedom," *Financial Times*, January 22, 2010, accessed September 22, 2017, https://www.ft.com/content/foc3bf8c-06bd-11df-b426-00144feabdco. On Clinton's Cold War reference points, see also Evgeny Morozov, *The Net Delusion: The Dark Side of Internet Freedom* (New York: PublicAffairs, 2011), 33–36.

2. Clinton briefly addressed cyberwarfare, while the *Citizens United* majority declared, "We need not reach the question whether Government has a compelling interest in preventing foreign individuals or associations from influencing our Nation's political process." In his partial dissent Justice Stevens indicated that the majority decision "would appear to afford the same [First Amendment] protection to multinational corporations controlled by foreigners as to individual Americans." Citizens United v. Federal Election Commission, 558 U.S. 310, 362, 424 (2010). On the bipartisan nature of American claims to the transformative impact of digital communications, see Morozov, *Net Delusion*, chap. 2.

3. Morozov, *Net Delusion*; Alexander Galloway, *Protocol: How Control Exists After Decentralization* (Cambridge, MA: MIT Press, 2004); Jaron Lanier, *You Are Not a Gadget: A Manifesto* (New York: Alfred A. Knopf, 2010).

4. For an insightful conceptualization of the connections between the "analog age," the "broadcasting logic" of one-way flows, and the short American century, see Brian T. Edwards, *After the American Century: The Ends of U.S. Culture in the Middle East* (New York: Columbia University Press, 2016), chap. 1.

5. Christian Henrich-Franke, "Jean d'Arcy et la naissance de l'Eurovision"; Myriam Tsikounas, "Le Tour de la France par deux enfants: Enjeux et contraintes du premier 'télé-feuilleton' franco-canadien," both in *Jean d'Arcy (1913–1983): Penser la communication au XXe siècle*, ed. Marie-Françoise Lévy (Paris: Publications de la Sorbonne, 2013). Hervé Bourges, *Decoloniser l'information* (Paris: Editions Cana, 1978), 47–48, 50; "Projet Socrate: Télévision Educative en Afrique Noire francophone: Etude économique comparative entre un Système à Satellite d'Education et des Chaines de Télévision éducatives nationales," report, Centre National des Etudes Spatiales (CNES) and ORTF, 1969, Inathèque de France, Paris, France.

6. Daniel T. Rodgers, *Atlantic Crossings: Social Politics in a Progressive Age* (Cambridge, MA: Belknap Press of Harvard University Press, 1998), chap. 11.

7. For a useful discussion of neoliberal evasions of international democracy, see Quinn Slobodian, *Globalists: The End of Empire and the Birth of Neoliberalism* (Cambridge, MA: Harvard University Press, 2018), chap. 7.

8. The phrase "quantitative politics" comes from Eugene Thacker, foreword to Galloway, *Protocol*, xv. For a lucid critique of the place of technology in American reactions to the Arab Spring, see Edwards, *After the American Century*, 34–49. On the State Department, see, e.g., Sam Gustin, "Digital Diplomacy," *Time*, September 12, 2011.

9. David Streitfeld, "European Court Lets Users Erase Records on Web," *New York Times*, May 13, 2014, accessed May 26, 2014, http://www.nytimes.com/2014/05/14/technology/google-should-erase-web-links-to-some-personal-data-europes-highest-court-says.html?hpw&rref=technology&_r=0; Editorial Board, "Ordering Google to Forget," *New York Times*, May 13, 2014, accessed May 26, 2014, http://www.nytimes.com/2014/05/14/opinion/ordering-google-to-forget.html?_r=0; Danny Hakim, "Right to Be Forgotten? Not That Easy," *New York Times*, May 30, 2014, B1; Frances Robinson, Sam Schechner, and Amir Mizroch, "EU Orders Google to Let Users Erase Past," *Wall Street Journal*, May 13, 2014, accessed January 26, 2019, https://www.wsj.com/articles/eu-says-google-must-sometimes-remove-links-to-personal-material-1399970326. The expert cited in the last two articles was James Q. Whitman.

10. Editorial Board, "Noisy America, Quiet France," *New York Times*, May 10, 2017, accessed October 5, 2017, https://www.nytimes.com/2017/05/10/opinion/noisy-america-quiet-france.html; Mark Scott, "In Europe's Election Season, Tech Vies to Fight Fake News," *New York Times*, May 1, 2017; Nick Kostov and Sam Schechner, "Europe Ponders Privacy's Scope," *Wall Street Journal*, July 20, 2017; Paul Mozur, Mark Scott, and Mike Isaac, "Facebook Faces a New World as Officials Rein in a Wild Web," *New York Times*, September 17, 2017, accessed October 5, 2017, https://www.nytimes.com/2017/09/17/technology/facebook-government-regulations.html.

11. Mozur, Scott, and Isaac, "Facebook Faces a New World"; Barry Lynn, *Cornered: The New Monopoly Capitalism and the Economics of Destruction* (Hoboken, NJ: Wiley,

2010); Ryan Grim, "Steve Bannon Wants Facebook and Google Regulated like Utilities," *Intercept*, July 28, 2017, accessed October 5, 2017, https://theintercept.com/2017/07/27/steve-bannon-wants-facebook-and-google-regulated-like-utilities/;   Editorial Board, "Big Tech Changes Tack on U.S. Privacy Regulation," *Financial Times*, October 3, 2018.

Selected Bibliography

ARCHIVAL COLLECTIONS

Archives and Special Collections, University of Stirling (Stirling, UK)
    John Grierson Archive
Archives Nationales (Pierrefitte-sur-Seine, France)
    Fonds Jacques Kayser (465AP)
Dolph Briscoe Center for American History, University of Texas at Austin (Austin, TX)
    Henry R. Cassirer Papers
Harvard University Law School Library (Cambridge, MA)
    Zechariah Chafee Papers
Inathèque de France (Paris, France)
    Fonds Jean d'Arcy
    Monographs Collection
    Periodicals Collection
Lyndon Baines Johnson Presidential Library (Austin, TX)
Manuscripts and Archives, Yale University Library (New Haven, CT)
    Harold Dwight Lasswell Papers (MS 1043)
National Archives and Records Administration (College Park, MD)
    Record Group 165
    Record Group 319
    Record Group 337
Rockefeller Archive Center (Sleepy Hollow, NY)
    Ford Foundation Records
    Rockefeller Foundation Records
Special Collections Research Center, Syracuse University Libraries (Syracuse, NY)
    Frank C. Laubach Collection

Special Collections Research Center, University of Chicago Library (Chicago, IL)
    William Benton Papers
UNESCO (United Nations Educational, Scientific, and Cultural Organization) Archives
    (Paris, France)

PUBLISHED SOURCES

Aalbers, Manuel B. "Regulated Deregulation." In *The Handbook of Neoliberalism*, ed. Simon Springer, Kean Birch, and Julie MacLeavy, 563–73. New York: Routledge, 2016.

Adas, Michael. *Dominance by Design: Technological Imperatives and America's Civilizing Mission*. Cambridge, MA: Belknap Press of Harvard University Press, 2006.

Alexandre, Pierre. "Francophonie: The French and Africa." *Journal of Contemporary History* 4, no. 1 (1969): 117–25.

Allbeson, Tom. "Photographic Diplomacy in the Postwar World: UNESCO and the Conception of Photography as a Universal Language." *Modern Intellectual History* 12, no. 2 (2015): 383–415.

Azzi, Stephen. "Negotiating Cultural Space in the Global Economy: The United States, UNESCO, and the Convention on Cultural Diversity." *International Journal* 60, no. 3 (2005): 765–84.

Ba, Ibrahima. "La télévision au service de l'éducation des masses." *Journal des Télécommunications* 37, no. 7 (1970): 479.

Bachmann, Sophie. "La suppression de l'ORTF en 1974: La réforme de la 'Délivrance.'" *Vingtième siècle* 17 (1988): 63–72.

Barnouw, Erik. *Documentary: A History of the Non-Fiction Film*. 2nd rev. ed. New York: Oxford University Press, 1993.

Barreto, Amílcar Antonio. *The Politics of Language in Puerto Rico*. Gainesville: University Press of Florida, 2001.

Barreyre, Nicolas, Manfred Berg, and Simon Middleton. "Straddling Intellectual Worlds: Positionality and the Writing of American History." In *Historians Across Borders: Writing American History in a Global Age*, ed. Nicolas Barreyre, Michael Heale, Stephen Tuck, and Cécile Vidal, 75–92. Berkeley: University of California Press, 2014.

Barry, William E., Sandra Braman, Clifford Christians, Thomas G. Guback, Steven J. Helle, Lewis W. Liebovich, John C. Nerone, and Kim B. Rotzoll. *Last Rights: Revisiting Four Theories of the Press*. Ed. John Nerone. Urbana: University of Illinois Press, 1995.

Bayley, Susan. "The Direct Method and Modern Language Teaching in England, 1880–1918." *History of Education* 27, no. 1 (1998): 39–57.

Bellos, David. *Is That a Fish in Your Ear? The Amazing Adventure of Translation*. London: Penguin, 2012.

Beltrán, Luis Ramiro. "La 'revolución verde' y el desarrollo rural latinoamericano." *Desarrollo rural en las Américas* 3, no. 1 (1971): 5–24.

Bennett, M. Todd. *One World, Big Screen: Hollywood, the Allies, and World War II*. Chapel Hill: University of North Carolina Press, 2012.

Berelson, Bernard, and Paul Lazarsfeld. *The Analysis of Communication Content*. N.p., 1948.

Berlin, Isaiah. *The Hedgehog and the Fox: An Essay on Tolstoy's View of History*. 1953. Princeton, NJ: Princeton University Press, 2013.

———. "Two Concepts of Liberty." 1958. In *Liberty*, 2nd ed., ed. Henry Hardy. Oxford: Oxford University Press, 2002.

Bernstein, Matthew. *Walter Wanger, Hollywood Independent*. Berkeley: University of California Press, 1994.

Blanchard, Margaret A. *Exporting the First Amendment: The Press-Government Crusade of 1945–1952*. New York: Longman, 1986.

Blondiaux, Loïc. "Comment rompre avec Durkheim? Jean Stoetzel et la sociologie française de l'après-guerre (1945–1958)." *Revue française de sociologie* 32, no. 3 (1991): 411–41.

Bollinger, Lee C. *Images of a Free Press*. Chicago: University of Chicago Press, 1991.

Bon Tempo, Carl J. "From the Center-Right: Freedom House and Human Rights in the 1970s and 1980s." In *The Human Rights Revolution: An International History*, ed. Akira Iriye, Petra Goedde, and William I. Hitchcock, 223–44. New York: Oxford University Press, 2012.

———. "Human Rights and the U.S. Republican Party in the Late 1970s." In *The Breakthrough: Human Rights in the 1970s*, ed. Jan Eckel and Samuel Moyn, 146–65. Philadelphia: University of Pennsylvania Press, 2013.

Bourély, Michel. "The Contributions Made by International Organizations to the Formation of Space Law." *Journal of Space Law* 10, no. 2 (1982): 139–55.

Bourges, Hervé. *Décoloniser l'information*. Paris: Editions Cana, 1978.

———. "Préface." *Histoire de la télévision en Afrique noire francophone, des origines à nos jours*, by Tidiane Dioh. Paris: Karthala, 2009.

Brattain, Michelle. "Race, Racism, and Antiracism: UNESCO and the Politics of Presenting Science to the Postwar Public." *American Historical Review* 112, no. 5 (2007): 1386–413.

Buchsbaum, Jonathan. *Exception Taken: How France Has Defied Hollywood's New World Order*. New York: Columbia University Press, 2017.

Burke, Roland. *Decolonization and the Evolution of International Human Rights*. Philadelphia: University of Pennsylvania Press, 2010.

Burton, Julianne, and Jean Franco. "Culture and Imperialism." *Latin American Perspectives* 5, no. 1 (1978): 2–12.

CAL (Center for Applied Linguistics). *Second Language Learning as a Factor in National Development in Asia, Africa, and Latin America: Summary Statement and Recommendations of an International Meeting of Specialists Held in London, December 1960*. Washington, DC: n.p., 1961.

Canham, Erwin D. "International Freedom of Information." *Law and Contemporary Problems* 14, no. 4 (1949): 584–98.

Cassirer, Henry R. "Radio in an African Context: A Description of Senegal's Pilot Project." In *Radio for Education and Development: Case Studies*, ed. Peter L. Spain, Dean T. Jamison, and Emile McAnany, 300–337. Washington, DC: World Bank, 1977.

Cate, Fred H. "The First Amendment and the International 'Free Flow' of Information." *Virginia Journal of International Law* 30, no. 371 (1990): 372–420.

Chafee, Zechariah. *Government and Mass Communications*. Vol. 2. Chicago: University of Chicago Press, 1947.

Chanet, Jean-François. *L'école républicaine et les petites patries*. Paris: Aubier, 1996.

Chansou, Michel. "Politique de la langue et idéologie en français contemporain." *Mots 6* (1983): 59–77.

Christol, Carl Q. "The 1974 Brussels Convention Relating to the Distribution of Program-Carrying Signals Transmitted by Satellite: An Aspect of Human Rights." *Journal of Space Law 6*, no. 1 (1978): 19–35.

Citizens United v. Federal Election Commission. 558 U.S. 310, 424 (2010).

Clark, Charles E. *Uprooting Otherness: The Literacy Campaign in NEP-Era Russia*. Cranbury, NJ: Associated University Presses, 2000.

Clinton, Hillary. "Remarks by Secretary of State Hillary Rodham Clinton on Internet Freedom." Speech at the Newseum, Washington, DC, January 21, 2010. Reprinted in "Statement: Hilary Clinton on Internet Freedom." *Financial Times*, January 22, 2010. Accessed September 22, 2017. https://www.ft.com/content/f0c3bf8c-06bd-11df-b426-00144feabdc0.

Cmiel, Kenneth. "The Emergence of Human Rights Politics in the United States." *Journal of American History 86*, no. 3 (1999): 1231–50.

——. "Human Rights, Freedom of Information, and the Origins of Third-World Solidarity." In *Truth Claims: Representation and Human Rights*, ed. Mark Philip Bradley and Patrice Petro, 107–30. New Brunswick, NJ: Rutgers University Press, 2002.

Cocca, Aldo Armando. *Consolidación del Derecho espacial*. Buenos Aires: Editorial Astrea, 1971.

——. *Derecho espacial para la gran audiencia*. Buenos Aires: Asociación Argentina de Ciencias Aerospaciales, 1970.

——. "The Supreme Interests of Mankind Vis-à-Vis the Emergence of Direct Broadcast." *Journal of Space Law 2*, no. 2 (1974): 83–94.

Cohen, Elie. *Le Colbertisme "high tech": Economie des Télécom et du Grand Projet*. Paris: Hachette, 1992.

Cohen, Lizabeth. *Making a New Deal: Industrial Workers in Chicago, 1919–1939*. Cambridge: Cambridge University Press, 1990.

Collis, Christy. "The Geostationary Orbit: A Critical Legal Geography of Space's Most Valuable Real Estate." In *Down to Earth: Satellite Technologies, Industries, and Cultures*, ed. Lisa Parks and James Schwoch, 61–70. New Brunswick, NJ: Rutgers University Press, 2012.

Commission on Freedom of the Press. *A Free and Responsible Press: A General Report on Mass Communication: Newspapers, Radio, Motion Pictures, Magazines, and Books*. Chicago: University of Chicago Press, 1947.

Conklin, Alice L. *A Mission to Civilize: The Republican Idea of Empire in France and West Africa, 1895–1930*. Stanford, CA: Stanford University Press, 1997.

Connelly, Matthew. *A Diplomatic Revolution: Algeria's Fight for Independence and the Origins of the Post–Cold War Era*. New York: Oxford University Press, 2002.

Cooper, Frederick. *Citizenship Between Empire and Nation: Remaking France and French Africa, 1945–1960*. Princeton, NJ: Princeton University Press, 2014.

——. "Development, Modernization, and the Social Sciences in the Era of Decolonization: The Examples of British and French Africa." *Revue d'histoire des sciences humaines 10* (2004): 9–38.

Cooper, Kent. *Barriers Down: The Story of the News Agency Epoch*. New York: Farrar & Rinehart, 1942.

Cumming, Gordon. *Aid to Africa: French and British Policies from the Cold War to the New Millennium*. Burlington, VT: Ashgate, 2001.

D'Arcy, Jean. "Direct Broadcast Satellites and the Right to Communicate." *European Broadcasting Union (EBU) Review* 118 (1969): 14–18.

——. *Jean d'Arcy parle: Pionnier et visionnaire de la télévision*. Ed. François Cazenave. Paris: La Documentation française, 1984.

Darré, Yann. *Histoire sociale du cinéma français*. Paris: La Découverte, 2000.

De Grazia, Victoria. *Irresistible Empire: America's Advance Through Twentieth-Century Europe*. Cambridge, MA: Belknap Press of Harvard University Press, 2005.

——. "Mass Culture and Sovereignty: The American Challenge to European Cinemas, 1920–1960." *Journal of Modern History* 61, no. 1 (1989): 53–87.

Denning, Michael. *Culture in the Age of Three Worlds*. London: Verso, 2004.

Diallo, Ibrahima. "Literacy and Education in West Africa: From *Ajami* to Francophonie." *Africa Review* 8, no. 1 (2016): 60–70.

——. *The Politics of National Languages in Postcolonial Senegal*. Amherst, NY: Cambria, 2010.

Dioh, Tidiane. *Histoire de la télévision en Afrique noire francophone, des origines à nos jours*. Paris: Karthala, 2009.

Doherty, Thomas. *Hollywood and Hitler, 1933–1939*. New York: Columbia University Press, 2013.

Dorfman, Ariel. *Heading South, Looking North: A Bilingual Journey*. New York: Penguin, 1999.

Dorfman, Ariel, and Armand Mattelart. *How to Read Donald Duck: Imperialist Ideology in the Disney Comic*. 1971. New York: I. G. Editions, 1991.

Dorn, Charles, and Kristen Ghodsee. "The Cold War Politicization of Literacy: Communism, UNESCO, and the World Bank." *Diplomatic History* 36, no. 2 (2012): 373–98.

Eckel, Jan, and Samuel Moyn, eds. *The Breakthrough: Human Rights in the 1970s*. Philadelphia: University of Pennsylvania Press, 2014.

Edwards, Brian T. *After the American Century: The Ends of U.S. Culture in the Middle East*. New York: Columbia University Press, 2016.

Edwardson, Mickie. "James Lawrence Fly v. David Sarnoff: Blitzkrieg over Television." *Journalism History* 25, no. 2 (1999): 42–52.

Eichengreen, Barry. *Globalizing Capital: A History of the International Monetary System*. 2nd ed. Princeton, NJ: Princeton University Press, 2008.

Eisele, John. "Whither Arabic? From Possible Worlds to Possible Futures." In *Applied Linguistics in the Middle East and North Africa: Current Practices and Future Directions*, ed. Atta Gebril, 307–42. Amsterdam: John Benjamins, 2017.

Ekbladh, David. *The Great American Mission: Modernization and the Construction of an American World Order*. Princeton, NJ: Princeton University Press, 2010.

Ellis, Charlie. "Relativism and Reaction: Richard Hoggart and Conservatism." In *Richard Hoggart and Cultural Studies*, ed. Sue Owen, 198–212. Basingstoke, UK: Palgrave Macmillan, 2008.

Ellis, Jack C. *John Grierson: Life, Contributions, Influence*. Carbondale: Southern Illinois University Press, 2000.

Engerman, David C. "American Knowledge and Global Power." *Diplomatic History* 31, no. 4 (2007): 599–622.

270 Selected Bibliography

Escobar, Arturo. *Encountering Development: The Making and Unmaking of the Third World.* Princeton, NJ: Princeton University Press, 1995.

Evans, Stephen. "Macaulay's Minute Revisited: Colonial Language Policy in Nineteenth-Century India." *Journal of Multilingual and Multicultural Development* 23, no. 4 (2002): 260–81.

Fein, Seth. "New Empire into Old: Making Mexican Newsreels the Cold War Way." *Diplomatic History* 28, no. 5 (2004): 703–48.

Finkelstein, Lawrence S. "Bunche and the Colonial World: From Trusteeship to Decolonization." In *Ralph Bunche: The Man and His Times*, ed. Benjamin Rivlin, 109–31. New York: Holmes & Meier, 1990.

Fisher, Desmond, and L. S. Harms, eds. *The Right to Communicate: A New Human Right.* Dublin: Boole, 1983.

Fitzpatrick, Sheila. *Education and Social Mobility in the Soviet Union, 1921–1934.* Cambridge: Cambridge University Press, 1979.

"Forty Years of Language Teaching." *Language Teaching* 40 (2006): 1–15.

Fousek, John. *To Lead the Free World: American Nationalism and the Cultural Roots of the Cold War.* Chapel Hill: University of North Carolina Press, 2000.

Fox, Melvin J. *Language and Development: A Retrospective Survey of Ford Foundation Language Projects, 1952–1974.* New York: Ford Foundation, 1975.

"From Audiolingual to Suggestopedia: The Varieties of Language Instruction." *Chronicle of Higher Education*, February 22, 1989.

Galloway, Alexander. *Protocol: How Control Exists After Decentralization.* Cambridge, MA: MIT Press, 2004.

Gary, Brett. *The Nervous Liberals: Propaganda Anxieties from World War I to the Cold War.* New York: Columbia University Press, 1999.

——. "The Search for a Competent Public: The Hutchins Commission and Post–World War II Democratic Possibilities." In *Democracy and Excellence: Concord or Conflict?*, ed. Joseph Romance and Neal Riemer, 75–90. Westport, CT: Praeger, 2005.

Geertz, Clifford. *The Interpretation of Cultures: Selected Essays.* New York: Basic, 1973.

Gertner, Jon. *The Idea Factory: Bell Labs and the Great Age of American Innovation.* New York: Penguin, 2012.

Gilman, Nils. *Mandarins of the Future: Modernization Theory in Cold War America.* Baltimore, MD: Johns Hopkins University Press, 2003.

Gitlin, Todd. "Media Sociology: The Dominant Paradigm." *Theory and Society* 6, no. 2 (1978): 205–53.

Glander, Timothy. *Origins of Mass Communication Research During the American Cold War: Educational Effects and Contemporary Implications.* Mahwah, NJ: Lawrence Erlbaum, 2000.

Go, Julian. "Chains of Empire, Projects of State: Political Education and U.S. Colonial Rule in Puerto Rico and the Philippines." *Comparative Studies in Society and History* 42, no. 2 (2000): 333–62.

Gordin, Michael. *Scientific Babel: How Science Was Done Before and After Global English.* Chicago: University of Chicago Press, 2015.

Grandin, Greg. "Human Rights and Empire's Embrace: A Latin American Counterpoint." In *Human Rights and Revolutions*, 2nd ed., ed. Jeffrey N. Wasserstrom, Greg Grandin, Lynn Hunt, and Marilyn B. Young, 191–212. Lanham, MD: Rowman & Littlefield, 2007.

Gray, James K. "The Groundnut Market in Senegal: Examination of Price and Policy Changes." PhD diss., Virginia Polytechnic Institute and State University, 2002.

Grierson, John. "The Film in British Colonial Development." *Sight and Sound* 17 (1948): 2–4.

——. "Production Unit Planned: Mass Media to Be Used for Peace." *UNESCO Courier* 1, no. 1 (1948): 3.

Guback, Thomas H. *The International Film Industry: Western Europe and America Since 1945*. Bloomington: Indiana University Press, 1969.

Hadley, Malcolm. "Promoting International Understanding and Cooperation: Richard Hoggart's UNESCO Years (1970–1975)." In *Re-Reading Richard Hoggart: Life, Literature, Language, Education*, ed. Sue Owen, 153–74. Newcastle upon Tyne, UK: Cambridge Scholars, 2008.

Hagège, Claude. *Contre la pensée unique*. Paris: Odile Jacob, 2012.

Hall, Stuart. "Richard Hoggart, *The Uses of Literacy*, and the Cultural Turn." In *Richard Hoggart and Cultural Studies*, ed. Sue Owen, 20–32. Basingstoke, UK: Palgrave Macmillan, 2008.

Hall, Stuart, Chas Critcher, Tony Jefferson, John Clarke, and Brian Roberts. *Policing the Crisis: Mugging, the State, and Law and Order*. London: Macmillan, 1978.

Hall, Stuart, Dorothy Hobson, Andrew Lowe, and Paul Willis, eds. *Culture, Media, Language: Working Papers in Cultural Studies, 1972–79*. London: Centre for Contemporary Cultural Studies, University of Birmingham, 1980.

Hamelink, Cees J. "The 2003 Graham Spry Memorial Lecture: Toward a Human Right to Communicate?" *Canadian Journal of Communication* 29, no. 2 (2004): 205–12.

Hartmann, Hauke. "U.S. Human Rights Policy Under Carter and Reagan, 1977–1981." *Human Rights Quarterly* 23, no. 2 (2001): 402–30.

Hay, James. "The Invention of Air Space, Outer Space, and Cyberspace." In *Down to Earth: Satellite Technologies, Industries, and Cultures*, ed. Lisa Parks and James Schwoch, 19–41. New Brunswick, NJ: Rutgers University Press, 2012.

Hazzard, Shirley. *Countenance of Truth: The United Nations and the Waldheim Case*. New York: Viking, 1990.

——. *The Defeat of an Ideal: A Study of the Self-Destruction of the United Nations*. Boston: Little, Brown, 1973.

——. *People in Glass Houses: Portraits from Organization Life*. New York: Knopf, 1967.

——. *We Need Silence to Find Out What We Think*. Ed. Brigitta Olubas. New York: Columbia University Press, 2016.

Headrick, Daniel. *The Invisible Weapon: Telecommunications and International Politics, 1851–1945*. New York: Oxford University Press, 1991.

Heil, Alan L., Jr. *Voice of America: A History*. New York: Columbia University Press, 2003.

Heilbron, Johan, Nicolas Guilhot, and Laurent Jeanpierre. "Toward a Transnational History of the Social Sciences." *Journal of the History of the Behavioral Sciences* 44, no. 2 (2008): 146–60.

Henrich-Franke, Christian. "Jean d'Arcy et la naissance de l'Eurovision." In *Jean d'Arcy (1913–1983): Penser la communication au XXe siècle*, ed. Marie-Françoise Lévy, 147–56. Paris: Publications de la Sorbonne, 2013.

Heyer, Paul, and David Crowley. Introduction to *The Bias of Communication*, 2nd ed., by Harold A. Innis, xxv–xlii. 1951. Toronto: University of Toronto Press, 2008.

Hoggart, Richard. *An Idea and Its Servants: UNESCO from Within*. New York: Oxford University Press, 1978.

——. *The Uses of Literacy*. 1957. New Brunswick, NJ: Transaction, 2000.

Hosenball, S. Neil. "Current Issues of Space Law Before the United Nations," *Journal of Space Law* 2, no. 1 (1974): 5–18.

Hyman, Sidney. *The Lives of William Benton*. Chicago: University of Chicago Press, 1969.

Immerwahr, Daniel. *Thinking Small: The United States and the Lure of Community Development*. Cambridge, MA: Harvard University Press, 2015.

Inglis, Ruth A. *Freedom of the Movies: A Report on Self-Regulation from the Commission on Freedom of the Press*. 1947. New York: Da Capo, 1974.

Innis, Harold A. *The Bias of Communication*. 1951. 2nd ed. Toronto: University of Toronto Press, 2008.

——. *Empire and Communications*. 1950. Toronto: University of Toronto Press, 1972.

Intelligence Unit of *The Economist*, UNESCO, and the FAO. *Paper for Printing—Today and Tomorrow*. Paris: UNESCO, 1952.

Iriye, Akira, and Petra Goedde. "Introduction: Human Rights as History." In *The Human Rights Revolution: An International History*, ed. Akira Iriye, Petra Goedde, and William I. Hitchcock, 3–24. New York: Oxford University Press, 2012.

Iriye, Akira, Petra Goedde, and William I. Hitchcock, eds. *The Human Rights Revolution: An International History*. New York: Oxford University Press, 2012.

Jarvie, Ian. *Hollywood's Overseas Campaign: The North Atlantic Movie Trade, 1920–1950*. Cambridge: Cambridge University Press, 1992.

Jay, Martin. "Adorno in America." *New German Critique* 31 (1984): 157–82.

Johns, Adrian. *Death of a Pirate: British Radio and the Making of the Information Age*. New York: Norton, 2011.

Jones, Colin. *Paris: The Biography of a City*. New York: Viking Penguin, 2005.

Jones, Phillip W. *International Policies for Third World Education: UNESCO, Literacy and Development*. London: Routledge, 1988.

Journal de l'année: 1er juillet 1968–30 juin 1969. Paris: Larousse, 1969.

Jowett, Garth S. "'A Capacity for Evil': The 1915 Supreme Court *Mutual* Decision." In *Controlling Hollywood: Censorship and Regulation in the Studio Era*, ed. Matthew Bernstein, 16–40. New Brunswick, NJ: Rutgers University Press, 1999.

Judt, Tony. *Postwar: A History of Europe Since 1945*. New York: Penguin, 2005.

Kalisman, Hilary Falb. "Bursary Scholars at the American University of Beirut: Living and Practising Arab Unity." *British Journal of Middle Eastern Studies* 42, no. 4 (2015): 599–617.

Kayser, Jacques. *Mort d'une liberté*. Paris: Plon, 1955.

Kennedy, Paul. *The Parliament of Man: The Past, Present, and Future of the United Nations*. New York: Vintage, 2006.

Kildow, Judith Tegger. *Intelsat: Policy-Maker's Dilemma*. Lexington, MA: Lexington, 1973.

Kline, Ronald R. "Cybernetics, Management Science, and Technology Policy: The Emergence of 'Information Technology' as a Keyword." *Technology and Culture* 47, no. 3 (2006): 513–35.

——. *The Cybernetics Moment: Or Why We Call Our Age the Information Age*. Baltimore, MD: Johns Hopkins University Press, 2015.

Klose, Fabian. "'Source of Embarrassment': Human Rights, State of Emergency, and the Wars of Decolonization." In *Human Rights in the Twentieth Century*, ed. Stefan-Ludwig Hoffmann, 237–57. Cambridge: Cambridge University Press, 2011.

Koeneke, Rodney. *Empires of the Mind: I. A. Richards and Basic English in China, 1929–1979*. Stanford, CA: Stanford University Press, 2004.

Kornbluh, Peter. *The Pinochet File: A Declassified Dossier on Atrocity and Accountability*. 2003. New York: New, 2013.

Kracauer, Siegfried. "The Challenge of Qualitative Content Analysis." *Public Opinion Quarterly* 16, no. 4 (1952): 631–42.

Kuczewski, Andre. "Review: *John Grierson and the National Film Board* by Gary Evans." *Film Quarterly* 39, no. 4 (1986): 59–60.

Kuisel, Richard. *Seducing the French: The Dilemma of Americanization*. Berkeley: University of California Press, 1993.

Küster, Sybille. "'Book Learning' Versus 'Adapted Education': The Impact of Phelps-Stokesism on Colonial Education Systems in Central Africa in the Interwar Period." *Paedagogica Historica* 43, no. 1 (2007): 79–97.

Laborie, Léonard. "Jean d'Arcy entrepreneur. Satellite, câble, vidéo: Nouvelles technologies et régulation audiovisuelle." In *Jean d'Arcy (1913–1983): Penser la communication au XXe siècle*, ed. Marie-Françoise Lévy, 201–15. Paris: Publications de la Sorbonne, 2013.

Lanier, Jaron. *You Are Not a Gadget: A Manifesto*. New York: Alfred A. Knopf, 2010.

Latham, Michael. *Modernization as Ideology: American Social Science and "Nation Building" in the Kennedy Era*. Chapel Hill: University of North Carolina Press, 2000.

Lebovic, Sam. *Free Speech and Unfree News: The Paradox of Press Freedom in America*. Cambridge, MA: Harvard University Press, 2016.

Lemberg, Diana. "The End of Empires and Some Linguistic Turns: British and French Language Policies in Inter- and Post-War Africa." In *British and French Colonialism in Africa, Asia and the Middle East: Connected Empires Across the Eighteenth to the Twentieth Centuries*, ed. James R. Fichter. Basingstoke, UK: Palgrave Macmillan, 2019.

——. "'The Universal Language of the Future': Decolonization, Development, and the American Embrace of Global English, 1945–1965." *Modern Intellectual History* 15, no. 2 (2018): 561–92.

Lerner, Daniel. "Communication and the Prospects of Innovative Development." In *Communication and Change in the Developing Countries*, ed. Daniel Lerner and Wilbur Schramm, 305–17. Honolulu: East-West Center, 1967.

——. *The Passing of Traditional Society: Modernizing the Middle East*. New York: Free, 1958.

——. "Technology, Communication, and Change." In *Communication and Change: The Last Ten Years—and the Next*, ed. Wilbur Schramm and Daniel Lerner, 287–301. Honolulu: University Press of Hawaii, 1976.

——. "Toward a New Paradigm." In *Communication and Change: The Last Ten Years—and the Next*, ed. Wilbur Schramm and Daniel Lerner, 60–63. Honolulu: University Press of Hawaii, 1976.

Lévy, Marie-Françoise. "La création des télé-clubs: L'expérience de l'Aisne." In *La Télévision dans la République: Les années 50*, ed. Marie-Françoise Lévy, 107–31. Brussels: Éditions Complexe, 1999.

Levy, Steven. "Hackers at 30: 'Hackers' and 'Information Wants to Be Free.'" *Wired*, November 21, 2014, accessed September 11, 2018, https://www.wired.com/story/hackers-at-30-hackers-and-information-wants-to-be-free/.

Literacy, 1969–1971: Progress Achieved in Literacy Throughout the World. Paris: UNESCO, 1972. Accessed January 30, 2017. https://unesdoc.unesco.org/ark:/48223/pf0000001736.locale=en.

Louis, Roger, and Joseph Rovan. *Television and Tele-Clubs in Rural Communities: An Experiment in France*. Paris: UNESCO, 1955.

Louis, William Roger, and Ronald Robinson. "The Imperialism of Decolonization." *Journal of Imperial and Commonwealth History* 22, no. 3 (1994): 462–511.

Lugard, F. D. "Education in Tropical Africa." *Edinburgh Review*, July 1925. Reprinted by the Colonial Office, August 1930, CO 879/123/12.

Lynn, Barry. *Cornered: The New Monopoly Capitalism and the Economics of Destruction*. Hoboken, NJ: Wiley, 2010.

Lyons, Eugene. *David Sarnoff: A Biography*. New York: Harper & Row, 1966.

Mabry, Tristan James. *Nationalism, Language, and Muslim Exceptionalism*. Philadelphia: University of Pennsylvania Press, 2015.

MacKenzie, David. "Canada's Red Scare, 1945–1957." Canadian Historical Association Historical Booklet 61. 2001. http://www.collectionscanada.gc.ca/obj/008004/f2/H-61_en.pdf.

Manning, Martin J., and Clarence R. Wyatt, eds. *Encyclopedia of Media and Propaganda in Wartime America*. Vol. 1. Santa Barbara, CA: ABC-CLIO, 2011.

Many Voices, One World: Towards a New More Just and Efficient World Information and Communication Order. New York: Unipub, 1980.

Matras, J. J. "Editorial." *Revue française de radiodiffusion et de télévision* 1, no. 4 (1967): 22–24.

Mattelart, Armand. *Agresión desde el espacio: Cultura y napalm en la era de los satélites*. 1972. Mexico City: Siglo Ventiuno Editores, 1998.

——. "Bataille à l'Unesco sur la diversité culturelle." *Le Monde diplomatique*, October 2005. Accessed April 15, 2014. http://www.monde-diplomatique.fr/2005/10/mattelart/12802.

——. "Communications sans frontières et impérialisme." *Le Monde diplomatique*, March 1978.

——. "The Nature of Communications Practice in a Dependent Society." Trans. Dana B. Polan. *Latin American Perspectives* 5, no. 1 (1978): 13–34.

Mattelart, Armand, and Michèle Mattelart. " 'L'aliénation linguistique,' d'Henri Gobard." *Le Monde diplomatique*, November 1976.

Maurel, Chloé. *Histoire de l'Unesco: Les trente premières années, 1945–1974*. Paris: L'Harmattan, 2010.

——. "Le 'droit de l'homme à la communication': L'action de Jean d'Arcy à l'Unesco." In *Jean d'Arcy (1913–1983): Penser la communication au XXe siècle*, ed. Marie-Françoise Lévy, 189–200. Paris: Publications de la Sorbonne, 2013.

Maxwell, Richard. *Herbert Schiller*. Lanham, MD: Rowman & Littlefield, 2003.

May, Glenn Anthony. *Social Engineering in the Philippines: The Aims, Execution, and Impact of American Colonial Policy, 1900–1913*. Westport, CT: Greenwood, 1980.

Mazower, Mark. *Governing the World: The History of an Idea*. New York: Penguin, 2012.

———. *No Enchanted Palace: The End of Empire and the Ideological Origins of the United Nations*. Princeton, NJ: Princeton University Press, 2009.

McAnany, Emile G. *Saving the World: A Brief History of Communication for Development and Social Change*. Urbana: University of Illinois Press, 2012.

McClatchy, J. D. "Shirley Hazzard: The Art of Fiction No. 185," *Paris Review* 173 (2005). http://www.theparisreview.org/interviews/5505/the-art-of-fiction-no-185-shirley -hazzard.

Meyen, Michael. "The IAMCR Story: Communication and Media Research in a Global Perspective." In *The International History of Communication Study*, ed. Peter Simonson and David Park, 90–106. New York: Routledge, 2016.

Milland, Jeffrey. "Courting Malvolio: The Background to the Pilkington Committee on Broadcasting, 1960–62." *Contemporary British History* 18, no. 2 (2004): 76–102.

Milward, Alan S., and George Brennan. *Britain's Place in the World: A Historical Enquiry into Import Controls, 1945–60*. London: Routledge, 1996.

Mitchell, Cheryl Brown, and Kari Ellingson Vidal. "Weighing the Ways of the Flow: Twentieth Century Language Instruction." *Modern Language Journal* 85, no. 1 (2001): 26–38.

Mitoma, Glenn. *Human Rights and the Negotiation of American Power*. Philadelphia: University of Pennsylvania Press, 2013.

Monsiváis, Carlos. "Notas sobre cultura popular en México." *Latin American Perspectives* 5, no. 1 (1978): 98–118.

Morin, Edgar. *New Trends in the Study of Mass Communications*. Birmingham: [Swift Print], 1968.

Morozov, Evgeny. *The Net Delusion: The Dark Side of Internet Freedom*. New York: PublicAffairs, 2011.

Moyn, Samuel. *The Last Utopia: Human Rights in History*. Cambridge, MA: Belknap Press of Harvard University Press, 2010.

Mulvey, Paul. *The Political Life of Josiah C. Wedgwood: Land, Liberty and Empire, 1872– 1943*. Woodbridge, UK: Boydell, 2010.

Navarro, José-Manuel. *Creating Tropical Yankees: Social Science Textbooks and U.S. Ideological Control in Puerto Rico, 1898–1908*. New York: Routledge, 2002.

Ninkovich, Frank. *The Diplomacy of Ideas: U.S. Foreign Policy and Cultural Relations, 1938–1950*. Cambridge: Cambridge University Press, 1981.

Nixon, Raymond B. "Factors Related to Freedom in National Press Systems." *Journalism Quarterly* 37, no. 1 (1960): 13–28.

Nocentini, Sara. "Building the Network: Raw Materials Shortages and the Western Bloc at the Beginning of the Cold War, 1948–1951." *Business and Economic History OnLine* 2, 2004. Accessed April 26, 2016. http://www.thebhc.org/sites/default/files /Nocentini_0.pdf.

Nord, Philip. *France's New Deal: From the Thirties to the Postwar Era*. Princeton, NJ: Princeton University Press, 2010.

Nordenstreng, Kaarle. "Institutional Networking: The Story of the International Association for Media and Communication Research (IAMCR)." In *The History of Media and Communication Research: Contested Memories*, ed. David W. Park and Jefferson Pooley, 225–48. New York: Peter Lang, 2008.

———. "Myths About Press Freedom." *Brazilian Journalism Research* 3, no. 1 (2007): 15–30.

Osgood, Kenneth. *Total Cold War: Eisenhower's Secret Propaganda Battle at Home and Abroad*. Lawrence: University Press of Kansas, 2006.

Oslund, Jack. "'Open Shores' to 'Open Skies': Sources and Directions of U.S. Satellite Policy." In *Economic and Policy Problems in Satellite Communications*, ed. Joseph N. Pelton and Marcellus S. Snow, 143–99. New York: Praeger, 1977.

Owen, Sue. "Introduction." In *Richard Hoggart and Cultural Studies*, ed. Sue Owen, 1–19. Basingstoke, UK: Palgrave Macmillan, 2008.

Palmer, Michael. "Jean d'Arcy et les acteurs internationaux de l'information." In *La télévision, le temps des constructeurs*, ed. Sylvie Pierre, 83–92. Paris: L'Harmattan, 2011.

Parker, William. *The National Interest and Foreign Languages: A Discussion Guide and Work Paper for Citizen Consultations*. 1954. Rev. ed. Washington, DC: [U.S. Government Printing Office], 1957.

Parmar, Inderjeet. *Foundations of the American Century: The Ford, Carnegie, and Rockefeller Foundations in the Rise of American Power*. New York: Columbia University Press, 2012.

Pasquali, Antonio. "Los medios de comunicación en la educación de adultos." *Convergence* 1, no. 2 (1968): 27–35.

Pedersen, Susan. *The Guardians: The League of Nations and the Crisis of Empire*. New York: Oxford University Press, 2015.

Pendergast, William R. "UNESCO and French Cultural Relations, 1945–1970." *International Organization* 30, no. 3 (1976): 453–83.

Persin, Jean. "Will Space Be Open to Piracy?" *Telecommunication Journal* 30, no. 4 (1963): 112–15.

Peters, John Durham. "Raymond Williams's *Culture and Society* as Research Method." In *Questions of Method in Cultural Studies*, ed. Mimi White and James Schwoch, 54–70. Cambridge: Blackwell, 2006.

——. *Speaking into the Air: A History of the Idea of Communication*. Chicago: University of Chicago Press, 1999.

Peters, Kimberley. "Sinking the Radio 'Pirates': Exploring British Strategies of Governance in the North Sea, 1964–1991." *Area* 43, no. 3 (2011): 281–87.

Petley, Julian. "Richard Hoggart and Pilkington: Populism and Public Service Broadcasting." *Ethical Space: The International Journal of Communication Ethics* 12, no. 1 (2015): 4–14.

Philipsen, Dirk. *The Little Big Number: How GDP Came to Rule the World and What to Do About It*. Princeton, NJ: Princeton University Press, 2015.

Pickard, Victor. *America's Battle for Media Democracy: The Triumph of Corporate Libertarianism and the Future of Media Reform*. Cambridge: Cambridge University Press, 2015.

Pigeat, Henri. "Jean d'Arcy: Le droit de l'homme à la communication, actualité d'une vision prémonitoire." In *Jean d'Arcy (1913–1983): Penser la communication au XXe siècle*, ed. Marie-Françoise Lévy, 217–26. Paris: Publications de la Sorbonne, 2013.

——. "Préface." In *Jean d'Arcy parle: Pionnier et visionnaire de la télévision*, ed. François Cazenave, 7–13. Paris: La Documentation française, 1984.

Pines, Burton Yale, ed. *A World Without a UN: What Would Happen If the UN Shut Down*. Washington, DC: Heritage Foundation, 1984.

Pinhas, Luc. "Aux origines du discours francophone." *Communication et langages* 140 (2004): 69–82.

Pohle, Julia. "Kêbé l'Inesko Fò!" *UNESCO Courier*, Sept. 2010.

Pool, Ithiel de Sola. "Direct-Broadcast Satellites and Cultural Integrity." 1975. *Society*, January/February 1998, 140–51.

——. "Direct Broadcast Satellites and the Integrity of National Cultures." In *National Sovereignty and International Communication*, ed. Kaarle Nordenstreng and Herbert I. Schiller, 120–52. Norwood, NJ: Ablex, 1979.

——. "The Necessity for Social Scientists Doing Research for Governments." *Background* 10, no. 2 (1966): 111–22.

——. "Scarcity, Abundance and the Right to Communicate." In *Evolving Perspectives on the Right to Communicate*, ed. L. S. Harms and Jim Richstad, 175–89. Honolulu: East-West Center, East-West Communication Institute, 1977.

——. *Technologies of Freedom*. Cambridge, MA: Belknap Press of Harvard University Press, 1983.

Power, Philip H., and Elie Abel. "Third World vs. the Media." *New York Times Magazine*, September 21, 1980.

Prendergast, Curtis. "The Global First Amendment War." *Time*, October 6, 1980.

Preston, William, Jr., Edward S. Herman, and Herbert I. Schiller. *Hope & Folly: The United States and UNESCO, 1945–1985*. Minneapolis: University of Minnesota Press, 1989.

Price, David H. *Cold War Anthropology: The CIA, the Pentagon, and the Growth of Dual Use Anthropology*. Durham, NC: Duke University Press, 2016.

Public Papers of the Presidents of the United States: Lyndon B. Johnson, 1967. Vol. 2. Washington, DC: U.S. Government Printing Office, 1968.

Queeney, Kathryn M. *Direct Broadcast Satellites and the United Nations*. Alphen aan den Rijn: Sijthoff & Noordhoff, 1978.

Rapport de la Commission des Besoins Techniques: Presse, film, radio après enquête dans dix-sept pays. Paris: UNESCO, 1948.

Rapport de la Commission des Besoins Techniques: Presse, radio, film après enquête dans douze pays dévastés par la guerre. Paris: UNESCO, 1947.

Rapports sur les moyens techniques de l'information: Presse, films, radio. Paris: UNESCO, 1951.

Records of the General Conference, Ninth Session, New Delhi, 1956: Resolutions. Paris: UNESCO, 1957. https://unesdoc.unesco.org/ark:/48223/pf0000114585.

Records of the General Conference of the United Nations Educational, Scientific, and Cultural Organization—Fifth Session, Florence, 1950. Paris: UNESCO, 1950.

Renoliet, Jean-Jacques. *L'Unesco oubliée: La Société des Nations et la coopération intellectuelle (1919–1946)*. Paris: Publications de la Sorbonne, 1999.

Ricci, Steven. *Cinema and Fascism: Italian Film and Society, 1922–1943*. Berkeley: University of California Press, 2008.

Rist, Gilbert. *Le développement: Histoire d'une croyance occidentale*. Rev. 4th ed. Paris: Presses de la Fondation nationale des sciences politiques, 2013.

Rockwell, Elsie. "Schools of the Revolution: Enacting and Contesting State Forms in Tlaxcala, 1910–1930." In *Everyday Forms of State Formation: Revolution and the Negotiation of Rule in Modern Mexico*, ed. Gilbert M. Joseph and Daniel Nugent, 170–208. Durham, NC: Duke University Press, 1994.

Rodgers, Daniel T. *Age of Fracture*. Cambridge, MA: Belknap Press of Harvard University Press, 2011.

——. *Atlantic Crossings: Social Politics in a Progressive Age*. Cambridge, MA: Belknap Press of Harvard University Press, 1998.

——. *Contested Truths: Keywords in American Politics Since Independence*. 1987. Cambridge, MA: Harvard University Press, 1998.

Rogers, Everett. *A History of Communication Study: A Biographical Approach*. New York: Free, 1994.

Rohde, Joy. "The Last Stand of the Psychocultural Cold Warriors: Military Contract Research in Vietnam." *Journal of the History of the Behavioral Sciences* 47, no. 3 (2011): 232–50.

Rosenberg, Emily. *Spreading the American Dream: American Economic and Cultural Expansion, 1890–1945*. New York: Hill & Wang, 1982.

Ross, Kristin. *May '68 and Its Afterlives*. Chicago: University of Chicago Press, 2002.

Sakr, Naomi. "From Satellite to Screen: How Arab TV Is Shaped in Space." In *Down to Earth: Satellite Technologies, Industries, and Cultures*, ed. Lisa Parks and James Schwoch, 143–55. New Brunswick, NJ: Rutgers University Press, 2012.

——. *Satellite Realms: Transnational Television, Globalization and the Middle East*. London: I. B. Tauris, 2001.

Santoro, Jean-Louis. "La liberté de l'information: Logiques institutionnelles et logiques professionnelles au plan international (1947–1972)." PhD diss., Université Michel de Montaigne, Bordeaux III, 1991.

Schiller, Dan. *Theorizing Communication: A History*. New York: Oxford University Press, 1996.

Schiller, Herbert I. *Communication and Cultural Domination*. White Plains, NY: M. E. Sharpe, 1976.

——. "Decolonization of Information: Efforts Toward a New International Order." *Latin American Perspectives* 5, no. 1 (1978): 35–48.

——. *Mass Communications and American Empire*. New York: Augustus M. Kelley, 1969.

Schmidbauer, M. "The Symphonie Project." *Proceedings of the Royal Society of London. Series A, Mathematical and Physical Sciences* 345, no. 1643 (October 7, 1975): 559–65.

Schramm, Wilbur. "In Memoriam: Ithiel de Sola Pool, 1917–1984." *Public Opinion Quarterly* 48, no. 2 (1984): 525–26.

——. *Mass Media and National Development: The Role of Information in the Developing Countries*. Stanford, CA: Stanford University Press, 1964.

Schramm, Wilbur, Friedrich Kahnert, Philip H. Coombs, and UNESCO. *The New Media: Memo to Educational Planners*. Paris: UNESCO, 1967.

Schramm, Wilbur, Lyle M. Nelson, and Mere T. Betham. *Bold Experiment: The Story of Educational Television in American Samoa*. Stanford, CA: Stanford University Press, 1981.

Schrecker, Ellen. *The Age of McCarthyism: A Brief History with Documents*. 2nd ed. Boston: Bedford/St. Martin's, 2002.

——. *Many Are the Crimes: McCarthyism in America*. Boston: Little, Brown, 1998.

Schudson, Michael. *The Rise of the Right to Know: Politics and the Culture of Transparency, 1945–1975*. Cambridge, MA: Belknap Press of Harvard University Press, 2015.

Schwoch, James. *The American Radio Industry and Its Latin American Activities, 1900–1939*. Urbana: University of Illinois Press, 1990.

——. *Global TV: New Media and the Cold War, 1946–69*. Urbana: University of Illinois Press, 2009.

Sedgewick, Augustine. "Against Flows." *History of the Present* 4, no. 2 (2014): 143–70.

Selcer, Perrin. "Beyond the Cephalic Index: Negotiating Politics to Produce UNESCO's Scientific Statements on Race." *Current Anthropology* 53, no. S5 (2012): S173–84.

——. "The View from Everywhere: Disciplining Diversity in Post–World War II International Social Science." *Journal of the History of the Behavioral Sciences* 45, no. 4 (2009): 309–29.

Shah, Hemant. *The Production of Modernization: Daniel Lerner, Mass Media, and the Passing of Traditional Society.* Philadelphia: Temple University Press, 2011.

Shale, Richard. *Donald Duck Joins Up: The Walt Disney Studio During World War II.* Ann Arbor: UMI Research Press, 1982.

Silberstein-Loeb, Jonathan. *The International Distribution of News: The Associated Press, Press Association, and Reuters, 1848–1947.* Cambridge: Cambridge University Press, 2014.

Simon, William E. "Foreword: An American Institution." In *The Power of Ideas: The Heritage Foundation at 25 Years,* by Lee Edwards, xi–xv. Ottawa, IL: Jameson, 1997.

Simpson, Bradley R. *Economists with Guns: Authoritarian Development and U.S.-Indonesian Relations, 1960–1968.* Stanford, CA: Stanford University Press, 2008.

Simpson, Christopher. *Science of Coercion: Communication Research and Psychological Warfare, 1945–1960.* New York: Oxford University Press, 1994.

Slobodian, Quinn. *Globalists: The End of Empire and the Birth of Neoliberalism.* Cambridge, MA: Harvard University Press, 2018.

Slotten, Hugh Richard. "The International Telecommunications Union, Space Radio Communications, and U.S. Cold War Diplomacy, 1957–1963." *Diplomatic History* 37, no. 2 (2013): 313–71.

——. "Satellite Communications, Globalization, and the Cold War." *Technology and Culture* 43, no. 2 (2002): 315–50.

Sluga, Glenda. "UNESCO and the (One) World of Julian Huxley." *Journal of World History* 21, no. 3 (2010): 393–418.

Smith, Donald L. *Zechariah Chafee, Jr.: Defender of Liberty and Law.* Cambridge, MA: Harvard University Press, 1986.

Smythe, Dallas. *Counterclockwise: Perspectives on Communication.* Ed. Thomas Guback. Boulder, CO: Westview, 1994.

——. "Preface." In *Mass Communications and American Empire,* by Herbert I. Schiller, vii–viii. New York: Augustus M. Kelley, 1969.

Snow, Marcellus S. *International Commercial Satellite Communications: Economic and Political Issues of the First Decade of Intelsat.* New York: Praeger, 1976.

Soni, Jimmy, and Rob Goodman. *A Mind at Play: How Claude Shannon Invented the Information Age.* New York: Simon & Schuster, 2017.

Sparrow, James T., William J. Novak, and Stephen W. Sawyer. "Introduction." In *Boundaries of the State in U.S. History,* ed. James T. Sparrow, William J. Novak, and Stephen W. Sawyer, 1–15. Chicago: University of Chicago Press, 2015.

Stamm, Michael. *Sound Business: Newspapers, Radio, and the Politics of New Media.* Philadelphia: University of Pennsylvania Press, 2011.

——. "The Space for News: Ether and Paper in the Business of Media." *Media History* 21, no. 1 (2015): 55–73.

Starosielski, Nicole. "Fixed Flow: Undersea Cables as Media Infrastructure." In *Signal Traffic: Critical Studies of Media Infrastructures,* ed. Lisa Parks and Nicole Starosielski, 53–70. Urbana: University of Illinois Press, 2015.

——. *The Undersea Network*. Durham, NC: Duke University Press, 2015.

Starr, Paul. *The Creation of the Media: Political Origins of Modern Communications*. New York: Basic, 2004.

Stephens, Cody. "The Accidental Marxist: Andre Gunder Frank and the 'Neo-Marxist' Theory of Underdevelopment, 1958–1967." *Modern Intellectual History* 15, no. 2 (2018): 411–42.

Stern, H. H. *Foreign Languages in Primary Education: The Teaching of Foreign or Second Languages to Younger Children*. London: Oxford University Press, 1967.

Terrou, Fernand. "Aspects législatifs et réglementaires de l'intervention de l'Etat dans le domaine de l'Information." *La Revue administrative* 6, no. 33 (1953): 259–64.

Terrou, Fernand, and Lucien Solal. *Legislation for Press, Film and Radio*. Paris: UNESCO, 1951.

Thacker, Eugene. "Foreword: Protocol Is as Protocol Does." In *Protocol: How Control Exists After Decentralization*, by Alexander Galloway, xi–xxiv. Cambridge, MA: MIT Press, 2004.

Torres Bodet, Jaime. "Half the World's Population Is Illiterate." *UNESCO Courier* 2, no. 8 (1949): 29.

Tsikounas, Myriam. "*Le Tour de la France par deux enfants*: Enjeux et contraintes du premier 'télé-feuilleton' franco-canadien." In *Jean d'Arcy (1913–1983): Penser la communication au XXe siècle*, ed. Marie-Françoise Lévy, 171–84. Paris: Publications de la Sorbonne, 2013.

Tupas, Ruanni, and Beatriz P. Lorente. "A 'New' Politics of Language in the Philippines: Bilingual Education and the New Challenge of the Mother Tongues." In *Language, Education and Nation-Building: Assimilation and Shift in Southeast Asia*, ed. Peter Sercombe and Ruanni Tupas, 165–80. Basingstoke, UK: Palgrave Macmillan, 2014.

Ulff-Møller, Jens. *Hollywood's Film Wars with France: Film-Trade Diplomacy and the Emergence of the French Film Quota Policy*. Rochester, NY: University of Rochester Press, 2001.

UNESCO (United Nations Educational, Scientific, and Cultural Organization). "Television Comes to the Land," film script, 1959. Accessed July 24, 2013. https://unesdoc.unesco.org/ark:/48223/pf0000180081.

United Nations Educational, Scientific, and Cultural Organisation: Report of the Director General on the Activities of the Organization in 1947. Paris: UNESCO, 1947.

United Nations Educational Scientific and Cultural Organization: Report of the Director General on the Activities of the Organization from April 1950 to March 1951. Paris: UNESCO, 1951.

U.S. Senate, Select Committee on Intelligence Activities. "Covert Action in Chile, 1963–1973." Accessed August 8, 2016. http://www.archives.gov/declassification/iscap/pdf/2010-009-doc17.pdf.

Van Vleck, Jenifer. *Empire of the Air: Aviation and the American Ascendancy*. Cambridge, MA: Harvard University Press, 2013.

Vasey, Ruth. *The World According to Hollywood, 1918–1939*. Madison: University of Wisconsin Press, 1997.

Vaughan, Mary K. *Cultural Politics in Revolution: Teachers, Peasants, and Schools in Mexico, 1930–1940*. Tucson: University of Arizona Press, 1997.

Verna, Chantalle F. "Haiti, the Rockefeller Foundation, and UNESCO's Pilot Project in Fundamental Education, 1948–1953." *Diplomatic History* 40, no. 2 (2016): 269–95.

Wagman, Ira. "Locating UNESCO in the Historical Study of Communication." In *The International History of Communication Study*, ed. Peter Simonson and David W. Park, 71–89. New York: Routledge, 2016.

Wanger, Walter. "Donald Duck and Diplomacy." *Public Opinion Quarterly* 14, no. 3 (1950): 443–52.

——. "120,000 American Ambassadors." *Foreign Affairs* 18, no. 1 (1939): 45–59.

——. "OWI and Motion Pictures." *Public Opinion Quarterly* 7, no. 1 (1943): 100–110.

Watras, Joseph. "UNESCO's Programme of Fundamental Education, 1946–1959." *History of Education* 39, no. 2 (2010): 219–37.

Watson, Alexander John. "Introduction to the Second Edition." In *The Bias of Communication*, 2nd ed., by Harold A. Innis, ix–xxiii. 1951. Toronto: University of Toronto Press, 2008.

Weber, Eugen. *Peasants into Frenchmen: The Modernization of Rural France*. Stanford, CA: Stanford University Press, 1976.

Weinstein, Brian. "Francophonie: A Language-Based Movement in World Politics." *International Organization* 30, no. 3 (1976): 485–507.

Westad, Odd Arne. *Global Cold War: Third World Interventions and the Making of Our Times*. Cambridge: Cambridge University Press, 2005.

White, Llewellyn, and Robert D. Leigh. *Peoples Speaking to Peoples: A Report on International Mass Communication from the Commission on Freedom of the Press*. 1946. New York: Arno, 1972.

Whitehead, Clive. "The Medium of Instruction in British Colonial Education: A Case of Cultural Imperialism or Enlightened Paternalism?" *History of Education* 24, no. 1 (1995): 1–15.

Williams, Raymond. *The Raymond Williams Reader*. Ed. John Higgins. Oxford: Blackwell, 2001.

Wilson, Kevin G. *Deregulating Telecommunications: U.S. and Canadian Telecommunications, 1840–1997*. Lanham, MD: Rowman & Littlefield, 2000.

Winkler, Jonathan Reed. *Nexus: Strategic Communications and American Security in World War I*. Cambridge, MA: Harvard University Press, 2008.

Wittern-Keller, Laura. *Freedom of the Screen: Legal Challenges to State Film Censorship, 1915–1981*. Lexington: University Press of Kentucky, 2008.

Wittern-Keller, Laura, and Raymond J. Haberski Jr. *The Miracle Case: Film Censorship and the Supreme Court*. Lawrence: University Press of Kansas, 2008.

World Communications: Press, Radio, Film. Paris: UNESCO, 1950.

Yust, Walter. Introduction. *Britannica Book of the Year*. Chicago: Encyclopedia Britannica, 1949.

Zick, Timothy. *The Cosmopolitan First Amendment: Protecting Transborder Expressive and Religious Liberties*. New York: Cambridge University Press, 2014.

Index